P9-ASC-665

Praise for Steven Greenhouse's

BEATEN DOWN, WORKED UP

"Riveting. . . . Over the past forty years, as union membership has declined, America's middle class has waned. Greenhouse outlines how a worker's movement could be rekindled and why it must be. Deeply inspiring and profoundly important."　　　　—Robert B. Reich,
former secretary of labor and author of *The Common Good*

"An excellent account of how important strong unions were in moving our nation 'toward greater economic and social justice,' and how their decline has increased 'inequality and unfairness.'"
—E. J. Dionne Jr., *The Washington Post*

"Paints vivid portraits of labor champions. . . . At the same time, there are searing accounts of the struggles of workers." —*Los Angeles Times*

"Greenhouse blends solid historical research with the intimate knowledge he has gleaned from twenty years of reporting on organized labor to tell an often deeply moving story that has much to say about whether the United States can address the dire inequality that is tearing apart the fabric of American democracy."　　　　—*Foreign Affairs*

"A great book to suggest to someone who doesn't know the first thing about the labor movement, but wants to learn." —*New Labor Forum*

"Powerful. . . . A combination of labor union history in America, investigative reporting about how rapacious employers and Republican governance have diminished labor unions, and an agenda for the revitalization of unions across the country. . . . Clearly written, impressively researched, and accomplished."
—*Kirkus Reviews* (starred review)

"Compelling. . . . [Greenhouse has] a journalistic flair for personal stories often absent from academic accounts. . . . An inspiring read."
—*The Indypendent*

"Helps us remember that labor unions really did build the middle class, raise the dignity of workers, and civilize workplaces."
—Robert Bruno, *Perspectives on Work*

"Riveting reporting and storytelling reminds a new generation why workers' and unions' concerns must be restored to the center of our politics and workplaces." —Katrina vanden Heuvel, editorial director and publisher of *The Nation*

"This is the one book you should read if you want to understand why so many American workers say they would vote to join a union if they could." —Leo W. Gerard, former international president of United Steelworkers

"Comprehensive, deeply informed, and empathic. . . . It's an inspiring, richly sourced account of what American work and workers really mean today." —Alissa Quart, author of *Squeezed: Why Our Families Can't Afford America*

"*Beaten Down, Worked Up* should be read by every American concerned about our nation's rising inequality and what should be done about it." —Cristina Tzintzún Ramirez, cofounder of the Workers Defense Project and founder of Jolt

"Exceptional. . . . Can a reinvigorated union movement reverse inequality? [Greenhouse] finds green shoots of hope today, such as the movement for a fifteen-dollar minimum wage." —Jeff Madrick, author of *Age of Greed*

"Greenhouse . . . has provided a human dimension to the tale of income inequality, wage stagnation, and employer disrespect for workers. . . . Informative." —*Booklist*

"Inspirational. . . . This collection will satisfy readers who seek an introduction to labor history or ideas about how American workers can regain some power." —*Publishers Weekly*

BEATEN DOWN, WORKED UP

The Past,
Present,
and Future
of American Labor

Steven Greenhouse

Anchor Books
A Division of Penguin Random House LLC
New York

FIRST ANCHOR BOOKS EDITION, JULY 2020

Copyright © 2019 by Steven Greenhouse

All rights reserved. Published in the United States by Anchor Books,
a division of Penguin Random House LLC, New York, and distributed in Canada
by Penguin Random House Canada Limited, Toronto. Originally published
in the United States in hardcover by Alfred A. Knopf, a division of Penguin
Random House LLC, New York, in 2019.

Anchor Books and colophon are registered trademarks of Penguin Random House LLC.

The Library of Congress has cataloged the Alfred A. Knopf edition as follows:
Names: Greenhouse, Steven, author.
Title: Beaten down, worked up : the past, present, and future of American labor /
    Steven Greenhouse.
Description: First edition. | New York : Alfred A. Knopf, 2019. | Includes
    bibliographical references and index.
Identifiers: LCCN 2018055786 (print) | LCCN 2018059815 (ebook)
Subjects: LCSH: Labor—United States—History. | Labor unions—United States—
    History. | Labor movement—United States—History.
Classification: LCC HD8072.5 (ebook) | LCC HD8072.5 .G739 2019 (print) |
    DDC 331.880973—dc23
LC record available at https://lccn.loc.gov/2018055786

Anchor Books Trade Paperback ISBN: 978-1-101-87279-6
eBook ISBN: 978-1-101-87444-8

Author photograph © Michael Lionstar
Book design by Anna B. Knighton

www.anchorbooks.com

Printed in the United States of America
10 9 8 7 6 5 4 3 2 1

For my wonderful children,
EMILY AND JEREMY

And for all others in their generation
who are fighting to create a better, fairer world

If there is no struggle, there is no progress.

—FREDERICK DOUGLASS

The only effective answer to organized greed is organized labor.

—THOMAS R. DONAHUE,
inauguration speech as AFL-CIO president,
August 1, 1995, Chicago

Contents

Introduction

Like millions of workers, I was stewing about my pay. It was 1977, and after eighteen months at my first newspaper job, I was earning $220 a week. Many of us reporters were putting in fifty- to sixty-hour weeks, often working from 1 p.m. to 1 a.m., researching and writing stories in the afternoon, covering town council and school board meetings in the evening, and then rushing back to the office to write stories about the evening's events. (Putting in for overtime was frowned upon—it could hurt your chances of getting ahead or getting a beat you coveted.)

A few of us discussed what to do about the low pay, and we looked into unionizing. We contacted the Newspaper Guild, and we scheduled a dinner at a local restaurant one Friday night to discuss the idea with a union organizer. If my memory is correct, about sixty reporters, copy editors, and photographers had signed up to attend.

That Friday afternoon, a notice appeared unexpectedly on the newsroom's bulletin board announcing that the newspaper was giving nearly everyone a 20 percent raise. We were thrilled (even though the announcement drained away most of the interest in unionization). That big raise showed what a union—or the threat of a union—could accomplish. It was an era when unions were far stronger and companies were far more scared of them.

Now, four decades later, labor unions are far weaker. The decline of unions, and of worker bargaining power in general, has taken a toll on our nation. It has contributed to many of the country's major problems: increased income inequality, wage stagnation, declining mobility, the high number of low-wage jobs, and the skewing of our politics in favor of corporations and wealthy campaign donors.

Millions of Americans know little about what unions have achieved over American history, how the labor movement has played an important, often unsung role in making America the great nation it is today.

Labor unions, and their ability to create a powerful collective voice for workers, played a huge role in building the world's largest, richest middle class. The success of American business of course played a major part as well, but it was unions' strikes, and the millions of workers who took to the streets, that pressured companies to share their profits more fairly after World War II. Unions also played a crucial role in achieving many things that most Americans now take for granted: the eight-hour workday, employer-backed health coverage, paid vacations, paid sick days, safe workplaces. Indeed, unions were the major force in ending sweatshops, making coal mines safer, and eliminating many of the worst, most dangerous working conditions in the United States. "Factory jobs didn't start as good jobs," one union leader told me. "They were shit jobs. People got killed all the time. Unionization caused them to change that." When the labor movement was robust, we as a nation moved toward greater economic and social justice, but with the union movement diminished—and with many billionaires and corporations seeking to cripple it further—we as a nation are moving toward more inequality and unfairness.

In the following pages, I tell the history of labor unions and worker power in America, focusing on pivotal episodes that built the union movement and gave workers a true voice and true power that lifted wages and benefits for millions of Americans. I write of key labor leaders and landmark confrontations—huge, riveting dramas in their day—like the women workers' Uprising of the Twenty Thousand of 1909–10, the Flint Sit-Down Strike of 1936–37, and the Memphis Sanitation Workers' Strike of 1968. I also explore the downward arc of the union movement and of worker power—why this has been happening and what it has meant for the nation. I explore the factors that have fueled this decline, including globalization, the rise of the atomized gig economy, and corporate America's war against labor unions. I devote several chapters to major episodes that badly set back labor, including the disastrous air traffic controllers' strike of 1981 and Scott Walker's crusade to cripple Wisconsin's government employee unions in 2011. As a result of these fights and forces, the United States now has the weakest labor movement of any advanced industrial nation, and that's a major reason why income inequality has grown worse in America than in any other industrialized nation.

Finally, I write about several unusually successful modern-day labor efforts that signal a hopeful path for workers—a path to lift wages, increase worker power, and improve jobs as well as workers' productivity and morale. I was the first journalist to write about the Fight for $15 when it was just getting started in 2012, and I take a close look at that fight, by many measures the biggest, most successful labor effort in decades. I also examine the Coalition of Immokalee Workers, which has done an astonishing job transforming the once-miserable jobs of tens of thousands of farmworkers. I look at Kaiser Permanente's Labor Management Partnership, probably the nation's best example of how management and workers cooperate closely to cut costs, boost efficiency, and improve service, morale, and wages. I also tell of the St. Paul Federation of Teachers, which has blazed a remarkable path, battling not just for teachers but for students, the community, and greater social justice as part of an innovative strategy known as "bargaining for the common good."

This is not a detailed, comprehensive history. For that, I recommend such excellent books as *Labor in America: A History* by Melvyn Dubofsky and Joseph A. McCartin, *State of the Union* by Nelson Lichtenstein, and *There Is Power in a Union* by Philip Dray. And because this is not a comprehensive history, I cannot do justice to some important groups and episodes in labor history, among them the Knights of Labor, the early railroad strikes, the Lawrence textile strike of 1912, the Wobblies, the general strikes in Minneapolis and San Francisco in 1934, and the Little Steel strike of 1937, in which ten unarmed workers and supporters were killed in Chicago.

I grew up in Massapequa, a part-working-class, part-middle-class town on Long Island, and I could see how unions helped many of the people living there—firefighters, police officers, construction workers, teachers. My father was a high school teacher, and I saw how his union went a long way to provide teachers with good pay, health insurance, solid pensions, and important protections against retaliation and dismissal if they wanted to speak out, for instance, against the Vietnam War.

My parents grew up during the Great Depression, when millions of struggling Americans poured into labor unions. I remember what my then-eighty-six-year-old mother told me during a phone conversation when I was in Wisconsin to cover Scott Walker's push to gut collective bargaining and cut public employees' health and pension benefits. She bemoaned the situation, saying, "When I was growing up, people used to say, 'Look at the good wages and benefits that people in a union have. I want to join a union.' Now people say, 'Look at the good wages and benefits that union members have. They're getting more than what I get. That's not fair. Let's take away some of what they have.'" Her comments captured an unfortunate loss of solidarity among Americans as well as a lamentable impulse not to lift each other up but to take away from other workers who might have it a little bit better.

During my nineteen years covering labor and workplace issues for *The New York Times,* I wrote about some amazing things unions did, like unionizing fifty-two hundred immigrant janitors in Houston. That effort showed how unionization could be a boon for marginalized workers—it ultimately doubled the pay of those janitors, provided them with valuable protections against abusive bosses, and gave many of them and their families health coverage for the first time in their lives. I also wrote about the downside of labor unions, doing many stories about union corruption—about labor leaders embezzling money, taking bribes from management, fixing union elections, and using strong-arm tactics. I have often debated the question of which group is more dishonest: politicians, business executives, or union leaders. There's no clear answer, but fortunately there is far less corruption in labor unions than there once was.

Pope Francis has championed unions, especially for workers on the bottom, calling them "prophetic" institutions. "There is no good society without a good union," he told Italian labor leaders. But Pope Francis warned that unions should be careful not to become tired and uncaring, like many politicians. He said unions need to help "the discarded" and "excluded," saying that labor does this best when "it gives a voice to those who have none" and "unmasks the powerful who trample the rights of the most vulnerable workers."

What Pope Francis decried has unfortunately become dismayingly common in the United States: powerful companies trampling on the rights of the most vulnerable workers. Far too many employers cheat workers out of overtime pay or illegally treat them as independent contractors to deny them benefits and legal protections. Many of the nation's leading corporations now prohibit employees from suing for wage theft or sexual harassment, forcing them instead into arbitrations behind closed doors, which generally tilt far more in employers' favor than do lawsuits, partly because employers have a major say in choosing the arbitrators. While corporate profits have soared, many companies have been depressingly tightfisted on raises—year after year pay for millions of workers lagged behind inflation. (Only recently, nearly ten years into an economic expansion, with the labor market unusually tight, have wage increases finally picked up.) Many corporate executives and Washington policy makers seem to have little inkling, or concern, about how tough it is for millions of American workers to get by. One in five adults say they can't pay the current month's bills, according to the Federal Reserve, and one in four skipped necessary medical care sometime in 2017 because they couldn't afford the cost.

Nowadays, much of the policy talk in Washington focuses on how to liberate corporations, scrap regulations, and reward investors, but if we are truly serious about making America a greater nation, wouldn't a good place to start be America's backbone, its more than 150 million workers? There seems to be ever more focus on maximizing profits and ever less talk about the common good and helping the less fortunate among us. In a time of record business profits and the greatest income inequality in a century, corporations and the wealthy have bounded forward, leaving tens of millions of workers in their wake, with many despairing over whether they and their children will ever achieve the American dream.

I wrote this book because I am deeply concerned about what is happening to many American workers. In my first book, *The Big Squeeze: Tough Times for the American Worker,* I showed the many ways that American workers—blue-collar workers, Walmart workers, young workers, older workers, immigrant workers, Midwest factory workers—were taking it on the chin. In this book, I seek to focus far more on *why* so many American workers have been squeezed so badly. I fear that if nothing is done to reverse the decline in worker bargaining power and workers' voice in politics and policy, our nation will become even more skewed, with even worse income inequality and even greater domination of politics and policy by corporations and wealthy donors. In these pages, I examine the roots of these problems and what we as individuals and as a nation can do to address and hopefully fix them.

Part One

STATE OF THE UNION

One

Losing Our Voice

THROUGHOUT MARY COLEMAN's six years as a cook at a Popeyes restaurant in Milwaukee, she remained stuck at the federal minimum wage of $7.25 an hour. One afternoon, when she arrived for her shift after an hour-long bus commute, her manager told her to go home without even clocking in. Business was slow, he said, and she wasn't going to be paid for the day.

◆

For ten years, Keith Barrett worked as a behind-the-scenes software engineer at Disney World in Orlando, helping monitor computers that handled ticket sales and hotel reservations. One day, Barrett and 250 fellow tech workers were stunned to receive layoff notices—Disney was replacing them with guest workers from India on temporary work visas. Many of the laid-off workers grew even more upset when Disney told them they wouldn't receive any severance unless they agreed to train their replacements.

◆

Jamie Workman became pregnant while working as a CVS cashier in Rocklin, California, northeast of Sacramento. Her eight-hour shifts soon became tiring and painful because she had to stand the whole time; her feet and legs became swollen. At one point, her shift supervisor gave her a stool to sit on for a few hours, but then the store manager ordered her to stop using it, telling her that cashiers weren't allowed to sit.

◆

Most mornings Jorge Porras reported to his car-wash job in Santa Fe at 8:15 A.M., as instructed, but his boss often didn't let him clock in until 11:00, sometimes not until noon, whenever customers began lining up. Many days his boss paid him for six hours of work, even though he had worked nine and a half. One day, when the heavy chain that pulled the cars forward got stuck, Porras tried fixing it, but the chain suddenly lurched forward and cut off the top of his right ring finger. That injury forced Porras to miss two weeks of work, during which he didn't receive any wages or workers' compensation. When he and several co-workers complained about the unpaid hours and unsafe conditions, the car-wash owner fired them.

◆

Patricia Hughes, a licensed practical nurse, came down with severe pneumonia while caring for a paraplegic in Thornton, Colorado. Coughing, vomiting, and with a 103 fever, Hughes called her manager to say she needed to miss work for two days. "I told him I was so weak that there was no way I could care for and move the patient," she said. "He responded, 'If you don't come in tomorrow, don't bother ever coming back.'" Too sick to work the next day, Hughes was fired, and as a result of losing that job, she was evicted from her apartment.

◆

John Billington, proud of his 4.9 rating as an Uber driver in Los Angeles, was shocked when Uber suddenly chopped its L.A. fares from $2.50 a mile to $1 a mile. As a result, his average weekly gross income fell from over $1,500 to around $750, and that's before subtracting the cost of gas, auto insurance, maintenance, and depreciation on his car. "Uber dictates everything," Billington said. "We don't get any input. It's unfair."

◆

After seventeen years of teaching, Laura Fox, an elementary school music teacher in a suburb of Phoenix, was having such a hard time making ends meet that she took a twenty-hour-a-week job at McDonald's. Fox, whose school district hadn't raised pay in a decade, often worked at McDonald's until 11:30 p.m., arrived home around midnight, and woke up at 6:30 to get ready for school. "Some days I was exhausted," she said. "I work to teach the people who are going to be the future of society. It makes me feel disrespected that they pay teachers so little."

◆

A week after graduating from college in North Carolina, Desmond Anthony moved to New York to pursue a career as an actor. To support himself, he took a job as a sales clerk and cashier at the Express clothing store in Herald Square. At first his boss assigned him thirty hours of work each week, but after several months his hours were cut to just twelve or fifteen, and some weeks he was assigned no hours at all. Working fifteen hours a week, Anthony earned around $500 a month, not enough to cover his $800 monthly rent, let alone the several hundred dollars more needed for phone, subway, and food. Some days he went hungry, and some weeks he had to ask his parents for money. Anthony repeatedly urged his boss to assign him more hours, but instead of giving him more hours, the store hired more part-time workers, giving it more flexibility to plug workers into its ever-changing schedule. Anthony quit in frustration.

———

In the United States, a country that by many measures is the world's richest, life has taken a wrong turn for millions of workers. For far too many, the land of opportunity has turned into a land of downsized hopes and shrunken mobility. Many Americans who struggle to pay each month's bills, who juggle two or three jobs, who bounce from one low-paid gig job to another, ask what has happened to this land of vaunted opportunity, a nation famed for its Horatio Alger credo: if you work hard, you will get ahead.

As the stories above make clear, something is fundamentally broken in the way many American employers treat their workers. Too often employers fail to show workers basic respect, too often they fail to heed workers' most fundamental concerns, too often workers are badly underpaid or cheated out of wages. Too often employers show utter contempt for the golden rule: do unto others as you would have them do unto you.

But something else is also fundamentally awry: corporate profits and the stock market have repeatedly climbed to new records in recent years, while wages for the typical American worker have either flatlined or inched up only slightly, after factoring in inflation. (The wage picture finally brightened recently when the job market tightened with the unemployment rate falling below 4 percent.) The share of national income going to business profits has climbed to its highest level since World War II, while workers' share of income (employee compensation, including benefits) has slid to its lowest level since the 1940s. Indeed, labor's share of national income has fallen at a faster rate in the United States than in any other major industrial nation since 1995. Little wonder that the income of the richest 1 percent has risen to its highest level since the 1920s. With so much of the policy talk in Washington focused on cutting taxes for corporations and the very wealthy when those two groups have done splendidly in recent years, it's palpable that the nation's priorities—and sense of fairness—are badly out of whack. While it's great to see workers pampered and paid well at elite corporations like Google and Facebook, we shouldn't forget the painful truth that four in ten American adults say they simply don't have the money to pay an unexpected $400 expense, according to the Federal Reserve. Forty million Americans—one in eight—suffer from food insecurity, that is, a lack of consistent access to enough food for an active, healthy life, according to the U.S. Department of Agriculture.

For decades, the United States was the world's economic beacon, the country with the largest and richest middle class, a land of rising wages and broad prosperity. But now millions of Americans are wondering what happened to that golden age of prosperity, to John F. Kennedy's exhortation that "a rising tide lifts all boats." American workers' pent-up frustration about stagnant wages and shuttered factories was a big factor in the 2016 election. That frustration helped push millions of blue-collar workers to vote for Donald Trump, a billionaire who wooed and wowed them by promising "to bring back the jobs," rev up manufacturing, and get tough on Mexico and China. Blue-collar whites gave Trump the margins he needed to win Michigan, Pennsylvania, and Wisconsin and, with those states, overall victory.

Though candidate Trump campaigned as a champion of workers, his administration has repeatedly sided with business over workers. It has scrapped numerous job safety regulations, pushed to take away health coverage from millions of families, and rolled back a rule that extended overtime pay to millions more workers. In a boon to Wall Street, the Trump administration has maneuvered to kill a rule requiring Wall Street firms to act in the worker's, not the investment firm's, best interests when managing retirement funds—a move that could potentially cost many workers tens of thousands of dollars. (Trump's tough trade actions have helped some steel, aluminum, and auto workers, but he has taken those actions in a blundering, blunderbuss way that has hurt many other workers and alienated and angered Canada and many other longtime allies.)

Trump's appointees have also moved aggressively to undermine the institution that is traditionally the biggest champion of workers: organized labor. Not only have his appointees to the National Labor Relations Board (NLRB) issued numerous rulings to weaken unions and make it harder for workers to organize, but his administration has pushed hard to undercut federal employees' unions (even ordering a wage freeze for federal workers). Taking the extraordinary step of reversing the previous administration's position before the Supreme Court, Trump's Justice Department urged the high court to issue two rulings that seriously hurt labor. One delivered a severe blow to the nation's public-employee unions, and the other, in a significant slap at workers' rights, permitted companies to bar workers from bringing class actions against wage theft, racial or sex discrimination, or other wrongdoing by employers. Neil Gorsuch, Trump's first nominee to the Supreme Court, cast the deciding vote in both 5–4 cases. It's plainly demagogic for President Trump to promote himself as a good friend of the American worker when his administration and appointees are pushing, in myriad ways large and small, to hobble labor unions and workers' ability to speak up.

———

There's a hugely important but often overlooked phenomenon that goes far to explain why so many bad things are happening to American workers, and that is the decades-long decline in worker power, both in the workplace and in politics and policy. Many industrial relations experts put it another way: they say there has been an undeniable decline in worker voice, the effective ability of workers to speak up and the willingness of many employers to listen to what workers have to say.

In their groundbreaking 1984 book on labor relations, *What Do Unions Do?*, Richard B. Freeman and James L. Medoff stressed the importance of voice, writing, "Voice means discussing with an employer conditions that ought to be changed, rather than quitting the job." As a result of the decline in worker voice in recent decades, there is far less of a brake to stop businesses from doing what they will vis-à-vis their workers, whether it's freezing pay or insisting that employees work sixteen-hour days.

As workers' power has waned, many corporations have adopted practices that were far rarer or largely unheard of three and four decades ago: hiring hordes of unpaid interns, expecting many workers to toil sixty or seventy hours a week, illegally treating many workers as independent contractors rather than as employees (and thus avoiding any obligation to contribute to their Social Security benefits or pay them overtime). In recent years, far more companies have reduced employees' mobility by making them sign non-compete clauses, with some employers requiring even fast-food workers and summer camp counselors to pledge not to work for competitors. And far more than in prior decades, many retailers and restaurants—in a practice known as "clopening"—are ordering employees to work until 11 p.m. or midnight to *close* up and then return at 7 or 8 a.m. to *open* up, meaning those workers are lucky to get five hours of sleep. And economists have recently documented how the excessive power of a few consolidated employers is holding down wages, a phenomenon known as monopsony. For instance, if one or two hospital chains dominate a metropolitan area, that might limit the ability of nurses or nurses' aides to move to other jobs in search of higher wages.

This lack of worker leverage helps explain what might be called America's anti-worker exceptionalism. The United States is the only industrial nation in which workers don't have a legal right to paid sick days (although several states and cities have enacted paid sick leave laws). Similarly, the United States is the only industrial nation not to give workers a legal right to any vacation, paid or unpaid. In France, by contrast, workers have a legal right to six weeks' paid vacation a year; in Britain, twenty-eight days; in Germany, four weeks. The United States is also the only industrial nation that doesn't have a law guaranteeing paid maternity leave; the average in European nations is more than twenty weeks. The only other countries in the world without paid maternity leave laws are Papua New Guinea, Suriname, and a few Pacific island states.

The decline in workers' bargaining power is of course closely related to the diminished might of America's labor unions. Labor unions represent just 6.4 percent of America's private-sector workers and 10.5 percent of workers overall. That's the lowest percentage in more than a century, and down from 35 percent in the 1950s. The United Automobile Workers (UAW) union has dwindled to 430,000 members from its peak of 1.5 million in 1979. The once-mighty International Ladies' Garment Workers' Union (ILGWU) shrank so much that it merged with several other unions, and its name and fame have faded into history.

"No one who looks at the American economy of the last generation can fail to be struck by the precipitous decline of organized labor," Jacob Hacker and Paul Pierson wrote in *Winner-Take-All Politics*. "While there are many 'progressive' groups in the American universe of organized interests, labor is the only major one focused on the broad economic concerns of those with modest incomes."

By uniting workers' collective power, unions have made many important advances for American workers—advances that many now take for granted. In the late 1940s and the 1950s, through landmark contracts with General Motors, Ford, and other industrial giants, unions played a decisive role in building the biggest, richest middle class the world had ever seen. Unions also played a pivotal role in winning enactment of the federal minimum wage, Social Security, unemployment insurance, Medicare, occupational safety laws, and the civil rights laws of the 1960s. (There is much truth to the bumper sticker: "Unions: The Folks Who Brought You the Weekend.")

Union members earn 13.6 percent more than comparable nonunion workers, after adjusting for education, age, and other factors. Seventy-five percent of unionized workers participate in employer-sponsored health plans, compared with just 49 percent of nonunion workers. Eighty-three percent of union members have an employer-sponsored retirement plan, while just 49 percent of nonunion workers do. Unions also help reduce the gender pay gap. Women workers in unions are paid, on average, ninety-four cents to the dollar paid to unionized male workers, while nonunion women earn seventy-eight cents to the dollar compared with nonunion working men. African American union members earn on average 16.4 percent more than comparable nonunion black workers.

Unions have played an important, but often unappreciated role in reducing inequality; the decades when unions were strongest—the 1940s through 1970s—were the decades when there was the least income inequality. One study found that the decline in union power and density since 1973 explains a third of the increase in wage inequality among American men and a fifth of the increased inequality among women. Two economists at the International Monetary Fund found that the "the decline in unionization" (and the concomitant decline in worker bargaining power) "explains about half of the rise in incomes for the richest 10 percent" in advanced industrial nations and about half the increase in those nations' main measure of income inequality. Unions often reduce inequality by pushing for higher pay for typical workers, more generous Social Security benefits, higher taxes on the rich, and greater restraints on executive pay.

Labor unions have done more than any other institution to mobilize average Americans to get involved in our democracy and elections, to vote, and to make themselves heard. Robert D. Putnam, author of *Bowling Alone,* has praised unions for building an important sense of community—with their meetings, marches, protests, and picnics—and also for serving as "schools for democracy," where workers get involved in everything from collective bargaining to canvassing in political campaigns.

While many unions engaged in deplorable race discrimination in decades past, organized labor has done more to bring together Americans of different races, religions, and nationalities than any other institution (except perhaps the military). Although Martin Luther King Jr. chided some unions for discriminating, he was an ally and champion of organized labor. When he was assassinated in Memphis in 1968, he was there to support a sanitation workers' strike. In a 1965 speech, King said,

> The labor movement was the principal force that transformed misery and despair into hope and progress. Out of its bold struggles, economic and social reform gave birth to unemployment insurance, old age pensions, government relief for the destitute, and above all new wage lev-

els that meant not mere survival, but a tolerable life. The captains of industry did not lead this transformation; they resisted it until they were overcome.

———

In their prime, unions regularly turned to their most powerful weapon—the strike—to fight for better pay and conditions. Nowadays, however, unions are so weakened that they rarely go on strike. From 2010 to 2017, there were fewer than 13 major strikes per year on average in the private sector (involving more than a thousand workers). That's less than one-sixth the average annual amount in the 1980s (83), and less than one-twentieth the yearly average in the 1970s (288). (The surprising surge of teachers' strikes in 2018 defied this trend; teachers in several states grew so fed up with meager pay and cuts in school spending that they felt an urgent need to walk out.)

Many forces have combined to reduce unions'—and workers'—power. Globalization has thrown American workers into direct competition with lower-wage workers in China, India, Mexico, and other countries, exerting a downward pull on pay. Partly because of imports and outsourcing, more than sixty thousand American factories have closed since 2000, causing many unions and workers to grow gun-shy about making aggressive pay demands, which could lead to even more jobs being shipped overseas. All told, manufacturing employment has fallen from 19.5 million in 1979 to 12.8 million today, badly eroding organized labor's longtime base.

Far-reaching changes across corporate America have also undercut workers' leverage. The C-suite's preoccupation with maximizing profits and stock prices has pushed companies to take a tougher stance toward wage demands and unions. Corporations have increasingly used temps, freelancers, independent contractors, and subcontractors—a practice (sometimes called fissuring) that has eroded the traditional employer-employee relationship and made many workers feel that their position is more precarious. (Indeed, a new term has been coined to describe today's ever-more-insecure workers: "the precariat.")

The advances in automation, robots, and artificial intelligence have added to this precariousness, making many workers fear that their job security is evaporating. Workers can't but be worried when they see experts like the McKinsey Global Institute forecast that automation will, by 2030, destroy more than 39 million jobs in the United States and 375 million worldwide, while two Oxford professors predict that 47 percent of U.S. jobs are at risk of being automated by 2033. Some economists say such estimates are outlandish, but it's hard to deny—just to take one example—that self-driving cars and trucks won't someday displace hundreds of thousands of taxi, truck, Uber, and Lyft drivers. Workers are paid such little heed nowadays that at the dozens of Future of Work conferences held each year to examine how robots and artificial intelligence will affect work, billionaire and millionaire tech executives are invariably invited to speak, but rarely even one worker representative.

As worker power has declined, we've seen many unfortunate trends for workers:

- From 1948 to 1973, worker productivity and hourly pay rose in tandem (productivity increased 95.7 percent during that span, while hourly compensation climbed 90.9 percent). But from 1973 to 2016, a period of waning union and worker power, productivity rose over six times as fast as compensation. This means that workers are receiving a far smaller share of the increased productivity that they're providing to their employers.
- Hard though it may be to believe, average hourly pay for American workers remains below the levels of 1973, after accounting for inflation.
- CEOs at the largest 350 corporations make 312 times as much as the average worker, up from 59 times in 1990 and 20 times in 1965.
- Nearly fifty million American workers earn less than $15 an hour. For a full-time worker, that translates to $31,200 a year.
- The top 1 percent of households received 22 percent of the nation's income in 2015, up from 9 percent in 1984. That's the highest percentage the 1 percent has received since the 1920s. The top 10 percent now receive nearly half of the nation's income (50 percent in 2015), up from one-third in the 1970s. (That of course leaves less for the bottom 90 percent of households.)
- Americans average 1,780 hours of work per year. That's 70 hours per year more than the Japanese, 100 hours (two and a half workweeks) more than British workers, 266 hours (six and a half workweeks) more than French workers, and 424 hours (ten and a half workweeks) more than German workers.

- For college graduates who entered the workforce in June 2018, average hourly pay ($20.37) was just 2.5 percent higher than seventeen years earlier, after adjusting for inflation. For high school graduates with no college credits, average hourly pay ($11.85 for entry-level jobs) was actually down 1.4 percent from 2001.
- The federal minimum wage of $7.25 is 37 percent below its 1968 level, after factoring in inflation. Indeed, the ratio of America's federal minimum wage to median hourly income is the lowest among thirty-six industrial nations—the ratio is just 35 percent in the United States, compared with 61 percent in France and 49 percent in Britain.

———

Even as unions have declined in size and power, corporate America and its conservative allies have stepped up efforts to hasten the demise of organized labor. Although the percentage of workers in unions has fallen to its lowest level in over a century, many corporations and business-friendly lawmakers insist that unions remain far too powerful. They complain that unions interfere with the free market, push up wages, and undercut profits and managerial flexibility (although they forget that unionization often leads to improved morale, less employee turnover, higher productivity, and stepped-up investment in workers). Labor's critics also say that unions perpetuate "big government" and "high taxes" by battling to protect Social Security, Medicare, and other safety net programs and by pushing for higher pay for public employees, whether firefighters, teachers, police, or social workers.

The right-wing billionaire Koch brothers and many other conservatives see unions as pillars of the Democratic Party—that helps explain the recent assault on unions in state after state. Republicans have pressed to enact anti-union-fee laws (commonly called right-to-work laws) wherever they can, having recently passed such laws in Kentucky, Michigan, Missouri, West Virginia, and Wisconsin (although Missourians overwhelmingly voted in 2018 to repeal such an antiunion law). These laws—which let workers opt out of paying any fees to the unions that negotiate their contracts—undermine unions, union treasuries, and labor's clout in bargaining and politics. In Wisconsin, Governor Scott Walker, strongly backed by several antiunion billionaires, pushed through a far-reaching law to cripple government employee unions.

Right-wing magnates also helped finance the *Janus* Supreme Court case in which the conservative majority dealt a severe blow to labor by barring any requirement that government employees pay union fees. That ruling is expected to cut many unions' treasuries by 10 to 30 percent.

At the same time in the private sector, major American corporations—among them Amazon and Walmart—have grown more expert and aggressive in beating back unionization drives. Many companies illegally fire pro-union workers to derail these efforts because these companies see that the penalties for such lawbreaking are puny. Walmart even went so far as to close the first Walmart store to unionize in North America (in Canada). When journalists at *Gothamist* and *DNAinfo* voted to unionize in 2017, the billionaire owner of those news websites immediately shut them down, throwing 115 people out of work.

As workers' leverage has declined, many companies have been paying less heed to workers' concerns, or even their physical well-being. Inside an Amazon "fulfillment center" in Pennsylvania's Lehigh Valley, temperatures sometimes soared to over a hundred degrees during the summer as workers raced hour after hour to pick goods from the shelves. So many "fulfillment" workers fainted or grew dehydrated that Amazon arranged to have paramedics parked in ambulances nearby. Only after a local newspaper published an exposé about the heat, fainting, and ambulances did Amazon install air-conditioning. According to a *New York Times* story about the brutal work environment at Amazon's Seattle headquarters, a white-collar employee who had breast cancer was told she had been put on a "performance improvement plan"—Amazon lingo for "you're in danger of being fired"—because "difficulties" in her "personal life" were getting in the way of fulfilling her job goals.

A biography of Tesla's co-founder Elon Musk tells of his scolding an assistant who had missed a corporate event to witness the birth of his child. The biography quotes an email that Musk reportedly sent to the employee: "That is no excuse. I am extremely disappointed. You need to figure out where your priorities are. We're changing the world and changing history, and you either commit or you don't." (Musk asserted that the story was "total BS.")

After the news media exposed Harvey Weinstein's horrific, decades-long history of sexual abuse, hundreds of women stepped forward with tales of abuse and harassment at their workplaces. The outpouring was so huge partly because many women didn't have a union or some other means to make their voices heard at work. Many employers had simply ignored women's complaints, and the victims had often been too scared to speak up. (Unions have sometimes been far too slow and reluctant to help when women complain of harassment.)

A notorious case involved Susan Fowler, who, while working as an engineer at Uber, complained to the human resources department that her direct supervisor had repeatedly propositioned her for sex. Uber's HR department gave her a choice: she could transfer to another team and not interact with that manager again, or she could stay on her current team, a team she liked working with. She was told that if she chose the latter, she risked getting a poor performance review from her supervisor. Fowler learned from other women that Uber's HR department had lied to her when it said her case was her supervisor's "first offense." A year after complaining to HR, Fowler wrote a blog post about her mistreatment that went viral. Only then did Uber act to stop its out-of-control harassment. (By that time, Fowler had left the company.)

The absence of an effective voice for workers has also led to deadly tragedies. On April 5, 2010, a coal dust explosion killed twenty-nine miners at Massey Energy's Upper Big Branch coal mine in West Virginia. A federal investigation found that the mine's ventilation system was inadequate and that explosive gases were allowed to build up. Workers at the nonunion mine knew about these dangers. Stanley "Goose" Stewart, an Upper Big Branch miner, told a congressional committee, "No one felt they could go to management and express their fears. We knew we'd be marked men and the management would look for ways to fire us. Maybe not that day, or that week. But somewhere down the line, we'd disappear."

The public can also pay a price when workers' lack of bargaining power leads to substandard pay and dangerous practices. Fifty people died in February 2009 when Continental Connection Flight 3407, originating in Newark, New Jersey, crashed into a house outside Buffalo. Afterward, the National Transportation Safety Board found that both the pilot and the co-pilot were probably suffering from fatigue. The night before, the co-pilot, Rebecca Shaw, had hopped aboard a FedEx flight from Seattle (where she lived) to Memphis and stayed in a crew lounge there from midnight to 4 a.m. She then flew to Newark Airport, arriving at 6:30, and hung out in the crew lounge there until 1:30 p.m., when she had to report to duty. Flight 3407 didn't take off until 9:15 p.m. because of weather delays. With her low salary of $23,900, Shaw couldn't afford a hotel or a place in the New York–New Jersey area. It was unclear where or how much Flight 3407's captain had slept, although he had logged on to a computer in the crew lounge at 3 a.m., making investigators suspect he had slept in the lounge.

In another tragedy, a Walmart truck driver plowed into Tracy Morgan's car on the New Jersey Turnpike in 2014, severely injuring him and killing a fellow comedian. Not only had the truck driver been working nearly fourteen hours straight, but he hadn't slept in twenty-eight hours. He had driven eight hundred miles overnight from his home in Georgia to a Walmart distribution center in Delaware to pick up his cargo and then set out for New Jersey. If drivers had more power vis-à-vis the trucking industry, it would make for tougher, more safety-minded regulations that wouldn't let drivers work fourteen-hour shifts.

Another glaring problem is the declining clout of workers in our political system. America's elected leaders have increasingly turned their backs on workers' concerns, a far cry from the days of Franklin D. Roosevelt, John F. Kennedy, and even Richard Nixon, a Republican who signed the landmark Occupational Safety and Health Act.

A survey done by the National Restaurant Association—echoing many other surveys—showed that Americans, by 71 percent to 22 percent, overwhelmingly support raising the $7.25 federal minimum wage to at least $10. A *New York Times*/CBS News poll found that Americans, by 85 percent to 14 percent, want a law that would guarantee paid sick leave for workers—60 percent of the nation's low-wage workers don't receive paid sick days. By 80 percent to 17 percent, that poll found that Americans want to require employers to provide paid leave to the parents of new children and to employees caring for sick family members. But barring a political earthquake, because of corporate America's huge power there seems little chance of Congress enacting either of these measures, fundamental worker protections that are nearly universal in other industrial nations.

Many corporations and conservatives deride "Big Labor's" clout in politics, but in fact business's contributions swamp labor's in election campaigns. In the 2015–16 election cycle, business outspent labor sixteen to one in the presidential, Senate, and House elections—$3.4 billion to $213 million—according to the nonpartisan Center for Responsive

Politics. All of the nation's labor unions taken together spend about $45 million a year for lobbying in Washington, while corporate America spends $3 billion. Little wonder that many lawmakers seem vastly more interested in cutting taxes on corporations and the so-called 1 percent than in helping the American worker. One Labor Day, the Virginia Republican Eric Cantor, while House majority leader, sent out a revealing tweet: "Today, we celebrate those who have taken a risk, worked hard, built a business and earned their own success." He was hailing business owners and didn't even refer to workers.

———

Some critics argue that unions are relics, archaic institutions that gum up the magic of the free market. The free market has indeed done wonders in creating wealth and lifting living standards, but an unrestricted market also leaves many workers unable to make ends meet. Labor unions first came into being more than two centuries ago to try to ensure that workers in the early Industrial Revolution earned enough to feed and shelter themselves and their families. And that's the role unions often still play today.

Sadly, the United States has, in contrast to Western Europe, become a low-wage, low-road economy for millions of workers. Europeans often deride America's $7.25-an-hour minimum wage jobs as McJobs, while McDonald's workers in highly unionized Denmark average more than $20 an hour. That's one reason that so many unions and worker advocates in the United States are pushing to raise the federal minimum wage. It would be great if all those $15-million-a-year CEOs and $250,000-a-year think tank senior fellows who denounce efforts to raise the minimum wage would spend a month or two living on $7.25 an hour. As for their oft-repeated advice that every $8-an-hour hamburger flipper, janitor, and home-care aide should go to college if they want to increase their pay, we as a nation are still going to need millions of hamburger flippers, janitors, and home-care aides, and we shouldn't consign them to poverty.

Free-market advocates often complain that unions push up pay and artificially set wages, forcing many companies to raise prices and sometimes rendering them uncompetitive. Increased prices are of course a concern, and a smart union will always seek to prevent employers from becoming uncompetitive. But with corporate profits repeatedly climbing to record levels in recent years and with the tax cuts enacted in 2017 giving profits a big boost, many companies should be able to raise wages substantially—and do so without raising prices much or at all—by accepting lower profits. Amazon's chairman, Jeff Bezos, the world's richest man and arguably its most successful capitalist, saw that such a move made eminent sense when he announced that Amazon would adopt a $15 minimum wage for its 350,000 U.S. employees. (Such a move might of course be hard for companies with low profit margins.)

Many corporate executives act as if there were a rule handed down from on high that corporations are supposed to be concerned only with maximizing their profits and share price. But the laws that govern corporations can be modified. Our democracy can enact fairer laws and rules for corporations to ensure that their goals and vision go beyond merely maximizing shareholder value. Just a few decades ago, American corporations used to say that their role was to serve multiple stakeholders, including workers and communities, and not just shareholders. But as America has moved away from its focus on the common good and on pulling together as a nation, a self-interested ideology focused on maximizing profits has taken firm hold, turbocharging the nation's income inequality. This profits-above-all philosophy has squeezed tens of millions of workers—on wages, health coverage, pensions, and much else—and has often hurt consumers, communities, and the environment. Senator Elizabeth Warren has a smart idea: workers at major corporations would elect two-fifths of the members of their corporations' boards in order to make companies less obsessed with maximizing profits and more concerned about the welfare of their workers and communities.

———

Even as the union movement has been hobbled, many innovative efforts to lift workers have sprouted across the United States. These efforts—some by unions, some by nonunion groups—have injected new life into worker advocacy. They are the foundation of a new and different labor movement.

- The Fight for $15 has been one of the largest, loudest, and most influential pro-worker campaigns in decades, helping millions of workers receive raises by getting a $15 minimum wage approved in Seattle, San Francisco, Los Angeles, Minneapolis, much of New York State, as well as statewide in California, Illinois, Maryland, Massachusetts, and New Jersey.

- The Coalition of Immokalee Workers has transformed Florida's tomato fields from having what were considered the worst farmworker conditions in the nation to having the best. That coalition has lifted pay for thirty-five thousand tomato workers and created a world-class monitoring system that has largely eliminated sexual abuses and modern-day slavery in Florida's tomato fields.

- The Los Angeles Alliance for a New Economy has been an extraordinary incubator of pro-worker ideas. It won enactment of a groundbreaking $15.37 minimum wage for L.A.'s hotel workers, and it created an innovative labor-environmental coalition that has transformed L.A.'s waste-hauling and port trucking industries, cutting pollution, raising wages, and spurring unionization. And with all the hopes of reviving manufacturing, an offshoot of that group has had spectacular success in getting Japanese and Chinese companies to open unionized rail and bus factories in the United States.

- In other efforts that are lifting workers, thousands of adjunct professors at Duke, Georgetown, Tufts, and other schools have unionized, with some startling results. Adjuncts at Fordham University negotiated a contract that raised the pay for many courses by 70 percent. The Teamsters have organized, and won big raises for, shuttle bus drivers for Facebook and Google in Silicon Valley, while digital media workers at *Slate, Salon, Huffington Post, Vox, Vice,* and other news sites have unionized, with some journalists winning raises of nearly 30 percent. The newsrooms at the *Los Angeles Times* and the *Chicago Tribune*—publications with a long, fierce antiunion history—unionized in 2018, and so did the editorial staff at *The New Yorker, New York* magazine, and *The New Republic.* In Las Vegas, the fifty-seven-thousand-member Culinary Union continues to show what a dynamic, well-run union can accomplish: winning middle-class wages for thousands of hotel housekeepers and building a political juggernaut that has gone far in turning Nevada from red to blue.

- Arguably the most robust and exciting exercise of worker power in recent years was the explosion of teacher walkouts in 2018 in West Virginia,

Oklahoma, Arizona, Colorado, Kentucky, and North Carolina, with tens of thousands of teachers, some making as little as $32,000 a year, taking to the streets and pouring into state capitals. More startling still, most of these walkouts erupted in deep red states, where unions are weak, but these actions show that when employers squeeze workers enough, especially proud professionals like teachers, at some point they're going to stand up and shout, "We're not going to take it anymore." Their efforts are paying off; as a result of the teachers' newfound militancy, Oklahoma's governor gave her state's teachers raises of 14 percent. In early 2019, more than thirty thousand Los Angeles teachers went on strike demanding not just raises, but far-reaching improvements for their students. To end that six-day walkout, L.A.'s school board agreed to cut class sizes and hire far more nurses, librarians, and school counselors.

These efforts are giving more power—and hope—to American workers. As we examine the history of America's labor unions and the rise and decline of worker power, it will become clear that unions have played a crucial role in creating a fairer nation with less income inequality and more prosperity for millions of workers and their families. Nonetheless, labor unions and worker power have grown far weaker in the United States than in any other advanced industrial nation. This leaves some big questions for our nation: Will American workers have a voice on the job and a voice in our politics? Will workers have a say as globalization, automation, and artificial intelligence eliminate millions of jobs and threaten many workers? If workers don't have a real voice, working conditions for millions of Americans will inevitably deteriorate, and corporations and the wealthy will gain even more control over our nation's politics and policies. In the balance is the future of our economy and our democracy.

Two

A Worker's Struggle Never Ends

MOST WEEKDAYS Terrence Wise left his Kansas City apartment at 6 a.m., before his three daughters woke up, to head to his job at Burger King. He took two different buses as part of his hour-long commute, and when his Burger King shift ended, usually at 3 p.m., he had a ninety-minute slog on three more buses to his second job, as a cook and deliveryman at Pizza Hut. Most nights his Pizza Hut shift finished after 11, and on nights when he had to make many deliveries, he'd finish as late as 1 a.m. He'd typically arrive home an hour later, long after his girls had gone to sleep.

"That was the most damaging part, not being able to be around my kids, not participating in their everyday activities," Wise said. "The kids started saying, 'Daddy, we never get to see you.'"

In the winter of 2014, Wise, his fiancée, Myoshia Johnson, and their three daughters lived in a cold, dark two-bedroom walk-up. The heating was so inadequate that during the fall and winter, in desperation, they covered all their windows with plastic sheeting to reduce the drafts. On the coldest nights, the three sisters slept together on a long sectional couch in the combined living room/dining room/kitchen because there was no radiator in their small bedroom. Those nights, the family turned the gas oven to four hundred degrees, leaving its door open.

Terrence and Myoshia sometimes fell behind in paying their monthly gas bill, struggling to juggle it with their $600 rent, the cost of food, phone, electricity, car insurance, and the $100-a-month outlay to rent their furniture. One November, after they had missed two months of payments, their gas bill had climbed to $348.

Wise, a wiry five feet eight with closely cropped hair, is by turns stoic and angry. He and his fiancée, a home health aide, were struggling to hold on to their apartment after getting evicted from their previous one because of a double dose of bad luck. Burger King abruptly cut back Terrence's weekly hours, and then Myoshia sprained her back lifting an obese patient, forcing her to miss work for three months. After being evicted, the Wise family moved in with Myoshia's brother, and suddenly there were eleven people crowded into a three-bedroom apartment.

As soon as Myoshia could return to work, the Wise family found a new apartment, the woefully underheated one. Terrence felt it was glaringly wrong that despite holding two jobs, he couldn't make ends meet. He was making $7.50 an hour at Pizza Hut after three years there, and $9.47 an hour at Burger King after nine years, but he still needed the government safety net of $240 in monthly food stamps to feed his daughters. The only way he could obtain health coverage for his daughters was through Medicaid. But he didn't have health insurance for himself; he told me he hadn't been to a doctor in fourteen years.

Terrence and Myoshia often couldn't afford new clothes for their daughters. Once when they didn't buy the girls new shoes for the coming school year, "the other kids teased them about that," Wise said. "My girls really cried. They go to school with other poor kids, but you can't stop mean kids." Nor was Wise able to afford ballet slippers for his daughter Déziana; a bighearted ballet teacher took pity and bought them for her.

Hunger was also a problem. "There were definitely days there wasn't enough for the family, so me and Moe [Myoshia], we would skip meals or not feed ourselves," Wise said. "We would always ensure that the kids could eat." Sometimes when he skipped meals at home, he would take some unusual steps. "Some of the things I had to do to feed myself I wasn't proud of," he said. "Fast-food restaurants often dump unsold food into big metal waste bins out back. Sometimes I'd sneak a sandwich that they trashed. It wasn't allowed, but I'd do it."

At Burger King, Wise worked the grill or fried the fries or made the sandwiches or worked the counter or cleaned up. "They call me 'Mr. Everywhere.' There is nothing in the store I cannot do," he said. Some days work was hugely stressful. "Sunday is the worst day. During the week, we have ten or twelve people working. But on Sunday we have three people to run the store. They really slice labor. When you have the K.C. [Kansas City] Chiefs playing football, this is a lively town on Sunday, and I do four people's jobs. I have to cook all the meat. I have to make all the sandwiches and do all the prep and do all the cleaning. It's crazy. These are tasks delegated to three or four people during the week."

Wise grew irked about the economics of the job. "We took in $1,200 the other day at lunch hour at my Burger King," he said. "The six workers there cost them $60 or so for that hour." To be sure, the franchise owner had to pay rent, insurance, franchise fees, and the wholesale cost of the meat, fries, and other food, but Wise was convinced that the franchise owner could pay his workers considerably more and still show a tidy profit.

Wise was haunted by the enduring frustration that his life was in ways a rerun of his mother's. He grew up in Columbia, South Carolina, and for years his mother, JoAnn Wise, juggled two restaurant jobs—at Hardee's and Waffle House. "She went to work every morning, early in the morning," Wise said. "She was immaculate in her uniform. Sometimes I'd see her at work; I'd see her at the counter. She was very quick and always smiling, and everybody knew her name, and everybody loved her," he said. When Wise was nine, his mother had a new man in her life, the chief cook at Fort Jackson, an army training center. They moved in with him.

"At the time, I didn't know, but our parents shielded us," Wise said, noting that many months they still didn't have enough to pay the bills. "You'd look at my mom, and you'd think she was just happy and life was great. But sometimes I'd go home with her, and the lights were off because we couldn't pay the electricity bill. Sometimes I'd sign for the food stamps book at our door when the mailman brought it when she was at work. Some days all there was to eat was the loaf of bread on top of the refrigerator." His mother worked at Hardee's for twenty-one years but retired from there without any savings, pension, 401(k), or health benefits.

"She suffered just like we did," Wise said. "It's systematic. I don't want my kids to grow up and work at the same place I did and get treated and get paid the same way I did.

"We bounced around from project to project," he added. "We never owned a house. We never owned a car. We had to walk everywhere. We had to take our clothes to the laundry in a shopping cart. We had to walk to the supermarket. It was really a bad neighborhood. They said the way out was to play sports or sell drugs."

His two brothers sold drugs, but Wise played golf and basketball. He was such a standout he was invited to a golf camp where "there were three hundred white kids and four to six black kids," he said. He was also invited into the Fellowship of Christian Athletes. "Until I was fifteen or sixteen, I was really committed to the Bible and learning the ministry," he said. "I was teaching it to the youth. They called me Bible boy. They teased me a bunch for playing golf."

Wise was placed in advanced classes. "I was in classes with the Chinese kids and white kids, me and another black student," he said. "I was all college prep. I'd read the newspaper front to back. I was like that." Still, he couldn't avoid the tensions at home. One brother was in prison for selling drugs, the other brother was in and out of jail, and his mother and stepfather often had screaming matches over how to pay the bills. "It was really hard in my house," Wise said.

He concluded that his life and studies would be easier if he moved out. While in tenth grade, he and an eighteen-year-old friend from the Fellowship of Christian Athletes took an apartment together. To help pay the rent, Wise took two fast-food jobs, at Wendy's and Taco Bell, while going to high school. "I worked thirty hours a week at each one," he said. "At Wendy's, we would close at 2 a.m. and then you clean up. Busy nights, we'd work until 4. I'd just stay up, not going to bed. That's better than going to bed at 5 and waking up at 7 for school. I took lots of Monster energy drinks."

Wise quit his exhausting Wendy's job because he was falling asleep in class and falling behind in school, but he ended up dropping out because he couldn't balance school with his thirty-hour-a-week job at Taco Bell. He was soon facing eviction. That Christmas, an uncle, a union bricklayer in Kansas City, heard about Wise's plight and invited him to move in with him.

At first, things went well in Kansas City; he made friends and played on the high school basketball team. Then his uncle told him he had to earn some money. So it was back to the fast-food world—first a KFC job, and then a second job, at Taco Bell. "I'd go to work at 4 and get off at 2 a.m., and then just crash," Wise said. "My uncle got up at 6 to go to work, and I'd tell him, 'I'm not going to school today. I worked too late last night.'" Wise tried to reduce his shifts, from eight hours to four, but Wendy's wouldn't let him. His grades suffered, and he dropped out. His hopes of college evaporated.

After quitting high school, Wise landed his best job ever—at a Red Lobster. As a charming, efficient waiter, he received his highest take-home pay ever: for thirty hours' work, he made $500 a week, including tips. Myoshia also worked there; that was where they met. She became pregnant, and they moved in together into a nice apartment, but then the Red Lobster closed, and it was back to the fast-food grind. He took a job with Burger King and then one at Pizza Hut, too.

"My thinking was, I'm going to go back to school before I'm thirty," Wise said. "Me and Moe would make plans: she not work for a year and go back to school. Moe was studying to be an LPN [licensed practical nurse]. She was supposed to go back to KU [the University of Kansas] the next year, but she couldn't afford it." They abandoned their plans.

"I didn't have the resources to stop working and go back to school and do it big like that," he added. "We never could just stop working. Life would always throw something at us."

Wise grew tired of people telling him that if he was unhappy with his low pay, he should go back to school. Those people are out of touch, he thought. "Sure, I still want to go back to school. But I can't work forty hours, raise three daughters, pay bills, and go to school at the same time. Who doesn't want to go back to school? Everyone wants to. Heck yeah."

Some days Wise raged about his family's situation. He was unhappy about living in a neighborhood where the schools were bad—where classes were large, students often fought, and the kids had to go through metal detectors each morning.

Like most Americans, Wise harbored his own version of the American dream: "We want to buy a house. That would be No. 1—a house and a car and a job."

He admitted to wanting one other thing: to marry Myoshia. "I tell her, 'Let's just go to the courthouse and get married,'" he said with a smile. "But she wants a big wedding. She wants a real wedding, and I tell her we don't have real money. It's going to cost over $1,000, not including invitations, wedding gown and tuxedo and kids' dresses and pretty flowers. That's a couple of grand there. No way we can afford that."

It was a scorcher—still ninety-nine degrees at 4 p.m.—and every time a car turned off Channahon Road to approach the Caterpillar factory gate, a dozen or so sweat-drenched strikers rushed over to shout "Scab!" as loudly and fiercely as they could. The drivers simply sped up and did their best to ignore them.

Outwardly, the strikers appeared casual—dressed in T-shirts, shorts, blue jeans, and baseball caps, some brims backward—but these strikers were battle-hardened, locked in a protracted industrial war that was playing out along a flat stretch of America's heartland, in Joliet, Illinois, thirty miles southwest of Chicago. They had stocked up on weapons to outlast the enemy: shade tents, folding chairs, coolers filled with Coke, Sprite, and orange juice, and, last but not least, Porta Potties. The strikers' picket signs proudly proclaimed, "On Strike for a Fair Contract," "I Am Solidarity," and "Fighting for Our Children's Future." The strikers shouted, marched, chatted, strategized, sat, napped, and picketed out front of a plant where, for years, they had made elaborate hydraulic parts and systems essential for much of Caterpillar's earthmoving equipment.

Eleven weeks into their strike, these workers—780 had walked out initially—were holding strong against one of the world's most powerful manufacturing companies, a behemoth with more than $45 billion in annual revenues, famed for its mighty yellow tractors. The strikers were furious that Caterpillar, in 2012, when it was crowing about record profits, was insisting on a *six-year* pay freeze for the factory's more senior workers, representing two-thirds of the workforce. Caterpillar was also demanding a pension freeze in perpetuity for these workers as well as a hefty $3,800 increase in each worker's annual contribution for health coverage. If acceded to, Caterpillar's demands meant that the strikers, members of the International Association of Machinists, would have their take-home pay chopped by 20 percent over the life of the contract, after factoring in inflation.

"It is never our objective to go on strike, but that's our only weapon, so we use it," said Allen Williams, the picket captain for the afternoon shift. "Considering the offer they gave us, it's a strike we had to have."

Williams, like those carrying picket signs alongside him, young and old, black and white, men and women, was convinced that the employee-employer relationship was dreadfully broken, that they had worked hard, had endured 5 a.m. shifts and midnight shifts, had suffered slipped disks and broken fingers, had done all this to help mighty Caterpillar make its record profits. Yet now this icon of American industry was seeking to seriously diminish them rather than reward them. This was not how America was supposed to work, not how the American dream was supposed to unfold—you work hard, you give your all, and in return you move ahead, and upward. For generations, that's what had made America great; people pulled together and then shared in the bounty, in the profits they produced.

For Williams, the walkout had taken a toll. After all these weeks on strike without his regular paycheck, he couldn't even afford the $40 equipment fee for his eleven-year-old to play Little League. Williams, sporting a bold, thick mustache and a black baseball cap that covered his shiny, bald pate, was both worn down and riled up. Before the strike, he was solidly in the American middle class, earning $26 an hour after nineteen years at Caterpillar, $54,000 a year before overtime. In previous contract fights, Caterpillar, unhappy about blue-collar paychecks that large, had pressured its labor unions into allowing a lower wage tier for newer workers, which started at $12 an hour and topped out at $19. Some of these younger factory workers lived in trailers; some needed food stamps to feed their children. In this fight, Caterpillar was refusing to promise raises to even these lower-tier workers, hinting that it might grant them pay increases, depending on vague "local market conditions."

Caterpillar workers have seen these hardball tactics before. In 1994, 13,400 of the company's blue-collar workers walked out at eight plants in three states, and Caterpillar ordered 5,000 white-collar employees to work on the factory floor to help win that seventeen-month-long strike. Those strikers were enraged by Caterpillar's demand for a contract with no guaranteed annual raises for six years, but Caterpillar emerged victorious on that demand and many others.

To Williams, Caterpillar's latest push for givebacks was a galling insult. The company's record profits that year amounted to $45,000 per employee, nearly as much as his base pay. "It's ridiculous. They're giving the CEO a 60 percent pay increase, and the employees who make the product are being asked to sacrifice," Williams said. "This is part of the climate across the country. Corporations are pushing to eliminate pensions and drive wages down."

In Caterpillar's eyes, the wages of Williams and the other experienced workers were out of line. "Paying wages well above market levels makes Joliet uncompetitive," the company warned in a statement. "Frankly, if we're not competitive, we're not gonna be here in the next thirty years," said Caterpillar's CEO at the time, Douglas Oberhelman.

The showdown in Joliet crystallized two views of the American economy: profit maximization versus shared prosperity. Caterpillar felt that no matter how high its profits rose, its wages should never exceed market levels, meaning the average amount paid by other factories in the area. This view underlined the primacy of shareholders and maximizing profits. "I always try to communicate to our people that we can never make enough money," Oberhelman said. "We can never make enough profit." This view allows little compassion for Caterpillar's workers, who happen to be his fellow citizens.

The workers, of course, believed passionately that the company should share with them the prosperity that the workers had helped to produce. To them, it was a matter of basic fairness and dignity.

"It is class warfare, really an attack on the middle class," said Tom Eley, who had worked at the plant for nineteen years.

"Basically," said Wayne Lander, a fellow striker, "the company is asking us to take less when they make record profits. How are they not competitive? Who are they trying to compete with, Walmart?"

Postscript: After Caterpillar had record net income in 2012, the year of the Joliet strike, its profits suffered an unanticipated decline in subsequent years because falling oil prices led to decreased orders for Caterpillar equipment and because Caterpillar made huge, ill-advised investments in China that largely fell flat. In 2015, three years after this strike, Caterpillar announced it would move most of the production operations from the Joliet plant to a new, lower-wage factory in Monterrey, Mexico. In February 2019, Caterpillar closed the sixty-eight-year-old plant.

―――――

Jennifer Sanders has a striking voice—smooth, modulated, beautiful— ideal for a radio host or for the pulpit. But in fact, she works at a General Motors plant, spending her days hoisting hundreds of heavy metal radiators into one truck chassis after another. She is a fifth-generation GM worker and speaks with pride that one of her great-great-grandfathers left a dirt-floor shack in Pennsylvania to work for GM in Michigan. In the summer of 2015, though, Sanders, then thirty-one, was deeply frustrated that GM workers in her generation were doing considerably worse than those in her father's and grandfather's generations.

Sanders began at GM in 2012 as a fill-in, having to learn forty different assembly-line jobs. She worked a ten-hour overnight shift, helping assemble Chevy Sonics and Buick Veranos at GM's plant in Orion Township, forty miles northwest of Detroit. She hired on as part of GM's second, lower-paid tier. By 2015, she was earning $17.53 an hour, but under GM's contract with the United Automobile Workers union, the most that second-tier workers could earn was $19 an hour, while workers in the upper tier typically made $29.

Sanders lived with her parents those first few years at GM, and that also frustrated her. "I've gone to college, I've had a career, and I moved back in with my parents," said Sanders, who has a strong, open face and straight brown hair falling to her shoulders. "It was not the American dream by any stretch. For the first year [2012], I was just a temp, not a permanent employee. And once I was hired permanently, it was still unstable." Sixth from the bottom on her plant's seniority list, she was repeatedly laid off, sometimes for months, because low gas prices had cut into sales and production of the fuel-efficient Sonics and Veranos. "That made it hard to move out from my parents," Sanders said.

In her eyes, her parents have lived the American dream. Her father, Roy Richard, retired at age fifty-five with a generous pension, having worked for GM for thirty-seven years, many of them as an expert tool-and-die maker. Her mother, Kris, had also worked at GM, putting in fifteen years there.

"I had a great life," Roy Richard said. "My father said I could go to college, but I wanted to work at GM instead. When I first hired into GM, it was the largest company in the country, and it was a good place to work with good pay and good benefits. You could raise a family on it. The biggest changes I see now is just the struggle for these younger workers to make ends meet. What we're seeing with Jennifer is she's pretty much living paycheck to paycheck."

Jennifer said of her father's generation at GM, "Everybody was able to have a vacation home up north and have Jet Skis and boats in those days. It was essentially middle-class. But now I wonder sometimes about what the auto industry has become and, because of the tier system, whether my generation of autoworkers will ever attain that."

She's outspoken and thoughtful, not bitter. Before going to work for GM, she had obtained a bachelor's degree in religious studies at a Baptist college in southwest Indiana. She got married and took a job as a youth pastor nearby. Seven years after she graduated, she and her husband divorced, and she and her daughter, Kendall, moved to Michigan in 2010. The state was still not close to recovering from the Great Recession.

"I was putting out résumés right and left," Sanders said. "Where they [employers] once had five or six people applying for each job, now they had a hundred." She settled for work as a substitute teacher for $75 a day, but seeing her struggle on that modest amount, her father told her he could try to get her a job with GM. She agreed.

She was surprised that she liked factory work. "I was fortunate," she said. "I'm a lot better off than I was substitute teaching." She was quick to add, though, that her second-tier wages were far from ideal. After falling into bankruptcy in 2009, GM said it would keep certain plants open, including Orion Township, only if the union helped GM cut its costs by agreeing to a lower wage tier. Some second-tier workers were furious at the UAW for agreeing to that, but not Sanders.

"I understand the tier system came into play because it was necessary," Sanders said. "But I very much feel it is not a necessity anymore. The auto industry has bounced back. They're making money. Now I feel they're making money off us lower-tier workers." In 2015, GM's profits were a record $9.7 billion, a huge turnaround from its loss of $5.3 billion in 2009 and its colossal $29 billion loss in 2008.

With so much union blood in her veins, Sanders became one of the more outspoken second-tier workers pushing for higher pay. She talks the language of solidarity, not resentment or division. Speaking of the higher-paid top tier, she said, "They haven't had a raise in ten years. We want them to get their raise, too. We want each other to have it better."

Considering Sanders's pedigree, it shouldn't be a surprise that she talks solidarity. One of her great-grandfathers, George Edmonds, participated in the Flint Sit-Down Strike of 1936–37, a historic labor victory in which GM workers struck for forty-four days in the dead of winter and got GM to finally recognize the UAW after GM had spent years trying to crush any attempts at unionization.

"Everything I have today is because of that sit-down strike," Sanders said.

Richard was with Jennifer as we talked one day. He told me how much things have improved for autoworkers. When he started in 1977, he had to work seven eleven-and-a-half-hour days each week. The UAW won the workers a day off. Wages had climbed steadily, he said, enabling him to take his family on vacations to Mexico and Europe. He said he has visited nonunion factories that seem like throwbacks to the 1930s. "You see [mechanical] presses running with no guarding, where you can get your hair and hands caught. You see guys climbing in the presses without locking them out [closing them down so the machines can't suddenly start up and maim someone]. We wouldn't stand for that in GM plants."

Richard told of his mother's grandfather and that grandfather's father: "They came out of coal mines in Pennsylvania. They got tired of the companies breaking the union. They were living in a dirt-floor shack. They moved to Michigan, and they were able to build a nice home, buy cars, buy guns, take vacations, go hunting—all the nice things they wanted to do. There was a strong union that helped people provide for their families."

Sanders nodded as her father talked. "The union is everything to me," she said. "My entire being revolves around what the union has done for us." She talked of how her parents could afford to send her and her sister (a schoolteacher) to college, and while the family didn't own a cabin in the woods, they did take vacations to Florida and overseas.

She often reflects on the problems her union faces. She told of a conversation she had with a co-worker when the UAW was seeking to raise dues to one and a half hours of pay per month, from one hour. "He was frustrated about it," she said. "He said, 'If I didn't have to pay union dues, I wouldn't. The union has never done anything for me. I've never been in trouble. I never needed a committeeman.'

"I said, 'If you did get in trouble, a committeeman would come out and help you.'

"I asked, 'Do you have a safe work environment?' He said, 'Yeah.' I said, 'The union did that for you.'

"And I said, 'Do you get paid overtime?' He said, 'Yeah.' I said, 'The union did that for you.'

"I said, 'Do you get your weekends off?' He said, 'Yeah.' I said, 'The union did that for you.'

"My generation doesn't realize that we wouldn't have these things if we didn't have unions."

On October 27, 2015, Sanders got some good news: after months of tense negotiations between GM and the UAW, the two sides agreed to phase out the lower-paid tier, raising everyone to $29 after eight years. "This was huge," Sanders said. (While most workers rejoiced that their pay would rise to $29, some complained that it would take eight years.) Sanders was also pleased that the lower-tier workers would be put into the same, far better health, vision, and dental plans as the top-tier workers.

Thanks to her greater income and job security, Sanders bought a modest house for $85,000 for herself and her daughter. It's filled with family photos and a piano. She also transferred to a GM plant in Flint, just ten minutes from her home, much better than her forty-five-minute commute to Orion Township. Now she helps assemble Silverado trucks, using a hoist and hook to lift radiators into the truck chassis.

She worries about the future of the UAW and unions in general. "My generation of autoworkers, they don't know the history of the UAW. They don't know the history of the sit-down strike. They don't want to know those stories," she said. "That's part of why the union is falling apart. There's not the strength that there was, because people don't care like they used to. Nobody realizes that all that we have is because of what was done before.

"I don't know what the future of the union will be," Sanders continued. "It's scary. My generation frightens me. I don't want to live in a world where there aren't unions. I don't want my daughter and my nieces to have to go into the workforce without the option of having union jobs. I fear that that's their future."

Three
_____

Helping Workers Hit the Jackpot

AT A TIME when much of organized labor is in a defensive crouch—walloped by falling membership, antiunion legislation, and hostile court decisions—a few unions are still flying high, none more so than Culinary Workers Union Local 226 of Las Vegas. Its membership has more than tripled since the late 1980s, soaring from eighteen thousand to sixty thousand today, making it one of the most powerful and fastest-growing union locals in the nation. Its contracts have catapulted thousands of dishwashers, waiters, and hotel housekeepers into the middle class, even though those are poverty-level jobs in many other cities. The Culinary Union, together with the city's casino-hotels, has created the trailblazing Culinary Academy of Las Vegas, where these workers can take free courses that train them for jobs such as chef and bartender that will often double or triple their incomes. It's a union of extraordinary diversity, with immigrant members from Latin America and Asia, blacks from the Deep South, and refugees from the Balkans and East Africa, representing 173 countries in all.

While the broader labor movement was humbled for failing to keep Michigan, Pennsylvania, and Wisconsin from falling into Donald Trump's column in 2016, the Culinary Union played a decisive role in turning another battleground state, Nevada, blue. Its foot soldiers knocked on 350,000 doors in the 2016 campaign—just one of the reasons it is widely viewed as an organizing and political juggernaut. The Culinary's reputation grew further in November 2018, when, with another all-out push, it played a pivotal role in flipping a U.S. Senate seat, the governor's mansion, and two House seats from red to blue;

indeed Nevada's Dean Heller was the only incumbent Republican senator to lose his race for reelection that year.

Francis Garcia, a thirty-nine-year-old housekeeper at the MGM Grand on Las Vegas's famous Strip, feels blessed to be a member of the Culinary Union. Garcia is short and stocky, with powerful shoulders, deep brown eyes, and long dark hair that she often wears in a bun. She is talkative and confident, even sassy at times. A native of Honduras, she crossed through Mexico and settled in Phoenix after Hurricane Mitch devastated her home country in 1998, killing over seven thousand people there and leaving more than one million homeless. "Honduras is a very poor place," she said. "I have nothing there. My parents are dead. I thought I would have a better opportunity over here."

Garcia was happy to land a $10-an-hour warehouse job in Phoenix, although in that job she strained to pay the $500 a month for health insurance, one-fourth of her pay. In Phoenix, she fell in love with a fellow immigrant from Honduras, a construction worker, and together they had three children. In 2007, her boyfriend, Juan, couldn't find work in Phoenix, so he moved to Las Vegas, where there were still plenty of construction jobs. Ultimately, Garcia and the kids also moved to Las Vegas, where she began looking for another warehouse job. But an acquaintance who knew her way around Las Vegas advised Garcia to go to the Culinary Academy.

There she took a free two-month course on how to be a guest room attendant. The course covered everything from how to lay out decorative pillows on a king-size bed to what cleaning solution to use on a bathroom's marble floor. Housekeepers and dishwashers can also take classes to become pastry chefs and more. A $35,000-a-year restaurant busser can train for a $60,000-a-year job as a waiter and then study to become a $90,000-a-year sommelier. (Each year the academy instructs sixteen hundred workers; it is financed by thirty-three casino-hotels, which are forever hungry for well-trained workers.)

Soon after completing her housekeeping course in 2007, Garcia landed a job at the MGM Grand. She started at $14.50 an hour. "The money you make over here is much better than in Phoenix, and the benefits are amazing," she said. Twelve years later, still working at the MGM Grand, she was making $19.54 an hour with a pension plan and Cadillac health coverage. Nationwide, median pay for hotel housekeepers is $11 an hour. The Culinary Union's contract guarantees housekeepers a forty-hour week, while at many nonunion hotels, housekeepers work twenty-five or thirty hours a week. Garcia earns over $780 weekly; many nonunion housekeepers earn just $330.

For the first time in her life, Garcia can afford to own a car—a Toyota Camry. She can also afford a comfortable three-bedroom apartment, which rents for $900 a month. Garcia gets one bedroom, her seventeen-year-old son gets another bedroom, and her two daughters—twenty-one and thirteen—share the third bedroom. The living room boasts an oversize TV and oversize brown leather couch. (Thrown out of work by the Great Recession, Juan moved back to Honduras in 2009.)

Garcia hasn't saved up enough to take advantage of one innovative, impressive Culinary benefit—its housing fund provides $20,000 in down payment assistance that has helped more than a thousand workers buy their own homes, an important step toward lifting them into the middle class. Culinary members don't have to repay that money unless they sell their homes.

Thanks to the good wages and benefits in her union's contract, Garcia can support a family without needing food stamps, Medicaid, or housing subsidies. The Culinary Union's health plan is a godsend for her and her family. Workers don't have to pay any premiums, and they pay just a few hundred dollars each year in co-payments for prescriptions, doctors' appointments, and hospital visits. Dental procedures often cost just $10, while workers at nonunion hotels often pay $400 or more. When Garcia's younger daughter was hit with a bad flu, she took her to one of the union's jewels: the Culinary Health Center. There, her daughter saw a doctor for free and received free prescription medication.

Garcia works 8:30 a.m. to 4:30 p.m. Sunday through Thursday; she goes to church on Saturday. Her job, she said, is a daily sprint to clean fifteen rooms in the allotted eight hours (which includes forty-five minutes for lunch and a fifteen-minute break). Housekeeping jobs are arduous—indeed, numerous academic studies have shown that those jobs have a dismayingly high rate of back and shoulder injuries. Five days a week, Garcia pushes a 300-pound cart through the halls of the MGM Grand; the cart is loaded with linens, towels, toiletries, tissues, bathrobes, glass cleaners, mop, vacuum cleaner, toilet brush, magazines, and bottles of water. And then there's the strain from repeatedly lifting the corners of 150-pound mattresses.

"Sometimes we rush, and it's easy to get hurt," she said.

One day while making a bed, she got a shock from static electricity and jerked her arm back so suddenly that she tore a shoulder muscle. She received a cortisone shot and physical therapy, but it was still hurting her a year later. Another day when she entered a bathroom to clean it, she slipped on a puddle of sunblock that a guest had spilled on the floor, and crashed to the floor, hurting her back.

Garcia takes pride in her ability to stand up for herself. "I like to fight about things that I think are wrong," she said. "I think nobody can fix your problem better than you." At one MGM Grand monthly meeting for housekeepers, Garcia spoke up loud and clear about mistakes that supervisors had made, making it hard for some housekeepers to clean all their assigned rooms in time. Dozens of other housekeepers burst into applause when Garcia finished. Having heard how bold and effective Garcia was about speaking up, a Culinary Union organizer asked her to become a shop steward so she could use her moxie to fight on behalf of others.

"I said no," Garcia recalled. "I like to fight, but I didn't want to deal with all that." She had a full-time job and three children to raise. A few days later, however, "the organizer came up to me and told me, 'Don't just think about you. You should think about the people you can help.' She made me think from a different point of view." Garcia agreed to become a shop steward, and in that unpaid position—she retained her regular job—she's responsible for twenty other guest room attendants. She listens to their concerns, conveys those concerns to union leaders, and keeps her twenty workers informed about everything from upcoming union protests to the Culinary Health Fund's annual Back to School Fair, where children get free inoculations and some free school supplies. As a shop steward, Garcia also has to fight for other workers, including housekeepers who face punishment for such things as failing to finish their assigned rooms within eight hours. "Some people don't know how to defend themselves," Garcia said. "I try to do that for them."

Francis Garcia is part of what is often considered the nation's most elaborate and effective network of shop stewards—the Culinary has more than a thousand of them. They serve as a central nervous system that helps to keep the union alert and strong, letting union leaders know what's going on inside the hotels. The Culinary Union further involves members by forming worker committees at each hotel and having rank-and-file workers serve on the bargaining team that negotiates contracts with the casino-hotels. As part of all this, the Culinary pursues a strategy that many other unions neglect: it trains rank-and-file workers to become leaders. Garcia has taken many courses that the union offers, including English literacy classes, a course on workers' rights, and one on how to be a shop steward. There, she learns about the details of the union's contract and how to be a more effective speaker and advocate.

The Culinary once sent Garcia to Washington as part of a delegation that met with members of Congress to push for immigration reform. Like eighty-six thousand other Honduran immigrants in the United States, she received temporary protective status after Hurricane Mitch ravaged Honduras. But President Trump canceled their protective status, and now Garcia fears being deported after two decades in the United States. "I'm scared of going back to Honduras with the gang violence there," she said.

She is heartened that the Culinary Union has done intensive lobbying and organized repeated protests to fight for immigrant workers like her. The union is also providing Garcia with some free legal assistance, hoping to help her obtain a permanent visa as the mother of three children born in the United States.

"I'm really afraid, but I'm not alone in this fight," Garcia said. "I have lots of support. I love that the union is fighting for me."

———

On the morning of Election Day 2016, the Culinary Union's headquarters was like a battle station. Color-coded maps lined the walls, with hundreds of pushpins indicating streets that had been canvassed. Some four hundred union members had crowded into the Culinary's "Big Hall" by 5 a.m., their bright red shirts proclaiming, "Defeat Trump." They carried handheld computers programmed to tell them which homes to visit in an effort to get people to vote. The union had acquired an arsenal of information—gathered from thousands of home visits and phone calls—about who had already voted (through early voting) and which voters were strongly or mildly for Hillary Clinton or Donald Trump and which supported the union's preferred candidate for Senate, Catherine Cortez Masto, a former Nevada attorney general. In the minutes before they fanned out across the city, the campaign workers erupted into a pep rally, chanting, *"Sí se puede"* (Yes, we can) and "226, 226, 226."

Culinary Local 226 certainly showed its political muscle in 2016. Its troops spoke to seventy-five thousand voters—Culinary members, family members, and workers in other unions. The Culinary and its affiliate, the Citizenship Project, also got eight thousand people to register to vote and shepherded twenty-five hundred members through the citizenship process. One of them was Xiomara Duenas, who emigrated from Cuba in 1996 and long thought her shaky English wasn't good enough for her to become a citizen. She was alarmed by Trump's anti-Hispanic rhetoric. "I didn't want him to become president," Duenas said. "But now I can vote." The Culinary says it got 54,000 early voters to the polls in 2016—a consequential number in a state where Clinton defeated Trump by 27,202 votes. (Cortez Masto also beat her Republican opponent by around 27,000 votes, making her the first Hispanic woman in the U.S. Senate.)

"The Culinary is the most potent grassroots organization in this state," said Jon Ralston, a Nevada political analyst. "It was really like an army knocking on doors," said Dina Titus, a Democratic member of Congress representing North Las Vegas. *The Washington Post* called it "the dominant political force in the state."

Recognizing the Culinary Union's clout, all of the Democratic presidential candidates made a pilgrimage to show their respect. When Clinton announced her plan to create a path to citizenship for undocumented immigrants, she did that in Las Vegas (the Culinary is 54 percent Latino). Bernie Sanders held a town-hall meeting on economic issues at the union's headquarters on the northern end of the Strip. When the Culinary was at war with the Trump International Hotel in Las Vegas because it wouldn't recognize the union, even though a majority of the hotel's workers had voted to join, Clinton and Maryland's governor, Martin O'Malley, rallied alongside union protesters outside the hotel.

The Culinary is a model for unions in politics, many political experts say. Three hundred members of the Culinary and its parent union, the UNITE HERE hospitality workers' union, took two months' paid leave (financed by the union) to work in the 2016 campaign. They, along with hundreds of union volunteers, did their utmost to educate rank-and-file members on the issues and then get them to vote. Yvanna Cancela, the Culinary's political director during the 2016 campaign, says the union's political success stems directly from the loyalty and trust that many members feel toward their union—both because of the excellent pay and benefits it delivers and because the shop steward network and hotel committees keep them informed and involved. "As a result of our very close relationship with members," Cancela said, "the union is able to explain to members why political work and voting are necessary to keep unions strong."

Part of the Culinary's gospel is if workers are to continue receiving good wages and benefits, they need to keep their union strong, and to do that, it's vital to defeat candidates who want to hobble unions and to elect candidates who want to strengthen them. The Culinary's all-out effort each election is predicated on the notion that Las Vegas is a big blue island in an overwhelmingly rural state with many deep red communities and that this blue island needs to maximize its turnout.

One of the Culinary's primary strategies is to "target low-propensity voters [often Latino, black, or young voters] that we think we can move with our message," Cancela said. "The Culinary—being the largest immigrant organization and the largest Latino organization in Nevada—has a history of organizing people in a longer-term and meaningful way, while other campaigns and national groups often try to organize on a one-off basis. As a result, our union has been able to move more voters."

Cancela is a precocious political dynamo. The daughter of Cuban immigrants, she grew up in Miami and fought for migrant farmworkers while in high school. She went to Northwestern University on a debating scholarship and got the political bug while doing a summer internship for Senator Harry Reid of Nevada. After college, she took a job as an organizer for the Culinary and was named its political director when she was just twenty-three years old. After a state senator from Las Vegas was elected to Congress in 2016, Cancela was appointed to replace him, making her the first Hispanic woman in the Nevada State Senate. (As a result of that move, she stepped down as the Culinary's political director.)

The Culinary places a big bet on early voting. "That is so important because a lot of time workers are working on Election Day," said D. Taylor, who ran the Culinary for two decades before becoming president of UNITE HERE. (Taylor uses his childhood nickname, D.) "People have several days to do early voting. It's convenient. The city sets up booths for early voting at supermarkets and malls." For two weeks before Election Day, the Culinary hires charter buses to carry housekeepers and kitchen workers from the casino-hotels to voting places at lunchtime (during those outings, the union provides them with a free box lunch). In 2016, the Culinary helped the Democrats do such a good job pulling out early voters that Trump was forty-six thousand votes behind in Nevada going into Election Day.

"Like most Americans, a lot of workers don't have the highest opinion of the candidates," Taylor said. "We always organize around the union and the issues, not around the candidate." One of the issues the union emphasized in 2016 was that Trump and the GOP had vowed to repeal the Affordable Care Act, a move that many Culinary members feared would undermine their health coverage.

The Culinary sometimes supports Republicans, most notably Nevada's two-term governor, Brian Sandoval, who bucked Trump by supporting immigration reform and opposing the repeal of Obamacare. But Taylor said it has become harder for unions to back Republicans because GOP politicians increasingly favor the rich, attack safety net programs, and push to weaken unions.

In Taylor's view, canvassers' repeated visits to Culinary members' homes are an important strategy, not just to get them to vote, but to strengthen ties between members and their union, even when the worker visited and the one visiting support different candidates. "People want to hear about the issues," Taylor said. "They also want to be listened to. They want to be heard."

Cancela said Nevada's right-to-work law has pushed the Culinary Union to draw closer to its members than many unions have. Because such laws mean that workers can't be required to pay any fees to the union that negotiates their pay and benefits, the Culinary pushes hard to communicate with workers and deliver impressive pay and benefits so workers value their union and agree to pay dues. As a result, more than 95 percent of the workers covered by the Culinary's contracts agree to pay union dues or fees. That is an unusually high percentage in an anti-union-fee, right-to-work state. It's also a strong vote of confidence in the Culinary, helping keep its finances strong.

Many of the Culinary's members favored Bernie Sanders in the Democratic primary in 2016, but the Culinary, nonetheless, got its members to vote massively for Clinton on Election Day. That effort got a lift from the union's battle with the Trump International Hotel. One evening the Culinary mobilized fifteen hundred people—including Francis Garcia and her daughters—to picket the hotel. Geoconda Argüello-Kline, a former hotel housekeeper and immigrant from Nicaragua who succeeded Taylor as head of the Culinary, said the union had a relentless message for its members: "We need to vote for Hillary because Trump is going to be really bad for workers and for immigrants."

Taylor is convinced that other unions can borrow the Culinary's strategies to have more success in politics. "Take Michigan, Ohio, Wisconsin, Pennsylvania—there are huge unions there," he said. "What we do can be replicated. The key thing is you shouldn't talk to your members and their families only around election time. If that's the case, that means for two years they're listening to whatever. You have to maintain a continual conversation with workers around economic issues."

———

In the Culinary's first three decades—it was founded in 1935—it played the unusual role of labor recruiter, finding workers for the new casinos that were sprouting in the desert, underwritten by gangster money. The Culinary grew steadily in the 1950s and 1960s as the Strip added casinos where the Rat Pack—starring Frank Sinatra, Dean Martin, Sammy Davis Jr.—and other entertainers often drew sellout crowds. Early on, Vegas's casino-hotel owners accepted the union because it helped recruit workers, but by the early 1980s some owners came to believe that the union had grown too powerful.

In the 1984 contract negotiations, eighteen casinos quickly settled with the Culinary, while thirteen set out to break the union. They demanded a series of painful, unpopular concessions that led the union to go on strike. Nine hundred strikers were arrested during the bitter, seventy-five-day walkout, which took a heavy toll on the casinos. The industry lost an estimated $60 million in tourism revenue, and with all the tensions and arrests, the casinos' image took a beating as they were seeking to shed their tainted past and project a more wholesome image.

The Culinary suffered, too. At six hotels, the workers, egged on by management, voted to decertify the union. That was a stinging setback.

Badly shaken, the Culinary elected new leaders and asked its parent union to send some help to strengthen the local. Headquarters dispatched some crack organizers and young activists, a team led by John Wilhelm, who had spearheaded the union's successful effort to unionize twenty-six hundred clerical and technical workers at Yale University. Taylor was sent in to run the Culinary's day-to-day operations.

Wilhelm and Taylor transformed the Culinary into a cohesive and mighty union that they hoped would never again lose a decertification vote. To that end, they created the elaborate system of shop stewards and union committees to involve the workers more and have the union serve them better. "The union was run more like a business union," Taylor said. "We decided to make it a rank-and-file union."

In 1989, the Culinary faced a make-or-break challenge with the opening of the Mirage, Las Vegas's first giant, themed casino-hotel, famous for its white tigers and erupting volcano. If the Culinary was to grow, it needed to organize the Mirage, which was ushering in a new era of mega-resorts on the Strip. Steve Wynn, the Mirage's owner, rebuffed the Culinary's demand: that the Mirage agree to "card check" neutrality (that is, that it wouldn't fight against unionization and would recognize the union once the Culinary got a majority of workers to sign cards supporting the union). The union persuaded Wynn to change his mind by offering two things he badly wanted: it agreed to rewrite archaic contractual language to whittle 134 job classifications down to 30, and it pledged to use organized labor's considerable clout to get Congress to block a plan that would have required that taxes be withheld whenever foreign gamblers racked up large winnings. (If such a rule took effect, it would chase away a highly profitable chunk of the Mirage's business.)

Soon after Wynn agreed to neutrality and card check, thirty-three hundred Mirage employees unionized. Seeking to avoid the Culinary's wrath and might, several other big new casino-hotels followed Wynn's lead and agreed to card check. As a result, the union added sixty-five hundred workers at the Excalibur, Treasure Island, and Luxor. A dozen other hotels still refused to accept card check, so the Culinary targeted one of them for a strike: the Horseshoe, an older downtown hotel not on the Strip. That walkout lasted nine months, causing the Horseshoe's business to plummet. Its owners ultimately capitulated and accepted card check, and most other hotels soon agreed to it as well. The Frontier, a Strip hotel with old-style cowboy owners, was the lone hold-out. The Culinary struck the Frontier on September 21, 1991, in what became one of the longest walkouts in American history—six years, four months, and ten days. Not a single one of the 550 Frontier strikers crossed the picket line. At one point, twenty thousand Culinary members and allies marched along the Strip in support of the Frontier strikers. Finally, in early 1998, the Frontier's business nearly ruined, its owners sold their casino-hotel. The new owners rapidly agreed to card check, and the union celebrated a long-awaited victory.

Two years into the Frontier strike, MGM was planning to open the MGM Grand on the Strip. Intent on keeping it nonunion, MGM hired many of the hotel's eighty-five hundred employees from Los Angeles, rather than union-friendly Las Vegas. Irked by MGM's antiunion maneuvering, the Culinary greeted the opening of the five-thousand-room MGM Grand—then the world's largest hotel—with a protest by five thousand members. The union even persuaded the governor and the mayor to skip the opening. Several months later, the Culinary held a rally in which five hundred people were arrested outside the hotel. These tensions embarrassed the MGM Grand, which was hoping to project a fun, family-oriented *Wizard of Oz* theme.

To ratchet up the pressure, the Culinary used research and politics in some sophisticated and potent ways. It prepared a report that it distributed to Wall Street investors, warning that MGM had high debt levels and that a Culinary strike could severely maim MGM's finances. The publication was called, "Would You Bet a Billion Dollars on a Single Roll of the Dice?" At the time, MGM was eager to expand in the Midwest as several Rust Belt cities were seeking to allow in casinos to boost their ailing economies. But UNITE HERE and its labor allies lobbied heavily in Detroit, Chicago, and several other cities to oppose MGM's efforts to win the right to open casinos.

This unrelenting pressure helped persuade MGM to oust the Grand's antiunion chairman. His replacement sued for peace and accepted card check—a move that helped persuade a new wave of mega-hotels to agree to card check. The Culinary added 4,150 workers at the Bellagio in 1998, and 5,600 at Mandalay Bay and the Paris in 1999. Today the Culinary represents workers at 95 percent of the casino-hotels on the Strip (the big exception being Sheldon Adelson's Venetian).

The MGM Grand's new chairman, J. Terrence Lanni, sang the praises of labor peace, noting it was far better to have satisfied workers than sulking ones. "The last thing you want is for people who are coming to enjoy themselves to see pickets and unhappy workers blocking driveways," Lanni said. "I swore then that we would never have such problems again." He added, "When you're in the service business, the first contact our guests have is with the guest-room attendants or the food and beverage servers, and if that person's unhappy, that comes across to the guests very quickly."

In the two decades since the Culinary unionized the MGM Grand, MGM's Las Vegas holdings have expanded to include such giant casinos as the Bellagio, Excalibur, Luxor, Mandalay Bay, the Mirage, and New York–New York. In the Culinary's 2018 contract negotiations with MGM, one of the hottest issues was the union's fear that many workers would lose their jobs to new technologies, like robots that vacuum hallways and make room service deliveries and touch screens where customers place restaurant orders. MGM and the Culinary, which has been one of the most farsighted unions on technology issues, agreed to create a committee that is studying how employees can be trained to harness—and work alongside—new technologies, instead of being replaced by them. The contract calls for giving the union 180 days' warning before MGM deploys new technologies and for MGM to try to find positions for any displaced workers. "You are not going to stop technology," Taylor said. "The question is whether workers will be partners in its deployment or bystanders that get run over by it. . . . At the end of the day, [MGM] can move forward, but this gives us time to understand the effects."

As Las Vegas has added new casino-hotels, the Culinary has rushed to organize them, determined to keep a huge swatch of the industry unionized. In 2016, it organized the Trump International Hotel (five hundred workers) and, in 2018, the Palms Casino Resort (nine hundred workers) and Green Valley Ranch, a new spa and casino (nine hundred workers).

With its devotion to organizing, the Culinary has created a playbook that could serve as a model for how unions can grow. One political science professor wrote,

The Culinary was among the pioneers of the strategies and tactics that are standard practices today: card check neutrality, corporate research and pressure, outreach to allies and others, and political pressure. Virtually all union organizing victories today rely on some combination of these tactics. Where these kinds of leverage are available, labor has proven it can win despite the hostility of employers and the inadequacy of the law.

Some labor experts argue, however, that other unions will have a hard time copying the Culinary's spectacular success because it has several distinct advantages. Las Vegas is in ways a hothouse, with its gaming and hospitality industry expanding rapidly in recent decades, helping fuel the Culinary's growth. (Tourism and the city's economy did stumble after the September 11 attacks and during the 2007–9 recession.) Moreover, many casino-hotels are highly profitable, and that enables them to afford generous pay and benefits. And the Culinary has unusual leverage over the hotels because they are so image conscious and vulnerable to political pressure (as well as embarrassment from strikes and picketing). In addition, Las Vegas's casino-hotels employ many Latinos, African Americans, and immigrants—groups that are generally sympathetic to unionizing.

But even if unions in other industries or cities don't have some of those advantages, they can certainly borrow from the Culinary's playbook. They can be more aggressive about organizing, be smarter about using research and political influence, and do a lot more to involve and mobilize their members.

"The Culinary is a great case study of what unions can achieve," said Jeff Waddoups, chairman of the economics department at the University of Nevada, Las Vegas. "Las Vegas is chock-full of what would be low-wage service jobs, but this union has given these workers so much bargaining power that their wages are significantly higher than they would be otherwise and their lives are so much better and more dignified than they would be otherwise."

Part Two ◆

_____

LABOR RAISES ITS VOICE

Four
———

The Uprising of the Twenty Thousand

CLARA LEMLICH was seventeen years old when she emigrated from the Ukrainian village of Gorodok to the United States in 1903, and within two weeks she was toiling in a New York sweatshop. Like thousands of other immigrant workers, she had to pay the boss for the needles and thread she used. Some apparel factories even charged workers for the chairs they sat on, and some charged five cents a week for drinking water from the faucet, at a time when many workers were making less than $5 weekly.

In factories that were often dark, dirty, and claustrophobic, many workers toiled from 7 a.m. to 7 p.m., hunched over sewing machines that they operated by foot power. Lemlich often worked seven days a week. "The shop we worked in had no central heating, no electric power," she said. "The hissing of the machines, the yelling of the foreman made life unbearable." To the foreman, Lemlich added, "the girls" are merely "part of the machines they are running."

Headstrong and barely five feet tall, Lemlich emigrated to escape poverty and discrimination. Growing up in a pious Jewish family, she helped her mother run a grocery store, while her father and brothers dedicated themselves to religious study. To earn extra money, she made buttonholes for tailors and wrote letters in Yiddish for illiterate neighbors whose children had immigrated to the United States. Barred from her village's public school because she was Jewish, Lemlich used her earnings to buy books by Tolstoy, Turgenev, and Gorky in defiance of her father's wishes. He was so enraged by Russia's pervasive anti-Semitism—Russia ruled Ukraine at the time—that he banned the

Russian language from his household. When her father discovered her trove of Russian-language books, he threw them in the fire.

Lemlich's family grew alarmed when Czar Nicholas II encouraged a wave of pogroms—essentially mass attacks against the region's Jews. In April 1903, a pogrom in Kishinev, a town not far away, left forty-nine Jews dead, nearly five hundred injured, and fifteen hundred homes and stores pillaged. Fearing more such onslaughts, Lemlich's family immigrated to New York, much like today's immigrants fleeing oppression, violence, and war. Lemlich thus joined one of the largest waves of migration in history, the two million Jews from Eastern Europe who moved to the United States.

Lemlich had dreams of becoming a doctor, but for a seventeen-year-old girl with no English and few skills, sweatshops were her only real option. Factory life was far worse than she had imagined. Foremen often rousted workers from the bathroom and hustled them back to work. The apparel workers—much like many low-wage workers today—were often cheated, not paid for all the piecework completed and hours worked. At one factory, a manager tricked the workers by moving the clock's hour hand to five o'clock when it was already six. At another, the boss required each newly hired employee to post a $25 security deposit that would be forfeited if she tried to unionize or protest the low wages. At many factories, the women complained of groping by managers and catcalls from male co-workers. Lemlich hated that the workers were searched like thieves at the end of each workday—to check that they weren't stealing any thread or apparel. Some factories locked their exit doors to ensure that workers didn't sneak away with garments.

Lemlich was struck by all the unfriendly factory signs: "Singing Is Forbidden." "Laughing Is Forbidden." "Talking Is Forbidden." She said "forbidden" was one of the first words she learned in English.

Lemlich took English classes and became involved with the Women's Trade Union League, a group of wealthy women who were eager to help lift their less fortunate sisters. Lemlich had a strong voice, a clever tongue, piercing brown eyes, and curly, dark hair that she tied back. She became a fiery street-corner speaker, and growing increasingly bold, she often led a band of young women from factory to factory. Once inside, she would leap onto a table and give a quick, passionate speech about the need to improve conditions, and then they'd dash out an exit when the boss appeared. One historian described Lemlich as "an organizer and an agitator, first, last and always," while David Von Drehle wrote, "She was a model of a new sort of woman, hungry for opportunity and education and even equality, willing to fight the battles and pay the price to achieve it."

In 1906, Lemlich was among the thirteen workers who founded Local 25 of the International Ladies' Garment Workers' Union, the first union local for female apparel workers in New York. The members— overwhelmingly immigrants, largely Eastern European Jews or Italians— lived by and large in lower Manhattan, many squeezing into squalid tenements on the Lower East Side, the residential/industrial neighbor- hood that was the heart of the garment trade. On some blocks, people lived eight hundred to an acre, making it the most densely populated neighborhood in the United States (with the world's largest concen- tration of Jews). In the late nineteenth and early twentieth centuries, garments were often produced in Lower East Side basements, kitch- ens, and bedrooms, in what was called "homework," with some work- ers toiling from 5 a.m. to 9 p.m., six or seven days a week. *McClure's Magazine* described it as "the lowest-paid, most degrading of American employment."

Labor reformers from the National Consumers League and the National Child Labor Committee publicized the plight of home- workers. Helped by muckraking journalists and reform-minded law- makers, their campaign pressured many manufacturers to move away from homework and into factories, where scores or hundreds of work- ers were brought together in one place, making it easier for them to talk, complain, and organize. By the age of twenty-one, Lemlich was already spearheading strikes. She became a major irritant to "rag trade" employers, and, not surprisingly, she was repeatedly fired. But with her expertise in dressmaking and draping, translating a designer's idea into actual garments by cutting and modeling pieces on a tailor's dummy, Lemlich could always find another job—where she would then plunge back into her crusade for better pay and conditions. In 1907, she led a ten-week strike at the Weisen and Goldstein factory, called to pro- test production speedups. The next year, she spearheaded a walkout at Gotham Waist, where the company was firing higher-paid men and replacing them with lower-wage teenage girls.

In July 1909, two hundred garment workers struck Rosen Brothers, which surrendered after five weeks, granting a 20 percent raise as well as union recognition. Inspired by that victory, the workers at Lemlich's factory, Leiserson's, a modern plant on West Seventeenth Street, went on strike in September because the owner had broken his promise to hire only union members. Lemlich was arrested seventeen times during the Leiserson walkout.

On the evening of Friday, September 10, she was leaving the picket line when Charles Rose, a thug hired by the factory owner, and William Lustig, a prizefighter friend of Rose's, savagely beat her, breaking six of her ribs and leaving her bleeding on the sidewalk. Lemlich was still living with her mother and unemployed father, but she didn't tell them about the beating because she feared they would forbid her to lead strikes or speak on street corners. "Like rain the blows fell on me," Lemlich described the scene years later to her grandson. "Unions aren't built easy."

The Leiserson strike dragged on. In October, workers walked out at what was New York's largest blouse factory, the Triangle Waist Company, which had more than four hundred employees. The Triangle made shirtwaists, which were, as Von Drehle wrote, "one of America's first truly class-shattering fashions," essentially long blouses (to be worn with skirts) that came to symbolize a step forward in women's liberation, rejecting the traditions and inhibitions of corsets, bustles, and hoops. The Triangle factory's owners, Max Blanck and Isaac Harris, were fierce opponents of unions and had created instead an ersatz "sweetheart" union run by relatives who worked in the factory. When Blanck and Harris heard that 150 of their employees had met after work with a union organizer, they warned the workers that if they ever sought to form their own union, they would be fired.

The workers defied that threat, and Blanck and Harris locked them out, temporarily closing the factory. The workers then declared a strike. As chronicled in newspapers at the time, the very next day Blanck and Harris hired prostitutes to accompany replacement workers— "scabs"—to the Triangle factory. When the prostitutes confronted the strikers, there was "kicking, punching, and tearing of hair; clawing and poking and jabbing with hat pins," as one historian wrote, and then some male thugs materialized to further pummel the strikers. When the police arrived, they arrested the strikers and let the prostitutes and goons walk away.

New York's newspapers largely ignored the Leiserson and Triangle strikes until Mary Dreier, a prominent social reformer who headed the Women's Trade Union League, was arrested while she was outside the Triangle factory supporting the strikers. The police testified that Dreier had told a scab, "I will split your head open if you try to go to work." Police headquarters and city hall soon faced acute embarrassment when front-page headlines screamed that the highly respected Dreier had been hauled in. She was quickly released. The Women's Trade Union League hired a detective whose investigation concluded that factory owners were indeed hiring "roughs and toughs" to break the strikes.

The Leiserson and Triangle strikers grew weary after weeks without paychecks. Eager to bolster those strikes and explore next steps, the International Ladies' Garment Workers' Union called a mass meeting at the Cooper Union's Great Hall, the cavernous space where Abraham Lincoln gave a major address in February 1860 that catapulted him into the national spotlight. On the evening of November 22, 1909, more than two thousand garment workers packed the hall.

The pressing question was whether to call an industry-wide shirt-waist strike that would support the Leiserson and Triangle strikers and broaden the field of battle. The roster of speakers included several socialist leaders along with Mary Dreier and Samuel Gompers, the founding president of the American Federation of Labor (AFL), the nation's main union federation. (Gompers immigrated to the United States from London in 1863 at age thirteen and within weeks was helping his father produce cigars in their apartment on the Lower East Side.) As Gompers spoke, excitement coursed through the hall, but the crowd grew restive as he waffled about the idea of a strike against all the shirtwaist factories. He was lukewarm about the prospect of thousands of women striking. In a book about pioneering female labor leaders, Annelise Orleck analyzed Gompers's ambivalence: "Most male labor leaders believed that women were, at worst, unorganizable and, at best, temporary members of the workforce who would soon marry and stop working. In their view women weren't worth expending energy or resources on because they weren't real workers."

After Gompers finished, a prominent socialist writer with a reputation as a windbag was just beginning to speak. Then a small, dark-haired woman deep in the audience blurted out, "I wanted to say a few words." Some women in the hall shouted to her, "Get up on the platform!" Then, as *The New York Call* wrote, "willing hands lifted the frail little girl with flashing black eyes to the stage." It was Lemlich, who feared that the crowd might soon disperse and that the electricity would be lost. Instead, she seized the moment and altered history for American workers and American women.

"I have listened to all the speakers, and I have no further patience for talk," Lemlich shouted in Yiddish. "I am a working girl, one of those striking against intolerable conditions. I am tired of listening to speakers who talk in generalities. . . . I offer a resolution that a general strike be declared—now."

More than two thousand workers jumped out of their seats. They screamed, stamped their feet, waved their hats and handkerchiefs. After a few minutes of pandemonium, the emcee, Benjamin Feigenbaum, urged the workers to deliberate a minute before they plunged into an industry-wide strike that could mean weeks, even months, without paychecks. Then Feigenbaum asked the workers to raise their right hands and take an oath: "If I turn traitor to the cause I now pledge, may this hand wither from the arm I now raise!" Over two thousand right hands shot into the air.

The next morning fifteen thousand workers—nearly 90 percent of them women—went on strike. That day, Lemlich rushed to a dozen union halls in lower Manhattan, exhorting the workers to stay strong and instructing them on the basics of picketing. On the second day, five thousand more workers walked out. Lemlich told them, "If we stick together, and we are going to stick, we will win."

Within days, the press was calling the strike "the Uprising of the 20,000," although by some counts more than 30,000 workers had walked out. It was, to that day, by far the largest industrial action by women in U.S. history. A journalist at Joseph Pulitzer's *World* called it "the Lexington and Bunker Hill of woman's revolution for her rights," while *Collier's* called it a show of women's power "such as has never been known since woman entered the Garden of Eden." Union leaders said half the strikers were nineteen or younger, and some Yiddish newspapers called it the revolt of the *"farbrente meydlekh,"* the "fiery girls."

These young strikers were demanding a fifty-two-hour workweek, a 20 percent raise, paid holidays, an end to paying for needle and thread, and recognition of the ILGWU as their union. Within two days, seventy factories, most of them small, accepted the strikers' demands.

Alarmed by this, Triangle's Blanck and Harris called an emergency meeting to firm up employer resistance. The hundred factories that joined their effort signed a "no surrender" pledge, and many hired thugs and paid off the police to arrest and undermine the strikers.

The strikers were well organized. Each factory had a strike committee, which met daily at a union hall, and those committees reported shortly before midnight to the strike's executive committee (on which Lemlich served). Each day speakers and pickets were assigned. (There was even a special Italian strike headquarters with Italian literature.) Lemlich "was up at six for the picket line," one chronicler wrote, and "out during the day to raise money and speak at meetings." The Women's Trade Union League collected $60,000 (more than $1.5 million today) to provide food and legal counsel for the workers. (One league leader, Mary Beard, and her husband, Charles Beard, a Columbia professor, both prominent historians, were so impressed with Lemlich that they offered to get her into Barnard and pay her tuition. Lemlich turned them down. "It was too late," she said. "I was swallowed up by the trade union movement.")

Many strikers were shocked by the hostility they faced from police and judges alike. The *New-York Tribune* quoted a police officer saying, "We ain't here to protect the strikers nor anybody belongin' to 'em. We're here to protect the scabs." The officer added, "You've no right to keep walkin' in front of this shop. Do you want to get t'rown in de gutter?"

A reporter for the New York *Sun,* McAlister Coleman, wrote of an incident outside a shirtwaist factory:

The girls, headed by teen-age Clara Lemlich [she was actually twenty-three], described by union organizers as a "pint of trouble for the bosses," began singing Italian and Russian working-class songs as they paced in twos before the factory door. Of a sudden, around the corner came a dozen tough-looking customers, for whom the union label "gorillas" seemed well-chosen.

"Stand fast, girls," called Clara, and then the thugs rushed the line, knocking Clara to her knees, striking at the pickets, opening the way for a group of frightened scabs to slip through the broken line. Fancy ladies from the Allen Street red-light district climbed out of cabs to cheer on the gorillas. There was a confused melee of scratching, screaming girls and fist-swinging men and then a patrol wagon arrived. They ran off as the cops pushed Clara and two other badly beaten girls into the wagon.

Frances Perkins, who was an investigator for an anti-sweatshop group at the time and later became Franklin D. Roosevelt's secretary of labor, was horrified by what she witnessed during the strike. "The brutality of the police was terrible," Perkins said. "They would take these young Jewish girls and bang them over the head with a nightclub [*sic*]. Pictures were taken of them bleeding with their noses broken open. It was pretty brutal."

One of the most famous strikers was sixteen-year-old Rose Perr, who worked at Bijou Waist. While picketing, Perr and her co-worker Annie Albert sought to talk to a replacement worker outside their factory, but when they approached her, they testified, a large man punched Albert in the chest, knocking her to the ground. Perr shouted for the police, and when an officer ran over, he arrested Perr and Albert. Magistrate Robert Cornell found Perr and Albert guilty of assaulting the man who had struck Albert. He sentenced Perr, "a wisp of a girl, with a high, gentle, and childlike voice" and long, braided hair, to five days of hard labor in the workhouse. Perr, who newspapers said looked closer to twelve than to sixteen, did her hard labor alongside prostitutes and robbers on Blackwell's Island in the East River.

In sentencing another teenage striker, Magistrate Willard Olmsted declared, "You are on strike against God and nature." Hearing of this, George Bernard Shaw, the British playwright, mocked Olmsted in a cable, writing, "Delightful. Medieval America is always in the most intimate personal confidence of the Almighty."

———

Without a paycheck, which meant little to eat, and with the police and judges siding with the factory owners, the strikers saw that their struggle was tougher than they had anticipated. On December 3, ten thousand strikers marched on city hall to protest the police department's hostility, but the mayor and the press largely ignored them. Then, unexpectedly, some of New York's wealthiest women threw their prestige and influence behind the strikers. This "mink brigade" included Anne Morgan, the thirty-six-year-old daughter of J. P. Morgan, America's wealthiest and most powerful banker, and Alva Vanderbilt Belmont, once the wife of William K. Vanderbilt, an heir to Cornelius Vanderbilt's railroad fortune, and later the widow of the millionaire banker O. H. P. Belmont.

"We can't live our lives without doing something to help them," Anne Morgan said. "Fifty-two hours a week seems little enough to ask. . . . The girls must be helped to organize, and if public opinion is on their side, they will be able to do it."

Alva Belmont rented the giant Hippodrome arena for December 6, and seven thousand people crowded in to hear bishops, suffrage leaders, and strikers. "All the powerful themes of the strike—sex, socialism, votes, and justice—were on display," one historian wrote. One speaker, Rose Pastor Stokes, an apparel worker turned journalist, put forward the slogan "Starve to win, or you'll starve anyhow."

The Hippodrome rally put the Uprising on the city's front pages. Several newspapers criticized Mayor George B. McClellan Jr. (son of the Civil War general) for not attending, while one minister castigated him for ignoring the "welfare of 40,000 striking girls."

Three weeks into the strike, the mink brigade sponsored a luncheon and fund-raiser at the luxurious Colony Club, where 150 ladies—the cream of New York's 400—listened as strikers told their sad stories. "I have a sick mother and two little sisters to support," a seventeen-year-old worker said. "I get three dollars and a half a week." Another told the ladies that when she arrived five minutes late to work, the bosses sent her home. A Triangle worker added, "We work from seven in the morning until very late at night, and sometimes we work a week and a half in one week."

The Colony Club ladies put $1,300 into a hat that was passed around—about $21,000 today—and Anne Morgan more than matched that. The mink brigade asked their friends to lend support, and soon students from Vassar, Barnard, and Wellesley joined the picket lines and donated money. The Shubert family, which controlled many Broadway theaters, pledged the profits from one week's run of a play. Morgan and company even organized a "motor parade" down Fifth Avenue to highlight their support. She rented seven stately automobiles and filled them with strikers, some wearing bronze medals saying "hardship . . . endured in a rightful cause."

Appalled by the arrests and harsh jail sentences, Alva Belmont sometimes went to the courthouse to watch the arraignments of the strikers. When a magistrate ordered four teenage strikers kept in jail because they didn't have the $100 bail, Belmont made headlines by pledging her famed mansion as collateral. (It would probably be worth over $100 million today.)

Some lauded the mink brigade's assistance; one commentator said that capital had never shown such solidarity with poor workers. But *The New York Call*, a socialist newspaper, mocked the "brigade," pointing to the jarring dissonance of the "bejeweled, befurred, belaced, begowned audience" at the Colony Club listening to "ten wage slaves, some of them mere children," who had been "mistreated, abused, enslaved by capitalism, poverty and police persecution."

In the strike's early weeks, the Blanck-Harris group had refused to negotiate. But the withering criticism from the press, religious leaders, and the mink brigade led the owners' group to say they would begin negotiations, and they hinted that the factories would grant raises and a shorter workweek. Seeking to divide the workers, the owners insisted on one precondition: there could be no discussion of granting union recognition to the ILGWU. The union rejected that condition, so there were no negotiations.

By Christmas, 723 strikers had been arrested, with 19 sent to the workhouse.

In January, anticipating a booming apparel season, dozens of factories settled and recognized the union. Blanck and Harris and scores of other owners held out. But by mid-February, with the hard-line owners facing more public outrage over thugs beating strikers and with many strikers pushed to the limit by thirteen weeks without pay, the two sides finally settled. The owners agreed to a fifty-two-hour workweek, raises of 12 to 15 percent, and four paid holidays. They also agreed to stop charging for needles and thread and to limit night work to no more than two hours per day. While most factories agreed to recognize and bargain with the ILGWU, the Blanck-Harris group refused to grant union recognition—although they, in a major step, no longer refused to hire union members.

Both sides insisted they had won. The ILGWU's membership soared from eighty before the strike to twenty thousand by strike's end. The muckraker Ida Tarbell praised the Uprising's strikers for their fortitude. "The only chance for fair treatment in their industry was in standing together," Tarbell wrote. "They were so convinced of this that they were willing to go hungry, if necessary, in order to see it established. If they stood alone, they would lose what they had." The writer Miriam Finn Scott hailed the strike as a breakthrough for women: "These young, inexperienced girls have proved that women can strike and strike successfully."

"They used to say that you couldn't even organize women," Lemlich said. "They wouldn't come to union meetings. They were 'temporary' workers; they would always undercut men. Well, we showed them!"

(The Uprising inspired the Cloakmakers Strike of 1910, in which tens of thousands of cloak and suit makers in New York, most of them men, won higher pay and a fifty-hour workweek. The settlement, called the "Protocol of Peace," created a grievance and arbitration mechanism that pioneered ways to settle disputes without strikes. A lawyer named Louis Brandeis, later to sit on the Supreme Court, played a key role in formulating this settlement.)

When the Uprising finally ended, a thoroughly exhausted Lemlich went to the country for a few months to recover. When she returned to New York, she learned that she had been blacklisted from the garment industry. The ILGWU hired her as a factory inspector, and she later became a paid organizer for the Women's Trade Union League, helping to fight for women's suffrage. In the 1920s, she bucked many of her socialist friends and became a Communist, helping to create the United Council of Working-Class Women, a group that held protests about bread and meat prices and rising rents. She ran unsuccessfully for the city council and led hunger marches during the Great Depression. Her husband, Joe Shavelson, a Russian immigrant who worked in the printing industry, became ill in the 1940s, and she found a job back in the garment industry while remaining a militant. Reflecting on her youth some four decades after the Uprising, Lemlich said, "Ah—then I had fire in my mouth!" When she was in a nursing home in her late seventies, she helped persuade the workers there to unionize. "I am still at it," she said.

Five

Out of These Ashes

IT WAS 4:42 ON A SATURDAY AFTERNOON, March 25, 1911, three
minutes before quitting time, and the workers on the eighth floor of
the Triangle Waist factory were readying themselves to leave. Most of
these workers—they included sleeve setters, lace runners, embroidery
trimmers, and buttonhole makers—were immigrant women in their
late teens or early twenties, roughly 60 percent from Eastern Europe
and 40 percent from Italy. Their factory filled the top three floors of a
spacious ten-story loft building on Washington Place, one block east
of Washington Square in Greenwich Village. In that era, those buildings were part of a new wave of steel-framed "skyscrapers." With high
ceilings, big windows, and electricity to power the sewing machines,
the Triangle factory was a definite step up from the dark, dusty factories heated by coal stoves. The factory's owners—Max Blanck and Isaac
Harris—were called the Shirtwaist Kings because the Triangle was New
York City's largest shirtwaist maker, producing more than a thousand
of those fast-selling blouses each day.

On the factory's eighth floor, a dozen long tables ran north to south,
perpendicular to Washington Place. Seven of the tables were for sewing
machine operators, and five were for the cutters, the "maestros" of the
apparel industry, who used sharp knives to carve ever so deftly through
layers of fabric to create the outlines of garments that would be stitched
into shirtwaists. The cutters tossed the leftover cotton scraps into bins that
ran underneath the long tables. More than a ton of such scraps had accu-
mulated at the factory since the scrap man last visited two months earlier.

One of the cutters, Isidore Abramowitz, had just finished laying out

120 layers of fabric to get a head start for the following Monday. The final minutes of the factory's six-day workweek were approaching. At that moment, the eighth floor's production manager, Samuel Bernstein, was deliberating over what base wage to pay a new seamstress. Suddenly Eva Harris, sister of one of the factory's owners, ran over to Berstein, shouting, "Fire!"

Seeing that a fire had ignited in a nearby scrap bin, Abramowitz hurried to an overhead ledge that held three emergency pails of water, and he threw the water onto the flames—to no avail. The fire raced through the bins, the cotton scraps serving as ideal tinder. (Fire investigators later concluded that a cutter had thrown a cigarette into a scrap bin, notwithstanding the many signs saying "No Smoking" in English, Yiddish, and Italian.) Bernstein rushed to the Greene Street staircase (to the east) and pulled out the eighth-floor fire hose, which was supposedly fed by a water tank on the roof. No water came out.

Hearing screams of "fire" and seeing smoke and flames, the 180 workers on the eighth floor rushed to flee. Some ran around the long tables, while some leaped onto them and awkwardly stepped from one table onto another. Many workers hurried toward the Greene Street staircase, and when too large a scrum formed there, others fumbled around the tables toward the front staircase along Washington Place. But the door to that staircase was locked.

Bernstein spotted Louis Brown, the mechanic in charge of maintaining the sewing machines, and yelled to him, "Try to get the girls out as quick as you can!" Brown bulled his way to the door near the Washington Place staircase.

"They were packed by the door, you couldn't get them any tighter," Brown later told Leon Stein, author of *The Triangle Fire,* a detailed 1962 account based on interviews with survivors. Brown somehow got the panicky workers to move away from the locked door, and he pulled out his key and opened it. The workers there rushed down the narrow Washington Place staircase.

Within three or four minutes, the fire had spread across much of the eighth floor. "The bins under the remaining cutting tables each represented a new firebomb," wrote David Von Drehle in *Triangle: The Fire That Changed America,* the definitive account of the tragedy. "Burning wisps of cotton and tissue paper swirled around the room. . . . Wherever these wispy torches touched down, they seeded fire."

A minute or two after the fire started, after an initial mix-up, Dinah Lipschitz, a bookkeeper on the eighth floor, telephoned the receptionist on the tenth floor, the executive floor, to alert her, though no one had notified the ninth floor, where more than two hundred sewing machine operators were working. The tenth-floor receptionist rushed into Max Blanck's office, and he immediately called the fire department, but it had already received word from people on the street. The fire that began minutes earlier two floors below had grown so intense that employees on the tenth floor could feel it—that floor held the owner's offices, a showroom for buyers, and a packing and shipping room. The building's air shaft served as a flue, and the fierce heat caused windows on the tenth floor to shatter, letting in drafts that spread the inferno.

At those crucial moments, the co-owners, Blanck and Harris, were at a loss about what to do. Suddenly Bernstein appeared, having clambered up the Greene Street stairs. He had hoped to alert employees on the ninth floor, but the fire was raging so fiercely there he couldn't do so. Upon reaching the tenth floor, Bernstein yelled to Blanck, Harris, and the others, "The only way for you to get out is the roof!" The tenth-floor workers fumbled to the stairs to the roof. The building just to the west housed New York University's law school, where Professor Frank Sommer, teaching a class, noticed several distraught workers on the roof next door. He and his students hurried to the roof of their building—which was one story above the roof of the Triangle building—and they lowered some ladders that, through a stroke of extraordinary good fortune, painters had left there the night before. Dozens of Triangle workers climbed the ladders to safety.

One of the seventy workers from the tenth floor died: twenty-two-year-old Clotilda Terdanova. Her hair caught fire from the spreading flames, and she grew so alarmed that she jumped out of one of the floor-to-ceiling windows. "She was young and very pretty," Bernstein later recalled. "She was to leave us next Saturday to be married three weeks later."

———

On the ninth floor, Anna Gullo, a supervisor, had just finished distributing that week's pay envelopes when windows began to burst because of the heat and flames rising from the floor below. Scraps of burning cotton floated in that ignited the cloth and scraps in the ninth floor's bins and baskets. There were over two hundred workers on the floor that day, spread along eight seventy-five-foot-long tables that each seated up to thirty sewing operators. The flames raced through the floor in minutes.

At first Gullo rushed toward the Washington Place stairway, but she was alarmed to discover that the door to that stairway was locked. She concluded that her only hope was the Greene Street staircase. Pulling her woolen skirt over her head, she raced to the staircase as flames lapped at her, and she made it to the ground floor.

Rose Glantz, a ninth-floor sewing machine operator, had gone to the dressing room to get her hat and coat. There, urged on by co-workers oblivious to the fire, she sang "Every Little Movement (Has Meaning All Its Own)." Finally, they heard screams and rushed out of the dressing room. "When we first saw the fire, it was already burning all around us," Glantz recalled years later.

She tried the Washington Place stairway, but she, too, was mortified to find the door locked. She somehow made it to the Greene Street stairs. "I pulled my scarf tighter around my head and ran right through it. It caught fire. I have a scar on my neck."

Rose Cohen, one of the terrified souls on the ninth floor, recalled years later, "Girls were lying on the floor, fainted. People were stepping on them. Other girls were trying to climb over the machines. Some were running with their hair burning." She reached the Greene Street stairs and scrambled up to the roof.

The building's two elevator operators, Joseph Zito and Gaspar Mortillalo, were heroes, rushing up and down repeated times despite the heat and flames. They must have saved over a hundred people. When Zito's elevator filled up on its last trip, Kate Weiner, desperate to escape the ninth floor, was unable to squeeze in so she dived onto the elevator as it was descending. "All the way down, I was on the people's heads. I was facing downward," Weiner told Leon Stein. (The elevator compartment didn't have a ceiling.)

Abe Gordon, who helped maintain the sewing machines, fled onto the fire escape; it was already packed with other workers. Gordon went down several flights, but, worried about the fire escape's stability, he stepped onto a window ledge on the sixth floor, seeing a broken window he could enter.

"I heard a loud noise," he said. "People were falling all around me, screaming all around me. The fire escape was collapsing." More than a dozen workers died when the rusting apparatus fell.

Many ninth-floor workers couldn't make it to the elevators, and the rampaging fire made the Greene Street stairway impassable. Many rushed toward the Washington Square stairway, but the door to the stairway was locked—a dozen burned bodies were later found near that locked door. Managers had often kept that door locked because they feared the workers would sneak out and steal garments or thread. After the fire, Blanck and Harris repeatedly insisted that they didn't know the ninth-floor door was locked that day.

Unable to reach the stairs or elevators, dozens of ninth-floor workers headed to the windows facing Washington Place, where the heat was less intense, at least at first. "Call the firemen!" some of those workers yelled to onlookers on the street below. "Save us!"

"The crowd yelled 'Don't jump!' but it was jump or be burned," *The New York Times* wrote the next day. With the flames and heat growing unbearable, several, and then many, workers climbed onto the ledge and jumped.

"I learned a new sound—a more horrible sound than description can picture. It was the thud of a speeding, living body on a stone sidewalk. Thud-dead, thud-dead, thud-dead, thud-dead sixty-two thud-deads." That was the eyewitness account of William G. Shepherd, a reporter for United Press, who was walking in Washington Square on that sunny afternoon when he noticed some smoke. He rushed over to the factory and phoned in his firsthand account, which was printed by newspapers across the nation.

"I even watched one girl falling. Waving her arms, trying to keep her body upright until the very instant she struck the sidewalk, she was trying to balance herself. Then came the thud—then a silent, unmoving pile of clothing and twisted, broken limbs," Shepherd wrote.

"The firemen raised the longest ladder. It reached only to the sixth floor," Shepherd added. "I saw the last girl jump at it and miss it." (In that era, the fire department's tallest ladders reached no higher than the sixth floor.)

Within fifteen minutes, firefighters got the fire under control. They found more than fifty bodies on the ninth floor. Fifty-three workers had jumped or fallen from the windows. Around twenty people died when the fire escape collapsed, and nineteen bodies were found in the elevator shaft.

All told 146 workers died in what was one of the worst industrial disasters in American history, before or since. All but twenty-three of those who died were women, and almost half were teenagers. The youngest, Rosaria Maltese, was fourteen; her mother and sister also died in the blaze.

The Triangle fire became an object lesson in inadequate safety precautions. If only the workers on the ninth floor had been alerted promptly. If only the door to the Washington Street stairway had not been locked. If only a ton of highly combustible scraps had not been allowed to accumulate for two months. If only a sturdy fire escape had been built. If only the factory had conducted fire drills. A prominent fire expert, H. F. J. Porter, had written to Blanck and Harris to urge them to conduct fire drills, but never heard back. In the months before the fire, safety experts and many workers grew more apprehensive about factory fires because four months before the Triangle disaster two dozen women and girls had died in an inferno at the Wolf Muslin Undergarment Company in Newark, New Jersey. Nineteen workers had jumped from the fourth floor to their deaths.

"The neglect of factory owners in the matter of safety of their employees is absolutely criminal," Porter said. "One man whom I advised to install a fire drill replied to me: 'Let 'em burn. They're a lot of cattle, anyway.'"

––––––

Two weeks after the fire, Blanck and Harris were indicted on manslaughter charges. They hired one of New York's best-known and most expensive lawyers, Max Steuer, to defend them. When the trial took place eight months after the fire, onlookers yelled "murderers" as the two defendants arrived in court. One prosecution witness after another described the horror and terror, but Blanck and Harris were helped immensely by the judge's instructions: the jury could find the Triangle owners guilty only if they concluded that the owners knew that the ninth floor's door to the Washington Place staircase was locked at the moment of the fire. Several prosecution witnesses testified that the door was always locked, but the defense put on several witnesses who said they often went through the door during the business day.

After deliberating a mere two hours, the jury announced its not-guilty verdict. The public was scandalized. New Yorkers were further enraged when Blanck and Harris's insurance company paid them $60,000 ($1.5 million today) beyond any losses that they could prove.

The Women's Trade Union League sponsored a mass meeting at the Metropolitan Opera House to honor the 146 dead. There, Rose Schneiderman, an immigrant from Poland and a former garment worker, made one of the most famous speeches in American labor history. Schneiderman told the wealthy and middle-class New Yorkers who filled the opera hall,

I would be a traitor to these poor burned bodies if I came here to talk good fellowship. We have tried you good people of the public, and we have found you wanting. The old Inquisition had its rack and its thumbscrews and its instruments of torture with iron teeth. We know what these things are today; the iron teeth are our necessities, the thumbscrews are the high-powered and swift machinery close to which we must work, and the rack is here in the firetrap structures that will destroy us the minute they catch on fire.

This is not the first time girls have been burned alive in the city. Every week I must learn of the untimely death of one of my sister workers. Every year thousands of us are maimed. The life of men and women is so cheap and property is so sacred. There are so many of us for one job it matters little if 146 of us are burned to death.

We have tried you citizens; we are trying you now, and you have a couple of dollars for the sorrowing mothers, brothers and sisters by way of a charity gift. But every time the workers come out in the only way they know to protest against conditions which are unbearable the strong hand of the law is allowed to press down heavily upon us. . . .

I can't talk fellowship to you who are gathered here. Too much blood has been spilled. I know from my experience it is up to the working people to save themselves. The only way they can save themselves is by a strong working-class movement.

Two years later, at their revived Triangle factory on Fifth Avenue, Blanck and Harris were found to have locked an exit door during working hours. The judge ordered the minimum fine: $20. The following year, the two co-owners were fined again for sewing counterfeit National Consumers League labels into their garments. (Such labels were to certify that the goods had been produced under decent workplace conditions.)

———

On the fateful Saturday of the Triangle fire, Frances Perkins was having afternoon tea at the elegant town house of her friend Margaret Morgan Norrie, a descendant of two signers of the Declaration of Independence. From that town house on Washington Square, they heard fire engines and screams, and the butler told them there was a big fire just east of the square. Perkins, then thirty years old and executive secretary of the New York Consumers League, an anti-sweatshop group, hurried to the Triangle factory and stood outside, shocked. Years later she described the scene:

> It was the most horrible sight. . . . People were hanging out the windows by their hand. . . . One by one the people would fall off. They couldn't hold on any longer. . . . Then there began to be panic jumping. People who had their clothes afire would jump. . . . It's that awful choice that people talk of.

For decades, that tragedy would haunt—and inspire—Perkins, who, twenty-two years later, would become the nation's first-ever female cabinet member. As secretary of labor for Franklin Delano Roosevelt, she was a crucial architect of the New Deal on issues ranging from Social Security to enactment of the first federal minimum wage. The fire, she said, "seared on my mind as well as my heart—a never-to-be-forgotten reminder of why I had to spend my life fighting conditions that could permit such a tragedy." Perkins later described that tragic Saturday as "the day the New Deal was born."

Born in Boston in 1880, Perkins grew up in Worcester, Massachusetts, the daughter of conservative, middle-class Republicans. Her father ran a stationery shop. She went to Mount Holyoke College in an era when few women went to college. She majored in physics with minors in chemistry and biology, but the course that most excited her was economic history. For that class, the students visited nearby factories and interviewed workers, and Perkins learned, in those pre-workers'-compensation days, that losing your hand at work could mean losing your livelihood. One of her most memorable moments in college came in February 1902, when Florence Kelley, a fiery Quaker lawyer who had been chief factory inspector for the State of Illinois and co-founded the National Consumers League, spoke at Mount Holyoke.

Pushed by her parents to become a teacher, Perkins took a job teaching chemistry at Ferry Hall, an elite girls' school north of Chicago. What impassioned her far more than teaching, however, were her weekend visits to Hull House, the settlement house that the trailblazing social reformer Jane Addams founded to lift and educate immigrants and the poor. As a Hull House volunteer, Perkins, a deeply religious woman, distributed milk and food baskets to hungry children and helped workers recover wages they were cheated out of. As part of her Hull House work, she visited several Chicago sweatshops, and even though her parents had warned her that unions were "an evil to be avoided," she became a supporter of organized labor, seeing how unions had improved wages and safety for Chicago's plumbers and carpenters. What Perkins saw as a Hull House volunteer transformed her, and to her parents' chagrin she decided to leave teaching and dedicate herself to the cause of workers and the poor.

In 1907, Perkins became general secretary of the Philadelphia Research and Protection Association. There she probed employment agencies that promised respectable jobs to young immigrant and African American women but then forced them into prostitution. One evening two owners of an agency, essentially pimps, followed Perkins home and attacked her. She screamed, and her assailants fled when neighbors opened their windows to investigate the ruckus.

Two years later, Perkins moved to New York to study for a master's degree in political science at Columbia University, taking courses in economics, sociology, and statistics and writing her thesis on childhood malnutrition in Manhattan's Hell's Kitchen neighborhood. At the time, New York was in a state of political, economic, and intellectual ferment with muckrakers, socialists, suffragists, trade unionists, up-and-coming writers, and, of course, robber barons. There, Perkins befriended Sinclair Lewis (who proposed marriage to her, unsuccessfully), the renowned dancer Isadora Duncan, and John Reed, author of an eyewitness account of the Russian Revolution.

In 1910, the National Consumers League hired Perkins as executive secretary of its New York operation, enabling her to work for Florence Kelley, who had so inspired her. (The league—and its calls to boycott goods made in sweatshops—was inspired by abolitionist boycotts of sugar and garments made of cotton produced by slave labor.) In her new job, Perkins focused on child labor, fire hazards, dismal conditions at cellar bakeries, and the long hours that many women worked. Through persistent lobbying and a willingness to work with some less-than-angelic folks in New York's Tammany Hall Democratic machine, Perkins persuaded the state legislature to establish a maximum fifty-four-hour workweek for women. Like her mentors, Addams and Kelley, Perkins combined passionate idealism with a practical bent and an ability to argue her cause intelligently and forcefully.

The day after the Triangle fire, several reporters contacted Perkins, who had become a factory safety expert thanks to her Consumers League position. She told the reporters that "there were hundreds of other factories in the State of New York, and probably the city, that were just as bad and where the same [kind of] fire might occur again." Viewing those words as an insult, the city's fire commissioner and buildings commissioner demanded that the league's wealthy benefactors shut Perkins down. The league backed her instead.

Days after the fire, the millionaire financier R. Fulton Cutting said he would donate $10,000 (about $250,000 today) to underwrite a blue-ribbon panel to investigate factory safety and make recommendations to prevent future factory disasters. New York's notables urged former president Theodore Roosevelt to head the panel, but he declined. At the urging of Addams and Kelley, he recommended Perkins to be the committee's executive director. She became chief investigator and whip hand for this Committee on Safety, which included Samuel Gompers, the bookseller Simon Brentano, and Mary Dreier of the Women's Trade Union League.

Soon Al Smith, a state assemblyman in whose district many of the Triangle dead had lived, gave Perkins a valuable tip: if she had any hope of getting the safety panel's recommendations enacted, she had better get the legislature to set up a parallel commission so that lawmakers could buy in and take credit for whatever recommendations were made. During her years at the Consumers League, Perkins befriended Smith and another up-and-coming Democratic politician, State Senator Robert F. Wagner. Smith later became New York's governor and the 1928 Democratic nominee for president, while Wagner became a U.S. senator and a pivotal Roosevelt ally on New Deal legislation. (He was the father of New York City mayor Robert F. Wagner Jr.) Thanks to Smith and Wagner, New York State set up the Factory Investigative Commission (which the two lawmakers headed). They named Perkins the commission's chief investigator, although some factory owners derided her as the "primary instigator." Perkins developed a reputation for being friendly and earnest, with one historian describing her as "plain-spoken, plainly dressed, and disarmingly direct."

Describing the commission's work, Perkins wrote,

> We used to make it our business to take Al Smith . . . to see the women, thousands of them, coming off the ten-hour night-shift on the rope walks [rope factories] in Auburn [New York]. We made sure that Robert Wagner personally crawled through the tiny hole in the wall that gave egress to a steep iron ladder covered with ice and ending twelve feet from the ground, which was euphemistically labeled "Fire Escape" in many factories. We saw to it that the austere legislative members of the Commission got up at dawn and drove with us for an unannounced visit to a Cattaraugus County cannery and that they saw with their own eyes the little children, not adolescents, but five-, six-, and seven-year-olds, snipping beans and shelling peas. We made sure that they saw the machinery that would scalp a girl or cut off a man's arm.

The commission visited 1,836 businesses, heard 222 witnesses, and produced thirteen volumes of research and recommendations. Guided by Smith and Wagner, the legislature enacted a series of landmark laws aimed at ensuring that there would never be another Triangle-like fire in New York (although there remain far too many such fires in Bangladesh, Pakistan, and other developing nations, disasters that would not have happened had the Western companies that buy apparel from those factories insisted that they adopt the elementary safety precautions that Perkins recommended more than a century ago). The New York legislature banned smoking in factories and required sturdy fire escapes, improved exits, periodic fire drills, occupancy limits, doors that open outward, and automatic sprinklers in buildings taller than seven floors. The legislature also required that factory rubbish be removed frequently and that factories be registered—there had been hundreds of unregistered factories, making it hard for state officials to inspect them. Decades later, Perkins commented, "In New York I could see a fire escape and say: I did that."

In 1913, she married Paul Wilson, a reform-minded economist who became budget secretary to New York City's mayor. In an unusual move for that era, Perkins kept her maiden name because relinquishing it would have meant losing valuable name recognition. The couple had one daughter, Susanna. Theirs was a strained marriage, with Wilson ultimately spending much of his life in mental hospitals with bipolar disorder.

When Al Smith was elected governor in 1918, he appointed Perkins to the state's five-member industrial commission. (That was the year after New York gave women the right to vote, and two years before the Nineteenth Amendment was ratified, giving all American women the right to vote.) In 1924, Perkins became the industrial commission's chair, and with a salary of $8,500 ($120,000 today) she became the nation's highest-paid female official. In 1928, when Franklin D. Roosevelt was elected New York's governor, he appointed Perkins the state's industrial commissioner, to run a department of eighteen hundred employees. Smith had warned FDR against the move, telling him that factory owners might rebel. "As a rule," Smith said, "men will take advice from a woman, but it is hard for them to take orders from a woman."

In 1929, the stock market crashed and the Great Depression hit, throwing fifteen million Americans out of work. To fight this devastating slump, Perkins, as Governor Roosevelt's right hand on economic and social matters, pushed him to experiment and innovate. New York became a national leader in creating not just a relief program but a public works program to put the jobless back to work. Perkins also pushed to create a state unemployment insurance program to provide much-needed money to the jobless. "Unemployment is just as much of an industrial hazard as accidents [a reference to workers' compensation], and therefore should be insured in advance," she said. (In 1932, Wisconsin became the first state to enact an unemployment insurance program, with New York following in 1935.)

Perkins pushed unsuccessfully to enact a state minimum wage and a law prohibiting retailers from forcing sales clerks to stand all day (an issue that plagues many retail workers even today). Perkins played a crucial role in winning enactment of workers' compensation, tougher factory safety protections, and, for women, a forty-eight-hour work-week and a ban on night work. (Perkins and the state legislature moved to protect women workers in particular because in 1905 the Supreme Court, in *Lochner v. New York,* had overturned a state law limiting bakery workers to ten hours a day as an unconstitutional violation of freedom of contract. Three years later, however, the Court, in *Muller v. Oregon,* upheld a law that set a ten-hour daily maximum for women workers as justified by the state's interest in protecting women's health.) Considering that New York was then the nation's most populous state, with powerful manufacturing and financial interests, Perkins said of the many worker-friendly programs and protections New York had enacted, "If it could be done there, it could be done anywhere."

————

From late 1929 through 1932, the nation remained mired in the Depression under Herbert Hoover. Although Perkins was a mere state industrial commissioner, she thrust herself into the national spotlight with a bold, direct challenge of Hoover. She held a news conference in December 1930 to criticize Hoover's boast that employment had jumped 4 percent and that the economy had turned a corner. She explained that the added jobs were merely temporary holiday season positions, and she said Hoover's misleading assertions were "cruel deceit" that would increase despair. The jobless, Perkins said, would worry, "'Why don't I get a job if things are better?'" and "Young people would read this story and say, 'Why doesn't Papa work?'"

In 1932, the Democratic Party nominated Roosevelt as its presidential candidate, largely because, as New York's governor, he had led the way with innovative programs to help the poor and jobless. Roosevelt crushed Hoover in a landslide, and within days his wife, Eleanor, Jane Addams, and many others were urging him to appoint Perkins secretary of labor. Roosevelt sent out feelers, but Perkins balked because she was reluctant to leave her mentally ill husband behind in New York. Moreover, she recognized that many people thought the secretary of labor should be a labor union official, and she cautioned Roosevelt that she was not a union person. Roosevelt told her that wasn't important, saying, "It was time to consider all working people, organized and unorganized."

Roosevelt summoned her to his town house on East Sixty-fifth Street in Manhattan. There, he asked her what she would hope to accomplish as labor secretary. Perkins had drawn up a far-reaching list of goals: She wanted general relief for the poor, a public works program to put people back to work, a federal minimum wage, a shorter workday (preferably eight hours), and prohibitions on child labor. (Child labor caused adults to lose jobs, she argued.) Perkins also wanted to create nationwide systems of unemployment insurance, health insurance, and old-age pensions. (That last idea would become Social Security.) As Kirstin Downey wrote in her excellent biography of Perkins, *The Woman Behind the New Deal,* "Ever mindful of the Triangle fire, she said she also would push for safety regulation in states across the country."

Knowing that her wish list was long, Perkins asked Roosevelt, "Are you sure you want this done, because you won't want me for secretary of labor if you don't want these things done?"

Valuing Perkins's service and loyalty and seeing eye to eye with her on many issues, Roosevelt said, yes, he would embrace her ideas. FDR had promised to improve the lives of Depression-pummeled Americans, and his trusted aide had laid out a path to do just that.

As Perkins was departing, she recalled, Roosevelt said of her proposals, "I suppose you are going to nag me about this forever."

One reason FDR chose her, she thought, was "he wanted his conscience kept for him by somebody."

When Roosevelt nominated Perkins, women and progressives were jubilant, but some labor bigwigs did indeed protest that a union official hadn't been chosen. William Green, the American Federation of Labor's president, said, "Labor can never become reconciled" to Perkins, while John L. Lewis, president of the United Mine Workers, dismissed her as a "mere social worker." (Perkins later remarked that those leaders would never have talked so dismissively if a man had been nominated.)

Perkins respected some union leaders—for instance, she worked closely with Sidney Hillman, president of the Amalgamated Clothing Workers, viewing him as smart, farsighted, and honest. To help his union's members, Hillman had his union build low-cost cooperative housing and create an unemployment insurance program and a consumer-friendly bank. But Perkins found many union officials incompetent, dishonest, or lacking in vision. She hadn't forgotten that unions had fought mightily against her push to enact a workers' compensation law to help all injured workers in New York. "They didn't care about the thousands of men who didn't belong to trade unions," Perkins said.

Gompers and many other early labor leaders had often opposed legislation that would lift workers in general because they feared that would make many workers conclude they didn't need a union. Perkins took a different view, believing that social reformers like herself could and should push through legislation that helps all workers. "One could not escape the fact that representation of working people through their own organizations was pathetically limited," she wrote. "I'd much rather get a law than organize a union," she added. This clash of visions still plays out today.

The press was fascinated by the nation's first female cabinet secretary, but she was famously unfriendly to reporters, chiding them for focusing too much on petty matters, like the felt tricorn hat she invariably wore, and not enough on the nation's grave problems. Once when asked if being a woman held her back in public life, she answered, "Only in climbing trees."

In March 1933, Roosevelt took the helm of a devastated nation, with fifteen million people out of work, long food lines, and one in six homes foreclosed upon. As FDR charted his course for his first hundred days and beyond, Perkins pushed hardest among the cabinet members for programs to help the poor, the unemployed, and workers in general. She turned many of Roosevelt's wishes on social and economic policy into programs by nudging the president, persuading other cabinet members, and lobbying Congress. In the New Deal's first month, while Roosevelt and his cabinet were rushing to rescue banks and family farms, Perkins was pushing for a cash relief program to ease the woes of the poorest families.

She played a major role in fleshing out Roosevelt's inchoate ideas for the Civilian Conservation Corps, an innovative and popular program that put three million young people to work in parks and forests. Perkins was also a crucial figure in persuading Roosevelt to embrace a trail-blazing $3.3 billion public works program ($64 billion today) to build and repair roads, bridges, and schools and thereby put hundreds of thousands of Americans back to work. Roosevelt put Perkins in charge of the initial push for public works, and she managed to rescue that program after FDR's conservative budget director, Lewis Douglas, had gone behind the cabinet's back and gotten Roosevelt to delete public works from his National Industrial Recovery Act legislation. Furious, Perkins outmaneuvered Douglas by arranging a private meeting with Roosevelt, where she convinced him that the program was essential to give the economy some badly needed upward thrust. That evolved into the much larger Public Works Administration, which built the Grand Coulee Dam, LaGuardia Airport, and hundreds of other major projects.

Perkins played an often-unappreciated role in another high-stakes battle—protecting labor's interests when the New Deal created national industry codes. These codes aimed to stabilize Depression-battered industries and stave off bankruptcies by letting competing companies essentially form cartels to set minimum prices. Corporate America loved this idea, and so did Roosevelt, but some progressives said this price-setting collusion violated antitrust law and would hurt consumers.

Eager to make the industry codes worker-friendly, Perkins pushed to have them include minimum wage and maximum hours' provisions. She approached her sometime critic William Green, the head of the American Federation of Labor, to ask him what organized labor would like included in the codes. Green recommended that every industry code guarantee workers the right to bargain collectively through representatives of their own choosing. Perkins embraced that idea and demanded that it be included in the codes. Then she got Senator Wagner to back the idea. It became Section 7A of the National Industrial Recovery Act and was hailed as the Magna Carta for American labor. It led to a surge in unionization, after union membership had plunged to two million in 1933, from four million in 1919.

After the conservative Supreme Court overturned key parts of the National Industrial Recovery Act as unconstitutional, Wagner inserted a pro-union provision nearly identical to Section 7A into the heart of the National Labor Relations Act (NLRA) of 1935. That provision became pivotal to organized labor's future growth and its hunger for a voice in the nation's workplaces. "We must have democracy in industry as well as in government," Wagner said. "Democracy in industry means fair participation by those who work in the decisions vitally affecting their lives and livelihood; and that the workers in our great mass production industries can enjoy this participation only if allowed to organize and bargain collectively through representatives of their own choosing."

There's a famous story about Perkins's pluck. In July 1933, the month after the National Industrial Recovery Act was signed into law, she went to Pennsylvania to solicit views to help formulate the industry code for the nation's steelmakers. She visited Homestead, where a fierce gun battle erupted in 1892 when Henry Clay Frick, who ran Andrew Carnegie's steel company, had sought to crush a strike by the fledgling steelworkers' union. At least seven steelworkers and three Pinkertons died (historical accounts differ on the death toll). Perkins met inside the town hall with Homestead's mayor and several of its leading citizens as some laid-off steelworkers clamored outside, hoping to talk with her. Perkins asked to meet with them, but the mayor, an ally of United States Steel, derided them as troublemakers and Communists and wouldn't let them in to speak with her.

Perkins asked if she could talk with them in a public park, but Homestead's mayor told her that public assembly wasn't permitted in the town's parks. Perkins spotted an American flag across the main square and realized it meant a post office. She told the mayor that he couldn't stop her from holding a meeting at the post office because it was federal property. There, with workers crammed into every last space, Perkins stood on a chair and listened as the laid-off steelworkers complained about Big Steel. In her short, heartfelt remarks to the workers, she made clear that the Roosevelt administration heard their concerns.

"I have come to the conclusion that the Department of Labor should be the Department FOR Labor," Perkins declared soon afterward. Her mission, she said, was "to render a service to wage earners who have no particular representative to speak for them."

———

Social Security is justly hailed as one of FDR's greatest achievements, although it is widely forgotten that it was Perkins who shepherded the idea from a vague notion into far-reaching legislation that has helped provide security to tens of millions of Americans.

In her initial interview with Roosevelt about becoming labor secretary, Perkins outlined her ambitious goal to create a national system of old-age pensions. FDR embraced it. Borrowing and embellishing her ideas, he envisioned a grand plan of "economic security" for the nation, of unemployment insurance, health insurance, aid to the poor, and old-age pensions. "I see no reason why every child, from the day he is born, shouldn't be a member of the social security system," Roosevelt said. "From the cradle to the grave they ought to be in a social insurance system."

It was a bighearted vision to lift the poor, assist orphans, and keep seniors from becoming paupers. The program was meant in part to enable many older Americans to stop working and thus open up more jobs for the unemployed. But FDR (in a fight that is still raging today) reluctantly abandoned his—and Perkins's—plan for universal national health insurance after the American Medical Association protested that Roosevelt's proposal would constitute "socialized medicine."

To transform his grand vision into reality, Roosevelt appointed Perkins to head the new cabinet-level Committee on Economic Security, tasking her to line up cabinet members behind the plan, assemble teams of experts, write legislative language, make sure the numbers added up, navigate past a contrarian, conservative Supreme Court, and rally public support to assure congressional passage.

"You care about this thing," Roosevelt told her. "You believe in it. Therefore, I know you will put your back to it more than anyone else, and you will drive it through."

There were complications galore. Regarding unemployment insurance, for example, Roosevelt didn't want to slight the states by denying them any role, and he also wanted to give richer states—that is, northern states—an opportunity to pay out higher jobless benefits. So Perkins, working with experts, actuaries, and state officials, developed an unemployment insurance system in which Washington would help pay for benefits administered by the states—the system that remains in place today. (This elaborate federal-state structure also aimed to ensure that the Supreme Court didn't find the program unconstitutional.)

At that time, for the great majority of workers, "the very thought of 'retirement' was unthinkable," the historian David M. Kennedy wrote, and "most elderly laborers worked until they dropped or were fired," at which point they often relied on the mercy of their families or local welfare agencies. Francis Townsend, a California physician, proposed that every American over age sixty receive a hugely generous government pension of $200 per month ($3,850 today), and hundreds of Townsend Clubs across the nation were putting pressure on Roosevelt. And so were backers of the Louisiana senator Huey Long's popular "Share Our Wealth" scheme.

While Roosevelt was determined to create an old-age pension, he was opposed to anything that looked like the dole. Instead, Perkins, heeding Roosevelt's wishes, oversaw development of an old-age pension system that would be financed by worker contributions.

Perkins was furious when Secretary of the Treasury Henry Morgenthau insisted that farmworkers, domestic servants, and workers in establishments with fewer than ten employees not be covered by Social Security. Morgenthau argued that it would be unduly difficult to collect Social Security contributions from these workers and their employers. He prevailed (many saw that as a sop to powerful southern conservatives); his move ultimately excluded 9.4 million people—a disproportionate number of them blacks and women—from Social Security pensions.

Roosevelt's economic security plan had broad public backing, but it faced opposition from key senators and business groups. Opponents argued that the nation couldn't afford such an expansive old-age pension. The National Association of Manufacturers slammed the "economic security" bill as "ultimate socialistic control of life and industry." To assure passage, Perkins went into overdrive—she organized the National Conference on Economic Security, made more than a hundred speeches, lined up fifty prominent Americans to sign a joint letter in support of the bill, and gave a national radio address on February 25, 1935. Perkins and Roosevelt managed to defuse the opposition, and Congress passed the bill overwhelmingly, with Roosevelt signing it into law on August 14, 1935. A *Washington Post* article declared it the "New Deal's most important act," adding that "its importance cannot be exaggerated . . . because this legislation eventually will affect the lives of every man, woman and child in the country."

Three years later, several other key parts of Perkins's original vision became reality with the enactment of the Fair Labor Standards Act. That landmark law created the first federal minimum wage, twenty-five cents, but rising to forty cents after two years—nearly $7 today. The law also called for a forty-four-hour workweek, soon declining to forty hours; time-and-a-half overtime had to be paid for additional work. The law also set a general ban on child labor under age sixteen.

Perkins's successes in battling for workers and the poor made her a nemesis to many on the right. Some congressional Republicans denounced her as a Communist and sought to impeach her after she didn't seek to deport Harry Bridges, the Australian-born president of the West Coast longshoremen's union, who was accused of being a Communist (a charge he repeatedly denied). Some conservatives asserted that Perkins was a Jew from Russia whose real name was Mathilda Watsky. Thrown on the defensive, Perkins released a genealogy of her New England Protestant ancestry going back to the seventeenth century. "If I were a Jew, I would make no secret of it," she said. "On the contrary I would be proud to acknowledge it."

Perkins was one of just two cabinet members who served Roosevelt for his full twelve years (the other was Secretary of the Interior Harold Ickes). She achieved nearly all of her ambitious, original goals, save for national health insurance. Assessing Perkins's record, *Collier's* magazine wrote in 1944, "The Roosevelt pattern of government contains more of her ideas than those of any other of the President's followers. . . . [W]hat this country has been operating under the past twelve years is not so much the Roosevelt New Deal as it is the Perkins New Deal."

Six

Standing Up by Sitting Down

IN 1936, *Fortune* magazine described General Motors as "not big, but colossal," "the world's most complicated and most profitable manufacturing enterprise." With sixty-nine auto plants in thirty-five American cities, GM had 250,000 employees and produced nearly half of the nation's automobiles. It was an icon of American industry and the world's largest company.

In sharp contrast, the United Automobile Workers was, at that time, a proverbial ninety-seven-pound weakling. Founded in 1935, the union emerged from a hodgepodge of other labor groupings that had floundered because of factional feuding and fierce opposition from GM and other automakers. Systematic company-sponsored espionage had badly undermined earlier efforts to unionize autoworkers. GM's spies posed as workers and joined fledgling union chapters so they could tell managers who the activists were. Inside the factories, these spies helped get union supporters fired by snitching to management whenever supporters broke a rule. Company spies sometimes even took positions as officials in union locals and deliberately sowed tensions to divide and weaken the locals. At times, an astonishing number of spies—two hundred—kept tabs on union activities in GM's plants, with the famed Pinkerton Detective Agency maintaining an office literally next door to the UAW's Detroit headquarters. "I know everything that is going on inside," one GM spy boasted. "I know every move."

GM's spies kept close tabs on union activities in Flint, Michigan, which was one of the auto giant's production hubs, with fifty thousand workers employed at GM's Chevrolet, Buick, Oldsmobile, Fisher Body, and AC Spark Plug plants there. In the mid-1930s, GM employed 80 percent of Flint's workforce, with one writer calling Flint, sixty-five miles north of Detroit, "a shabby shrine to the automobile." Many of Flint's autoworkers were transplants from Appalachia and the Ozarks, searching for a better life. In 1930, when a predecessor union to the UAW staged a walkout in Flint, police on horseback rode down the strikers, while other police officers arrested union leaders, seized the local's membership rolls, and prohibited union meetings within city limits.

GM's spying was so elaborate that in 1936 five of the thirteen executive board members of the UAW's Flint local were either GM agents or Pinkerton spies. One union supporter told a Senate committee that because of all the surveillance, many autoworkers were too scared to openly back the UAW. "You don't know who you're talking to," he said. "You never take a chance. . . . You get suspicious of everybody." According to a Senate committee report, spying and union busting had been so successful that auto union membership in Flint had plummeted from several thousand in 1934 to a mere 120 in 1936.

Flint's union rolls shriveled even as autoworkers complained bitterly of dehumanizing conditions. One Chevy worker said, "Where you used to be a man . . . now you are less than their cheapest tool." A *New York Times* reporter who visited a GM plant in Flint was shocked to see the beehive-like swarm of workers and the speed and monotony of their labor. That reporter, Russell B. Porter, wrote of "thousands of men . . . perform[ing] the same operation all day or night, five days a week, the year round." Completing sixty cars an hour, "they seem to work on strings as a monster jerks them back to begin another car," Porter added. "Speed, speed, speed—that is Flint morning, noon and night."

One Buick worker complained, "We didn't even have time to go to the toilet . . . if there wasn't anybody to relieve you, you had to run away and tie the line up, and if you tied the line up, you got hell for it." A Chevrolet worker said, "The supervisors . . . were just people with a bullwhip, so to speak. All they were interested in was production. They treated us like a bunch of coolies. 'Get it out. Get it out. If you cannot get it out, there are people outside who will.'"

GM's foremen had nearly absolute power to hire, fire, and discipline, which led to resentment, favoritism, and kickbacks to keep one's job. Some foremen fired higher-paid, longtime workers and then rehired them at entry-level pay. "We was only beggars . . . with no power to demand anything that we asked for," said James Mangold, a Chevy worker in Flint.

Many autoworkers said they could hardly support their families because of the severe seasonal employment that resulted from GM's frequent plant closings (usually to retool for new models). While GM boasted that it had the highest hourly wages in the industry, many GM workers complained of meager annual earnings. In a 1936 speech in Detroit, President Roosevelt said one autoworker had told him that he worked just sixty-eight days the previous year, meaning he earned around $680 (about $12,000 today).

After having been beaten down in the early years of the Depression, autoworkers were, by 1936, slowly gaining courage, buoyed by the enactment of the National Industrial Recovery Act in 1933 and the National Labor Relations Act in 1935. These laws gave workers a federally protected, New Deal–blessed right to unionize. Even with these laws encouraging unionization, the American Federation of Labor, the nation's main labor federation, was making depressingly little headway in organizing the auto industry. John L. Lewis, the president of the United Mine Workers, a powerful, well-financed union, was eager to fill that vacuum.

A man of booming voice, uncommon vision, and monumental ego, Lewis founded the Committee for Industrial Organization (CIO) in 1935 to do mass organizing in that era's major industries, adopting a far different strategy from the AFL. Lewis wanted to do "wall-to-wall organizing" in auto, steel, rubber, and elsewhere—for example, to organize all five thousand workers at an auto plant into one union, eschewing the AFL's traditional approach of craft-by-craft organizing, that is, the fifty electricians at a plant would join one union, the fifty carpenters another, and the five hundred assembly-line workers yet another. The brilliant and bombastic Lewis clashed repeatedly with the AFL, most famously at a labor convention where he began a fistfight with the president of the carpenters' union. In 1938, the CIO, which had renamed itself the Congress of Industrial Organizations, broke away from the AFL. It included Lewis's mine workers, the UAW, the steelworkers, Sidney Hillman's clothing workers, and several other major unions. (The CIO merged with the AFL in 1955.)

The CIO and the UAW assigned two organizers to Flint to rally workers behind the fledgling autoworkers' union, which only a tiny fraction of those eligible had joined. To avoid detection by GM's spies, those organizers, Robert Travis and Roy Reuther, usually met with workers at the workers' homes, often in the basement. In the fall of 1936, the union activity began reaching critical mass, with many Flint workers growing less frightened and many even wearing UAW buttons into the plants.

The workers desperately wanted to improve factory conditions, and they knew they needed to somehow band together to get GM to bargain with them. Seeing how GM had crushed previous strikes and organizing drives, UAW leaders were eager to devise a strategy that would get GM to recognize their union and agree to nationwide bargaining. One historian wrote, "A moderately conservative bookmaker in the summer of 1936 might have offered 100 to 1 odds against the union." (At the end of 1932, George Barnett, then the president of the American Economic Association, said he saw "no reason" why labor would "revolutionize itself" to "become in the next decade a more potent social influence." "We may take it as probable that trade unionism is likely to be a declining influence in determining conditions of labor," Barnett declared.)

UAW strategists analyzed GM's industrial structure and recognized that there were two facilities absolutely essential to overall production: the plants in Flint and Cleveland that stamped out auto bodies and body parts for Chevy, Buick, Pontiac, and Oldsmobile. "We knew that if we could tie up these two shops, then General Motors would come to a halt," said Wyndham Mortimer, one of the UAW's top organizers.

UAW leaders saw that a bold labor tactic was catching fire. Workers at the Goodyear tire plant in Akron, Ohio, had conducted several sit-down strikes in the spring of 1936, while French workers had staged a huge wave of such protests that May and June. The sit-down had many advantages over traditional strikes. In typical strikes, workers trudged back and forth in front of their workplace, exposed to cold, rain, and snow. The police often attacked them, and replacement workers could easily take their jobs while the strikers picketed outside. With sit-downs, however, the workers were comfortably indoors, staying at or near their machines so "scabs" couldn't take their jobs. Management was reluctant to send in the police to oust sit-downers out of fear that the company's valuable machinery would be damaged or sabotaged. With most workers still too scared to stand up in favor of a union, it often took only a few dozen militant unionists to shut down an entire factory through a sit-down.

GM officials showed utter contempt toward the sit-down strikes in France. "That could not happen in the United States," said GM's executive vice president, William S. Knudsen. "The American people would not stand for them." Just the same, UAW strategists grew more enamored with sit-downs that November when a nine-day sit-down at a Bendix auto-parts plant in South Bend, Indiana, got that company to finally recognize and bargain with the UAW after several failed attempts.

That fall the union repeatedly asked GM to agree to a national bargaining conference to discuss wages, line speed, and seniority. GM rebuffed the union, saying those subjects could be discussed only at the individual plant level. The company also rejected the UAW's demand to recognize it as the "exclusive bargaining agent" for the autoworkers in Flint.

With this rejection, union leaders knew it was time to turn to their most potent weapon: a strike at GM's gigantic Flint complex. UAW strategists wanted to delay any stoppage until January because they didn't want to spoil the workers' Christmas holiday or prevent workers from getting their Christmas bonuses. Moreover, the union thought it wise to wait until January 1, when Michigan's newly elected governor, Frank Murphy, a New Deal progressive known for being sympathetic to workers, was to be inaugurated. Undermining that schedule, several dozen workers at GM's body-stamping plant in Cleveland began a sit-down on December 28, forcing seven thousand people there to stop work. The Cleveland strikers faced fierce pressure from GM and Cleveland's mayor to engage in plant-level bargaining to settle the dispute. The UAW and CIO leaders who were insisting on nationwide bargaining vigorously debated whether to wait until January 1 to begin a sit-down in Flint, but the matter was decided for them.

On the morning of December 30, fifty workers, spoiling for a fight, sat down at the Fisher Body No. 2 plant in Flint, which produced 450 Chevy bodies a day, angry that three workers had been transferred for refusing to quit the union. UAW leaders knew it was far more important to shut down the Fisher Body No. 1 stamping plant, which employed seventy-three hundred workers and produced 1,400 Buick bodies a day. Travis, the UAW/CIO organizer, grew alarmed when a worker called him to say that GM was loading critical body-stamping dies onto rail-cars in Flint. This aroused suspicions that GM was shipping the dies to plants in Pontiac and Grand Rapids with the goal of transferring production and undermining any possible strike.

Travis summoned workers to an urgent meeting. "What do we want to do?" he asked.

The workers shouted, "Shut her down!"

They soon poured into Fisher Body No. 1, stopping the machines, as union officials waited nervously outside.

Soon a shout came from a third-floor window: "She's ours!"

———

Within days, sit-downs and conventional strikes erupted at GM plants in Detroit, St. Louis, Janesville, Wisconsin, and Toledo and Norwood, Ohio. By the end of the first week of January, one labor historian wrote, "the great General Motors automotive system had been brought to its knees." What a prominent economist called "the most critical labor conflict of the nineteen thirties" was under way.

From the very first day, as Sidney Fine explains in *Sit-Down: The General Motors Strike of 1936–1937*, the strike became a huge story, the lead article in newspapers across the nation. The sit-downers occupied the north end of the giant Fisher No. 1 plant because that section had the cafeteria and many finished car bodies to sleep in. The workers formed a fourteen-member governing council and a dozen commit-tees: for food, education, press, sanitation, recreation, postal services, and more. The governing council banned liquor and established daily cleanup crews and six-hour-long patrols to watch for counterattacks and company spies. The sit-downers even set up a reading room—the chairs were car seats—and invited theater groups to perform. And the sit-downers sang. One song that became popular was this:

When the speed-up comes, just twiddle your thumbs,
Sit down! Sit down!
When the boss won't talk, don't take a walk,
Sit down! Sit down!

A nearby restaurant turned over its facilities to the UAW. With a former chef of the high-end Detroit Athletic Club in charge, the union served three hot meals a day to the roughly two thousand sit-downers. The strikers had guards who let union leaders, entertainers, and food deliverers in and allowed sit-downers out (and back in) to deliver messages to the union. The sit-downers' many outside supporters formed numerous committees, including ones for defense, picketing, publicity, and welfare for the strikers' families. Lewis, the CIO's president, said the sit-downers were "undoubtedly carrying through one of the most heroic battles that has ever been undertaken by strikers."

It's sexist by today's standards, but the strikers told Fisher Body's three hundred women workers not to join them, to stay home with their families. Nonetheless, the women played a major role during the strike, with the Women's Auxiliary creating a first aid squad and a speakers' bureau that championed the strikers' cause across the nation. The auxiliary also established the Women's Emergency Brigade, a "flying squadron" that rushed to the plant at critical times to create a human barrier out front. Genora Johnson, a sit-downer's wife, said, "We will form a line around the men, and if the police want to fire, then they'll just have to fire into us."

America's corporate leaders condemned the sit-down, with one business group commenting that if workers "can seize premises illegally, hold [them] indefinitely, refuse admittance to owners or managers . . . and threaten bloodshed [in] all attempts to dislodge them . . . then freedom and liberty are at an end, government becomes a mockery, superseded by anarchy, mob rule and ruthless dictatorship."

Outraged by the sit-down, GM executives sought an injunction to have the Flint strikers removed for trespassing. The union argued that this wasn't trespassing because the sit-downers had legally reported to their workstations, and besides, didn't the strikers have "a property right" to their jobs? State Circuit Court Judge Edward D. Black quickly rejected the UAW's arguments, and on January 2 he ordered the strikers to evacuate. His injunction appeared to be a devastating blow to the union. But the union's lawyers soon discovered that Judge Black owned 3,665 shares of GM stock worth $219,900 (around $3.6 million today). That was a huge embarrassment to GM; the company had the case transferred to another judge, and thrown on the defensive, it didn't even ask to have Judge Black's injunction enforced.

GM soon grew impatient and decided to try to force the workers out. On January 11, with the temperature just sixteen degrees, GM shut off the heat in Fisher No. 2. At 6 p.m. that day, company police blocked delivery of dinner to the strikers inside the plant. Furious, thirty strikers went downstairs, confronted the GM police, and told a GM police captain to stop blocking the gate. When he refused, they shoved the gate open, and he called Flint police headquarters for help. The Flint police rushed to the scene and started firing tear gas, often through the plant's windows. The strikers fought back from Fisher No. 2's roof, throwing milk bottles, cans, and rocks and soaking the police with high-pressure hoses. They also turned inner tubes into slingshots to fling one-and-a-half-pound door hinges.

To keep the police out, union supporters rushed to barricade the plant's gates with their cars. As the battle raged, a UAW organizer, Victor Reuther, used an impromptu sound truck to tell the strikers what the police were doing and where to aim their projectiles. Reuther shouted, "We wanted peace! General Motors chose war. Give it to them."

Unluckily for the police, the wind changed direction and blew the tear gas back at them, forcing them to retreat. Several policemen opened fire, and fourteen strikers and strike sympathizers were injured, thirteen by gunshot. Nine police officers were hurt. But when the fighting ended after midnight, the strikers still held Fisher No. 2. They declared victory in what was called the Battle of the Running Bulls. ("Bulls" was slang for police.)

Governor Murphy, fearing that the violence would escalate, ordered the National Guard to Flint, and by the next day 1,200 troops had arrived, the total eventually climbing to 3,454. GM supporters pressed Murphy to have the Guard evict the strikers, but Murphy's instructions were that "everything be done by the troops to avoid bringing on a conflict." He added, "The state authorities will not take sides," and the National Guard were there "only to protect public peace." Many GM supporters found Murphy's behavior maddening and cowardly. They asserted that his policy of neutrality was in effect a pro-strike stance because it failed to restore private property to its rightful owners.

A close ally of President Roosevelt's, Murphy would play a decisive role in this showdown. He had previously been a federal prosecutor, mayor of Detroit, and governor-general of the Philippines. Ascetic, soft-spoken, and patient, he made no secret that he hoped to someday become the nation's first Roman Catholic president. Devoutly religious, he was a lifelong bachelor and teetotaler. His favorite line from the Bible was "But with righteousness he shall judge the poor, and decide with equity for the meek of the earth" (Isaiah 11:4). Complicating Murphy's role, he owned $104,775 worth of GM stock ($1.8 million today) when the sit-down began. He sold off his holdings on January 18.

Murphy's overriding goal was to end the standoff peacefully, through a negotiated settlement. To his eyes, GM's position was a formidable obstacle—it vowed not to bargain unless the sit-downers first evacuated (it said it was willing to meet with UAW officials only to discuss how to get the strikers to leave). "Collective bargaining cannot be justified if one party, having seized the plant, holds a gun to the other party's head," GM's Knudsen said.

Murphy summoned top GM and UAW officials to Lansing, the state capital, and after sixteen hours of talks he announced a settlement at 4:30 a.m., January 15. The union agreed to vacate the plants, and in return GM promised fifteen days of formal bargaining, not to remove the crucial dies during that time, and not to fire any union activists.

Many sit-downers bridled at the deal, fearing that the UAW would be surrendering its leverage—the sit-down—without achieving any of its goals on wages, line speed, or other matters. Nonetheless, on January 16, the union began pulling its strikers out of several plants, including the Cadillac and Fleetwood plants in Detroit and GM's Guide Lamp plant in Anderson, Indiana.

Also on January 16, GM's Knudsen met with the leaders of the Flint Alliance, a GM-backed, anti-UAW "union," to reassure them that they wouldn't be shunted aside and that GM would negotiate with them, too. The alliance's leaders asserted that it was independent of GM, although its head had once been a Buick executive, it shared a public-relations firm with GM, and many GM factory foremen had urged workers to sign cards to join the alliance. The UAW and the Flint Alliance detested each other, with the UAW angry that the alliance was spearheading a "back to work" movement to sabotage the strike. Union officials also thought the alliance had encouraged vigilantes to physically attack UAW activists, including Roy Reuther. When UAW leaders learned of Knudsen's meeting with the Flint Alliance, they were livid, feeling undermined and betrayed. They told the sit-downers not to vacate Fisher 1 and 2, causing the January 15 settlement to collapse.

At that point, Secretary of Labor Frances Perkins decided to get far more involved because the strike was spreading economic pain across the nation. She persuaded GM's chairman, Alfred Sloan, to meet with her in Washington; she left Roosevelt's second inauguration before it ended to meet Sloan inside a private railcar at Union Station. Her goal was to get GM to bargain with Lewis and top UAW officials *even with* the plants still occupied.

President Roosevelt disliked GM's stance. According to Perkins, he found it "stuffy," faulting the company for being overly concerned with the legal technicalities of trespass. Perkins described FDR's position this way:

> And what do you do when a man trespasses on your property? Sure, you order him off. But shooting it out and killing a lot of people because they have violated the law of trespass somehow offends me. . . . There must be a better way. Why can't these fellows in General Motors meet with the committee of workers? Talk it out. They would get a settlement. It wouldn't be so terrible.

A week after meeting with Perkins, Sloan told her that he would meet with UAW leaders and Lewis, but Sloan soon reversed himself, saying it was indefensible for the sit-downers to throw so many other GM employees out of work. His about-face enraged Perkins. In a phone conversation, she told Sloan, as she later recalled, "You are a scoundrel and a skunk, Mr. Sloan. You can't do that kind of thing. That is a rotter. . . . You don't deserve to be counted among decent men. Decent people don't do such things. . . . You have betrayed your government. You have betrayed the men who work for you."

Sloan was appalled, telling Perkins, "You can't talk like that to me! I'm worth $70 million, and I made it all myself. You can't talk like that to me! I'm Alfred Sloan."

It was back to stalemate. Now the sit-downers' spirits were flagging. Their wives and children missed them, the public was turning against them, and GM signaled that it would seek another injunction. The UAW's leaders grew convinced that they needed to take some bold action to improve the strikers' spirits—and leverage. A handful of union strategists hatched an idea. Notwithstanding the sit-down, one of the most important GM plants in Flint continued to operate: Chevy

No. 4, which made all of Chevy's engines, one million a year. If the workers could seize that plant, they would totally shut down Chevy, which was by far GM's best-selling brand.

Cunningly, UAW officials leaked inaccurate plans to the press, indicating that workers planned to seize another, far less important Flint plant, Chevy No. 9, a ball-bearing plant. As union officials expected, GM learned about the leak. At the designated time on February 1, GM and the City of Flint sent hundreds of police to Chevy No. 9 to prevent the anticipated sit-down there. Then several hundred UAW members rushed in and took over Chevy No. 4; fifty of those sit-downers came from a UAW local in Detroit that was headed by Walter Reuther (Roy and Victor Reuther's brother). In capturing that plant, the union again seemed to have the momentum.

The very next day, however, GM persuaded Judge Paul V. Gadola to issue a sweeping injunction. Gadola not only ordered the strikers to vacate the plants but prohibited the UAW from doing peaceful picketing anywhere in Michigan (an evident violation of the First Amendment). The sit-downers pledged not to vacate, all but inviting a bloody confrontation. They sent Governor Murphy a telegram: "We have decided to stay in the plant. We have no illusions about the sacrifices which this decision will entail. We fully expect that if a violent effort is made to oust us, many of us will be killed."

Adding to the pressure, the CIO's Lewis, with his flair for the dramatic, warned Murphy that if he ordered troops to oust the strikers,

> I shall then walk up to the largest window in the plant, open it, divest myself of my outer raiment, remove my shirt and bare my bosom. Then when you order your troops to fire, mine will be the first breast that those bullets will strike.

At the same time, GM's corporate and conservative supporters were pushing Murphy to send in the Guard and get those lawbreaking strikers to comply with the injunction. One critic called Murphy "a Yellow-Bellied Cur Dog."

With Judge Gadola ordering the Flint workers to vacate at 3 p.m. on February 3, the UAW urgently summoned members and supporters to converge on Flint. At the appointed time, with the temperature close to zero, more than three thousand union supporters, some carrying clubs, pipes, and hammers, massed outside the plant. Fearing a huge outbreak of violence, the sheriff and the National Guard decided against trying to eject the sit-downers.

Many GM supporters viewed that as another abject breakdown in law and order. Flint's fiercely antiunion city manager, John Barringer, was furious, warning, "We are going to go down there shooting. The strikers have taken over this town, and we are going to take it back."

Fearing mayhem and fatalities, Murphy redoubled his efforts to resolve the dispute through negotiation. "You can't put those men out by force without killing them," he told a congressman. And he told a friend, "I'm not going down in history as 'Bloody Murphy.' If I sent those soldiers right in on the men, there'd be no telling how many would be killed. It would be inconsistent with everything I have ever stood for."

Although GM had sought Judge Gadola's injunction, the company's executives were torn about having troops remove the strikers. On the one hand, GM was hurting badly; the Flint sit-down and related strikes had idled 136,000 of its workers and caused its production to plunge to fifteen hundred cars and trucks a week in early February from fifty-three thousand in mid-December. On the other hand, GM feared that a bloody ejection of the sit-downers would be a lasting stain on the company's image and would damage its sales in the long term. GM was inching toward a willingness to bargain, even with the sit-downers still in the plants. Eager to save face about such a huge reversal, top GM officials told Perkins that they would agree to negotiate with the UAW and Lewis, but only if President Roosevelt personally requested them to do so. Perkins told GM that, yes, the president wanted that to happen, and within days the two sides began talking in earnest.

Now the union erected a major, new obstacle, insisting that GM recognize it as the sole bargaining agent at the seventeen plants where workers had gone on strike that winter. For years, GM had vigorously opposed exclusive representation, maintaining that some workers could have UAW representation if they wanted, while others should be able to have other unions represent them, including a company-backed union.

During the week of February 3, Murphy, GM executives, and union officials spent fifty hours negotiating—swapping proposals, swatting down ideas, and screaming at each other in search of a settlement. That whole week, many GM backers continued their anti-Murphy diatribes, calling him spineless for failing to enforce the injunction. On February 11, Murphy finally announced a settlement. The sit-downers would vacate after forty-four days, without a single life lost.

The deal was a complex compromise. GM still wouldn't officially accept the UAW as the exclusive bargaining representative, but it did agree to recognize the UAW as the bargaining agent for any employees who wanted the UAW to represent them. GM also promised that at the seventeen plants where workers had struck, it would not talk to any other union for the next six months. For all intents and purposes, that would make the UAW the exclusive bargaining agent because the UAW was, in those six months, likely to sign up the lion's share of those plants' workers as union members for two reasons: first, the workers were no longer scared to openly back a union, and, second, the workers were impressed that the union had just defeated GM in a colossal showdown. As part of the settlement, GM also promised not to retaliate against any strikers and not to interfere with the UAW's unionization efforts. GM refused, however, to grant the eight-hour day the union was seeking, although it did agree to a 10 percent raise. The UAW trumpeted that raise as a major victory, although GM insisted that the 10 percent was merely a response to wage hikes at Chrysler.

The day of the settlement, the sit-downers marched triumphantly out of the Flint plants, proud that they were not vacating under a sheriff's order. Thousands of supporters cheered them as the strikers sang "Solidarity Forever." Outside the plant hung a fifty-foot banner proclaiming, "VICTORY IS OURS." Roy Reuther described the scene: "I never saw a night like that and perhaps may never see it again. I liken it to . . . a country experiencing independence."

Suddenly thousands of autoworkers who had been too scared to support the union or who had doubted that it could succeed flocked into the UAW's ranks. Its membership nationwide soared from 88,000 in February 1937 to 400,000 in October. By late 1941, it had jumped to 649,000.

Nelson Lichtenstein, a labor historian, called the Flint sit-down "undoubtedly the most significant work stoppage in twentieth-century American history." It inspired a tidal wave of other sit-downs and strikes, with nearly five million workers participating in job actions in 1937 and nearly three million workers joining unions that year. "Sitting down has replaced baseball as a national pastime," *The Detroit News* declared. The UAW's breakthrough in Flint helped lead to epic unionization wins at Chrysler in 1939 and at Ford in 1941. Sidney Fine, author of *Sit-Down*, said one of the showdown's most important results was "that the decision-making power in large segments of American industry where the voice of labor had been little more than a whisper, if that, would henceforth have to be shared in some measure with the unions in these industries."

Alfred Lockhart, a Fisher Body worker who had initially opposed the strike and the UAW, was overjoyed. "The inhuman high speed is *no more*," Lockhart wrote to a friend. "We now have a voice. . . . [We] are now treated as human beings, and not as part of the machinery. . . . It proves clearly that united we stand, divided or alone we fall."

Seven

Walter Reuther, Builder of the Middle Class

DURING WORLD WAR II, America's military might and courageous fighting men played a crucial role in defeating Germany, Italy, and Japan. America's manufacturing prowess—the many factories that churned out bombers, tanks, and machine guns—also played a big role. At war's end, with many of Europe's and Japan's industries decimated, the United States emerged as the world's preeminent economic power. But even as Americans celebrated victory, many government officials and economists quietly worried that the nation would slide into recession and perhaps back into a second Depression once the factories that made all those warplanes, tanks, and bombs were shut down and hundreds of thousands of workers were laid off. For the nation's labor unions, this was a huge concern, and they wanted to do their utmost to prevent the economy from entering a tailspin.

Unions emerged from the war far stronger than they were before the war. Union membership rose 63 percent (from 8.7 million in 1940 to 14.3 million in 1945) as wartime employers, eager to maintain labor peace and maximize production, did little to resist organizing efforts. The Roosevelt administration had invited union leaders to help plan the war effort, while many corporations at the time viewed unions not as adversaries but as partners to help plan production and assure victory.

Unions worked closely with management to help factories convert to a war footing. To support the war effort, labor leaders agreed to unpopular wage controls and no-strike clauses (although there were plenty of short wildcat strikes, for instance, when rank-and-file workers erupted in response to a firing or a worker suffering a severe injury). Unions became a vital and visible partner in many tripartite government-business-labor efforts. Powerful federal agencies like the War Production Board, the War Labor Board, and the Office of Economic Stabilization helped convert industries to military use as well as allocate resources, maintain labor peace, and administer wage and price controls. In all these efforts, labor had a strong voice. FDR's military planners even borrowed from a proposal that a brainy, thirty-three-year-old UAW official had put forward in December 1940—it called for converting the nation's auto plants so they could produce five hundred warplanes a day.

At war's end, millions of Americans were hungering for a substantial raise. Despite FDR's pledge to maintain a fair balance between wages and prices, many workers were convinced that their pay had not nearly kept up with inflation. Moreover, many Americans' workweeks had dropped from forty-eight hours to forty because the years of push-it-to-the-max war production had ended, causing their paychecks to decline. All this fueled huge pent-up frustration and militancy on the labor front.

At the vortex of many of these pressures was Walter Reuther, the UAW official who would soon emerge as one of the nation's most visionary and effective union leaders. (Reuther was the young UAW official who had made the five-hundred-planes-a-day proposal five years earlier.) When Japan surrendered, Reuther was head of the UAW's General Motors department, meaning he led the largest division of the nation's most dynamic union. Put another way, he was in charge of labor's dealings with the world's largest corporation, a colossus that had produced 12 percent of all the metal goods that America's armed forces used during World War II. GM and its workers had produced 13,000 bombers and fighter planes, 206,000 aircraft engines, 97,000 aircraft propellers, 1.9 million machine guns, 190,000 cannons, 854,000 trucks, and 14 million shells.

Several weeks after V-J Day, Reuther plunged into that year's contract talks with GM on behalf of the 175,000 UAW members there. Unlike many labor leaders, he didn't see unions as merely a mechanism to put more money in workers' pay envelopes. He "rejected the cash-register approach alone and always argued that labor should seek to build a better world," wrote Damon Stetson, a longtime Detroit and labor correspondent for *The New York Times*. *Harper's Magazine* wrote,

"The smart, dancing-eyed Reuther is something special among labor leaders, a person who moves in a world of ideas that includes a concept of the general welfare as distinct from short-term labor welfare."

Known for his down-to-earth eloquence (and red hair), Reuther championed a public-minded unionism. "We are not going to operate as a narrow economic pressure group, which says 'we are going to get ours and the public be damned' or 'the consumer be damned,'" Reuther said. "We . . . want to make progress with the community and not at the expense of the community." (UAW leaders had urged the federal government to exempt Reuther from serving overseas during the war, saying he was needed to help maintain production and labor peace at home.)

Reuther was a font of ideas about how to convert the wartime economy to peacetime with as little pain and unemployment as possible. He proposed that war factories be converted to produce railcars and housing. He called for creating the Peace Production Board, a government/business/labor/consumer agency that would plan production, oversee factory conversions, and set wages and prices. Even as some economists warned of a possible second Depression, Reuther argued that technological advances could assure long-term prosperity. In his view, there was plenty of productive capacity to guarantee broad prosperity. The problem, he argued, was that not enough wealth was getting to consumers (and workers) to keep the prosperity machine humming, because "the corporate elite" sought to "maximize profits by pursuing policies of 'planned scarcity.'" He asserted that corporations artificially pushed up prices while cutting the number of jobs. Showing his socialist tendencies, Reuther argued that "there can be no permanent prosperity" so "long as the controls of production remain in the hands of a privileged minority."

Reuther's leftist ideas, and his success in conveying them, unnerved many in corporate America. George Romney (Mitt's father), then the general manager of the Auto Manufacturers Association, said, "Walter Reuther is the most dangerous man in Detroit because no one is more skillful in bringing about the revolution without seeking to disturb the existing forms of society." Barry Goldwater, the conservative senator from Arizona, maintained that Reuther was a "more dangerous menace than the Sputnik or anything Soviet Russia might do to America."

Reuther had trade unionism in his blood, as Nelson Lichtenstein explains in his richly detailed biography, *The Most Dangerous Man in Detroit*. Born in Wheeling, West Virginia, in 1907, Reuther was the son of German immigrants. His father, Valentine, was a leader of the United Brewery Workers and an ardent socialist who often had his family discuss politics and unionism at the dinner table. "At my father's knee," Reuther recalled, "we learned the philosophy of trade unionism. We got the struggles, the hopes, and the aspirations of working people every day." At age sixteen, Reuther dropped out of school and became an apprentice for a steelmaker in Wheeling. He emerged as an expert tool-and-die maker, although he lost his right big toe when he and two co-workers dropped a four-hundred-pound die that they were trying to lift. At age nineteen, Reuther moved to Detroit, landing a job at the notorious Briggs auto body plant, where he often worked thirteen-and-a-half-hour overnight shifts. Attracted by the higher pay, he soon moved to Ford's River Rouge plant in Dearborn, just west of Detroit.

Not surprisingly, this son of a union leader became a union militant, describing the auto industry as a "social jungle" in which workers were "nameless, faceless clock numbers." His brothers Roy and Victor followed him to Michigan, and they, too, became union activists. Ford fired Walter in 1932 for being a leftist agitator, and he and Victor took their savings and went to Europe for two years and eight months. There they witnessed Hitler's rise in Germany and worked for two years at a Ford-backed auto plant in Gorky (now Nizhny Novgorod) in the Soviet Union, helping train its workers. The two brothers returned to Michigan in 1935, and soon, as we saw, they and brother Roy played important roles in the Flint Sit-Down Strike. All were climbing the UAW ladder, with Walter serving as president of a UAW local in West Detroit.

Walter's fame skyrocketed in May 1937 when Ford's ferociously anti-union private "police" force—Ford called it its "Service Department"—beat, kicked, and bloodied him and three other UAW officials as they sought to launch a unionization drive by distributing handbills on a public overpass outside Ford's River Rouge complex, by far the world's largest manufacturing complex. The next morning, newspapers across the nation ran graphic front-page photographs of the brutal mauling, in what became known as the Battle of the Overpass. Reuther wrote, "They picked my feet up and my shoulders and slammed me down on the concrete and while I was on the ground, they kicked me again in the face, head and other parts of my body. This process went on about eight times. . . . And all the time I had the permit to distribute the leaflets in my pocket, but no one would look at that."

In the fall of 1945, just weeks after the war ended, Reuther was pushing two highly ambitious bargaining demands that he hoped would chart a course for postwar industrial America. First, he sought a 30 percent raise for the UAW's 175,000 members at GM (equivalent to thirty-three cents an hour). GM's workers were feeling explosive frustration after years of a no-strike pledge and wages lagging behind inflation. Moreover, Reuther argued that GM could afford to grant large raises while keeping its prices frozen because its production had risen 50 percent since 1941, its productivity was climbing by nearly 3 percent a year, and it had a 28 percent return on investment in some quarters. He believed passionately that workers should share in the benefits of their own and their company's increased productivity. Second, Reuther demanded that GM agree not to raise its sticker prices, fearing that if the nation's largest corporation hiked its prices, it would generate a wave of me-too price increases across America. That, Reuther feared, would wipe out much of the raises the workers received. That second demand grew directly out of the wartime practice of administering, and limiting, price increases. Indeed, Reuther pressed President Harry S. Truman's Office of Price Administration to back him by ordering GM not to raise its prices. That second demand also reflected Reuther's, and much of labor's, view at the time that unions should have a real voice on fundamental issues like production and prices.

GM vigorously disagreed with Reuther. It offered a thirteen-and-a-half-cent raise (a 12 percent raise) and scoffed at the demand that it not raise its sticker prices. Joined by other automakers and the steel industry, GM urged the Truman administration to eliminate price controls. (To help raise take-home pay, GM also proposed getting Congress to legislate a forty-five-hour workweek to replace the existing forty-hour week. Reuther denounced that proposal as a major step backward, saying that GM was baiting the union and asking for a strike.) Reuther told GM that he would lower the UAW's demand for a 30 percent raise if GM opened its books to demonstrate that it couldn't afford such an increase. GM insisted that wages should have nothing to do with profit levels and refused to open its books or up its wage offer. "I am greatly exercised—perhaps unduly so—by the philosophy of 'capacity to pay,'"

Alfred Sloan wrote to another CEO. (Many workers saw GM's stance as manifestly unfair, although GM's view from the 1940s has come to dominate corporate America's current view, with many companies refusing to give their workers raises large enough to keep up with inflation, even when their profits are soaring. That's one of the factors fueling today's income inequality.) Charles E. Wilson, GM's president, told Reuther, "We shall resist the monopolistic power of your union to force this 30 percent increase in basic wages." "Automobiles," Wilson added, "would shortly cost 30 percent more to produce."

With a chasm dividing the two sides, GM workers voted overwhelmingly to strike. On November 21, 1945, 175,000 UAW members walked out at eighty GM plants and warehouses in nineteen states. That strike turned into a titanic conflict, but one that was far more peaceful and orderly than the Flint Sit-Down Strike.

As many business leaders, Republican politicians, and editorial writers demonized unions as selfish, as seeking a larger slice of the economic pie than they deserved, Reuther insisted that the autoworkers were merely seeking their fair share. In speech after speech, he argued that if the UAW could win a large raise from GM while getting the automaker not to raise its prices, that would become a model for other companies and an inspiration for millions of workers across the United States. Other workers, Reuther asserted, would receive similar, me-too raises, creating a nationwide surge in consumer buying power. Borrowing a page from the British economist John Maynard Keynes, Reuther believed that increased consumer purchasing power would in turn benefit industrial production. This virtuous cycle, he argued, would guarantee that America's postwar economy would not slide back into recession or depression. One of the strike's slogans became "Purchasing power for prosperity," with Reuther proclaiming, "Mass purchasing power is our new frontier." In an article for *The New Republic,* he wrote, "Labor is not fighting for a larger slice of the national pie. Labor is fighting for a larger pie."

GM's negotiators resisted and sniped at Reuther's demands and Keynesian vision. At one bargaining session, Reuther said, "Unless we get a more realistic distribution of America's wealth, we won't get enough to keep this machine going." GM's chief negotiator, Harry Coen, fired back that Reuther was again "exposing" his "socialist desires." Reuther responded, "If fighting for a more equal and equitable distribution of the wealth of this country is socialistic, I stand guilty of being a Socialist."

Reuther recognized that to maximize the UAW's chances of winning this showdown, the union needed support from the Truman administration and the public. The UAW set up the National Committee to Aid the Families of GM Strikers, which included Eleanor Roosevelt, the theologian Reinhold Niebuhr, the former Treasury secretary Henry Morgenthau, the former interior secretary Harold Ickes, and Henry Luce, the powerful publisher of *Time, Life,* and *Fortune.* Luce put Reuther on the cover of *Time,* while *Life* lauded him as a visionary who was "battling to attack the great problems of the national economy." *Fortune* wrote that Reuther's objective was "to gain for labor—and thus, he believes, for the consumer—a true partnership in the U.S. productive machine."

Eager to end this protracted strike, Truman appointed a fact-finding board that recommended a nineteen-and-a-half-cent raise for the autoworkers (translating to nearly 18 percent). The panel agreed with Reuther that an increase in GM's car prices was not justified. Even though the recommended raise fell short of the strike's goals, Reuther felt constrained to accept the board's findings. GM, however, rejected the board's recommendations, giving itself a black eye with the public.

A rush of events soon weakened Reuther's hand. In January 1946, 750,000 steelworkers went on strike, shutting down that crucial industry. Desperate to end that work stoppage, the Truman administration quickly proposed a compromise: the workers would receive an eighteen-and-a-half-cent-an-hour raise, while the steelmakers would get a green light to raise prices by five cents a ton. Management and union embraced that deal, ending a four-week strike. The steel walkout and the GM strike, together with a coal strike and a nationwide rail strike, were part of an extraordinary explosion of strikes in 1946—the largest strike wave in U.S. history. There were 4,985 strikes that year, involving 4.6 million workers. The public was growing angry about all the strikes and disruption.

Further weakening Reuther's position, Ford, Chrysler, and General Electric, in their contract talks, agreed to raises of eighteen or eighteen and a half cents—all lower than the nineteen-and-a-half-cent raise that Truman's fact-finding board had recommended for the

UAW at General Motors. Moreover, the United Electrical Workers—a Communist-dominated union that was no fan of the anti-Communist Reuther—undercut him and the UAW by settling for an eighteen-and-a-half-cent raise for its thirty thousand members who worked for GM.

Reuther found himself boxed in. He didn't want to accept less than the recommended nineteen and a half cents, but he could hardly insist on a deal more generous than those received by the other unions. After the UAW's picket lines had held strong for nearly four months, Reuther reluctantly accepted the eighteen-and-a-half-cent raise (17 percent) as part of a settlement that did nothing to stop GM from increasing its prices. That bitter strike had lasted 113 days.

As Reuther predicted, an 18 percent spike in inflation in 1946 wiped out the value of the hard-won raises. And even though the settlement fell far short of Reuther's goals, he was seen as doing such an impressive job leading the troops, strategizing, and communicating to the nation during the strike that he won the UAW's overall presidency in March 1946. Reuther was just thirty-eight at the time.

———

Reuther was not the only one in Detroit with a bold vision. GM's president had an unusually audacious vision of his own. Engine Charlie Wilson, as he was known, wanted to invest $3.5 billion (more than $35 billion today) to expand GM's production capacity by more than 50 percent. He was eager to make this great investment leap because he could see that with millions of veterans returning home, there was huge pent-up consumer demand. And with the rapid growth of the nation's suburbs and highways, he saw an unprecedented surge in demand for automobiles.

Wilson was fearful that Reuther and his union would sabotage Wilson's grand project with new and devastating walkouts. To Wilson's mind, two heavyweight boxers had slugged it out for twenty-five rounds during the strike, with both fighters emerging battered and weaker. Wilson, desperately wanting to avoid more such knockdown fights, knew that the UAW was still strike-happy; its many locals had authorized 409 strikes in 1947 and 1948. But he also felt that Reuther, despite their major ideological differences, was a pragmatist, someone he could work with. He also recognized that Reuther, having won overwhelming reelection as UAW president in 1947, was a force he would have to reckon with for years to come.

Wilson realized that he wasn't dealing with just another run-of-the-mill labor leader but someone who was increasingly respected, even revered as a hero. On the evening of April 20, 1948, Reuther had returned home from a UAW executive board meeting and was opening his refrigerator door when a twelve-gauge shotgun blast smashed through his kitchen window. Four buckshot pellets tore into his right arm, and another pellet plowed through his chest. If he had not turned at the last second to say something to his wife, May, all five shots would have hit him in the chest. Reuther received three pints of blood and was in traction for weeks. Thirteen months later, his brother Victor was shot by a shotgun of the identical make while he was reading at home. He lost his right eye. Neither shooting was ever solved, with suspects ranging from auto industry goons to Communist opponents to mobsters unhappy that Reuther was cracking down on their illicit operations in Detroit's factories.

While Walter Reuther was convalescing, Wilson was eager to nail down a new contract without another painful strike. So he made the UAW an offer that Reuther could hardly refuse, an offer that showed that the 113-day strike was having a time-delayed payoff. Wilson proposed a highly innovative deal aimed at assuring two years of labor peace. Until then, almost all UAW contracts lasted just one year, necessitating laborious bargaining each year and new worries about new walkouts. In exchange for a guarantee of two years of no strikes, Wilson offered a groundbreaking and unusually generous deal: a raise of eleven cents an hour, a quarterly cost-of-living adjustment, and a radical new idea—a 2 percent annual improvement factor. That meant a 2 percent additional raise that enabled the autoworkers to share in the strong productivity growth GM was enjoying. It was an offer that Reuther and the union's members happily accepted. Wilson's innovative contract proposal addressed two of Reuther's long-standing concerns: that workers share in their employer's increased productivity and that their paychecks be protected against inflation.

The 1948 contract was a huge breakthrough, containing some landmark gains. But the visionary Reuther had his eye on a new and arguably bigger prize: vastly improved benefits. After the war ended, Reuther had hoped that Truman and Congress would enact a universal national health system, much like Britain's National Health Service Act, enacted under Labour Party rule in 1946. Reuther also hoped that Congress would make Social Security far more generous—with inflation raging, monthly benefits for the typical retiree had eroded to a paltry 11 percent of average income.

In November 1946, Republicans won control of both houses of Congress for the first time since 1930. Campaigning on a "Had Enough" slogan, the GOP appealed to the public's anger over double-digit inflation and the hugely disruptive wave of strikes that year. The new Republican Congress moved quickly to hobble the fast-growing union movement by enacting the Taft-Hartley Act, which labor and Reuther bitterly opposed. The act allowed individual states to pass anti-union-fee, right-to-work laws and prohibited foremen from unionizing; when foremen joined unions, it gave unions a huge boost and made their strikes far more effective. Taft-Hartley banned secondary boycotts, a powerful tool in which a union picketed and pressured companies that did business with another company the union was on strike against. Taft-Hartley also required that all union leaders sign affidavits saying they were not Communists, a move that forced many Communists out of the union movement, many of them among its most effective and dedicated organizers. (Taft-Hartley in this way ironically strengthened Reuther's hand because some of his fiercest opponents within the UAW were Communists.) The Republican Congress passed the law over Truman's veto in June 1947, sapping labor's momentum. Today, more than seven decades later, Taft-Hartley continues to have a lasting effect in holding back labor.

The Republican-led Congress also took discussion of a British-style national health insurance system off the table. A significant increase in Social Security benefits was also unlikely. Reuther concluded that because Congress would not deliver better social benefits, he would seek to win those benefits at the bargaining table.

Meanwhile, Charlie Wilson wanted to build on the innovative two-year 1948 deal. For the 1950 contract round, he was eyeing an unprecedented five-year contract that would assure sixty months of labor peace. In exchange for that, Reuther was intent on winning generous pension and health coverage. At the time, those were rarities in union contracts, although Reuther and the UAW had, in 1949, gotten Ford to agree to a landmark $100-a-month pension ($1,000 today) to workers with thirty years of service. Much like today's union leaders, Reuther used some robust rhetoric to pressure and embarrass Wilson and GM. Angry that Wilson was refusing to agree to pensions for GM's blue-collar workers, Reuther mocked Wilson's anticipated $25,000-a-year pension, then considered an outlandish amount ($250,000 today). "If you make $258 an hour, they give it to you," Reuther said. "If you make $1.65 an hour, they say, 'You don't need it . . . and we are not going to give it to you.'"

To persuade Reuther to accept a five-year contract, Wilson ultimately agreed to a considerably richer deal than the 1948 contract. Not only did the new contract include a better cost-of-living adjustment and a greater annual improvement factor, but it included the most generous pension in all of American industry: $125 a month ($1,250 today) after thirty years on the job. Moreover, GM agreed to pay for 50 percent of each worker's health insurance—another trailblazing provision. The deal guaranteed a stunning 20 percent increase in autoworkers' income over the next five years (after factoring in inflation). This contract astonished many in business and labor because it was so much longer and more generous than other collective bargaining agreements.

The deal was so widely celebrated that there was talk of Reuther running for president. *Business Week* hailed the deal as "industrial statesmanship of a very high order," while *The Washington Post* said it was "a great event in industrial history." The deal became known as the "Treaty of Detroit"—*Fortune* magazine's famous term—because it signaled a peace agreement after years of labor-management hostilities. Daniel Bell, a *Fortune* magazine writer and later a sociology professor at Harvard, wrote, "GM may have paid a billion for peace but it got a bargain" because it "regained control over one of the crucial management functions," especially "long range scheduling of production."

The Treaty of Detroit served as both a foundation and a model that produced the world's largest, richest middle class as hundreds of companies followed or partly followed the GM-UAW innovations on pay and benefits. By the early 1960s, over half the nation's collective bargaining agreements contained similar annual improvement factors and cost-of-living adjustments, while one-third of the overall workforce had some pension coverage. Moreover, many companies that were eager to remain nonunion copied (or nearly copied) the package of benefits won by the UAW. One business school professor who analyzed corporate compensation trends in the 1950s, 1960s, and 1970s wrote, "The activities of many unions in the United States are benefiting many nonmembers; in other words, unions are doing much good for people who do not pay them any dues."

The autoworkers (along with the steelworkers) became the lords of the labor world, paid handsomely for assembly-line jobs that were often mind-numbingly dull. (They were paid and treated light-years better than the Flint autoworkers were just fifteen years earlier.) But when Germany and Japan finally recovered from World War II, Detroit's automakers, with their higher labor costs, eventually felt intense pressure from those two nations' lower-cost automakers, resulting in a wave of plant closings. In this way, the UAW was a victim of its own success.

———

In the years after the Treaty of Detroit, some scholars talked of the emergence of an unofficial "social contract" in which corporations, seeking stability and labor peace, shared their increased prosperity, profits, and productivity as never before. From 1948 to 1973, as we discussed, worker productivity and wages rose hand in hand, with both nearly doubling. (Worker productivity overall increased by 96 percent, while median hourly pay climbed by 91 percent, after accounting for inflation.) Reuther's success in getting GM and, indirectly, corporate America to share their prosperity gave America's leaders plenty of economic ammunition to use in their ideological battle with the Soviet Union. At a speech in Detroit in 1960, President Eisenhower told those at the National Automobile Show's dinner, "Other peoples find it hard to believe that an American working man can own his own comfortable home and a car and send his children to well-equipped elementary and high schools and to college as well. They fail to realize that he is not the downtrodden, impoverished vassal of whom Karl Marx wrote. He is a self-sustaining, thriving individual, living in dignity and freedom." In 1959, in his much-acclaimed kitchen debate with the Soviet premier, Nikita Khrushchev, Vice President Richard Nixon, in a jab at Marxism, added, "The United States comes closest to the ideal of prosperity for all in a classless society."

To be sure, the United States was not a classless society. Millions of blacks, farmworkers, and domestic workers were left behind and stuck on the bottom. The rising tide had missed their boats. Nonetheless, thanks to unions lifting millions of workers in the bottom half, it was an era known as the Great Compression, in which income inequality narrowed and the poorest fifth of households had their income increase by 42 percent, and the richest fifth by just 8 percent.

Reuther hardly hesitated to use the UAW's might and money to spread the prosperity. The UAW helped to finance Cesar Chavez and the United Farm Workers (UFW) in their early days. It also financed much of the famed 1963 March on Washington, where Reuther spoke shortly before Martin Luther King Jr., telling the crowd of 250,000, "This rally is not the end, it's the beginning of a great moral crusade to arouse America to the unfinished work of American democracy."

Reuther and his wife, May, died in a plane crash in 1970 as they were heading to the UAW's education center in northern Michigan. He was sixty-two. He was eulogized by friend and foe. His frequent adversary, Henry Ford II, who succeeded his father as Ford's chairman, called him "an extraordinarily effective advocate of labor's interest." But perhaps the greatest tribute came years earlier from *Fortune* magazine, which wrote that Reuther's landmark Treaty of Detroit had "made the worker to an amazing degree a middle-class member of a middle-class society."

Eight

I *Am* a Man

ELMORE NICKLEBERRY served proudly in the Korean War as a corporal in the Eighth Armored Division. So he was understandably dismayed with what he encountered upon returning to Memphis, his hometown, in 1953.

"People would call you 'boy,'" said Nickleberry, who was twenty-two years old when he returned. "They'd say, 'Do this, boy. Come here, boy.' They treated me better overseas than I was treated in Memphis." Nickleberry is soft-spoken and disarmingly friendly, with short silver-charcoal hair, still fit and trim, even though he is in his eighties.

Like many young African Americans, Nickleberry, the grandson of a slave, found it hard to land a job because blacks, in that Jim Crow era, were typically the last ones hired. His brother Roosevelt worked in the city's sanitation department, and even though Elmore had hoped to find a better job, after eight fruitless months of looking for work, he settled on getting a job there, too. Every morning for three weeks, he stood outside one of the city's sanitation garages, making his availability known, as he watched the big yellow trucks rumble out to the city's neighborhoods.

One morning a foreman finally approached him and said, "Boy, you been here two or three weeks standing outside this gate. You want a job?"

"Yes, sir," Nickleberry said.

The foreman responded, "Come in, boy, I'll give you a job."

He started at seventy-five cents an hour ($6.85 today). That was in July 1954, two months after the Supreme Court decided *Brown v. Board of Education,* rendering school segregation illegal, and the same month that Elvis Presley gave his first public performance, at a park in Memphis.

For Nickleberry, the new job was humbling. "Everybody called us 'boy,'" he said in an interview more than six decades later. "The supervisors [all of them white] also called us 'boy.' You'd tell them 'I ain't no "boy." I am a man.' And they'd keep calling you 'boy.'"

Nickleberry was a tub toter. His job was to go into people's backyards, transfer their garbage into a seventeen-gallon, round, plastic tub, and then carry the tub to the truck in the street. The sanitation workers frequently filled their tubs with thirty, even forty pounds of garbage, often carrying the tubs on their backs or shoulders, often on top of their heads. Because the tubs got banged around, "there would often be holes in the tub, and the garbage and maggots would crawl down your back and onto your clothes," Nickleberry recalled, with a scowl. "A lot of the people weren't nice," he said. "They'd say, 'Boy, you left some garbage behind. How about picking that stuff up?'" He hated when homeowners called him "garbage man," as if he were just garbage.

The toters, virtually all of them black, complained that the sanitation garages didn't even have showers for them after their sweaty days hauling garbage. "So we just had to get on the bus after work," Nickleberry said. "We smelled real bad. Nobody wanted to sit near us." Because many bus passengers steered clear of him, even sneered at him, he often skipped the bus and trudged the six miles home. When he arrived home, his wife, Mary, didn't exactly rush to hug him. "I'd take my clothes off in the backyard because I stink so bad," he said. "I'd take off everything but my underclothes."

The pay was as humbling as the working conditions. In 1968, after fourteen years on the job, Nickleberry was earning $1.65 an hour, five cents more than the federal minimum wage. (That $1.65 translates to $12.20 today.) The pay was so low that 40 percent of the trash collectors' families fell below the poverty line, with many qualifying for welfare and food stamps. Some homeowners took pity and gave hand-me-downs to their "garbage men." "You could tell a worker when you saw him in the streets because his hat was too big, his coat was too long, his shoes were too big," said Clinton Burrows, a fellow sanitation worker.

Workers who called in sick for a day or two were often fired. Nickleberry remembers missing one day because he had to see a doctor about a painful boil on his buttocks. His boss fired him, but Nickleberry cajoled his boss into taking him back.

If a crew was working the 7 a.m. to 3 p.m. shift and their truck broke down at 2 p.m., they sometimes had to stay until 5 or 6 p.m., until it was towed away. They didn't receive pay for those extra hours. "We'd never got paid overtime," Nickleberry said. Sometimes when workers confronted their supervisor about all the unpaid hours they had worked, the supervisor would retaliate by sending them home early, meaning they'd miss even more hours of pay.

"You work two weeks, and payday your money ain't right," said James Robinson, a tub toter. "You go in there and tell the man, 'Look, I worked eighty hours this payday, how come I ain't got but sixty?' "

Robinson's foreman would respond, "Get out of here, you don't know what you're talkin' about." Sometimes when workers arrived a minute late, their supervisor sent them home for the day.

One scorching day, Robinson and several other toters were taking their fifteen-minute lunch break under a shade tree. When a white woman complained that they were too close to her property, the crew chief ordered them to finish their lunch crouched under their garbage truck—even though, Robinson said, the truck "had maggots and things all fallin' out of it."

One day a sanitation supervisor sent twenty-two black sewer and drainage workers home around 9 a.m. ostensibly because he thought the morning rain would impede their work. They received two hours' show-up pay for the day. But the department's white sewer and drainage workers weren't sent home; they received a full day's pay.

The insults and indignities piled up, but it was hard to do anything about it. "We didn't have no voice, period," Nickleberry said. Taylor Rogers, a co-worker, agreed. "Anything that you did that the supervisor didn't like, he'd fire you, whatever. You didn't have no recourse. . . . We just got tired of all that," he said.

———

On February 1, 1968, with the rain pouring down, Echol Cole and Robert Walker, their workday nearly over, sought shelter by climbing inside the barrel-shaped compartment in the back of their sanitation truck.

That putrid compartment had a powerful hydraulic plate that compacted the garbage. All of a sudden the plate started up and crushed Cole and Walker to death. Cole was thirty-six; Walker, thirty.

Neither Cole nor Walker had workers' compensation coverage because of a loophole in the law. That meant no death benefits for their families. Nor were Cole and Walker able to afford the life insurance the city offered. Their families were left in penury, receiving just one month's salary and a $500 special payment—not even enough to cover burial expenses. Walker's wife was pregnant at the time.

Investigators concluded that an electrical short had caused the truck's compactor to malfunction. A defective sanitation truck had killed two workers four years earlier, causing many workers to urge the city to invest in new equipment, but city officials ignored their pleas. The city's thirteen hundred black sanitation workers were stunned and furious about Cole's and Walker's deaths, as well as all the other indignities. Aware of this, T. O. Jones, a union organizer, rushed around Memphis to meet with and rally hundreds of workers. Five years earlier, Jones and thirty-two other Memphis sanitation workers were fired after a snitch informed on them for attending a meeting to discuss unionizing. Jones rejected the city's offer to return to his job as a tub toter, dedicating himself instead to trying to organize a sanitation workers' union under the aegis of the American Federation of State, County and Municipal Employees, known as AFSCME.

At Jones's behest, eight hundred sanitation workers packed into the city's Labor Temple on the evening of Sunday, February 11, ten days after Cole and Walker died. For many, it was their first union meeting. Presiding, Jones, a short, rumpled, deep-voiced man, laid out a long list of grievances: unsafe, obsolete equipment, wages of less than $70 a week, pay not guaranteed on rainy days, scant opportunity for promotion, repeated firings for expressing support for a potential union. The workers were spoiling to go on strike, but Jones told them he first wanted to talk with the city's public works commissioner in the hope that the city would address their concerns. The commissioner, however, was decidedly unhelpful; he said the city's budget deficit prevented it from giving anything but skimpy raises. Returning to the Labor Temple after 11 p.m., Jones told the men that the public works commissioner was offering mere crumbs. One man in the crowd yelled, "He gives us nothing, we'll give them nothing." The workers immediately started shouting for a walkout. The sentiment was so overwhelming that there was no need to put it to a vote.

The next morning, 1,144 of the city's 1,330 sanitation workers went on strike, with the number increasing the next day. Paraphrasing one of Martin Luther King Jr.'s aphorisms, Taylor Rogers explained why they were going on strike: "You keep your back bent over, somebody's gonna ride it."

In his excellent book, *Going Down Jericho Road: The Memphis Strike, Martin Luther King's Last Campaign* (from which I draw heavily here), Michael K. Honey noted that officials at AFSCME headquarters in Washington knew nothing about this strike until a newspaper reporter called to ask about it. Peter J. Ciampa, AFSCME's director of field operations, was dispatched to Memphis to help, but he quickly grew worried because these workers were undertaking a poorly planned walkout in the fiercely antiunion South.

"My God, what in the hell am I going to do with a strike in the South?" Ciampa said. "I had a feeling of impending doom before I even started."

But the workers were focused on justice, not strategy. From day one, Mayor Henry Loeb took a hard line. Time and again he asserted that the strike was illegal, even immoral, because Tennessee law prohibited government employees from striking. Loeb, who had inherited his father's large laundry business, scorned the workers' demands for union recognition and dues checkoff (which would mean having the city deduct dues from the workers' paychecks to finance their union). An acquaintance of Loeb's explained his intransigence: "His daddy would turn over in his grave if he knew that he had ever recognized a damned union."

Early on, Loeb was accused of acting like a plantation owner. "I represent these men," he said, suggesting that he knew what was best for the workers. On the strike's second day, Loeb insisted on meeting with the strikers, and he sternly told hundreds of them, "City employees can't strike against their employer. This you can't do!" Loeb was stunned when the workers laughed and jeered him. Jesse Epps, an AFSCME organizer, said, "That was the first time . . . in Loeb's life that he was no longer the master. There was an insurrection among the slaves."

Loeb's I-know-what's-best-for-you attitude angered James Lawson, one of the South's leading civil rights activists and pastor of Centenary

United Methodist Church in Memphis. "When a public official orders a group of men to 'get back to work, and then we'll talk' and treats them as though they are not men, that is a racist point of view," Lawson said. "The heart of racism is the idea that a man is not a man." Loeb echoed GM's truculent stance during the Flint Sit-Down Strike. He, too, said he wouldn't bargain "with anyone who is breaking the law." To that, AFSCME's Ciampa replied, "What crime have they committed, Mr. Mayor? They are saying they don't want to pick up stinking garbage for starvation wages. Is that a crime?"

The city's white residents cheered Loeb for standing firm against the strikers and what many believed were outside union agitators greedy for union dues. The city's largest newspaper, *The Commercial Appeal,* denounced the walkout as "a shallow attempt at blackmail" and likened the strikers to the Vietcong (Communist guerrilla forces in South Vietnam). That newspaper maintained that outsiders from AFSCME were trying to capitalize on a New York City sanitation strike that had won major gains just days before. The Memphis workers insisted that they, not outsiders, had engineered the strike.

In Memphis, which was 40 percent African American, just three of the city council's thirteen members were black, and they supported the strikers. The white council members were far less sympathetic, but they, too, wanted to find a way to end the walkout. As hundreds of sanitation men crowded into the council's chambers on February 22, threatening a sit-in, the council's black members persuaded a council subcommittee to approve an ordinance that would end the strike by granting union recognition and dues checkoff. The workers were elated, having been assured that the full council would approve the subcommittee's measure the next day.

The next morning, *The Commercial Appeal* denounced the subcommittee's move, saying it was surrendering to a threatened sit-in. The *Appeal* ran a cartoon, widely derided as racist, with the headline "Threat of Anarchy," showing a thuggish, animalistic figure resembling T. O. Jones astride a garbage can. Mayor Loeb also condemned the subcommittee's vote. The next day, the full council defied the seven hundred strikers attending the council meeting by declining to approve the subcommittee resolution that would have ended the strike.

The workers felt betrayed. Furious, they set out on a three-mile protest march, locking arms, four abreast. Police cars drove just inches from the marchers, trying to nudge them toward the curb. Suddenly a woman shrieked; a patrol car had driven onto the foot of one of the city's African American leaders, Gladys Carpenter, a veteran of the famed 1965 Selma march. A dozen protesters surrounded the police car and began rocking it, and then pandemonium erupted. Police jumped out of their cars and began clubbing and bloodying the marchers, dozens of them. They also sprayed Mace at scores of people, often singling out strike leaders, even attacking black ministers and a federal civil rights official.

The strikers and clergymen insisted that it was an indefensible, out-and-out police assault, but Loeb defended the police, saying they had responded appropriately. The Reverend Ralph Jackson, a black minister with close ties to the city's white establishment, was outraged that the police had attacked and maced him. "This was done to me for one reason, and that's because I was black," Jackson said.

Loeb and the police continued to maintain that outsider agitators were stage-managing the strike. They even threatened to throw AFSCME officials in jail. Fearing that such arrests would cripple the strike, the city's African American ministers stepped up and assumed a leadership role. The day after the march and police violence, the ministers formed a new group, Community on the Move for Equality, known as COME, inspired by the biblical phrase "Come let us reason together." The ministers called on Memphis's blacks to boycott white businesses as a way to pressure Loeb. That same day, a minister, Malcolm Blackburn, had the idea of printing up hundreds of placards voicing the workers' earnest desire to be treated with dignity. The placards read, "I Am A Man."

Day after day, the strikers marched through the city single file in silence, carrying those placards in a terse, powerful demand for respect. But even as the sanitation workers stood solid and strong, many strike supporters wondered whether the workers could hold on long enough to achieve victory. AFSCME didn't have a strike fund to sustain them (even though the union considered them official union members), and Loeb cut off food stamps to the strikers' families. Meanwhile, Loeb was hiring replacement workers, and five weeks into the walkout 80 of the city's 180 sanitation trucks were back on the streets. (Memphis's AFL-CIO labor council strongly backed the sanitation workers, although the overwhelmingly white unions from the construction trades shunned their cause.)

The city's African American leaders concluded that the strikers needed outside help and attention. Jesse Turner, the president of the Memphis NAACP, reached out to Roy Wilkins, that group's national president, and Bayard Rustin, the main behind-the-scenes organizer of the 1963 March on Washington. Wilkins and Rustin heeded Turner's request for help, and in rousing speeches to five thousand people at Mason Temple on March 14 the two civil rights leaders inspired the strikers. "If you can't get a decent salary for men who are working, in the name of God, how the hell are you gonna get rid of poverty?" Rustin told them. "This fight is going to be won because the black people in this community and the trade unions stand together."

The strikers got a bigger boost when, thirty-four days into the strike, the Reverend Dr. Martin Luther King Jr. agreed to Lawson's pleas that he come to Memphis, even though it was a particularly trying time for King. Having led the struggle to persuade President Johnson and Congress to enact landmark civil rights legislation, King was deeply frustrated that African Americans were still far from achieving economic equality. Eager to focus the nation's attention on black Americans' economic woes—their poverty and unemployment rates were twice those of whites—King set out to organize a big, new protest: the Poor People's Campaign. Three thousand poor Americans were to assemble in a tent city in front of the Lincoln Memorial in late spring with the goal of pressuring Congress to take major steps to lift blacks economically. In seeking to rally people behind the campaign, King said, "If America doesn't use its vast resources and wealth to bridge the gap . . . between the rich and poor in this nation, it, too, is going to hell."

Lawson's invitation arrived as King was rushing from city to city, seeking to drum up support for the Poor People's Campaign. Many King aides implored him not to go to Memphis, not to get distracted by the sanitation strike, not only because he was overstretched and exhausted, but also because he was having trouble attracting enough people to go to Washington for the Poor People's Campaign. Adding to King's difficulties, members of the Black Power movement, led by H. Rap Brown and Stokely Carmichael, were loudly attacking his strategy of nonviolence as inadequate. At the same time, King faced a wall of hostility from southern whites, many of whom accused him of showboating to promote his ego.

King quickly recognized that the Memphis struggle was very much part of the poor people's cause he was battling for—economic justice for blacks. "Memphis is the Washington campaign in miniature," King said. Moreover, he had long championed an alliance between the civil rights movement and the labor movement, even as he decried the racial discrimination in numerous unions. In a 1961 speech, King told the AFL-CIO, "You can't win without us, and we can't get a damn thing without you."

Tense and worn down, King was buoyed immensely by what he encountered when he went to Memphis on March 18—a huge, enthusiastic crowd of five thousand inside the Mason Temple. "I've never seen a community as together as Memphis," he said. In a stem-winder that repeatedly brought the crowd to its feet, King told the strikers and supporters, "You are demanding that this city will respect the dignity of labor. . . . You are here to demand that Memphis will see the poor." He heaped praise on the sanitation workers: "You are reminding the nation that it is a crime for people to live in this rich nation and receive starvation wages." He then said that winning civil rights, as immense as that victory was, was not enough. "It isn't enough to integrate lunch counters," King said. "What does it profit a man to be able to eat at an integrated lunch counter if he doesn't earn enough money to buy a hamburger and a cup of coffee?" King next emphasized the importance of solidarity:

> Now let me say a word to those of you who are on strike. You have been out now for a number of days, but don't despair. Nothing worthwhile is gained without sacrifice. The thing for you to do is stay together, and say to everybody in this community that you are going to stick it out to the end until every demand is met, and that you are gonna say, "We ain't gonna let nobody turn us around."

To step up pressure on Mayor Loeb, King called on Memphis's African American community to stage a one-day general strike and protest. March 28 was chosen as the day. He told the Mason Temple crowd,

We can all get more together than we can apart; we can get more organized together than we can apart. And this is the way we gain power. . . .
What is power? Walter Reuther said once that "Power is the ability of
a labor union like UAW to make the most powerful corporation in the
world, General Motors, say 'Yes,' when it wants to say, 'No.'" That's
power. And I want you to stick it out so that you will be able to make
Mayor Loeb and others say, "Yes," even when they want to say, "No."

————

The nonviolent protest that King called for March 28 began inauspi-
ciously. Early that morning, black students at Hamilton High School
threw rocks at a Memphis sanitation truck and at several cars with
white drivers. Police cars sped to the school just as two hundred students were starting to march toward downtown. The police sought to
push them back to the school, but the students resisted, some throwing rocks. The police began hitting students with their nightsticks, and
soon a fourteen-year-old student, Jo Ann Talbert, was rushed to the
hospital after a police baton or a rock hit her in the head. Inaccurate
rumors spread that the police had killed a student.

By 9:30, more than three thousand strikers and supporters had
assembled at Clayborn Temple, a giant African Methodist Episcopal
church downtown. Organizers delayed the march because King was
late arriving from Atlanta, but the crowd was growing so impatient that
the organizers let the march begin without him. Landing at 10:28, King
rushed from the airport and joined Lawson at the head of the march.
Minutes later, just as the march reached Main Street, there was a disqui-
eting sound: shopwindows were being smashed on famed Beale Street,
at the Harris Department Store, Schwab's Sundries, and other stores.
King, the apostle of nonviolence, was horrified, and Lawson hurried to
get him away from the march, concerned that he might get injured and
shouldn't be leading a protest that had turned violent.

At 11:18, a police chief ordered the marchers to disperse, and in the
disorder the police again began clubbing and macing scores of protesters. The marchers suffered concussions, broken bones, broken teeth,
and cuts on their heads and shoulders. Many also suffered damage
to their faces and lungs from Mace. A seventy-five-year-old man was
beaten. The police shot and killed a sixteen-year-old, asserting that he

was looting and armed. Hundreds of demonstrators sought refuge back at Clayborn Temple, but when a few protesters threw rocks at the police from the temple's front steps, the police entered the building, clubbing people and shooting tear gas in the sanctuary.

Once again, the city's blacks said the police had engaged in a police riot. One student leader said the cops seemed to chase everybody except the looters. Once again, Loeb defended the police, while *The Commercial Appeal* praised them for "exercising restraint." The newspaper accused King of instigating a riot. As part of its long campaign to undermine King, the FBI sent out memos to "cooperative news sources," saying that the result of King's "famous espousal of nonviolence was vandalism, looting, and riot." Hours after the violence, Tennessee's governor, Buford Ellington, declared a state of emergency and sent in the National Guard. Soon tanks rolled into Memphis, and bayonet-carrying soldiers lined downtown streets.

For King, the March 28 protest was a debacle. *The Dallas Morning News* mocked him as the "headline-hunting high priest of nonviolent violence," while Senator Robert Byrd, a West Virginia Democrat, said King had maneuvered people into trouble "and then [took] off like a scared rabbit." *The Commercial Appeal* ran a headline, "Chicken à la King."

King and his allies explained that he had left the march because he led only nonviolent protests. King-hating southern politicians professed alarm that the Poor People's Campaign would turn violent just like the Memphis march. King soon concluded that he needed to organize a new, peaceful march in Memphis, first, to demonstrate to the nation that he led a nonviolent movement and, second, to restore confidence that the Poor People's Campaign would be disciplined and peaceful. One union official recalled King saying, "Either the movement lives or dies in Memphis."

Aides who had weeks earlier implored the Nobel Peace Prize winner not to go to Memphis now descended on the city to help make sure the second march would be nonviolent. They trained parade marshals, talked with high school students, and met with militant groups to get them to pledge to eschew violence during the march. King had expansive ambitions for the second Memphis march, which was scheduled for Monday, April 8. He wanted it to be a huge, symbolic national event, much like the 1965 Selma march.

On April 3, King returned to Memphis, his plane from Atlanta delayed by a bomb threat. Exhausted, he was planning to skip the rally at Mason Temple that evening, but Ralph Abernathy—King's right-hand man and secretary-treasurer of the Southern Christian Leadership Conference—seeing an enthusiastic crowd and more than two hundred journalists inside the temple, phoned King at the Lorraine Motel and implored him to come speak.

With the church windows rattling from a fierce storm—a tornado killed three people nearby that night—King gave an extraordinary speech. "We've got to march again" to "force everybody to see that there are 1,300 of God's children here suffering, sometimes going hungry," he said. "For when people get caught up with that which is right and they are willing to sacrifice for it, there is no stopping short of victory. . . . Nothing would be more tragic than to stop at this point in Memphis," King continued. "We're got to see it through. And when we have our march, you need to be there. . . . [E]ither we go up together, or we go down together."

Invoking the biblical tale of the Good Samaritan, King said that he and all of Memphis had a moral obligation to help the sanitation strikers. "If I do not stop to help the sanitation workers, what will happen to them? That's the question," he said. In his concluding words, he made clear that mortality was on his mind, no doubt a result of the many death threats he had received:

> Like anybody, I would like to live a long life. Longevity has its place. But I'm not concerned about that now. I just want to do God's will. And He's allowed me to go up to the mountain. And I've looked over. And I've seen the Promised Land. I may not get there with you. But I want you to know tonight, that we as a people will get to the Promised Land. And so I'm happy tonight. I'm not worried about anything. I'm not fearing any man. Mine eyes have seen the glory of the coming of the Lord.

With those majestic words, King stepped off the podium and collapsed into his seat, sobbing.

His next day, April 4, was filled with meetings, including an intense afternoon session with the Invaders, a group of young black militants from Memphis. They had been blamed for provoking the window breaking at the March 28 march, and King implored them to forswear violence at the upcoming march. That meeting over, King got dressed for the dinner he was to attend at the home of a Memphis pastor. He then stepped onto the balcony outside his room at the Lorraine Motel, and from there he began talking to a bandleader in the parking lot below, telling him to play "Precious Lord, Take My Hand" at the strike rally scheduled for that evening.

"I want you to play it real pretty," King said.

Moments later, a bullet ripped into his jaw, tearing into his jugular vein and spinal cord. Within an hour, King was declared dead.

"Nonviolence was murdered in Memphis last night," said Julian Bond, a civil rights leader. Rage and violence erupted in 125 cities across the nation. There were 5,117 fires and 1,928 homes and businesses destroyed. There were forty-three deaths, two thousand injured, and twenty thousand arrests, prompting the biggest domestic deployment of the army and National Guard since the Civil War.

In his eulogy, King's mentor, Morehouse College's former president Benjamin Mays, said, "He believed, especially, that he was sent to champion the cause of the man farthest down. He would probably say, 'If death had to come, I am sure there was no greater cause to die for than fighting to get a just wage for garbage collectors.'"

The morning after the assassination, a shaken President Johnson asked Undersecretary of Labor James Reynolds why in the world the Labor Department hadn't settled the Memphis dispute. Reynolds explained that the federal government doesn't involve itself in municipal labor disputes, unless invited. Nonetheless, Johnson, desperate to quell the tensions, ordered Reynolds to Memphis to somehow settle things.

Upon arriving in Memphis, Reynolds rushed to meet with Loeb and union officials. Loeb still refused to budge. Reynolds remembered Loeb saying, "We are not going to recognize this union. . . . I committed myself in the election that this city would never recognize this union." But the city's white establishment and white council members, seeing the devastation the dispute had done to Memphis and its image, had parted ways with Loeb. They desperately wanted a settlement.

On April 8, four days after King was killed, thousands of people marched through Memphis—the police said nineteen thousand; organizers said forty-two thousand. Civil rights and labor leaders came from out of state, including Rosa Parks, Harry Belafonte, and Walter Reuther, with Reuther giving the sanitation workers a $50,000 check from the UAW ($360,000 today). Reuther told the thousands gathered, "I say to Mayor Loeb, even though this may be painful, before this fight of the sanitation workers is over, we're going to drag you into the twentieth century."

Thanks to Reynolds's ingenuity as a mediator and the city council's eagerness to end the confrontation, a deal was finally reached. Unlike Loeb, the council agreed to bargain with the sanitation workers' union and allow a dues checkoff. The council said the city was too financially strapped to grant anything but meager raises because it had spent so much on police overtime during the strike. Fortunately, a bighearted industrialist, Abe Plough, chairman of a large pharmaceutical company, donated nearly $60,000 ($430,000 today) to pay for an immediate raise for the sanitation workers. That made it possible to increase pay by ten cents an hour on May 1 and five cents more on September 1 (Loeb had originally offered a raise of eight cents an hour).

The settlement gave the tub toters much of what they wanted, including union recognition, elaborate grievance procedures, and strict protections against racial discrimination. The agreement included an important provision stating, "The city shall make promotions on the basis of seniority and competency." That meant promotions would not be based on race. "White supremacy thus fell, in twelve simple words," Michael Honey wrote in *Going Down Jericho Road*. Jerry Wurf, AFSCME's national president, hailed the agreement. This, he said, was "our Flint sit-downs" and "our Hart Schaffner & Marx" (a landmark apparel workers' victory in Chicago in 1911). At a mass meeting of the strikers, AFSCME leaders read the contract provisions aloud. Then T. O. Jones put it to a vote. All those who approve the agreement, please stand, Jones said. Not one striker remained seated.

"We have been aggrieved many times," Jones said to conclude the meeting—and the strike. "We have lost many things. But we have got the victory." Then he sat down and sobbed.

Elmore Nickleberry was of course pleased that the union had won its battle, although at a terrible cost. He was devastated by Dr. King's death. "It hurt me. It really did something to me," he said. Then he added, "If it weren't for him . . ." He dropped off and cried for a few minutes, never finishing his thought.

The sixty-five-day strike had been an arduous struggle for Nickleberry and his family. He, too, was beaten and maced by the police. To feed his five children during the strike, he made money chopping wood and selling sweet potatoes from his father's farm. Nickleberry spelled out the benefits that the contract and the union had brought the workers. "With the union, we got a good raise," he said. "We got showers. We got better working conditions. We got health benefits. Before we had to pay doctor bills ourselves." The biggest thing the union won, Nickleberry said, was dignity: "The union came in and we got respect. They stopped calling us 'boy.' They started calling us 'A Man. A Sanitation Man.'" (Nickleberry was eventually promoted to crew chief on a truck.)

Half a century later, he voiced disappointment that many young sanitation workers know little about the struggles and hardships that he and thirteen hundred other strikers endured. "The union did a great job," Nickleberry said. "If we didn't have a union, we would get nothing. We'd be in the same shape as before. You got a union to back you, you achieve more. The more people you have in a union, the more you get. They can talk for you more than you can talk for yourself."

Part Three

HARD TIMES FOR LABOR

Nine

Mighty Labor Strikes Out

AFTER SERVING IN THE AIR FORCE during the Vietnam War, Bob Butterworth was thrilled to land a job as an air traffic controller in Southern California in 1967. But on his very first day, he felt seriously disrespected—the tower's manager mocked his flattop haircut, told him he had to change it, and also told him to wear a white shirt, necktie, and name tag. Some controllers were ordered to shave off their beards. "I was sent home from work one day because I forgot to wear my name tag," Butterworth recalled. "That's insanity. That's the type of working conditions we had."

At the time, the nation's air traffic controllers were a macho group. Many of them were military veterans; many had served in Vietnam. They were fiercely proud of their skills, able to juggle the flight paths of up to thirty aircraft at a time and guide them safely, knowing that hundreds of lives depended on their getting it right every time. This daunting responsibility produced considerable stress, and that was doubly true at the busiest airports, like O'Hare in Chicago, where at peak times control towers had to handle a takeoff or landing every twenty seconds.

Many controllers described a vicious cycle. Towers were often understaffed, heightening the controllers' stress. Many controllers quit as a result, aggravating the staffing problem, and those who remained frequently had to work mandatory overtime, further ratcheting up the stress and exhaustion. Butterworth said a lack of breaks greatly exacerbated the situation. "You might work hours and hours without a break, sometimes even a whole day," he said.

At that time, the novel *Airport* was the nation's best-selling book. One of its main characters was a controller who guided a badly damaged airliner to a safe landing during a severe snowstorm at a major Chicago airport. One day, frazzled from all the pressure, the heroic controller takes off his headset, throws his pills in the trash, and heads out the control tower door, never to return.

In the mid-1960s, with an eye to reducing stress and winning more respect, several dozen New York–area controllers began pushing to create a nationwide labor union. Many of them came from blue-collar families, and many saw how teachers and transit workers in New York had achieved big gains through public-employee unions. After months of patient organizing, on January 11, 1968, in a hotel ballroom in New York, seven hundred controllers from twenty-two states gathered for a founding convention. They named their union the Professional Air Traffic Controllers Organization (PATCO) to connote their desire to be considered professionals. In a rousing speech, the union's first president—F. Lee Bailey, a renowned trial lawyer who piloted his own Learjet—appealed to their pride and to their conviction that they were undervalued. "You should be treated like a pilot," Bailey said. "You should get a salary like a pilot."

The fledgling union hardly hesitated to show its militancy. A three-week slowdown in July 1968 infuriated the Federal Aviation Administration (FAA) and the airlines. But that action brought the FAA to the bargaining table for the first time and won the workers the right to overtime pay as well as a dues checkoff to sustain PATCO's finances.

Afterward, controllers continued to complain as much as ever about on-the-job stress. The FAA did little to address their concerns. So in March 1970, twenty-five hundred controllers joined a sick-out that also got results, even though a federal judge ruled it illegal. The FAA and Congress agreed to hire more controllers, install new, automated equipment, and increase pay to attract and retain controllers. But the FAA fired eighty controllers for participating in the sick-out.

In 1972, a commission the FAA set up to study the controllers' working conditions issued a stunning report—the commission's members said they had never seen "as much mutual resentment and antagonism between management and its employees." The commission added that the controllers were frustrated by "their inability to communicate upwards." Its members were shocked to learn that Las Vegas blackjack dealers got far more rest breaks—often every forty minutes—than air traffic controllers, who often went four hours without a break. Notwithstanding the commission's report, Butterworth and other controllers continued to chafe under their managers' gruff military style; they were often treated more like grunts than like professionals. Moreover, many controllers were convinced that management felt emboldened to boss them around because, as federal employees, controllers were prohibited from going on strike.

When Jimmy Carter, a Democrat, was elected president in 1976, the controllers hoped that after eight years of Republican presidents, Carter would bargain over wages (something not previously allowed under federal rules) and would move hundreds of controllers into higher job classifications to lift their pay. But Carter did neither thing. The 1979 oil shock pushed inflation to double-digit levels, and to help keep the budget deficit from soaring, Carter turned stingy on federal employee raises. From 1973 to 1981, federal employees' pay slipped 3.1 percent a year, after factoring in inflation. This infuriated the controllers, who were already upset that they earned 18 percent less on average than private-sector air traffic controllers.

Carter's embrace of airline deregulation made the controllers' on-the-job stress even worse. Deregulation increased air traffic, encouraging the creation of low-cost airlines like People Express, which had a $29 fare from Newark to Boston and a $39 fare from Newark to Columbus, Ohio. Deregulation also spurred large airlines to develop a hub-and-spoke strategy, which meant a stress-inducing surge in takeoffs and landings each morning and late afternoon at many airports.

As Joseph McCartin wrote in *Collision Course: Ronald Reagan, the Air Traffic Controllers, and the Strike That Changed America,* a richly detailed book on the controllers and the PATCO strike, the FAA under Carter took numerous other steps that infuriated the controllers. It scrapped a popular early retirement program as well as a program that protected controllers from retaliation when they reported safety-related mistakes. The FAA further irked controllers by launching investigations into who was taking drugs; some had turned to illicit pills to help with their exhaustion and stress.

Many controllers felt that their pride, professionalism, and paychecks were under attack. The discontent grew so great that some controllers began floating the idea of going on strike when their contract expired in June 1981, even though federal law barred them from walking out. The strike talk upset the FAA's administrator, Langhorne Bond, who responded by developing an elaborate plan to keep the control towers operating during a walkout. Bond's move further provoked the controllers because they felt he was seeking to undermine their bargaining leverage. Many controllers grew angrier still at Bond when he said their work was no more stressful than driving a bus in New York City.

Within PATCO, a debate began to rage about the pros and cons of going on strike. John Leyden, who was PATCO's president during the 1970s, had seen how the courts had used injunctions to shut down and punish PATCO for its sick-outs and slowdowns, and he warned that a strike could have ruinous results. Moreover, many controllers balked at striking because they had to sign a no-strike pledge when they were hired. Leyden stepped down from PATCO's presidency in August 1980 in the face of a challenge from more militant controllers.

His successor, Robert Poli, an air force veteran who had been a controller in Pittsburgh and Cleveland, was an outspoken cheerleader for a strike. Poli asserted that the controllers' ambitious demands would never be granted unless they mounted a crippling walkout. With the skies shut down by a strike, he argued, the FAA would be so eager to bring the controllers back that it would surrender to PATCO's demands and not punish the strikers. "Our studies show that the only ILLEGAL strike is an unsuccessful one," Poli said. He had the union distribute flyers saying, "Strike is not a dirty word" and "Politicians will react to only one concept—CLOUT." Convinced that PATCO had exhausted its use of slowdowns and sick-outs, Mike Rock, one of the union's founders, said if the controllers wanted to win "a substantial amount of money and benefits," the best way was to strike and "shut the entire country down."

———

It is often forgotten that PATCO's relations with Jimmy Carter grew so poisonous that PATCO endorsed his opponent in the presidential election of 1980, making it one of the few unions to back Ronald Reagan. To help clinch PATCO's endorsement, Reagan sent the union a letter that pledged "a spirit of cooperation" and expressed sympathy for the controllers with regard to their "unreasonable hours" and "obsolete equipment." "You can rest assured that if I am elected president," Reagan wrote, "I will take whatever steps are necessary to provide our air traffic controllers with the most modern equipment available and to adjust staff levels and work days so that they are commensurate with achieving a maximum degree of public safety." After he trounced Carter in a landslide, PATCO's leaders felt confident that Reagan would reward their union handsomely in their contract talks.

The first bargaining session took place in February 1981, a month after Reagan's inauguration. With a large militant faction pressuring Poli to think big, PATCO put forward what Joseph McCartin called the "most far-reaching set of demands ever made by a union of federal workers." The controllers, whose pay averaged $36,600 a year ($105,000 today), demanded an immediate $10,000 across-the-board raise for every controller (which translated into a raise averaging 27 percent). They also demanded a 10 percent raise in the contract's second year and a cost-of-living adjustment that would lift pay by 1.5 percent for each 1 percent increase in prices. The controllers also demanded a four-day workweek with three consecutive days off.

Some controllers warned that these demands were totally unrealistic. A controller in Florida described the demand for an immediate 27 percent raise as "almost an embarrassment," while a Los Angeles controller said, "Our greed should not exceed those of our fellow federal workers. If it does, then are we willing to go it alone on the suicide mission of all time?" Poli defended the union's stance, saying, "Some had said that our demands are unrealistic—pie in the sky pipe dreams! I don't believe that and neither should you."

In May, after several months of largely fruitless negotiations, federal mediators warned the White House that an illegal strike was a real possibility. Reagan's aides estimated that a strike would take a $150 million daily toll on the nation's economy, while granting all of PATCO's demands would cost the federal government $300 million to $1 billion a year. The administration also feared that if it agreed to most or all of what PATCO sought, the much larger postal workers' unions, with more than 400,000 members (PATCO had 16,000 members), would demand similar outsize raises that would cost billions more.

Reagan's aides viewed PATCO's demands as outlandish, but they remained eager to avoid a strike. With Secretary of Transportation Drew Lewis taking the lead, the administration took several unorthodox steps toward reaching an agreement. Even though federal rules barred the government from bargaining over wages and benefits, Lewis quietly offered PATCO an 11 percent raise, double what other federal employee unions were receiving. Lewis, a former railroad executive with long experience dealing with unions, also offered a night differential, more generous severance pay, exemption from a cap on overtime pay, a guaranteed, paid half-hour lunch, and other add-ons. Lewis rejected PATCO's demand for a four-day workweek—a key union demand—but he promised that controllers at the busiest airports wouldn't be required to spend more than six and a half hours a day handling flights. Lewis's offer, McCartin writes in *Collision Course,* "crossed into uncharted territory, winning approval from a conservative president for a contract offer that far exceeded anything the federal government had offered a union before."

PATCO's leaders were nonetheless far from satisfied. When Lewis told Poli that the administration couldn't go any further, Poli replied, "We'll work that out on the picket line." He repeatedly warned that unless the administration showed more flexibility, "I vow to you that the skies will be silent." On June 17, five days before the strike deadline, Poli's bargaining team, full of militants with little negotiating experience, walked out of the talks.

Shortly before the June 22 strike deadline, Lewis offered a few sweeteners, but Poli said they fell far short of what the union wanted. A strike seemed inevitable, but Poli first needed to hold a rank-and-file vote. PATCO's rules required that at least 80 percent of its members support a strike because the union felt it couldn't sufficiently cripple the nation's airports unless four-fifths of the membership joined a strike. To Poli's shock, only 75 percent of the controllers voted to endorse a strike. A humbled Poli then told the Reagan administration that PATCO would accept the deal that he had lambasted a few days earlier.

PATCO's militants were furious that Poli had accepted the deal, with some calling the deal an insult. PATCO's leaders had created a powerful group of militants known as the Choirboys, whose role was to mobilize controllers behind a potential strike, but the Choirboys were so gung-ho, so adverse to compromise and moderation, that their militancy overwhelmed Poli. They rallied the controllers so effectively that the membership voted 13,495 to 616 to reject the deal. Then, in a startling about-face, Poli and the union's board now voted unanimously to reject the deal they had accepted. Poli reported this to Lewis and told him that PATCO had set an August 3 strike date, leaving just four days to negotiate. Lewis concluded that Poli couldn't control his union and couldn't be trusted. Moreover, Reagan's Office of Management and Budget backed a hard-line stance, saying the controllers were "perhaps the most overpaid, pampered employees in the nation." The Reagan administration grew more resolute. Reagan's aides feared that if the new president granted further concessions in the face of an unlawful strike, it would, McCartin wrote, "call Reagan's resolve into question and send the message to foreign powers that the American president lacked toughness."

———

On the evening of August 2, Bob Butterworth gathered alongside a hundred other controllers at a union hall in Oakland, California. They came from half a dozen control towers in the Bay Area and were ready to walk out, though they were still hoping for a last-minute settlement. Early the next morning, the call came from Washington. The strike was on.

"When we got the word, there was jubilation, high-fiving," Butterworth said. "We almost had this New York Yankees' attitude. We were so used to winning. We got everything we wanted from the slowdown. We got everything we wanted from the sick-out. We thought our battle was with the FAA, and not the president of the United States, and we were used to kicking the FAA's ass. We definitely thought this thing couldn't last more than three days, that there wouldn't be any airplanes in the air. We never considered the possibility of losing."

Thirteen thousand air traffic controllers walked out on August 3. They sought to close down the world's largest air traffic system, stretching from Alaska to Puerto Rico and from Maine to Guam. On a typical summer day, the system handled thirty-three thousand departures.

From the moment the walkout began, it riveted the nation's attention like no other strike since World War II. Controllers picketed airports across the nation. More than 90 percent walked out at JFK, LaGuardia, O'Hare, Denver, LAX, Pittsburgh, and Miami airports, though less than 75 percent went on strike in Washington, Atlanta, Kansas City, Philadelphia, and Dallas/Fort Worth. That first day, Lewis informed

Reagan that half of the 14,200 scheduled daily commerical flights had taken off. "Better than anticipated," Lewis said. He also had a warning for Poli: "You're making a mistake for the country by doing this, you're making a mistake for the union by doing this."

When the strike began, Butterworth was convinced the administration would agree to a fair settlement because Reagan had once headed a labor union, the Screen Actors Guild, and had led that union's first industry-wide strike (in 1960). Moreover, Reagan had championed Lech Walesa's Solidarity union in Poland and had promised the controllers during the campaign that he'd help them achieve their goals. Butterworth was confident that Reagan would stand aside and let the union and the FAA slug it out. He couldn't have been more wrong.

Less than four hours after the strike began, Reagan appeared in the White House Rose Garden and, speaking in a calm but determined voice, portrayed the controllers as selfish villains engaged in an illegal walkout. He explained that a settlement had been reached at one point, granting a $40 million increase in salaries and benefits. "This is twice what other government employees can expect," he said. "Now, however, the union demands are seventeen times what had been agreed to—$681 million. This would impose a tax burden on their fellow citizens, which is unacceptable."

The president spoke of one controller who had told a TV reporter that morning that he had resigned from PATCO and reported to work, saying, "How can I ask my kids to obey the law if I don't?" Reagan explained that the government is not like a factory: "It has to provide without interruption the protective services which are government's reason for being. It was in recognition of this that the Congress passed a law forbidding strikes by government employees against the public safety." Reagan next read aloud the no-strike oath that each controller took upon being hired. He concluded with an ultimatum that stunned the strikers: "I must tell those who fail to report for duty this morning they are in violation of the law, and if they do not report for work within forty-eight hours, they have forfeited their jobs and will be terminated." His three-minute speech turned the public decisively against the strikers.

During the Q&A that followed, a reporter asked Reagan a question that must have been on many controllers' minds: "Mr. President, why have you taken such strong action as your first action? Why not some lesser action at this point?"

Reagan responded, "What lesser action can there be? The law is very explicit. They are violating the law."

His words frightened many strikers, but galvanized others. In Tampa, after watching Reagan's opening remarks, controllers drowned out the ensuing Q&A by singing Johnny Paycheck's country-and-western hit "Take This Job and Shove It." Poli denounced Reagan's remarks, calling them "the most blatant form of union-busting I have ever seen." He added, "It will not end the strike." But Mike Rock, a PATCO founder, disagreed. "It's all over now," he said. "You put the president of the United States publicly in a corner. He can't back down."

Throughout the dispute, Reagan maintained that he didn't fire the controllers so much as they had forfeited their jobs by violating their no-strike oath. David Gergen, Reagan's spokesman, said the president "believes this is desertion in the line of duty."

PATCO knew that more than 150,000 postal workers weren't fired after their illegal wildcat strike in 1970. Indeed, Nixon's labor secretary, George Shultz, blessed the deal that raised their wages and took steps to improve labor-management relations. PATCO also knew that Reagan not only had signed the law giving California's state employees the right to bargain but hadn't fired anyone during the more than one hundred illegal walkouts by state and local government employees during his eight years as California's governor. Meanwhile, the Reagan administration was confident that its forty-eight-hour ultimatum would get many controllers to return to work. Reagan had reminded his cabinet that as governor he had pressured five hundred striking state employees into returning to work by threatening them with dismissal within five days.

The day the strike began, the AFL-CIO's executive council was meeting in Chicago, and labor leaders there were stunned that any union would call "a strike of such magnitude" without lining up support from other unions and "in open defiance of both the law and a popular president," who was being lionized as a hero for having survived an assassination attempt four months earlier. Those labor leaders thought that many union members would oppose PATCO, because the controllers not only were breaking the law but earned considerably more than most unionized workers. One AFL-CIO emissary had warned Poli, "You can't win this strike." During the strike's first week, the UAW's president, Douglas Fraser, said the walkout could mean "massive damage to the labor movement."

With Reagan's forty-eight-hour ultimatum approaching, Butterworth was dismayed that fourteen controllers from his California facility had reported to work after originally walking out.

System-wide, about thirteen thousand controllers had walked out the first day, while three thousand stayed on the job. Ultimately, about 10 percent of those who struck on day one returned to work to avoid termination. (Lewis had predicted that 50 to 80 percent would.)

As soon as the strike began, the FAA rushed to implement its crisis plan. It kept the system operating by using 4,669 non-striking controllers, 3,291 supervisors, 800 controllers in the military, 1,500 furloughed airline pilots, and 1,000 newly hired controllers. They often worked five twelve-hour days each week, with cots set up in some control towers. The Reagan administration ultimately sent out 11,345 dismissal notices to striking controllers. It also arrested dozens of PATCO officials and strikers.

After three days, the FAA said it was handling 75 percent of the normal air traffic nationwide—far more than PATCO had anticipated—although the agency was keeping the number of flights at the major airports to 50 percent of normal. That percentage rose week by week. The nation's airlines cooperated with Reagan and the FAA, taking advantage of a welcome opportunity to reduce overcapacity and drop unprofitable routes.

The controllers' big hope was that the Air Line Pilots Association, with forty thousand members, would honor their picket lines and decline to fly. That would have assured a PATCO victory. But the pilots' union, which PATCO had done little to cultivate, was angry because the controllers went on strike during the peak summer flying season, when pilots' hours and earnings soared. In a crushing blow to the strike, the pilots decided against honoring PATCO's picket lines.

The controllers received some support, though not all-out backing, from other unions. After the AFL-CIO's leaders ended their meeting in Chicago, they took buses back to Washington, joining PATCO rallies in Cleveland and Pittsburgh. The Communications Workers of America donated $1 million to the strikers, while the New York City electrical workers' union sent a $25,000 check. In several cities, unions gave free office space to PATCO locals. But in a sharp breach of solidarity, the United Brotherhood of Carpenters didn't withdraw its invitation to Reagan to be the featured speaker at its hundredth anniversary convention. There, on September 3, Reagan defended the PATCO firings, saying, "We cannot, as citizens, pick and choose the laws we will or will not obey."

Speaking at that convention, Charles T. Manatt, chairman of the Democratic National Committee, slammed Reagan, saying, "The President of the United States ought to be a bigger individual than to praise Polish workers for striking against their government and then jail American workers for doing the same thing."

———

After the first week, Butterworth still thought PATCO would emerge with major gains. "I had already lived through two weeks of being threatened during the sick-out, and the outcome was fine," he said. "From my experience, I thought it would just take longer than we thought. I thought they can't fire all of us. I was of the opinion we were going to hurt, but it would turn out all right."

Day by day, the controllers' hopes and spirits flagged. After a fortnight, Butterworth grew disheartened. "Nobody showed any compassion for our situation," he said. "The public was pissed at us. Commerce wasn't affected. Air traffic wasn't affected after a few weeks. At this point, Reagan has no reason to lose this thing. He has the game won. He's up sixty-eight to nothing. All he has to do is hold on to the ball and let the clock run out. I was absolutely devastated. I never saw this outcome."

The strike took a heavy toll on Butterworth and his family, hastening the demise of his marriage. Butterworth's eleven-year-old daughter was badly shaken when he and four other Bay Area strikers were arrested on felony charges. They faced a year in prison for contempt of court and for helping to lead an illegal strike. Butterworth was released on bail, but he remained in a terrifying limbo for more than a year. He ultimately agreed to a plea bargain of a hundred hours of community service, which he fulfilled by coaching Little League.

"The strike was tough to get through," Butterworth said. "We had bankruptcies by the thousands. We had people commit suicide. Everything changed overnight. We were out there scrambling. It became a life where you did without things, like going out to restaurants. Driving newer cars came to an end. Going on vacation came to an end. Buying new clothes came to an end." He began living off credit cards. "We'd borrow money from friends and pay it back $10 at a time," he said. His income plunged from $40,000 a year to next to nothing. For the first six months of the strike, PATCO paid him $1,000 a month to help run its West Coast office.

The strike proved to be a resounding victory for the president. *The Washington Post* noted that PATCO, like the rogue states of North Korea and Libya, had served as a perfect foil for Reagan. The courts ordered PATCO to pay the airlines $28.8 million in damages, and on October 22 the government officially decertified PATCO, putting the union out of business.

Butterworth regrets that the PATCO strike led to some profound, negative changes for organized labor. He is convinced that some top Reagan aides were eager to take on a union to throw the whole labor movement for a loss.

"I don't think that any other strike ever affected employers so much," Butterworth said. "Employers began to get a lot of courage from Ronald Reagan. Employers suddenly woke up and saw that strikes are really something not to be afraid of, that strikes can be used to fire people, to teach people a lesson. They realized that there's another side to a strike—if these fools want to go on strike, I'll let these strikers go to hell, and I'll hire these other people out there. I can end up better off. There was an attitude change that never existed before 1981."

In his book on the PATCO strike, *Silent Skies,* Willis J. Nordlund, a business school professor, concurred with Butterworth's analysis. "The administration," Nordlund wrote, "wanted to send a strong, unambiguous message to organized labor . . . that organized labor—unionism—was essentially incompatible with the emerging free-market philosophy of the administration."

To McCartin, the labor historian, PATCO's loss was a colossal earthquake that undermined labor's confidence and foundations for years afterward. "Reagan's breaking of the PATCO strike more than any other act of his presidency . . . announced the dawn of a conservative era," McCartin wrote. "It was among private-sector union workers that the influence of the controllers' strike proved enduringly devastating, for PATCO's destruction marked the beginning of the end of one of organized labor's most reliable weapons, the strike."

Ten

Labor's Slide Picks Up Speed

"SUDDENLY PEOPLE REALIZED, hell, you can beat a union. Time was, big unions were considered invincible. We demonstrated that nobody was invincible." Thus spoke Richard Moolick, the president of the Phelps Dodge Corporation, the nation's second-largest copper mining and smelting company, after it trounced a coalition of twelve unions in an extraordinary twenty-month strike in southern Arizona. During that unusually bitter conflict, the strikers threw thousands of rocks, the police used tear gas, the governor called in the National Guard, and Phelps Dodge evicted dozens of strikers from company-owned homes.

Soon after the 2,900 miners walked out on July 1, 1983, Phelps Dodge embraced a tactic that American companies had rarely used before: it hired 1,345 *permanent* replacement workers to keep its mines running. (They were not typical, temporary replacements; they would permanently take the strikers' jobs.) With this move, Phelps Dodge was displaying a new, hard-nosed managerial militancy. In the years after the PATCO strike, one Fortune 500 company after another—including International Paper, Eastern Airlines, Greyhound, the Chicago Tribune, and Boise Cascade—successfully used this tool to defeat walkouts. This was a far cry from the 1950s and 1960s, when workers typically got their jobs back as soon as a strike was settled. Commenting on this new corporate aggressiveness, *Fortune* magazine wrote, "Managers are discovering that strikes can be broken, that the cost of breaking them is often lower than the cost of taking them, and that strike-breaking (assuming it to be legal and nonviolent) doesn't have to be a dirty word. In the long run, this new perception by business could turn out to be big news."

Martin Jay Levitt, an antiunion consultant who wrote a book about combating unions, said corporate America's militancy was a direct response to the PATCO strike. "Ronald Reagan recast the crimes of union busting as acts of patriotism," Levitt wrote. Martin F. Payson, an attorney with Jackson Lewis, a firm representing employers, agreed that the PATCO dispute had emboldened companies: "If the President of the United States can replace" strikers, then "this must be socially acceptable, politically acceptable, and we can do it, also."

In previous decades, corporations were often wary of using permanent replacements because that undermined two long-standing management goals: stable tenure and good employee morale. James Brudney, a Fordham law professor, noted that before the PATCO strike employers were eager to "maintain an image as corporate 'good citizens.'" "Managers," Brudney wrote, "generally had long-term ties to their communities, and most employers saw it as socially unacceptable to banish employees who had spent years contributing to the company over a temporary, albeit intense, economic dispute."

Elmer Chatak, an AFL-CIO official, noted ruefully in 1986 that many workers had long viewed crossing picket lines as unethical, even traitorous, but that more and more workers were willing to cross because many "workers are desperate." Labor solidarity was in decline, he said, after wage stagnation and unemployment had squeezed many workers and families.

Phelps Dodge had all but invited the walkout by its twenty-nine hundred miners, most of them Mexican Americans. Having lost $74 million in 1982, largely because of a flood of low-cost imported copper, the company insisted on a wage freeze and scrapping its cost-of-living adjustment—one of labor's prized achievements. Phelps Dodge also demanded cuts in health coverage, holidays, and starting pay. A coalition of twelve unions accepted the call for a wage freeze but rejected the other demands. George B. Munroe, the company's chairman, said the unions were "not in tune with economic realities." (The other major copper companies had demanded their workers accept a wage freeze but not the other concessions that Phelps Dodge was seeking.)

Confronting this impasse, Phelps Dodge's miners walked out. Tempers flared when management brought in strikebreakers, who were attacked by furious, rock-throwing union members. One hundred strikers were arrested, and Arizona's governor, Bruce Babbitt, twice called in the National Guard.

Phelps Dodge soon demonstrated to the strikers that it could operate the mines without them. With the strikers badly squeezed after months without work, the union coalition reluctantly agreed to accept the company's demand to eliminate the cost-of-living adjustment. Phelps Dodge rebuffed that concession, however, and let the strike continue because, as Moolick, the company's president, explained, "I had decided to break the unions."

Fifteen months after the walkout began, in a devastating blow to labor, the permanent replacement workers and six hundred original strikers who had crossed the picket line to save their jobs voted 1,906 to 87 to oust their unions. Alex Lopez, chairman of the twelve-union coalition, warned that the workers would regret that vote, saying that decertifying the unions would give Phelps Dodge "a free hand" to cut wages and benefits whenever it wished.

That same summer, seventeen hundred employees at Louisiana-Pacific, the nation's second-largest wood products company, walked out at seventeen sawmills in Washington, Oregon, and Montana. Louisiana-Pacific provoked the strike by quitting the industry's eight-company joint-bargaining association and scoffing at the other companies' contract offer, which called for freezing wages at nearly $10 an hour. Louisiana-Pacific instead insisted on chopping pay to $7 an hour. The company quickly hired five hundred replacement workers at $7 an hour, and before long it had gotten most of the seventeen sawmills up and running again. Within six months, one-third of the original strikers had returned to work, and within eighteen months, in a rolling series of votes, a majority of workers at nearly all of the seventeen struck mills voted to decertify their unions.

In the fall of 1983, Greyhound, the nation's largest intercity bus company, pursued the same aggressive battle plan. When the union representing 12,700 Greyhound drivers and other workers struck, the company quickly hired 1,291 replacement workers, enabling it to resume limited service in twenty-seven states. Hurt by the deregulation of bus service, Greyhound complained that it had lost $16 million the previous year and that its wages were 30 percent higher than those at Trailways, its main competitor. The Amalgamated Transit Union, which called the strike, had no effective answer to Greyhound's tactics; union leaders and members were stunned by the company's hard-nosed strategy and success at restoring service. So in December 1983, a month after the strike began, the union's humbled leaders accepted Greyhound's demand for a 7.8 percent pay cut. Just two weeks earlier, 96 percent of the union's members had voted to reject that cut.

Greyhound's hard-charging CEO, John W. Teets, boasted of his victory. "The ultimate weapon of the union is to strike," he said. "The ultimate weapon of management is to operate the company during a strike." "There's been a place for unions," he added, "but they've gone too far."

Robert M. Baptiste, a lawyer who represented employers and later became the National Labor Relations Board's chairman, pointed to a hardening of corporate attitudes. During strikes in decades past, Baptiste said, "there was always a sense that people would eventually say, 'Enough, let's sit down and get serious.'" But now, Baptiste explained in a 1990 interview, "companies just want to get rid of unions." As organized labor suffered a string of devastating defeats, it became increasingly clear that the tide was ebbing for union power. As Bill Keller, then *The New York Times*'s labor reporter, wrote, "Union members and leaders are approaching Labor Day 1984 with a growing feeling that the balance of power in the workplace has shifted dramatically in favor of employers."

In the 1970s, unions averaged 289 large strikes per year involving a thousand or more workers. In the decade after the PATCO strike, the number of work stoppages per year plunged to an average of 58. Unions had grown gun-shy about using their most powerful weapon—strikes—because they were losing too many of these high-stakes battles. The decline in strikes was good for companies and overall economic efficiency, but there was a cost for workers; those who participated in strikes generally had higher wages than comparable workers who hadn't gone on strike. Walkouts had pried extra pay and benefits out of companies. Jake Rosenfeld, a labor relations expert at Washington University, said that for the overall union movement, "falling strike activity" represents "a real financial loss, and a clear sign of declining power."

Over the past decade, there have been just thirteen major strikes a year on average. A weapon that was long labor's powerful sword has largely disappeared from America's industrial landscape (although there was a surprising surge of teachers' strikes in 2018).

———

In many ways, the 1970s were a precursor of labor's calamitous 1980s. As the 1970s began, organized labor still had plenty of clout and was even able to get Republican presidents to sign significant pro-worker legislation. It is often forgotten that Richard Nixon was attentive to worker concerns. He signed the Coal Mine Health and Safety Act of 1969 and the Occupational Safety and Health Act in 1970, probably the most important pro-worker legislation since the New Deal. And Gerald Ford, Nixon's successor, also heeded worker concerns, signing the Employee Retirement Income Security Act in 1974. That landmark law, sponsored by a Republican senator, Jacob Javits of New York, sought to safeguard employee pensions after Studebaker, an automaker, collapsed, leaving forty-one hundred of its workers with just 15 percent of their promised pensions.

Also in the 1970s, American industry first felt the bite of imports in a serious way. In the previous two decades, the United States was the world's unchallenged industrial colossus as Europe and Japan recovered from the ravages of world war. But in the 1970s, American manufacturers confronted a rising tide of imports: Volkswagens from Germany; Hondas, Toyotas, and Sony televisions from Japan; and steel from Belgium and Romania. In 1971, the United States experienced its first trade deficit since the late nineteenth century. Indeed, starting in 1976, the nation has run a trade deficit every year.

In 1973 OPEC ordered an oil embargo against Western nations after the Arab-Israeli War of that year, and that was followed in 1979 by a second oil crisis caused by plummeting production in Iran after the mullahs swept to power. Those shocks caused oil prices to skyrocket from $3 a barrel to $31. That sent inflationary waves through the economy and set the stage for a deep recession that devastated workers and unions alike.

Other far-reaching trends also undercut labor in the 1970s. Productivity growth slowed to a 1 percent average annual increase, down from a nearly 3 percent annual clip during the 1950s and 1960s. The corporate rate of profit was falling, too, and many companies, alarmed by these trends, started resisting unionization and began driving a harder bargain in contract negotiations.

In the 1980s, everything seemed to go wrong for labor. A confluence of forces—recession, imports, deregulation, technological change—clobbered the nation's unions. After the 1979 oil shock, consumer prices jumped by 12 percent in 1980, and the Federal Reserve set out to break the back of inflation. The Fed raised interest rates to a record high of 20 percent, slamming the brakes on consumer spending and throwing the economy into a severe slump. The nation's jobless rate climbed to 10.8 percent, the highest level since the Great Depression. Paul Volcker, the Fed's chairman, warned that to bring inflation down, "the standard of living of the average American has to decline."

That brutal downturn and the surge in imports devastated the industrial Midwest, as well as organized labor's core membership: factory workers. The unflattering term "Rust Belt" was invented as steel mills, auto assembly plants, and machine shops shuttered in community after community as a result of the huge overcapacity caused by recession and imports. Between 1979 and 1983, 2.7 million manufacturing jobs vanished, with Michigan's jobless rate climbing to a chilling 16.5 percent at one point. One of the era's most painful moments came in 1983, two days before Christmas, when United States Steel, an icon of American industry since the days of Andrew Carnegie, announced that it was shutting down nearly one-fifth of its steelmaking capacity and laying off 15,000 workers. The number of steelworkers nationwide plunged from 450,000 in 1980 to 170,000 at decade's end, and the steelworkers' average hourly wage shrank by 17 percent, after accounting for inflation. Auto industry employment also fell sharply, from 760,000 in 1978 to 490,000 three years later. By decade's end, foreign cars had captured 30 percent of the U.S. auto market, up from 20 percent in 1980.

Corporations now repeatedly demanded concessions. In late 1979 and early 1980, with Chrysler on the verge of bankruptcy, the UAW agreed to over $650 million in wage and benefit concessions to keep the company afloat. GM and Ford weren't in Chrysler's parlous condition, but they nonetheless obtained similar givebacks. In return for GM's promise not to close several assembly plants, the UAW agreed to defer its cost-of-living adjustment and to eliminate the cherished annual improvement increases that Walter Reuther and GM's Charles E.

Wilson had championed. That move seemed to unofficially sever an important link—that as productivity rose, worker pay would rise along with it.

As Nelson Lichtenstein points out in his insightful book *State of the Union: A Century of American Labor*, the competitive challenge from Europe and Japan called into question the raison d'être of America's unions and of the New Deal legislation that promoted them—the notion that "unions are good for industrial society because they raise wages, not only for union members themselves, but for the entire working population." In Reuther's era, many Americans viewed union wage increases as an unalloyed good because they helped build the middle class, spur consumer demand, lift living standards, and spread prosperity.

In the 1950s and 1960s, the raises that unions won hardly endangered companies in core industries like autos, steel, and tires, where competition was anything but fierce because they were largely oligopolies. If wage hikes pushed up prices, it was easy enough for GM or Goodyear to pass that on to the consumer. That changed when American industry began facing fierce competition from Europe and Japan. Many manufacturers warned that wage hikes and generous benefits not only undercut their competitiveness but jeopardized the survival of their operations.

It was true, as labor's many critics pointed out, that higher-paying unionized factories were often the first to close due to lower-priced imports (union members often hesitated to have their pay and benefits cut to make their companies more competitive). But many nonunion factories shuttered as well. That was true of many garment companies, which couldn't compete with factories in China, Honduras, Vietnam, and Bangladesh, countries where workers often earn a fraction of what American workers earn. Manufacturing had long been the heart of organized labor, so the wave of factory closings caused a concomitant drop in union membership. In the two decades after 1973, the International Ladies' Garment Workers' Union lost nearly 400,000 members (two-thirds of its membership), while the UAW lost 500,000 members, and the International Association of Machinists lost 300,000.

Deregulation also walloped unions. President Reagan continued Jimmy Carter's push to deregulate key industries in order to spur competition and cut costs for consumers. In doing so, Reagan shook up several highly regimented and highly unionized industries, most notably airlines, trucking, railroads, and telecommunications. Deregulation ended restrictions on where trucking companies could dispatch their eighteen-wheelers and which cities airlines could fly to. As intended, deregulation spurred an influx of lower-cost competitors, putting immense pressure on many long-insulated unionized companies. Some well-known corporations collapsed—Pan Am and Eastern Airlines among them—while many companies demanded far-reaching givebacks from workers to stay competitive. In the airline industry, annual wages and benefits averaged nearly $42,000 per worker in 1982; at the new, nonunion carriers, total compensation averaged just $22,000. That of course fueled demands for painful concessions from labor.

The International Brotherhood of Teamsters prided itself on having the clout to get hundreds of trucking companies to sign on to a nationwide standard in the form of a master freight agreement. In 1979, that agreement covered 285,000 long-haul drivers. A decade later, after deregulation, that agreement covered just 165,000 drivers because many unionized trucking companies went out of business. A big factor: the pay at nonunion carriers was 25 percent to 40 percent lower. In 1979, before deregulation, 50 percent of U.S. trucking tonnage was hauled by Teamster drivers; five years later, just 23 percent was.

Drew Lewis, who became president of Union Pacific Railroad after serving as Reagan's transportation secretary, noted that rail and truck deregulation was pushing down railroads' volume and the rates they charged. "The only way we can increase earnings is going to be cutting labor costs," Lewis said.

A. H. Raskin, the dean of American labor journalists, saw how the 1980s was having a devastating effect on workers and worker power: "The Gompers gospel of 'more' as the main function of unionism has become a shaky proposition . . . when many unions find it necessary to settle for less under the hammer blows of mass unemployment, savage trade competition, and the threatened extinction of highly unionized industries that had been traditional frontrunners in wages and benefits."

———

Then, as now, corporate America was overflowing with upbeat talk about how automation and technological change would bring a brighter tomorrow. New production techniques swept through many industries in the 1970s and 1980s, and that, too, took a heavy toll on unions—and, of course, many workers.

There is a famous anecdote about a Ford Motor Company executive goading Walter Reuther about how automation would undermine labor unions. While giving Reuther a tour of a Ford plant in Cleveland in the 1950s, the Ford official pointed to some early robots that did various assembly-line tasks. He asked Reuther, "How are you going to collect union dues from these guys?"

Reuther responded, "How are you going to get them to buy Fords?"

A new production technique developed by Iowa Beef Processors (IBP) revolutionized the meatpacking industry and hobbled its unions. Eschewing the longtime practice of having skilled butchers take apart a whole animal, IBP created assembly lines (actually disassembly lines) where unskilled workers did the same simple tasks day after day to take apart a steer—a worker might do the same knife cut ten thousand times a day. This new method meant that IBP could use lower-paid workers. IBP usually built its slaughterhouses in lower-wage rural areas, forcing many high-paying, unionized slaughterhouses and packinghouses in Chicago, Omaha, and elsewhere to shut down, eliminating thousands of unionized butcher jobs. (This new system, and the box beef it shipped, also eliminated many unionized butcher jobs in supermarkets.) One of IBP's many ripple effects was that where meatpackers were unionized, management demanded big wage cuts; Hormel Foods, for instance, demanded a 23 percent wage cut at its plant in Austin, Minnesota, in 1985, igniting an extraordinarily divisive six-month strike.

Containerization—shipping goods in large metal containers instead of as separate pieces—changed the landscape, too. According to one study, in 1969, it took 500 workers three months to unload a nine-hundred-foot cargo ship through traditional "break bulk" practices that relied on manual labor to remove individual items or boxes. Several decades later, after the containerization revolution, it took just 10 workers twenty-four hours to unload such a ship as large cranes lifted and moved one fifteen-ton, forty-foot-long container after another. As a result, the number of longshoremen in the Port of New York and New Jersey plunged from 35,000 in 1954 to 2,700 five decades later, while the tonnage unloaded more than tripled and production per worker increased more than thirty-fold. Similarly, the number of West Coast dockworkers plunged from 100,000 in the 1950s to 10,500 in the early twenty-first century.

The nation's seaports boomed as more American companies— Walmart, Macy's, Nike, General Electric (and later Apple)—looked overseas to source what they sold, whether blouses, blue jeans, running shoes, radios, or iPhones. Thanks to globalization and new technologies like containerization, faxing, and email, American companies could now often locate an operation abroad more profitably than in the United States. That, too, reduced the number of American factory jobs and, along with them, organized labor's membership and strength. (Recently we've seen the same trend with call centers.)

There are thousands of examples of American companies moving operations abroad—to make televisions in China, refrigerators in Mexico, or shirts and slacks in Bangladesh. Many corporations told unions to swallow concessions or else they would move production overseas. Here's one example: In 1988, General Electric said it would close an aging factory in Fort Wayne, Indiana, that made electrical motors and relocate abroad unless the union agreed to a 12 percent pay cut. "There's a bunch of guys in Thailand, Korea, and Brazil who get up every morning and try to figure out how to eat your lunch and take your market share," said David C. Genever-Watling, the head of GE's motor division. The Fort Wayne workers voted by more than two to one to accept an 11 percent pay cut to save their jobs. "It used to be that companies had an allegiance to the worker and the country," said Jim Daughtry, a leader of the factory's union. "Today, companies have an allegiance to the shareholder. Period." Those words were prescient.

Globalization reduces American workers' bargaining power as well as their wages. A study by three Harvard economists—George J. Borjas, Richard B. Freeman, and Lawrence F. Katz—concluded that for every 1 percent drop in an industry's employment because of imports or factories gone overseas, wages are pushed down by half of 1 percent for the workers who remain in that industry. Robert A. Johnson, a New York financier, described how globalization has tilted the playing field against labor. "Now capital has wings," Johnson said. "Capital can deal with twenty labor markets at once and pick and choose among them. Labor is fixed in one place. So power has shifted."

———

A profound change in American capitalism—its swing from managerial capitalism to investor capitalism (also known as financial capitalism)—has undercut workers and unions alike. As a result of this shift, corporations have focused far more on maximizing their profits and share price, and in doing so, they have generally taken a tougher stance on labor costs and unions. In the postwar era of managerial capitalism, CEOs had firm control of their companies. With corporate headquarters often adjacent to a major factory, top executives were frequently supportive and generous toward their employees. In that era, it was easier for CEOs to be generous to their workers because executives went largely unchallenged by shareholders. From that era come tales of greater social solidarity, of future CEOs who had fought alongside blue-collar soldiers in World War II, and of those CEOs making sure two or three decades later that they treated their blue-collar workers fairly and well, even if it meant somewhat lower profits.

Corporate America's behavior changed with the rise of institutional investors. Now corporate executives came under fierce pressure to focus on maximizing profits and share price. CEOs knew that if they didn't get profits up and keep them up—and that often meant squeezing labor costs—they risked being ousted, either by corporate takeover or by a peeved board of directors. In 1965, 84 percent of stock in publicly traded corporations was owned by individuals and just 16 percent by institutional investors. By 2010, institutional investors owned 67 percent. All this gave fund managers a much larger say, and they often didn't hesitate to unload on CEOs who fell short of quarterly earnings forecasts.

For many in corporate America, Jack Welch, General Electric's CEO, was the model to follow. In his first six years at GE's helm, Welch aggressively shut or shrank lagging businesses, eliminating 130,000 jobs, one-fourth of the company's workforce. During his reign from 1981 to 2001, GE's valuation went from $13 billion to $500 billion—the highest in the world. While many workers called Welch heartless, *Fortune* magazine hailed him as "far and away the most influential manager of his generation."

The compensation system for CEOs further fueled the focus on maximizing profits and share price (and squeezing down costs). From 2006 to 2014, the five hundred highest-paid U.S. corporate executives received 76 percent of their income in stock options and other stock-based compensation, creating huge incentives for them to push share prices ever higher. Taken together, CEOs' desire for more stock-based pay and corporate America's preoccupation with maximizing share prices have fueled a surge in stock buybacks—more than $5 trillion worth over the past decade. Instead of further enriching shareholders, some of that money could have gone to workers' raises and helped end years of wage stagnation.

In 1990, the Business Roundtable, an association of the CEOs of the nation's leading companies, stated, "Corporations are chartered to serve both their shareholders and society as a whole." In other words, top corporations were not to focus only on share price; they should also serve the "company's employees, customers, suppliers, creditors and the community where the corporation does business." The Roundtable added, "The central corporate governance point to be made about a corporation's stakeholders beyond the shareholders is that they are vital to the long-term successful economic performance of the corporation."

By 1997, the Roundtable had changed its tune and adopted an overriding focus on serving shareholders, thus turning its back in large part on other stakeholders, including workers. In the intervening years, many CEOs had felt considerable heat from activist shareholders and corporate raiders who often complained that companies' share prices were too low because they weren't focusing enough on shareholders. These activists drew fuel from the economists Milton Friedman and Michael C. Jensen, who argued that corporate executives' sole duty was to shareholders. "The paramount duty of management and boards of directors is to the corporation's stockholders," the Roundtable said in its 1997 statement. "The interests of other stakeholders [including workers] are relevant as a derivative of the duty to stockholders." It concluded, "The notion that the board must somehow balance the interest of other stakeholders fundamentally misconstrues the role of the directors." So much for the notion of the common good upon which America was predicated.

———

For two years, Chris Cummings typically worked six days a week, from 7 a.m. to 7 p.m., to help his company, Allegheny Technologies, prepare for the opening of a gargantuan $1.2 billion steel mill in Pennsylvania that stretches the length of four football fields, its bright white walls jutting forty feet into the air. Many weeks, however, Cummings, whose job was to maintain and repair elaborate steelmaking machinery, had to work double shifts, which meant putting in a sixteen-hour day. Many days he didn't see his young son or daughter, because by the time he returned from work, they were asleep. He said his wife often complained that she felt "like a single mom."

At age thirty-eight, he was fuming because his company, a leading producer of stainless steel, had locked him out of his job four months earlier, leaving him and his family without a paycheck. Indeed, on August 15, 2015, Allegheny had locked out twenty-two hundred steelworkers at twelve plants in six states after the workers had voted overwhelmingly to reject Allegheny's contract proposal, which called for a four-year wage freeze and having many workers pay an additional $2,000 each year toward their health coverage. The company was also insisting on a two-tier contract that would give future hires far worse health and pension plans.

Allegheny Technologies told the United Steelworkers union that it needed those concessions because it was losing money. It was hurt by a 30 percent plunge in the price of stainless steel, largely the result of a surge in low-cost imports from China. After eight years with the company, Cummings said he understood Allegheny's need to stay competitive, but he nonetheless thought its demands for concessions were draconian. "This is our reward for putting in all this overtime to help open the new mill," Cummings said angrily.

Outside the shiny new steel mill, located in Brackenridge, Pennsylvania, twenty-two miles upriver from Pittsburgh, Cummings and other locked-out workers took turns picketing as temporary replacement workers came and went. The locked-out union members had set up burn barrels and built temporary sheds to shield them from December's cold, wind, and snow. Nailed to the sheds were signs saying, "Danger: Scabs Trying to Run Mill" and "Scabs Equal Dishonor." (Jack London once wrote, "After God had finished the rattlesnake, the toad and the vampire, he had some awful substance left with which he made a Strikebreaker.")

The lockout, once rare, is now a common tool for American employers who are eager to show who has the upper hand. From the National Football League to Sotheby's rarefied auction house, more and more employers are locking out workers when their collective bargaining agreement expires without having agreed on a new contract. "This is a sign of increased employer militancy," said Gary Chaison, an industrial relations professor at Clark University.

This strategy denies workers their paychecks with the goal of pressuring them to surrender on management's terms. John Budd, a business school professor at the University of Minnesota, said lockouts aim for the "unconditional surrender of the union."

In recent years, the National Basketball Association locked out its players for 161 days and the NFL for 130 days; the National Hockey League has locked out its players three times since 1994, with its 2004–5 lockout canceling an entire season. DeMaurice Smith, executive director of the NFL Players Association, said lockouts put "huge pressure on athletes whose professional careers typically last just a few years." National Grid locked out 1,250 gas workers in Massachusetts for six months when they wouldn't accept a two-tier contract, while Kellogg's locked out 225 workers at its plant in Memphis. Long Island University kept out 400 professors at its Brooklyn campus for twelve days, while the Minnesota Orchestra locked out its musicians for sixteen months. Even New York's famed Metropolitan Opera locked out its singers and orchestra for a week before reaching a settlement.

In one of the longest lockouts in American history, American Crystal Sugar, the nation's largest sugar beet processor, locked out thirteen hundred unionized workers in North Dakota, Minnesota, and Iowa for twenty months. The workers had rejected management's demands, which included higher payments for health coverage, greater flexibility to outsource jobs, and the ability to ignore seniority in making promotions. The company used replacement workers during the lockout. (Unlike employers hit by strikes, employers that lock out workers are prohibited from using replacements to permanently take away jobs.) Paul Woinarowicz, an American Crystal worker, called the lockout "just another way of trying to break the union." After twenty arduous months, the thirteen hundred locked-out workers voted 55 percent to 45 percent to approve a concession-filled contract that they had previously rejected four times, once by 96 percent to 4 percent.

At Allegheny's headquarters in Pittsburgh, Bob Wetherbee, its executive vice president in charge of the flat-rolled steel division, asserted that the lockout was needed to reduce what the company said were bloated labor costs. Wetherbee said the steelworkers averaged $70 an hour in compensation, including pensions, health coverage, overtime, and paid time off. The workers ridiculed that number as vastly exaggerated, noting that their base pay was $24 an hour. With one-third of Allegheny's blue-collar workers eligible to retire before 2020, Wetherbee said it made sense to seek a two-tier contract—something the steelworkers' union detests because it drives a wedge between lower-paid new hires and longtime workers. "We're faced with a once-in-a-generation opportunity to bend the cost curve on a major part of our costs," Wetherbee said. "If we're going to be competitive, we have to be in a position where we have a different benefit structure for the next generation we hire." Paul Clark, director of Penn State's School of Labor and Employment Relations, said Allegheny seemed to be seizing on a temporary drop in stainless steel prices to extract deep and lasting cuts. "They're using the excuse of the industry downturn, not just to adjust to the new situation," Clark said. "They want to go well beyond what's justified by the downturn."

In most lockouts, the workers come out on the losing end. But they are not a foolproof weapon for employers. At times, employers are so eager to lock out their workers that they violate some laws. Allegheny's steelworkers, thanks to some smart lawyering, were able to emerge from their six-month lockout largely victorious, beating back most of the company's demands for concessions. Richard Brean, the steelworkers' general counsel, convinced the NLRB's regional director that Allegheny had unlawfully bargained in bad faith to precipitate a lockout. The NLRB's regional director stunned Allegheny by saying not only was the lockout illegal, but the company would owe back pay to all twenty-two hundred steelworkers from the day the lockout began six months earlier, at a potential cost of over $40 million.

With that potential penalty hanging over its head, Allegheny agreed to a new contract that eliminated or reduced many of the concessions it had previously demanded. The company retreated from its demand that it have wide latitude to impose onerous work schedules, such as double shifts. The agreement called for the workers to pay significantly less toward health coverage than the company had wanted. Allegheny also abandoned its idea of future hires being in a lower pay tier, except for one small wrinkle. Mindful of keeping Allegheny competitive, the steelworkers' union agreed to forgo regular raises for several years and instead accepted lump-sum payments and profit sharing (which came to about 4 percent of pay the first year). The union also agreed that retirees would pay somewhat more toward their health coverage. Leo Gerard, the union's president, called the result "a tremendous victory for a very brave group of workers."

Tom Conway, the steelworkers' vice president who oversaw the negotiations, said Allegheny had made a big mistake by locking out its workers: "The sad part is the people hate the company's guts now, and they will hate them for the rest of their lives. It was all so unnecessary."

Eleven

Corporations Turn Up the Heat

SPEAKING AT A NEWS CONFERENCE for the very first time, Takele Gobena, an Uber driver in Seattle, awkwardly approached the microphone to convey two messages: first, that Uber drivers needed a union and, second, that Uber paid miserably. Gobena, a gangly, twenty-six-year-old refugee from Ethiopia, said his hourly earnings came to less than the minimum wage after factoring in gas, insurance, and other expenses. Fearing retaliation, Gobena said, "I know Uber will probably deactivate me tomorrow. But I'm ready because this is worth fighting for."

It didn't take that long. At 6:50 that evening, a few hours after several websites posted articles about the news conference, Uber emailed Gobena to notify him he had been deactivated, Uber lingo for being fired. The company said his auto insurance had expired.

Within minutes, Gobena grabbed his smartphone, photographed his insurance card (which showed that his insurance policy was still in force), and emailed the photo to Uber and to Mike O'Brien, the city councilman who had organized the news conference. O'Brien sent the photo to several journalists to show that Uber's reason for firing Gobena was poppycock. Badly embarrassed, Uber reinstated Gobena the next day. Uber vigorously denied that it had retaliated against Gobena, insisting it was all a mistake.

◆

Josh Coleman excelled as a customer service representative at T-Mobile's call center in Wichita, so much so that the company awarded him its top prize for performance: a trip to Puerto Rico. To celebrate his success, the company placed Coleman's face on billboards and computer screens, and his co-workers paraded him around the call center. A month later, however, a T-Mobile manager informed Coleman that the company was canceling his trip. That was days after Coleman first appeared in a union video urging his co-workers to join the Communications Workers of America. Several months later, T-Mobile fired Coleman, saying it was for poor performance in handling phone calls. The NLRB accused T-Mobile of illegally firing Coleman for being a union supporter. Months later, the company agreed to pay Coleman $40,000, without admitting any wrongdoing.

———

In no other industrial nation do employers fight so hard to defeat, indeed quash, labor unions. Whether in Anglophone countries like Australia, Britain, and Canada, or in continental European countries like France, Germany, and Sweden, or in Asian countries like Japan and South Korea, employers generally see unions as legitimate institutions that represent workers' interests and that businesses need to work with, if sometimes unenthusiastically. In the United States, however, the common (though not universal) corporate view is that unions are the enemy, an illegitimate nuisance that should be wiped out. Within corporate America, senior executives, by and large, abhor the idea of having to discuss or negotiate issues with union officials. They view that as an improper invasion of their autonomy, flexibility, and managerial prerogatives. "We like driving the car, and we're not going to give the steering wheel to anyone but us," said Lee Scott, when he was Walmart's CEO.

Many companies take aggressive steps to make sure that no union is going to share the driving with them. Menards, a Wisconsin-based home-improvement chain, was so intent on keeping out unions that its employment contracts said that any store managers whose employees unionized would have their salaries chopped by 60 percent. Imagine what lengths Menards' store managers must have gone to in order to defeat unionization drives. As soon as that contract provision was leaked to the press, an embarrassed Menards eliminated the provision. At many companies, managers know that if a majority of workers at their store, restaurant, hotel, or factory vote to unionize, they are likely to be demoted or even fired.

To shine a spotlight on corporate America's antiunion behavior, the Teamsters union asked several truck drivers in Georgia to secretly record what managers were telling them about unions. The drivers recorded union-bashing speeches at FedEx, Coca-Cola, and Staples distribution centers and warehouses. As Dave Jamieson wrote in *The Huffington Post,* the companies' central message was that unions weren't seeking to help workers but rather just trying to make money for themselves. "It is no secret that the Teamsters' first priority is to collect employee dues," one FedEx manager told the drivers. "They will do anything to get those dues." The manager then mocked the Teamsters because its membership, like many unions', has been declining. "The Teamsters are literally a bunch of losers," he said.

At a second meeting, another FedEx manager was more emphatic. "We do not want a union at FedEx Freight, not under any circumstances," he said. "This company, by any legal means necessary, will fight that. And everybody in this room and everybody who works for this organization needs to understand that. . . . We don't think it fits with our business model. We don't think it's good for you or your families."

At a Coca-Cola distribution center in Atlanta, a company representative spoke from a similar script: "They may claim they want to represent you, and give you a voice in the workplace, but at least my experience is, at the end of the day, it's all about the money." At a Staples warehouse, the drivers were told that "unions are divisive" and "can pit associates against one another." The Staples manager added, "Unions are a business that needs your money. Don't be fooled: Unions are first and foremost a business." (After those highly opinionated remarks, the Staples official added, "I'm trying to give you an objective opinion.")

Seven hundred miles up the East Coast, in Middletown, Delaware, Kellen Wadach, an Amazon warehouse manager, told several hundred workers a disturbing story. Based on the account of three Amazon workers, *The New York Times* wrote, "Flashing a photograph of himself as a boy with his father, Mr. Wadach said the union did not help his family financially after his father died suddenly in front of their house, not even bothering to send a condolence card." After his tale aroused suspicions, several workers discussed their doubts with an organizer for the machinists' union. The union tracked down an obituary of Wadach's father. The obituary noted that he had died while jogging during a family vacation in South Carolina, not in front of their house. Moreover, Wadach's father was not in a labor union; he was a partner in an insurance agency. The story was a fake.

Martin Jay Levitt, a longtime management consultant who wrote a tell-all book, *Confessions of a Union Buster,* said companies often lie to defeat unionization drives. "Union busting is a field populated by bullies and built on deceit," Levitt wrote. "A campaign against a union is an assault on individuals and a war on the truth. As such, it is a war without honor. The only way to bust a union is to lie, distort, manipulate, threaten, and always, always attack."

Union busting has become a sizable industry in the United States, with scholars estimating that companies spend over $200 million a year on "union-avoidance" firms and consultants. The industry has exploded in size from a hundred antiunion specialists in the 1960s to more than two thousand today. They range from shady outfits that routinely break the law to some of the nation's most respected law firms.

Kate Bronfenbrenner, a Cornell University researcher who has conducted several nationwide studies on unionization drives, found that during such campaigns 89 percent of employers required workers to attend antiunion meetings, much like the ones that FedEx and Staples held for their drivers. According to Bronfenbrenner, 57 percent of employers threatened to close operations if workers voted to unionize, while 47 percent threatened to cut wages or benefits. That study also found that 63 percent of employers interrogated workers in one-on-one meetings about whether they supported a union, 34 percent fired union supporters, 28 percent attempted to infiltrate the union organizing committee, and 22 percent used "bribes and special favors" to help persuade workers to oppose unionization.

Bronfenbrenner described some especially intimidating tactics. Facing a unionization drive, ITT Automotive parked thirteen flatbed tractor trailers with shrink-wrapped production equipment in front of its plant in Oscoda, Michigan, and next to those trucks it posted large hot-pink signs reading, "Mexico Transfer Job." ITT also flew workers in from its Mexican factory to videotape its Michigan workers on the production line, saying the company was "considering moving to Mexico."

When a Fruit of the Loom factory in the Rio Grande valley in Texas confronted an organizing effort, it posted yard signs in the community saying, "Keep Jobs in the Valley. Vote No." Fruit of the Loom also hung a banner across the factory saying, "Wear the Union Label. Unemployed."

Managers at a Continental General Tire factory in Mount Vernon, Illinois, were surprisingly blunt in their antiunion pitch, telling workers at a large meeting: "We are not competitive as a company, and we can't afford to pay the wages and benefits the union will impose on us. We will have to close, and we already have facilities overseas."

In response to an organizing drive by the Service Employees International Union (SEIU), Avanté, a nursing home in Lake Worth, Florida, distributed a flyer about a shrimp-processing plant, Kitchens of the Oceans, that suddenly shut down after its two hundred employees had voted in favor of unionizing. In bold letters, the Avanté nursing home flyer screamed, "The Union *never* got a contract—as it had promised! The Union *never* got any wage increases—as it had promised! The Union *never* got shorter hours—as it had promised! Here's what did happen: The plant was shut down! 200 jobs were lost!"

Many of the tactics that American companies use to beat back unions are illegal, whether firing workers for backing a union, spying on union supporters, asking workers to disclose whether they favor a union, or threatening to close a plant if workers unionize. Many companies use these tactics for a simple reason: they often work, and the "penalty" for breaking labor laws is rarely more than a slap on the wrist—the NLRB often just orders management to post a notice on the bulletin board in which the company admits it violated the law and promises not to do it again.

Walmart, the world's largest retailer, is an avowed enemy of unions. During its orientation, tens of thousands of cashiers and stockers have had to watch a video in which a professional actress says some startling things about unions. "I always thought that unions were kind of like clubs or charities that were out to help workers," the actress says. "Well, I found out that wasn't exactly the case. The truth is unions are businesses, multimillion-dollar businesses that make their money by convincing people like you and me to give them a part of our paychecks." Such antiunion videos are required viewing during orientation at many U.S. companies. In Walmart's case, some of what the actress said wasn't exactly true. Thomas A. Kochan, an MIT professor who is one of the nation's foremost experts on industrial relations, said the Walmart video "insults any new hire's intelligence." "Everyone knows that labor unions aren't clubs or charities," Kochan said. "They're organizations in which workers join together with the goal of improving wages and working conditions."

In February 2000, butchers in the meat department of a Walmart in Jacksonville, Texas, voted 7–3 to join the United Food and Commercial Workers International Union. Two weeks later, even though Walmart had recently invested in new equipment for the Jacksonville meat department, the retailer announced it was closing down the meat department at that store and 180 other stores in Texas and neighboring states. Union leaders said this showed how far Walmart would go to snuff out unions, but Walmart said it had merely decided to switch to prepackaged cuts of meat. "Our decision to expand case-ready meat has nothing to do with what went on in Jacksonville," Jessica Moser, a Walmart spokeswoman, said.

One Walmart store manager in Kentucky told of discovering a flyer in his store's bathroom that said, "This store needs a union." He called Walmart's antiunion hotline, and the next day an antiunion SWAT team arrived at his store, flown in by corporate jet. The spread of thousands of Walmart stores has meant fierce, low-price, low-wage competition for unionized supermarkets across the United States, pushing many to clamp down on wages and pushing some out of business. In September 2004, the United Food and Commercial Workers racked up a huge victory, winning a unionization drive at a Walmart store in Jonquière, Quebec, making it the first Walmart store to be unionized in North America. Walmart closed that store seven months later, shortly before an arbitrator was going to decide on contract terms for the store's 190 employees. Walmart said the store was losing money.

Stuart Appelbaum, president of the Retail, Wholesale, and Department Store Union, said, "Walmart has sent a clear message to working people: Walmart would rather shut its operations than allow its employees to exercise their legal right to form a union."

Juan Carlos Cardenas grew up in Cuba and went to the University of Havana to study classical literature. There, he was arrested and expelled for writing "subversive" poetry. "It was pretty critical of the government," he said. "It dealt with the lack of freedom to express ourselves."

After being sent to a "re-education" farm for two months, Cardenas was desperate to escape Cuba. With the help of a friend, he stole onto a freighter heading to Jamaica, burying himself under sacks of sugar in the cargo hold. In Jamaica, he managed to stow away on a cruise ship going to Florida. Upon arriving in Miami, he achieved his longtime dream: he was officially admitted into the United States as a refugee from Communism. He was twenty-two at the time.

Cardenas studied to become a physical therapist, taking a job at Pan American Hospital, which served Miami's Cuban community. Facing a financial squeeze because of a disastrous acquisition, the 750-employee hospital infuriated its workers by suddenly eliminating end-of-year bonuses, slashing overtime hours, cutting workers' annual vacation by a week, and reducing the number of paid sick days. Outraged, the workers began a unionization drive. Popular among his co-workers and unafraid to speak up, Cardenas became a leader in the effort. "I had been there for ten years," he said. "I knew everybody. Everybody knew me. I knew the patients. I knew the community." Cardenas posted pro-union literature on the employee bulletin board and asked co-workers to sign cards calling for a vote to join the Union of Needletrades, Industrial, and Textile Employees, known as Unite.

"We wanted a voice," Cardenas explained. "We're the people closest to the patients, and we have no voice. How can you fix the system if the people carrying the system day to day could not say anything? It's a disservice to the hospital if we just come here and accept things like they are and not try to make them better."

To discredit the unionization drive, the hospital's managers circulated flyers that likened unions to Communism. "They associated anything that has to do with social justice with Communism," Cardenas said. In a particularly heavy-handed move, the hospital's top executive sent out a letter saying the union local's "president used to work for a union that goes by an acronym borrowed from a statue of Karl Marx in Moscow imploring the workers of the world to UNITE." In a further slap, the hospital's top executive complained that too many hospital workers "champion the causes of communist organizations [that is, unions]." Management's hardball tactics surprised Cardenas. Then came another big surprise: the hospital fired him two days before the unionization vote.

Proud and defiant, he wrote an impassioned letter to his co-workers. "Many years have passed and now we are no longer in Cuba, but here we also find the likeness of Cuba's repressive policies," he wrote. "Like in Cuba, the obvious intention for the recent firing of employees . . . has been to intimidate us, as a way to silence our rights and our ideals." Cardenas argued that the best way to stand up to such repression was to vote for the union. "To vote yes means to assert our rights and freedom of speech and ideas, our rights of not having to work under threat and intimidation," he wrote.

When companies fire the leaders of unionization drives, that often hobbles such efforts, but the hospital's decision to fire Cardenas backfired. Its move rallied workers behind their beloved friend and his cause. More than 90 percent of Pan American's workers voted in favor of unionizing. Fifteen months after Cardenas was fired, an NLRB judge ruled that the hospital had illegally dismissed him and five other workers for backing a union. "I was and still am a very idealistic person," Cardenas said. "When I left Cuba and came to the United States, I never expected to be punished for exercising my freedom of speech."

When confronted by unionization drives, many employers conclude that a smart way to cripple them is to fire the most outspoken union activists. One study found that one in three companies facing unionization drives discharges union supporters. A 2007 study concluded that one in fifty-three union supporters gets fired during unionization campaigns, but rank-and-file "union organizers and activists" who lead organizing drives "face a 15 to 20 percent chance of being fired."

America's labor laws provide little deterrent to such firings. Many corporate executives—along with their lawyers and antiunion consultants—conclude that the advantages far outweigh the disadvantages when it comes to illegally firing pro-union workers. Dismissing workers who spearhead a drive often chills fellow workers, making them all the more scared to speak out, while at the same time throwing the union organizing drive into disarray. Under federal labor law, employers can't be fined for such illegal firings; they can only be ordered to reinstate the worker and pay back wages, and that amount can be modest, even minuscule.

Take the case of Ernest Duval, a Haitian immigrant who was the leader of a drive to unionize the King David Nursing Home in West Palm Beach, Florida. Duval was fired, allegedly for choking a nurse. After five and a half years of costly litigation, the NLRB ruled on Duval's behalf, concluding that the "choking" accusation was a total fabrication and that he—and six other union supporters—were fired illegally because they were campaigning for a union. Even though it was nearly six years since Duval was fired, the NLRB ruled that he was entitled to just $1,305 in back wages (plus $493 interest). The award was so small because under federal law the nursing home was required to pay him the back pay due him *minus* all that he had earned working other jobs after being dismissed. Soon after Duval was fired, Catholic Charities hired him as a translator; he speaks English, French, Creole, and Spanish. "They were supposed to punish them for that wrong-doing, but there was really no punishment," Duval said. Many employers realize, as Jacob Hacker and Paul Pierson wrote, that "defying the law was far cheaper than risking any prospect of unionization."

The right of American workers to unionize is systematically violated, so often and with such impunity that the United States falls short of international human rights standards. A Human Rights Watch report said that "for many employers" the modest back-pay award for firing a few union activists "is a small price to pay to destroy a workers' organizing effort." Lance Compa, the report's author, said, "Firing is the single most potent anti-union weapon. The upshot is many employers can achieve their goal of remaining union-free by breaking the law."

John-Paul Ferguson, a professor at Stanford Business School, did a fascinating study of all the unionization drives reported to the NLRB from 1999 through 2004. He found that unions filed 22,382 petitions for unionization elections but that only about two-thirds of those petitions led to union elections (14,615 of them). Unions often withdraw election petitions in the face of management's hard-hitting tactics. Ferguson found that unions won 8,155 of those elections (55.8 percent), and that after winning, unions obtained collective bargaining agreements 4,592 times. That means unions won first contracts just 56.3 percent of the time they won elections. All told, Ferguson found, workers who petitioned for a union election from 1999 to 2004 ultimately won first contracts only 20 percent of the time, and even when union elections were held, they got first contracts only 31 percent of the time.

(Employers often stoutly resist agreeing to a first contract in an effort to convince workers that unions won't do much for them and that they should ultimately vote to decertify—that is, get rid of—their union.)

"Employers have perfected the antiunion playbook in the United States in a way that they haven't elsewhere," said Jake Rosenfeld, a labor expert at Washington University.

When the UAW sought to unionize Volkswagen's billion-dollar assembly plant in Chattanooga in 2014, Republican politicians stepped in to lead the fight when they saw that labor-friendly VW didn't oppose the union (as nearly all American corporations do). State Senator Bo Watson, who represented a Chattanooga suburb, warned that if VW's workers voted to unionize, that would make it "exponentially more challenging" for the Republican-dominated legislature to approve tens of millions of dollars in anticipated aid to help the plant expand. Watson's threat made many Volkswagen workers worry that the future of the plant—and their jobs—would be imperiled.

Tennessee's governor, Bill Haslam, also indicated that $300 million in planned aid to help VW add a second production line was contingent on the union drive "being concluded to the satisfaction of the state"—that is, defeated. Haslam told Tennessee newspapers that unionizing the plant could undercut the state's ability to attract investment. "When we recruit other companies, that comes up every time," he said. Senator Bob Corker chimed in against unionization. "We're concerned about the impact," Corker said, adding, "Look at Detroit"—a reference to the city's many shuttered factories and its decades of decline. Union-averse companies, when deciding where to expand operations, often look to see how prevalent unionization is in a state. They ignore the fact that German companies like BMW and Daimler are heavily unionized and phenomenally successful.

Upset that VW wasn't battling the unionization drive, several corporate and conservative groups entered the fray. The Competitive Enterprise Institute, a group backed by business and conservative billionaires, sponsored a billboard near the plant saying, "Auto Unions Ate Detroit. Next Meal: Chattanooga." Grover Norquist, the antitax crusader, created the Center for Worker Freedom to fight the UAW; Norquist worried that if a progressive union like the UAW won, it would help bring more social programs, bigger government, and higher taxes to Tennessee. His group held antiunion meetings and put up thirteen billboards, with some calling the UAW "United Obama Workers" and saying, "The UAW Spends Millions to Elect Liberal Politicans [*sic*]." Another billboard said, "Detroit: Brought to You by the UAW," and showed a photograph of a Packard plant that was shuttered in the 1950s.

"Unions are a big driver of government," said Matt Patterson, executive director of Norquist's group. "Unions are very political. . . . If they help elect politicians who pass huge government programs, that requires taxes."

The UAW lost narrowly at VW, 712–626, with many workers saying that politicians' threats had influenced their vote.

When the UAW sought a unionization vote at the giant Nissan plant in Canton, Mississippi, in 2017, the Republican governor, Phil Bryant, weighed in by calling UAW supporters "socialists" and declaring, "I don't think we need a union to come in there and tell us how to make a better automobile." In a gibe at northern cities, Bryant added, "Detroit is the perfect example of the damage the United Auto Workers can do to automotive manufacturing." (Bernie Sanders went to Mississippi to campaign for unionization.) Nissan ran an intense antiunion campaign, and when the workers voted in August 2017, the UAW lost badly, 2,244–1,307.

This wasn't the first time southern politicians battled against unionization; they fought mightily when organized labor made its biggest effort to organize workers in the South—a historic campaign called Operation Dixie that began in 1946. The CIO sent about twenty organizers to each state; they were spread too thinly to make major inroads in the face of implacable opposition from the police, press, clergy, business, and local officials, who often condemned organizers as Communists. The police tapped organizers' phones and, to intimidate workers, jotted down the license plates of vehicles at union gatherings. They started bonfires near where CIO organizers were giving out flyers as a hint that there was a handy place to discard them. In *There Is Power in a Union,* Philip Dray wrote that "the insular South," with its "legacy of slavery, sharecropping, convict labor, and states' rights, had rejected labor unionization as doggedly as it defended racial segregation." Because of such truculent resistance, the CIO's Operation Dixie was largely unsuccessful, leaving the South an overwhelmingly non-union region that has helped pull down wages and undercut unions across the country.

As governor of South Carolina, Nikki Haley vehemently resisted union advances. In a speech about economic development in 2012, she declared, "We'll make the unions understand full well that they are not needed, not wanted, and not welcome." When the International Association of Machinists and Aerospace Workers signaled plans to unionize the $6 billion Boeing plant in North Charleston, Haley voiced similarly strong views—views highly popular with the GOP's leaders and donors. "You've heard me say many times, I wear heels. It's not for a fashion statement. It's because we're kicking them [labor unions] every day, and we'll continue to kick them."

The machinists withdrew their initial petition for a vote at Boeing, partly because there was such fierce opposition from political leaders. When they mounted a new drive in early 2017, Boeing responded with an all-out antiunion campaign that included 485 television ads aimed at the plant's three thousand blue-collar workers. The political arm of a leading business group, the South Carolina Manufacturers Alliance, ran more than 350 antiunion TV spots, including one during the Super Bowl. "Organized labor has no place down here," said Lewis Gossett, president of the Manufacturers Alliance. "We don't need them to replicate what they've done in the Midwest and the Northeast. The governor gets that. And she's taken some very strong stands about it, and we love it."

Politicians are free to fight against unionization drives, although some academics argue that their antiunion comments can so poison the atmosphere that it could prevent a fair vote, as required by the National Labor Relations Act. As organized labor grows weaker and states vie ever harder to attract investment, more governors might copy Haley's and Haslam's antiunion tactics. This will make labor's hoped-for rebound even more difficult. As unions continue to shrink in the South and elsewhere and as fewer Americans know what unions have achieved over the years, it may well become harder to persuade workers to vote to join a union.

"The local students are violently opposed to unions," said Hoyt N. Wheeler, an emeritus business professor at the University of South Carolina. "They kn[o]w absolutely nothing about them, but they ha[ve] strong opinions. . . . One of the things that happens in a state like South Carolina where you don't have organized workers is it's hard for people to learn anything about a union. . . . You don't have neighbors, friends, relatives in a union." In decades past, that wasn't the case. But nowadays, in states like South Carolina and North Carolina—in both states just 2.7 percent of the workers belong to unions—unions face longer and longer odds.

Twelve

Labor's Self-Inflicted Wounds

CLARA LEMLICH, Walter Reuther, A. Philip Randolph, Cesar Chavez—indeed, all the key figures who built America's labor movement were fearless fighters. They knew how to organize and how to mobilize. They stood on soapboxes, shouted into bullhorns, and stared down strikebreakers. They carried the fight to fields and factories, to the streets and sweatshops.

Many of today's labor leaders are a different lot. Fewer are inspiring fighters; more are cautious figures overseeing cumbersome bureaucracies. Today's union leaders often focus far more on securing that extra 0.5 percent wage increase for their members than on inspiring the unorganized to organize. To be sure, this change stems in part from the transformation of labor unions from rebellious upstarts to sturdy institutions often viewed as part of the establishment.

The labor movement mushroomed from 3.5 million members in 1935 to nearly 15 million at the end of World War II, with more than one in three workers belonging to a union. For the first time in American history, labor unions were truly a powerful force—and voice—in the nation's economy, politics, and policy making. Corporations and government had to reckon with organized labor, whether about how workers should be treated or how the nation's economic pie should be divided. The economist John Kenneth Galbraith lauded unions for being a countervailing power that helped check the might of ever-expanding corporations.

Labor leaders were potent, unions a source of social and cultural influence. Sidney Hillman, the visionary president of the textile workers' union, became part of FDR's kitchen cabinet. John L. Lewis and Walter Reuther were household names, and so was the Teamsters' notorious president Jimmy Hoffa. Workers joined union bowling leagues and credit unions, and in the decades before television Americans regularly attended union meetings and picnics. There they often sang "Which Side Are You On?" and "Union Maid," with its refrain, "Oh, you can't scare me, I'm sticking to the union." Such pro-labor singers as Woody Guthrie, Pete Seeger, and Paul Robeson were famous, while *The Pajama Game*, a musical about a garment workers' strike, was a Broadway hit in 1954.

There is considerable debate about how soon after World War II labor's decline started, but it's hard to underestimate how much unions have sunk in power, prestige, and prominence since then. As we've seen, much of labor's slide was fueled by such forces as imports that caused factory shutdowns and corporate America's increased aggressiveness in combating unions. At the same time, unions and union leaders were responsible for some of labor's decline—too often guilty of corruption, a lack of vision, increasing inertia and bureaucratization, a tendency to alienate potential progressive allies, and all-too-frequent discrimination against women and workers of color.

After the remarkable surge of union growth during the late 1930s and the 1940s, and after the extraordinary economic gains made in the 1950s, many labor leaders became dangerously self-satisfied. Too many seemed convinced that they and their newly powerful unions could rest on their laurels. Instead of remaining the organize-the-unorganized, fight-like-hell unions of old, many unions embraced a small-bore, bureaucratic approach that focused on handling grievances or getting an additional quarter-percent raise. Those matters are important, but if unions are to remain effective champions of workers, it's vital that they not lose their fight and fire or their broader social vision.

In 1960, the sociologist Daniel Bell warned of the "desiccated" aspects of collective bargaining, saying its focus on contractual details and minutiae could be "a trap" that drained labor's energy and inspiration and made unions focus less on "economic and social justice." Alice and Staughton Lynd pointed to other conservatizing influences. The spread of union contracts sapped labor militancy by taking away the right to strike during the two, three, or four years of a collective bargaining agreement. Moreover, the automatic dues payments that companies forwarded to union treasuries meant that many labor leaders grew less attentive to workers and their concerns. Many activists complained that labor had forsaken social movement unionism for what was called "business unionism," running unions like a business.

With considerable myopia, George Meany, the AFL-CIO's president from 1955 to 1979, thought organized labor was doing just fine during those years. Meany, the most powerful labor leader of his era, evidently forgot that greater numbers mean greater power. "Why should we worry about organizing people who do not appear to want to be organized?" he asked in 1972. Frankly, "I used to worry about the membership, about the size of membership. But quite a few years ago I just stopped worrying about it, because to me it doesn't make any difference." (Meany's mentality grew out of the AFL's old focus on unionizing only skilled craftspeople, a group that's hard to replace in a strike. Meany began as a plumber in the Bronx.) Meany also seemed to forget that there would always be forces seeking to tear down labor. He uttered those why-should-we-worry words when unions represented 25 percent of the workforce, not realizing that in future decades union membership would fall to a mere 10.5 percent of the workforce and 6.4 percent in the private sector.

The cantankerous Mr. Meany didn't project an inspiring or ennobling image for labor. He was frequently photographed chomping on a cigar, often at union conventions in Miami Beach. The great labor reporter A. H. Raskin wrote, "In appearance, he is a cross between bull and bulldog." Meany even boasted, rather perversely for a labor leader, that he had never led a strike or walked a picket line. For all his faults, Meany, a staunch anti-Communist, was respected for being an influential political insider in Washington and an outspoken foe of union corruption.

In the Meany era and after, many unions spent a mere 3 percent of their budgets on organizing, even though more than two-thirds of the nation's workforce was nonunion. In sharp contrast, in the 1930s, many unions spent over half their budgets on organizing new members. The CIO, which stressed organizing, merged with the AFL in 1955, and within four years Meany had slashed the number of organizers (most of them from the CIO) from 355 to 157, and half of those organizers' time was not spent organizing. (Not one of those organizers was female.) Observing all this, the sociologists Rick Fantasia and Kim Voss wrote that unions' organizing muscles "tended to enter a state of atrophy." Reuther frequently criticized Meany's leadership, saying, "The AFL-

CIO lacks the social vision, the dynamic thrust, the crusading spirit that should characterize the progressive modern labor movement."

Labor's many successes, especially in bettering workers' lives, took an inevitable toll on unions' and workers' vigor and militancy. From the 1930s through the 1960s, as millions of workers went from being discontented souls barely able to feed their families to being solid members of the middle class, many workers lost their anger, fire, and urge to fight management. As a result, many workers felt less impetus to participate in their unions and in their unions' battles, and many union leaders seemed content to have a disengaged rank and file. Many a labor leader realized that an engaged, mobilized membership might rise up and threaten an incumbent's hold on power. *Labor Notes,* a respected chronicler of the union movement, wrote that "business unionism" had demobilized unions and left workers "disarmed on the shop floor when the attacks of the Reagan era began."

Some industries, including steel, auto, rubber, and paper, became more than 80 percent unionized. As a result, many labor leaders in those industries thought they no longer needed to worry about organizing, even as company after company began opening plants in the antiunion South. From coast to coast, there were still tens of millions of workers who could have benefited from unionization—department store workers, janitors, hospital aides, bank tellers, supermarket cashiers, restaurant cooks and waiters—and for decades organized labor did little to unionize them. Many of those workers were paid far less than factory workers.

It was an era when more and more Americans came to view union members as a high-paid, grasping elite. Some viewed them with admiration, some with resentment, some with a mixture of both. In his book *State of the Union,* Nelson Lichtenstein noted that many intellectuals, journalists, academics, and politicians came to see unions "as little more than a self-aggrandizing interest group, no longer a lever for progressive change." Lichtenstein wrote, "The unions were now 'Big Labor': in the 1950s and 1960s it seemed to many former allies that caution, bureaucracy, and self-interest had replaced the visionary quest for solidarity and social transformation that had been a hallmark of the depression decade."

Herbert Harris, a labor expert, wrote in *Harper's* in 1964 that unions had lost the support of intellectuals because "the American labor movement is sleepwalking along the corridors of history."

In the 1950s, even as the UAW, United Steelworkers, and other unions raised workers' living standards to new heights, labor's image suffered a devastating setback because of rampant union corruption. As unions grew, they became honeypots of money—dues money, health-care money, pension money, political money—which were temptations not just for ethically challenged union officials but for organized crime. The East Coast longshoremen's union became closely tied to the Mafia and notorious for shakedowns, cargo theft, and violence. *On the Waterfront,* Elia Kazan's epic 1954 film starring Marlon Brando, focused on union corruption in New York and New Jersey and gave the longshoremen's union—and all of labor—a black eye.

In 1956, in a particularly horrific episode, Victor Riesel, a New York–based syndicated columnist on labor issues—his column appeared in more than two hundred newspapers—was permanently blinded when a Mafia hit man threw sulfuric acid into his eyes outside Lindy's, a well-known Times Square restaurant. Days before, Riesel had written a hard-hitting column about corruption in the mob-tainted International Union of Operating Engineers. Three Genovese crime family members were later convicted for ordering the hit.

That attack spurred Congress and investigative reporters to delve deeper into union corruption. Between 1957 and 1960, a Senate committee led by John McClellan, an Arkansas Democrat, held 270 days of hearings into labor racketeering and corruption. With Robert Kennedy as the committee's general counsel, the 1,526 witnesses who testified focused on the International Brotherhood of Teamsters and exposed a cavalcade of corruption: work slowdowns to extort money from companies, kickbacks to union leaders so they wouldn't push hard in contract talks, goods mysteriously disappearing off the backs of trucks, beatings and killings of union dissidents who spoke out against corruption. In those televised hearings, the senators—and the nation—heard about the plundering of tens of millions of dollars from Teamster pension funds to finance casinos and other Mafia-backed businesses. For years, the Mafia had handpicked the Teamsters' president and the heads of many of its locals. (Jimmy Hoffa, the Teamsters president, went to prison for jury tampering, and after his release he mysteriously disappeared in 1975 outside a Michigan restaurant in what many believed was a rubout by rival union leaders and the Mafia.)

One historian wrote that the McClellan hearings "had a devastating impact on the moral standing of the entire trade-union world, belying labor's claim that it constituted the most important and efficacious movement for democracy and social progress." In February 1957, just before the McClellan hearings began, the public's pro-union sentiment reached an all-time high, 75 percent. That sentiment fell sharply during the hearings, never to return to its earlier level.

Unfortunately, there were hundreds of tales of union corruption. Another ghastly episode occurred in the United Mine Workers. Its autocratic president, Tony Boyle, detested the stream of criticisms coming from Joseph "Jock" Yablonski, a union democracy activist. In 1969, Yablonski ran against incumbent Boyle for the union's presidency. Boyle was declared the winner, but Yablonski asked the Labor Department to investigate the election for fraud. Thirteen days later, on New Year's Eve, three men sneaked into Yablonski's home and killed him, his wife, and their twenty-five-year-old daughter. Boyle and the three men were convicted, with Boyle found to have embezzled $20,000 in union funds to pay the killers.

There is far less union corruption nowadays, thanks in large part to a decades-long federal effort to clean up the Teamsters, the Laborers' International Union (a construction workers' union), and the East Coast longshoremen's union. In July 2017, however, federal prosecutors brought charges against Fiat Chrysler's top labor negotiator, accusing him of making more than $1.2 million in payoffs to the UAW's chief negotiator with Chrysler, General Holiefield, and his wife, including $262,219 to pay off the mortgage on the Holiefields' home. Holiefield's wife was indicted, too (Holiefield had died two years before the indictments). The indictments said the money was siphoned from a UAW-Chrysler training fund. The news broke shortly before more than thirty-five hundred workers at Nissan's assembly plant in Canton, Mississippi, voted on whether to join the UAW. Nissan repeatedly pointed to this scandal to help sway workers against unionizing. The UAW, as we saw, lost that vote, 2,244–1,307.

With labor's approval ratings plunging after the McClellan hearings, one might have thought that Meany and other union leaders would take some steps to increase labor's popularity, perhaps by reaching out to other progressives. Instead, Meany and his confederates seemed happy to alienate, even to insult, many of their potential allies.

The AFL-CIO and Meany angered progressives and much of the younger generation by vigorously supporting the Vietnam War. The barons of labor turned a blind eye when two hundred unionized construction workers beat up antiwar demonstrators at a 1970 protest on Wall Street, injuring seventy people. Meany defended the Chicago police's savage attacks against antiwar protesters outside the 1968 Democratic National Convention. He derided the protesters as a "dirty-necked and dirty-mouthed group of kooks." In 1972, Meany seemed to take relish in insulting young people who were backing George McGovern, the Democratic nominee for president, a fierce opponent of the Vietnam War. Meany mocked them as "people named Jack who look like Jill and smell like johns." Meany and the AFL-CIO tacitly backed Nixon that year. As a result of Meany's actions, many Democrats, progressives, young people, and intellectuals resented and distrusted organized labor for the next quarter century. Many viewed labor's top officials as mean-spirited, intolerant, and vindictive.

Only when John Sweeney became the AFL-CIO's president in late 1995 did a thaw begin as Sweeney courted progressives. Indeed, he voiced regret, saying labor's relations with its "natural allies" were "torn apart in the 1960s and 1970s," and "the labor movement became isolated and introverted." Under Sweeney, the AFL-CIO encouraged the creation of labor-religion coalitions in several states. It formed a formal alliance with scores of professors, and it created Union Summer, which immersed hundreds of undergraduates in the labor movement. In October 1996, seventeen hundred people thronged into an auditorium at Columbia University for a so-called teach-in with labor, called the Fight for America's Future. It had an electricity rare for a labor event. Among those who spoke were Betty Friedan and Cornel West.

Michelle Sieff, a political science graduate student at Columbia, came away encouraged. "It's been very inspiring to see labor back on American campuses," she said. "Students are reaching for something right now. There's a lot of apathy, as we all know, but there's a desire to find an alternative to the M.B.A.–law school track of life." (There's been a huge recent burst of labor activity on campuses, with the unionization of thousands of adjunct professors as well as graduate student workers at Brandeis, Columbia, Harvard, New York University, Tufts, and several other schools.)

In 1996, Union Summer hosted twelve hundred undergraduates who spent three weeks interning with labor and assisting organizing drives. Helen Petrozzola, a junior at Marymount Manhattan College, went to Mobile, Alabama, where she was inspired by a campaign to unionize low-wage, African American nursing-home workers. "For a lot of students, there is the stereotype that unions mean big Cadillacs and Mafia control," she said. "Union Summer has dispelled those ideas for me. It shows me that the union is the workers."

For far too many years, however, much of organized labor didn't welcome women, blacks, Latinos, or Asian Americans, with many unions engaging in outrageous, overt discrimination. In 1941, for instance, men at the Kelsey-Hayes Wheel plant in Detroit went on strike, insisting on "the removal of all girl employees from machine work." That helped persuade the UAW's national convention that year to approve a resolution opposing "any attempt to train women to take the place of men on skilled jobs until such time as the unemployed men have been put back to work." At that time, women were pouring into the workforce, the number of women employed soaring from eleven million in 1940 to eighteen million in 1945 as many Rosie the Riveters became a vital part of the war effort. This made many union leaders rethink their discriminatory attitude toward women. Indeed, worried that this influx of women workers would undercut men's wages, unions suddenly became champions of "equal pay for equal work."

During the 1950s and 1960s, Meany not only rejected a push to appoint an AFL-CIO assistant for women's affairs but also refused to develop programs to get unions to stop discriminating against women. Barbara Easterling, an official with the Communications Workers of America, said that naming women to top leadership positions was "just something that wasn't done." That was one reason more than three thousand women gathered in Chicago in 1974 to found the Coalition of Labor Union Women, a group meant to give women a larger voice in the labor movement. Addie Wyatt, an official with the meat cutters' union who was elected vice president of the new coalition, said, "The slogan 'You've come a long way, baby,' isn't quite true."

During the 1970s, many women were asking why the AFL-CIO hadn't named even one woman to its thirty-five-person executive council. It was not until 1980, the year after Meany retired, that the executive council added Joyce Miller, the second-ranking official in the Amalgamated Clothing and Textile Workers Union.

Meany's successor, Lane Kirkland, also showed little interest in women's issues, resisting pressure to create an AFL-CIO women's department. In 1990, after millions more women entered the workforce the previous decade, an AFL-CIO economist declared that women workers were the key to reinvigorating the labor movement. At the time, there were just two women on the AFL-CIO's executive council, even though 38 percent of all union members were women. (Today 45 percent are.) Karen Nussbaum, co-founder of 9to5, a group that addressed challenges that female office workers faced, said that women often got the cold shoulder from union organizers. She recalled a Teamsters leader telling her, " 'You can't organize women, because they think with their cunts, not their brains.' . . . We ran into that a lot, actually."

———

In 1902, W. E. B. Du Bois, the African American writer and civil rights activist, noted that forty-three national unions had no black members and that twenty-seven didn't allow black apprentices. Three years later Du Bois joined with other intellectuals in the Niagara Movement, a black civil rights group, to condemn "the practice of labor unions in proscribing and boycotting and oppressing thousands of their fellow-toilers, simply because they are black."

Some major unions welcomed blacks as members. In the 1880s, the Knights of Labor, and then in the early twentieth century the Industrial Workers of the World (the Wobblies), stressed the idea of solidarity for all workers and were eager to have blacks as members.

To be sure, many employers deliberately fomented tensions between black and white workers. In the early decades of the twentieth century, companies repeatedly sought to undercut unions and strikes (and higher wages) by bringing in black workers, and sometimes Chinese workers, desperate for jobs. Samuel Gompers, the AFL's founding president, sometimes showed stunning hostility toward these minorities, even though he at times called for nondiscrimination and sought to expel unions that discriminated against blacks. Gompers said in 1899 that blacks were a "convenient whip placed in the hands of the employers to cow the white man." In 1905, he said, "Caucasians are not going to let their standards of living be destroyed by [N]egroes, Chinese, Japs, or any others."

In 1917, one of the nation's most horrific racial incidents occurred, spurred in part by white union leaders. Workers at the Aluminum Ore Company went on strike in East St. Louis, Illinois, and management brought in blacks from the South to serve as strikebreakers. Union leaders responded by "provok[ing] a veritable hysteria of race hatred," an NAACP official wrote. After one union meeting, three thousand whites marched into East St. Louis, shooting and lynching blacks and setting fires that destroyed whole neighborhoods, causing ten thousand blacks to lose their homes. The journalist Ida B. Wells estimated that between 40 and 150 African Americans were killed.

A. Philip Randolph, one of the greats of the labor movement—as well as the civil rights movement—abhorred the way that companies, time and again, pitted the races against each other. "If employers can keep the white and black dogs on account of their race prejudice fighting over a bone, the yellow capitalist dog will get away with the bone—the bone of profits," Randolph wrote in 1919 for the Harlem newspaper that he edited.

In 1925, Randolph began a struggle to win union recognition for the Brotherhood of Sleeping Car Porters. (The porters had tapped him to be president of their union because he, not being a Pullman employee, couldn't be fired or harassed.) Finally, in 1937, the Pullman Car Company recognized that overwhelmingly African American union, and only then, after years of resisting, did the AFL agree to admit the Brotherhood into the federation.* In 1936, Randolph urged the AFL at its convention to let the Brotherhood join and to expel unions that dis-

---

* A little-known fact about Randolph's Brotherhood of Sleeping Car Porters is that years after its founding, E. D. Nixon, a porter and the head of the Brotherhood's Alabama branch, helped select and coach Rosa Parks for her historic act of civil disobedience in Montgomery in 1955. Nixon, who also headed the NAACP in Alabama, helped get Parks out on bail and find her a lawyer after she was arrested for refusing to surrender her bus seat to a white. Nixon also enlisted a then-little-known pastor named Martin Luther King Jr. to lead the Montgomery bus boycott in 1955.

criminated against black workers. "White and black workers . . . cannot be organized separately as the fingers on my hand," he said. "They must be organized altogether, as the fingers on my hand when they are doubled up in the form of a fist. . . . If they are organized separately, they will not understand each other. They will fight each other, and if they fight each other, they will hate each other. And the employing class will profit from that condition."

In 1941, Randolph angered President Roosevelt by threatening to mobilize 100,000 people for a march in Washington to press the government to end segregation in war industries. Roosevelt pressured Randolph to call off the march, but Randolph agreed to cancel it only after FDR issued an executive order that called for an end to segregation in America's defense industries. Randolph's agitation also went far to persuade President Truman to end segregation in the armed forces in 1948.

Throughout the 1940s and 1950s, Randolph pressed the AFL and then the merged AFL-CIO to crack down on national unions that had discriminatory constitutions and segregated locals. Randolph got support from the famed Swedish sociologist Gunnar Myrdal, who wrote in his landmark 1944 book, *An American Dilemma: The Negro Problem and Modern Democracy,*

> The fact that the American Federation of Labor as such is officially against racial discrimination does not mean much. The Federation has never done anything to check racial discrimination exercised by its member organizations.

At the 1959 AFL-CIO convention in San Francisco, Randolph again took up the fight, urging George Meany to expel two unions that allowed segregated locals. Meany, upset by Randolph's assertiveness, angrily barked at him, "Who the hell appointed you the guardian of all the Negroes in America?" Coming out of a union, the plumbers, that was notorious for discriminating against blacks, Meany had a checkered history toward African Americans. In a slap at the civil rights movement, he and the AFL-CIO refused to endorse the 1963 March on Washington for Jobs and Freedom; indeed, when put to a vote, only two of the thirty-five members on the AFL-CIO's executive council voted to back that historic march: Walter Reuther and A. Philip Randolph.

When Martin Luther King Jr. spoke at the AFL-CIO's convention in Miami Beach two years later, he criticized Meany's harsh words to Randolph, reminding Meany that Randolph was an unstinting champion of labor for decades. Picking up Randolph's fight, King chided the assembled labor leaders for failing to stamp out blatant racism inside the house of labor:

> Discrimination does exist in the labor movement. It is true that organized labor has taken significant steps to remove the yoke of discrimination from its own body. But in spite of this some unions, governed by the racist ethos, have contributed to the degraded economic status of the Negro. . . . In every section of the country, one can find local unions existing as a serious and vicious obstacle when the Negro seeks jobs or upgrading in employment. Labor must honestly admit these shameful conditions.

Randolph was the main organizer of the 1963 March on Washington, and Reuther's UAW provided much of the financing for it. Meany wasn't even in Washington the day of the march, even though Randolph and Reuther were among the speakers. Prodded by Randolph and Martin Luther King Jr., the AFL-CIO ultimately threw its lobbying clout behind the landmark civil rights legislation enacted in the 1960s.

In many parts of the labor movement, there had been racial progress. Within the CIO, workers called each other "brother" and "sister," regardless of race. In 1941, despite the Ford Motor Company's efforts to divide the races, the UAW and the CIO pulled off a successful strike by black and white workers at Ford's colossal 85,000-employee River Rouge plant in Dearborn, Michigan. That strike caused the vehemently antiunion Henry Ford Sr. to surrender and grant union recognition to Ford's 130,000 factory workers.

For each step forward, though, there was often a step or two back. In 1944, the Philadelphia Transportation Company, bowing to Roosevelt administration pressure, promoted eight African Americans to streetcar motormen. The Transit Workers Union supported those promotions, but forty-five hundred white workers, opposed to the promotions, went on strike, preventing 300,000 people from getting to work and disrupting war production. Union leaders were unable to persuade the strikers to return to work, and the federal government sent in more than five thousand soldiers to help end the strike.

In 1959, Herbert Hill, the NAACP's labor director, wrote an article for *Commentary* magazine saying that some unions "conscientiously worked to eradicate institutionalized job bias." He praised the UAW, the United Rubber Workers, and the United Packinghouse Workers. Hill then listed fourteen unions that "practice either total exclusion of the Negro, segregation (in the form of 'Jim Crow' locals, or 'auxiliaries'), or enforce separate, racial seniority lines." Here he cited mainly rail and construction unions, including the electrical workers, the ironworkers, the operating engineers, and the plumbers.

It was not until 1964, as Congress was passing its civil rights laws, that the final, foot-dragging labor unions removed the "whites only" clause from their constitutions and bylaws. It was federal pressure and the tenor of the times, not George Meany, that made this happen.

King certainly saw the many shortcomings in labor, but he also saw it as a great friend of African Americans. In a speech to the AFL-CIO in 1961, he said,

Our needs are identical with labor's needs: decent wages, fair working conditions, livable housing, old-age security, health and welfare measures, conditions in which families can grow, have education for their children, and respect in the community. That is why Negroes support labor's demands and fight laws which curb labor. That is why the labor-hater and labor-baiter is virtually always a twin-headed creature spewing anti-Negro epithets from one mouth and anti-labor propaganda from the other mouth.

———

American labor also had a dismal early history with regard to Asians and Latinos. Sadly, Samuel Gompers shared much of his era's prejudice toward Chinese immigrants, who, in the 1870s and 1880s, were heavily employed in railroad construction and agriculture. Gompers, who went to work in a New York cigar factory at age fourteen, wrote in his autobiography that in 1878 one-fourth of the nation's forty thousand cigar makers were "Chinamen" on the West Coast and that during strikes "we had to meet the threats of employers to import Chinese strike breakers." Gompers and many unions championed the Chinese Exclusion Act of 1882, with one writer calling him "perhaps the most important of the advocates of Chinese exclusion and author of some of the most racist demagoguery presented during the anti-Chinese movement." Gompers once wrote that the Chinese "as a race were cruel and treacherous" and called them "this Asiatic contamination" in which "gambling hells, opium joints, dens of iniquity and vice" abound. A report of the AFL's convention in 1905 said, "Surely, America's workmen have enough to contend with, have sufficient obstacles confronting them in their struggle to maintain themselves . . . without being required to meet the enervating, killing, underselling, and under-living competition of that nerveless, wantless people, the Chinese."

Three decades after the Chinese Exclusion Act of 1882, immigrants from Mexico, Japan, and Korea had filled many of the jobs once held by Chinese workers. Again complaining that immigrants were taking jobs and depressing wages, unions helped win passage of the Emergency Quota Act of 1921, which set severe limits on immigration from Asia and southern Europe. But with farms in the Southwest relying on Mexican immigrants, the U.S. Chamber of Commerce persuaded Congress to exempt Mexicans from those quotas. Unhappy about that exemption, William Green, Gompers's successor as head of the AFL, went to Mexico to seek to persuade government and labor leaders there to suppress immigration into the United States, but he had little success.

As the immigrant population from Mexico rose, American unions often shunned Latino workers. Some unions organized them, often into segregated locals, fearing that these Latino workers might become strikebreakers. It was only after Communist organizers—some of the nation's most effective organizers—began unionizing farmworkers in the 1930s and led several strikes, which the growers and police crushed, that the AFL began organizing Latino farmworkers, albeit halfheartedly. The CIO, however, with its vision of wall-to-wall unionizing, eagerly organized Hispanic as well as black and Asian American workers. By 1942, the CIO had unionized fifteen thousand Mexican workers in Los Angeles.

After the attack on Pearl Harbor, millions of Americans joined the armed forces, and the nation's farmers were desperate for workers. In response, the federal government created the bracero program, which brought in as many as 200,000 low-paid Mexican "guest workers" some years. This often-exploitative program—the braceros frequently lived in labor camps—lasted from 1942 until 1964. Unions complained that employers sometimes used the braceros to undercut strikes, and it was only when the program ended that the AFL-CIO grew serious about unionizing farmworkers. The AFL-CIO gave financial backing to the Agricultural Workers Organizing Committee, a group that focused on organizing Filipino farmworkers in California. When that union struck grape growers in and around Delano in 1965, a second struggling union—the National Farm Workers Association, founded by Cesar Chavez and Dolores Huerta—joined the strike. (The two unions later merged and renamed themselves the United Farm Workers.) That grape strike lasted five years and became a crusade, which included a dramatic three-hundred-mile march from Delano to Sacramento and inspired one of the most successful consumer boycotts in American history. Two hundred UFW supporters fanned out to supermarkets and houses of worship across the country, persuading millions of Americans to shun table grapes. The United Auto Workers pledged $5,000 a month to the farmworkers' strike fund. "You're going to win this strike," the UAW's Walter Reuther told one strike rally. "And we're going to stay with you till you do." Stung by the boycott, twenty-six table grape growers signed union contracts in July 1970, increasing the percentage of the industry that was unionized to two-thirds.

As a boy, Cesar Chavez picked cotton, carrots, strawberries, and other crops in California after his family had lost its 120-acre farm in Yuma, Arizona. He served in the navy and then got involved in community organizing. Dolores Huerta quit her job as an elementary school teacher to devote herself to lifting farmworkers. "I couldn't tolerate seeing kids come to class hungry and needing shoes," she said. "I thought I could do more by organizing farm workers than by trying to teach their hungry children." Though self-effacing and ascetic, Chavez became the UFW's inspiring leader; Huerta became its chief organizer and negotiator. Chavez and the union won national, even international support as he engaged in long, harrowing fasts that drew attention to *la causa*. *The New York Times* wrote that Chavez "blend[ed] the nonviolent resistance of Gandhi with the organizational skills of his mentor, the social activist Saul Alinsky."

Chavez played a pivotal role in cementing, indeed expanding, ties between Latinos and the labor movement. He also became an icon for

Latino rights and recognition. "The union's survival, its very existence, sent out a signal to all Hispanics that we were fighting for our dignity," Chavez said. "That we were challenging and overcoming injustice, that we were empowering the least educated among us, the poorest among us."

A high point came in 1975 when Governor Jerry Brown signed a landmark law giving California's farmworkers a government-backed right to bargain collectively when a majority of workers at a farm vote to unionize. (That provision resembled the National Labor Relations Act, which excluded farmworkers.) At its zenith, the UFW bargained for about one-fourth of California's 200,000 farmworkers. The union's numbers and influence waned in the 1980s, however, undercut by employer opposition and the Teamsters' maneuvering to sign contracts with many growers. Chavez said the Teamsters were seeking to destroy his union and steal its members, with many growers preferring the Teamsters, viewing it as easier to deal with and less demanding. (The growers also liked that the Teamsters were not mounting highly publicized crusades that made them look bad.) Internal tensions within the UFW also badly weakened the union; Chavez accused numerous aides of disloyalty and fired them. The union's membership had fallen below ten thousand by the time of Chavez's death in 1993.

In 2000, with illegal immigration rising, the AFL-CIO adopted a bold new policy on immigrants, casting aside its often hostile attitude. The labor federation called for amnesty and a path to legalization for the six million undocumented workers in the United States at the time—most of them from Latin America and Asia. Labor leaders saw how these immigrants were often horribly exploited. They also viewed such workers as an important part of labor's future. "With this resolution, the AFL-CIO proudly stands on the side of immigrant workers," said Linda Chavez-Thompson, the AFL-CIO's executive vice president and the highest-ranking Hispanic in the federation's history.

Unions have come a long way. Of the nation's four largest unions, three are headed by women (one of them Hispanic), and the fourth is headed by an African American. What many critics were saying about union leaders just a few years ago—that they were overwhelmingly "pale, male and stale"—is no longer nearly as true.

Thirteen

The Assault on Public-Sector Unions

LEAH LIPSKA IS AGHAST at what has happened to her union local since Wisconsin's then-governor, Scott Walker, set out to cripple the state's public-sector unions in February 2011. Its membership has nose-dived to just eighty, from eleven hundred.

Lipska's local is the first and original local of the nation's largest union of state and local government workers, the American Federation of State, County and Municipal Employees. Her local was founded in 1932 to battle efforts to undermine the landmark civil service law that Wisconsin's great Progressive governor, Robert La Follette Sr., signed in 1905. That law ensured that there would be more merit and less partisanship and patronage in government hiring.

Lipska, a computer specialist for the Wisconsin Department of Corrections, became Local One's president when she was twenty-nine years old. Like many union members, she reacted with fury when Walker unveiled his antiunion plan, which called for prohibiting public-sector unions from bargaining about virtually everything that unions normally bargain about: health coverage, pensions, vacation days, overtime, safety issues, staffing levels, and, for teachers, tenure and class size. Walker's proposal limited public-sector bargaining to just one item, wages, and it prohibited unions from receiving raises higher than inflation.

The week after Walker announced his plan, tens of thousands of angry union members and their allies took to Madison's streets and filled the majestic State Capitol. They lofted banners saying, "United We Bargain, Divided We Beg." They chanted, "Hey, hey, ho, ho, union busting's got to go." "It was empowering to be part of that," Lipska said. "It was awesome."

Notwithstanding the biggest, loudest labor protests the nation had seen in decades, Walker managed to push his antiunion plan through the Republican-dominated legislature.

"They crammed it through," Lipska said. As a result, the take-home pay from her job fell by around 10 percent; the new law required her and tens of thousands of other Wisconsin public employees to begin contributing 5.8 percent of their salary toward their pension while doubling what they paid in health-care premiums. The law, known as Act 10, also froze their wages for two years.

The legislation so devastated Local One's membership and finances that Lipska had to forgo her $3,000-a-year union salary. Her overall take-home pay, from her job and union position, dropped by nearly 20 percent ($8,400 a year). "Financially, it's been horrific for me," she said.

With two sons and pregnant with a third when Act 10 was passed, Lipska suddenly qualified for food stamps, federal home-heating aid, and federal nutrition assistance to low-income women who are pregnant. Her husband, Mickey, runs a computer-installation business, and at the time it was struggling to recover from the Great Recession. To help make ends meet, Lipska took a third job, as a $9.50-an-hour waitress. "We cut what we could," she said. "We cut a landline. We got rid of one of our two cars. We never go out much anymore. When we go out now, it's to eat at Taco Bell. For our anniversary, all we did was go out to a diner."

Lipska's current take-home pay is around $1,000 every two weeks, after taxes, pension deductions, and health premiums are taken out. Her family frequently runs out of money before her next paycheck arrives, and there's often a mini-crisis, for instance when one of her kids needs new shoes. That often means turning to her parents for help (her mother works at a Target, and her father is retired, after managing a McDonald's for thirty years). With some embarrassment, Lipska admits that she sometimes goes to food banks. She was livid when Walker sought to win support for his antiunion legislation by saying, "We can no longer live in a society where the public employees are the haves and taxpayers who foot the bills are the have-nots."

"My running joke," Lipska said, "is, I *have* no money. That's how I'm a have."

Lipska is short and intense; she exudes warmth but is quick to anger when confronting injustice. She wears stylish black glasses and has a butterfly tattoo on her right arm. After high school, she went to Edgewood College, a Roman Catholic school in Madison, where she planned to major in music (she plays violin). She worked forty hours a week during college to help pay her tuition but had to drop out after a year because it was too great a financial burden.

At age nineteen, she took a job with the Wisconsin Department of Corrections, but she quickly grew exasperated with her boss. "He treated me like a kid," she said. "He was on me about everything." He was angry when she stayed home sick and angry when she reported to work with a bad cough. "I got lectured by my boss," she said. "I got condescended to. I didn't know how to handle it." She would come home crying on a regular basis. "My husband said one day, 'Don't you have a union?' He said, 'Let's do something about it.'"

She studied the details of Local One's contract in order to defend herself from her boss. She also took a course to become a union steward and soon began representing co-workers when they filed complaints about how they were treated. "I quickly turned it around and became one of the biggest pains in the butt in the office," she said with a defiant laugh. "Our family is not a get-pushed-around family. We're a push-back family." Because of her passion and smarts, Lipska was soon elected vice president of Local One. Right before Act 10 was passed, she became president.

When Act 10 became law, she was earning $18.62 an hour. Five years later, she received a promotion to program and policy analyst, overseeing computer services for the Wisconsin prison system's manufacturing program. She orders supplies, coordinates with customers, and ships finished products. Her new position pays $21.51 an hour, around $44,500 a year. "My take-home pay is finally back to where it was before Act 10," Lipska said.

One of her main goals now is to rebuild Local One's membership, an uphill battle in large part because Act 10 essentially prevents public-sector unions from doing what unions do, that is, bargain collectively. What's more, Act 10 includes an ingenious—some say insidious—provision that has, in effect, put many union locals out of business. To be able to continue bargaining, a union must hold a recertification vote every year and win the backing of a majority not just of all the workers who vote but of all the workers in the bargaining unit, which can mean all the workers in several statewide agencies. That's a dauntingly high hurdle. So high, Lipska notes, that few members of Congress or the Wisconsin legislature meet it—few have won a majority of all of the voters in their districts. "They knew that was an impossible task," Lipska said. "That was intentional." AFSCME reluctantly decided not to attempt these annual elections, knowing it would mean expensive year-round campaigning.

"We're technically still a union, but only sort of," Lipska said. "We can't bargain at all. We do grievances and that type of work when we can." The state used to give union leaders like Lipska time off to meet with agency officials to discuss workers' grievances. But now she usually has to use her own vacation time to do that. Lipska said the eighty dues-paying workers who remain in Local One "have stayed because they believe in the union. They are members who are loyal and diehard." Lipska often asks workers to rejoin Local One, but many say they simply can't afford the $39 in monthly dues ($468 a year) when many earn less than $40,000 a year. "Even some of the diehards," she says, "are having to choose between union dues and rent, utility bills, and basic necessities. People ask, 'Why should I join the union?' I struggle to answer that every day. It's hard to tell someone why they should give us $39 a month when we can't even bargain for them. We say, 'It's insurance. We will fight for you if you get in trouble.' But a lot of people say, 'I never get in trouble.'

"We look out for the little guy, and we fight these fights," Lipska said. "But we can fight them a lot better if we all stand together."

———

Four days before making his bombshell of a plan public, Scott Walker invited his cabinet to dinner at the governor's thirty-four-room, lakeside mansion. It was February 7, 2011, five weeks after his inauguration, and Walker was feeling his oats. Republicans had won the political trifecta in Wisconsin: flipping the governor's mansion and both legislative houses to GOP control. At the dinner, Walker held up a photograph of his idol, Ronald Reagan, and told his cabinet that the previous day would have been Reagan's hundredth birthday. Walker then boasted that his bold antiunion plan would be a watershed, much like Reagan's battle with the air traffic controllers.

A few days after that dinner, Walker explained some of the thinking behind his antiunion plan:

> This may sound melodramatic, but thirty years ago Ronald Reagan . . . had one of the most defining moments of his political career, not just his presidency, when he fired the air traffic controllers. To me, that moment was more important than just for labor relations or even the federal budget. That was the first crack in the Berlin Wall and the fall of communism because from that point forward, the Soviets and the Communists knew that Ronald Reagan wasn't a pushover. . . . This may not have as broad of world implications, but in Wisconsin's history . . . this is our moment, this is our time to change the course of history.

The day before "dropping the bomb," to use Walker's phrase, he met with Republicans in the state senate to explain his antiunion plan. He called it a "budget-repair bill," saying it was needed to balance the state's budget. Not only would it curb public-sector unions' ability to bargain, but it would undercut their finances and political power. Republicans hated those unions' electoral clout: public-employee unions had contributed nearly 20 percent of the campaign money that the Wisconsin Senate's Democrats received in 2010.

Among its many provisions, Walker's antiunion bill would prohibit the state and its localities from doing something they had done for decades: withhold union dues from employees' paychecks and forward that money to union treasuries. Walker's plan would also bar any requirement that government employees pay dues or fees to the unions that represent them. (Labor leaders protested that this would let many government employees become "free riders" who wouldn't pay anything for the services that unions provide for them.) Walker called for requiring annual secret-ballot votes at every public-sector union to determine whether a majority of workers wanted to keep their union. His plan would also prohibit unions from signing two-, three-, or four-year contracts, forcing them instead to negotiate new contracts every year, often an arduous, time-consuming process.

Because Republicans had large majorities in both houses, Walker was confident he could get his plan enacted within a week of introducing it. In their in-depth book about the war over Act 10, *More Than They Bargained For: Scott Walker, Unions, and the Fight for Wisconsin*, Jason Stein and Patrick Marley explain that many Republicans applauded his proposal, but several warned Walker that he was misjudging how it would be received. "My God, this is going to cause a firestorm," said Mike Ellis, president of the state senate.

Hours before announcing the plan, Walker met with the legislature's top two Democrats. Peter Barca, the assembly minority leader, told him, "This is going to be met with massive resistance," while Mark Miller, the senate minority leader, warned, "You're going to blow up the state." Walker charged ahead nonetheless. His plan exempted the state troopers' and local police and firefighters' unions from the anti-union provisions; Walker's critics said that carve out was blatant political payback because the troopers' union and the police and firefighters' unions in Milwaukee had endorsed him for governor. Walker denied any political motivation, insisting that he was exempting those workers to make sure they remained on the job in case other unions went on strike and the state erupted.

Walker announced his plan on Friday, February 11. That weekend, a thousand members of the state's most powerful union, the Wisconsin Education Association Council, sprang into action, phoning and email-ing teachers across the state, urging them to join protests in Madison that Monday. The Wisconsin State AFL-CIO used its new phone and email tree to mobilize labor's masses, while University of Wisconsin students pushed to vastly expand the rally they were already planning for that Monday to protest Walker's cuts to the university's budget. At a union strategy meeting in Madison that weekend, some activists called for a general strike, but that idea—last carried out in 1946 in Oakland, California—went nowhere because many union leaders feared that it would be illegal and impossibly ambitious.

That Monday, and every day for the next month, Madison was a madhouse of protest. Thousands crammed into the majestic, marble-halled State Capitol that La Follette's progressives had built in 1906 as "a temple to democracy." In a raucous march, protesters carried a giant banner saying, "This Is What Democracy Looks Like." They chanted, "What's disgusting? Union busting." The capitol's main floor became a scrum of thousands—a primal protest of drums, air horns, bagpipes, vuvuzelas, shouting, and chants. More than a hundred students camped out on the third and fourth floors, above the governor's office and legislative chambers. The anti-Walker forces swarmed onto Twitter, urging one and all to join the protests. They used the hashtags #NotMyWI, #killthebill, and #WeAreWI, while Walker's supporters fired back with #standwithwalker.

Day after freezing day, protesters poured into Madison. Some rallies attracted 30,000, some 50,000, and the largest, nearly 100,000, with a dozen farm tractors joining the action. "This is a King moment," Jesse Jackson said at one protest. "When our political leaders fail us, we must march, we must rally." Loudspeakers blared Twisted Sister's "We're Not Gonna Take It." AFSCME's national president, Gerald McEntee, told the protesters, "We know what this is about. . . . It's about making sure the only people who have a say in American politics are the well-heeled and the politically connected." McEntee later told reporters, "If they succeed in Wisconsin, the birthplace of AFSCME, they will be emboldened to attack workers' rights in every state."

AFSCME was founded in Madison in 1932, and in 1959, Wisconsin became the first state to let public-sector workers bargain collectively. The National Labor Relations Act, enacted under Franklin Roosevelt in 1935, gave that right to most private-sector workers but not to public-sector workers. Walker and his allies repeatedly noted that FDR opposed the idea of public-sector unions. Viewing government employees as loyal servants of the state and the people, Roosevelt once wrote, "The process of collective bargaining as usually understood cannot be transplanted into the public service." FDR added that it would be "unthinkable and intolerable" for government employees to strike.

Walker insisted that Act 10's objective was not to cripple unions. He warned that Wisconsin faced a deficit of $137 million in 2011 and a shortfall of $3.6 billion over the following two years. He maintained that it wasn't enough to get workers to make the two big concessions on pension and health contributions that would badly squeeze Leah Lipska and 175,000 other government employees. Although those measures would save the state $3 billion over four years, Walker said he still needed to gut collective bargaining. He argued that union intransigence would make it hard for the state and its cities, seventy-two counties, and 464 school districts to balance their budgets.

A powerful Walker ally let slip that there were political motives behind Act 10. Scott Fitzgerald, the state senate's majority leader, said, "If we win this battle, and the money is not there under the auspices of the unions . . . President Obama is going to have a much more difficult time getting elected [in 2012] and winning the State of Wisconsin." Obama won Wisconsin in 2012, but Donald Trump narrowly won it in 2016. Act 10 has badly hobbled Wisconsin's unions and their treasuries. For example, the state's main teachers' union has lost more than half of its members, with its dues income dropping by $12 million a year. Indeed, union membership overall has fallen at a faster rate in Wisconsin than in any other state since 2009—by 43 percent, or 166,000 workers. Now just 8.1 percent of Wisconsin's workers are in unions, meaning for the first time in more than a century Wisconsin's unionization rate is below the national average.

Many Wisconsinites were angry that Walker had proposed such far-reaching, controversial legislation without even hinting at it during his gubernatorial campaign. If he had, labor unions would have no doubt thrown far more resources into trying to defeat him.

In an editorial, *The Sheboygan Press,* which had endorsed Walker, wrote,

> It appears Walker's motive all along was union busting. . . . We fully support the idea of public employees paying a greater share of the cost of their health insurance and funding at least part of their own pension. . . . But the way things have gone these last three weeks, it appears Walker's motive all along has been equally focused on union busting as budget balancing. . . . Like many others who supported Walker and Republicans last fall, we are feeling like we've been duped.

Walker issued a stern warning to Wisconsin's unions: unless Act 10 was passed, he would be forced to lay off six thousand state workers. "I'm just trying to balance my budget," he said. "To those who say why didn't I negotiate on this? I don't have anything to negotiate with. We don't have anything to give. Like practically every other state in the country, we're broke."

Democratic lawmakers, labor leaders, and newspaper fact-checkers rejected Walker's claim. "Wisconsin can balance its budget. We've actually dealt with more serious shortfalls," said Mark Pocan, a Democratic assemblyman during the Act 10 battle and former co-chair of the legislature's Joint Finance Committee. "This isn't about revenue and spending. This is about finding an excuse to take away collective bargaining rights and destroy unions as a political power." The shortfall Walker faced was smaller than one faced by his predecessor, Jim Doyle, a Democrat, who sorted it out with assistance from the state employee unions that included wage freezes and unpaid furlough days.

Walker and many Republicans condemned some of their adversaries' tactics. Some protesters likened Walker to Hitler, and some at the State Capitol blocked legislators from getting to their offices and cars, forcing many to trudge through an underground tunnel. In La Crosse, Wisconsin, several demonstrators surrounded Walker's car, rocked it, and beat on its windows. Walker said that he and his family received anonymous death threats.

Notwithstanding their colossal protests, Wisconsin's unions realized that it would be hard to block Walker's plan because Republicans had such large majorities in the state senate and assembly. Marty Beil, the president of the Wisconsin State Employees Union, a branch of AFSCME, announced that the public-sector unions, "to help bring our state's budget into balance," would reluctantly accept the painful concessions that Walker was demanding on pensions and health. But Beil rejected Walker's plan to eviscerate unions, declaring, "We will not be denied our God-given right to join a real union. . . . We will not be denied our rights to collectively bargain."

The Democrats saw only one way to stop Walker: deny the Republicans the quorum needed. To that end, fourteen Democratic senators fled to northern Illinois—beyond the reach of the state troopers that GOP leaders had dispatched to haul them back to Madison. The "Wisconsin Fourteen" stayed away for twenty-one days, but the Republicans ultimately outmaneuvered them by stripping budget provisions from the antiunion bill, thereby reducing the quorum requirements. In that way, Walker won passage of Act 10.

Walker hailed it as a great achievement. Three years after Act 10 was passed, Walker told me in an interview, "The reforms have done exceptionally well in terms of the financial benefits they provided. Many people don't fully realize that the lasting reform of Act 10 is it helps communities balance their budget."

Walker pointed to what happened in West Bend, a community of thirty-one thousand north of Milwaukee. Before Act 10, its school district had reduced course offerings and increased class sizes. But after Act 10, the district saved $250,000 a year by revamping its health plan and raising the retirement age for teachers. "We couldn't negotiate or maneuver around that when there was [collective] bargaining," said Ted Neitzke, the district's superintendent. "We've been able to shift money out of the health plan back into the classroom." (Some city and county officials complained, however, that Walker's sharp cuts in state revenue sharing to their communities more than offset the labor cost savings stemming from Act 10.)

Everyone agreed that Act 10 was a huge smackdown of labor. James R. Scott, the Walker-appointed chairman of the Wisconsin Employment Relations Commission, said, "As a result of Act 10, the advantages that labor held have been diminished. It's fair to say that employers have the upper hand now." William Powell Jones, who was a history professor at the University of Wisconsin during the battle over Act 10, was blunter about the law's consequences. "I don't see how unions can survive," he said. "This bill is designed to make it almost impossible to operate a union."

―――――

If Scott Walker had a mentor or a sponsor, it was Michael Grebe. Grebe was chairman of Walker's gubernatorial campaign committee and president of the Lynde and Harry Bradley Foundation, a Milwaukee-based foundation with an endowment of over $800 million that has been described as an "ideological behemoth" on behalf of conservative causes. Grebe, a West Point graduate, Vietnam veteran, and former general counsel to the Republican National Committee, also headed Walker's gubernatorial transition committee, helping select his cabinet. Grebe and his foundation played a pivotal role in laying the groundwork for Act 10. Before Walker's election, the Bradley Foundation gave $2 million to the Madison-based, free-market MacIver Institute and the Wisconsin Policy Research Institute. Both vigorously oppose public-sector unions, and both gave valuable policy advice to Walker. Bradley also gave $520,000 to the Americans for Prosperity Foundation, a Koch brothers affiliate that championed Act 10.

The political action committee at Koch Industries, the brothers' mammoth conglomerate, was the second-biggest donor to Walker's gubernatorial campaign. That PAC also gave $1 million to the Republican Governors Association, which spent heavily to help elect Walker. John Menard Jr., Wisconsin's richest man, famously antiunion, donated $1.5 million to the Wisconsin Club for Growth, a PAC that also spent generously to elect Walker. (For many years, Menard's chain of home-improvement stores had an illegal policy of refusing to hire anyone who had ever been in a labor union.)

In her important book *Dark Money*, Jane Mayer wrote that Walker won "on a wave of dark money, ready to implement policies [that contributors] had painstakingly incubated in conservative nonprofits for decades." Mayer added that the Bradley Foundation "provided the playbook for many of Walker's policies."

Soon after Walker won, the MacIver Institute posted an op-ed that urged him to launch a frontal assault on public-sector unions. The article, by Brian Fraley, a MacIver senior fellow, said that "public employee unions skew the labor-management equation through their political muscle" and obtain better wages and benefits "at the expense of the taxpaying public." Fraley complained that public-sector unions gained "power through taxpayer paid union dues, which in turn are used to leverage policies that lead to the increase in the size, scope, and cost of government, which means more public employee union members."

Some of Act 10's antiunion provisions were proposed by the Bradley-funded Wisconsin Policy Research Institute. James R. Klauser, the institute's chairman, said, "Some people in the Walker campaign were scratching their heads about how to deal with union health and pension costs, and we supplied the ideas."

Another billionaire Walker backer was Diane Hendricks, co-founder of ABC Supply, the nation's largest roofing wholesaler. In 2011, several weeks after Walker was inaugurated, Hendricks met with him and asked, "Any chance we'll ever get to be a completely red state and work on these unions?" Forgetting that he was in front of a video camera, Walker responded, "We're going to start in a couple weeks," as part of his budget bill. "The first step is we're going to deal with collective bargaining for all public-employee unions, because you use divide and conquer." Walker said he wanted to work with private-sector unions and would never let a right-to-work law get to his desk—private-sector unions detest such laws. Despite that vow, Walker, pressed by conservative donors, signed a right-to-work bill in 2015.

Walker's antiunion crusade caused many conservatives to rally behind him when unions put a recall vote on the ballot in 2012. Hendricks gave $500,000 to Walker's anti-recall effort (and later $5 million to a super PAC backing his unsuccessful 2016 presidential campaign). The casino billionaire Sheldon Adelson gave $250,000 to fight the recall, and so did Dick DeVos, a Michigan billionaire married to Betsy DeVos, President Trump's secretary of education. The Texas billionaire Bob Perry, who bankrolled the deceitful "Swift Boat" attacks against John Kerry in 2004, gave Walker $500,000. In all, Walker raised over $30 million, more than seven times what the pro-recall forces raised. Walker defeated the recall with 53 percent of the vote.

Walker won the governorship in November 2010 as part of a wave election for Republicans at the state level—they won control of the governor's mansion and the state legislature in Wisconsin and twelve other states where there had been divided government. It soon became clear that GOP lawmakers and their financial backers were spoiling to launch an offensive against public-sector unions, and Walker led the way. In a candid moment, he admitted that Act 10 was "pushing the envelope" with its antiunion tactics. He added, "I hope I'm [an] inspiration" for others.

Wisconsin's Act 10 was the culmination of decades of GOP and conservative anger at public-sector unions. While private-sector unions had taken a drubbing, public-sector unions were going strong, with 37 percent of government employees in unions. For GOP lawmakers and conservative donors, attacking government unions was the key to further undermining labor. For them, it would be a trifecta: it would weaken a financial pillar of the Democrats, undercut a vocal supporter of "big government," and hobble those unions' ability to win pay increases that often lead to higher taxes.

Critics of public-sector unions often pointed to the hefty pensions received by some government employees, like the yearly pensions of over $100,000 for many Suffolk County, New York, police and California Highway Patrol retirees. Critics complained that such generous pensions led to problems like the $130 billion shortfall in the State of Illinois's public-employee pension plan. Conservative think tanks, GOP politicians, and many parents (including some Democrats) also criticized teachers' unions for often using tenure protections to delay or prevent the firing of teachers who did a poor job educating children or had been charged with misbehavior.

At the time Walker was first elected governor, many private-sector workers in Wisconsin were reeling from layoffs due to recession and factory shutdowns, with many losing their health coverage and seeing their pensions endangered. A good number of them resented that government workers contributed nothing toward their pensions. As Leah Lipska said, Walker tapped into that by repeatedly attacking government employees as the "haves." At a time when many Wisconsinites were hurting economically, Dave Weiland, a teacher in Oconomowoc, said public-sector unions were stuck in a mind-set from a more generous era. "The gravy train was running, and they didn't see the curve," Weiland said. (A 2012 study by three business school professors found that overall compensation for state and local public employees was between 1 and 5.6 percent less than for comparable private-sector employees, depending on which data set was used.)

Days after Walker unveiled Act 10, Republican lawmakers in Tennessee and Idaho moved to strip public school teachers of their bargaining rights, while Indiana's governor, Mitch Daniels, proposed limiting teachers' bargaining to just wages and benefits. The Ohio state legislature and Governor John Kasich enacted a bill even more far-reaching than Wisconsin's, stripping all government employees, including police and firefighters, of their ability to bargain. (Because the Ohio Constitution, unlike Wisconsin's, allows ballot initiatives to repeal laws, Ohio's unions put a repeal measure on the ballot. In November 2011, Ohioans voted by 62 percent to 38 percent to erase their state's antiunion, anti-bargaining law.) In February 2017, Iowa lawmakers enacted a far-reaching antiunion law much like Act 10.

Grover Norquist, the antitax crusader, said that as a result of Act 10, 135,000 government workers in Wisconsin stopped paying union dues. He celebrated that this had cut union revenues by an estimated $135 million a year. Noting that Republican governors in Kentucky and Missouri hoped to enact similar legislation, Norquist predicted, "If Act 10 is enacted in a dozen more states, the modern Democratic Party will cease to be a competitive power in American politics. It's that big a deal."

Public-sector unions have faced attacks not just in Republican-led states but also in the Supreme Court, which dealt them a severe blow in a 2018 ruling. In that case, *Janus v. AFSCME,* Mark Janus, an Illinois child support worker, asked the justices to ban any requirement that public employees pay fees to the unions that bargain for them. By a 5–4 vote, the Court ruled that any such requirement violates government employees' First Amendment rights because the union might espouse positions—like preserving tenure or seniority protections— that a worker disagrees with. The Court struck down an Illinois law that required government workers to pay unions "their proportionate share of the costs of the collective bargaining process" and "contract administration." At the time, twenty-two states had laws requiring public employees to pay such fees, known as "agency fees" or "fair share fees."

In an op-ed, Janus explained his position:

> Government unions have pushed for government spending that made the state's fiscal situation worse. How is that good for the people of the state? Or, for that matter, my fellow union members who face the threat of layoffs or their pension funds someday running dry? The union voice is not my voice. The union's fight is not my fight. But a piece of my paycheck every week still goes to the union.

(Later, when interviewed by several journalists, Janus had a kinder take, saying, "I'm not anti-union. . . . Collective bargaining is beneficial to people and workers.") Mark Mix, president of the National Right to Work Legal Defense Foundation, which helped argue Janus's case, called the ruling "a landmark victory for rights of public-sector employees coast-to-coast that will free" them "from mandatory union payments."

Labor unions attacked the *Janus* decision, worried that it would encourage many public employees to become "free riders" who would receive union benefits without paying for them. Labor experts predicted that between 10 and 30 percent of government employees would opt out of paying union fees. In the Court's majority opinion, Justice Samuel Alito mocked the "free rider" notion, writing that Janus "is not a free rider on a bus headed for a destination that he wishes to reach but is more like a person shanghaied for an unwanted voyage." (The Court overturned its unanimous forty-one-year-old *Abood* ruling that upheld laws requiring government workers to pay union fees; the *Abood* court viewed those laws as a way to promote labor peace and enable unions to get monetary support from all of the workers they represented.)

Dissenting in *Janus,* Justice Elena Kagan wrote that the majority decision "wreaks havoc" on thousands of union contracts nationwide. She slammed the majority as "black-robed rulers" who were "overriding citizens' choices" and "weaponizing the First Amendment, in a way that unleashes judges, now and in the future, to intervene in economic and regulatory policy." Randi Weingarten, the president of the American Federation of Teachers (AFT), said *Janus* wasn't "a case brought by individuals trying to have a voice, it's a case brought by wealthy forces to eliminate worker voice and power."

Ten minutes after the Court issued its ruling, President Trump tweeted, "Big loss for the coffers of the Democrats!" *Politico* wrote that public-sector unions were "keeping the labor movement afloat," but "now the Supreme Court just took a sledgehammer to that pillar." A who's who of conservative groups and billionaires had helped underwrite the case, hoping it would severely weaken unions' finances. The funders included the Koch network, the Bradley Foundation, the Richard and Helen DeVos Foundation, and Richard Uihlein, a right-wing Illinois industrialist.

Even before *Janus* was decided, public-sector unions were moving to counteract the anticipated result. They reached out to hundreds of thousands of members to urge them to recommit to their union and to paying dues. At the time *Janus* was decided, the AFT said 530,000 members had recommitted to the union. Nonetheless, the National Education Association predicted it would lose about 340,000 of its 3 million members.

Days after the ruling, a right-wing nonprofit, the Freedom Foundation, said it would send eighty canvassers to knock on government employees' doors in three union strongholds—California, Oregon, and Washington—to urge those workers to quit their unions and stop paying dues. The group, funded by a billionaire-backed conservative network, said it hoped its campaign would reduce union ranks in those states by 127,000 members. The Freedom Foundation's CEO, Tom McCabe, once wrote a fund-raising letter saying it had a "proven plan for bankrupting and defeating government unions," and its Oregon coordinator said, "Our No. 1 stated focus is to defund the political left."

Bob Schoonover, who works as a heavy equipment mechanic for the City of Los Angeles and heads an SEIU local there, condemned these efforts. "They're really not advocating for the employees at all—they're advocating for unions to lose their power," he said. "They want to silence the working class. It just so happens that unions are the ones that stick up for the working class."

———

Few people know the problems government employee unions face better than Paul Spink, a thirty-nine-year-old Milwaukee resident who looks like a rugby player, with his reddish-brown beard and burly frame. In 2015, Spink was elected president of AFSCME's beleaguered statewide operations in Wisconsin largely because he is so good at explaining what public-sector unions need to do to win public support and beat back conservatives' attacks. In addition to his union post, Spink holds a full-time state job inspecting children's day-care centers across Wisconsin to ensure that they're safe and comply with the law.

Spink and his union face a mountain of problems. Since 2011, AFSCME's membership in Wisconsin (which includes Leah Lipska's local) has plunged from sixty-three thousand to below twenty thousand statewide, and its budget has fallen by around 75 percent. Many government workers keep asking why they should belong to a union and pay dues when public-employee unions can hardly bargain anymore in Wisconsin.

As AFSCME's most visible leader in Wisconsin, Spink focuses on reaching two audiences: public employees and the public. "We don't have very good public relations. We don't have a very good public image," Spink acknowledged, talking in his cramped union office in a blue-collar Milwaukee neighborhood. "We don't know how to talk to our members about what a union is for. All that has to change. In the past, it was very easy to tell people, 'Join the union. We will get you a good contract. This contract will make your life significantly better.' Now the message has to be different, when we don't have the ability to just say, 'We're going to get you a contract.' Now we're trying to find that next new message."

In Spink's view, too many members of the public fail to appreciate government employees or understand what they do. As a result, when things go wrong, for instance, when a recession causes a big budget deficit, it makes it easier for politicians to blame government employees and their unions. "We are going to continue to be the scapegoats for bad policy; public workers are no one's natural constituency," Spink said. "No one is going to speak up for city workers out of the goodness of their heart. Unless we come together to amplify our voice, we're going to be an easy scapegoat. We have to let the public know what we do. How many people know what the government is doing for them behind the scenes? If you ask people, they would just assume that these massive day-care chains do everything out of the goodness of their hearts. They don't understand how many regulations it takes and how many workers it takes to make sure that their children are safe at these day-care centers."

While Walker used a divide-and-conquer strategy that categorizes public-sector workers as the haves, Spink has adopted a reassuring public-relations message: that what public employees do is good for the public, indeed essential for the public, whether it's firefighters extinguishing fires, police officers snagging muggers, sanitation workers collecting trash, social workers helping badly abused children—or Paul Spink inspecting to make sure day-care centers are safe for kids. Spink further maintains that when there aren't public-employee unions to speak for workers, that's bad for the public as well as the workers. He noted, for example, that in his department, child protective services workers used to have an average caseload of fifteen abused or neglected children, but their caseloads soared to forty or fifty. That, Spink said, is bad for children, workers, and the public.

Many individual workers were scared to speak up about the heavy caseloads, fearing that they would anger their bosses and perhaps get fired. Spink and other union officials seized the moment and made a lot of noise about the issue, testifying at hearings and speaking to the press. The result: even though Walker cut the overall state workforce by four hundred slots, he added a dozen more child protective services workers to reduce the onerous caseload.

Spink says that workers are far more willing to speak out about work-place problems and about public services—for instance, how to improve education at a middle school or reduce crime in a neighborhood—when they have a union to protect them against a supervisor who might punish them for speaking out. Without union protections, Spink said, "if you go into your boss and say, 'You should change your policies, things could be better,' then your boss says, 'Would you like to pack your desk now or after lunch?'"

As evidence of what can go wrong when public employees are too scared to speak up, Spink pointed to a scandal at a youth correctional facility that rocked Wisconsin and badly embarrassed Walker (who lost his bid for a third term in 2018). Spink maintains that the scandal could have been prevented if the facility, essentially a state-run juvenile prison, still had a labor union and if prison officials—and Walker administration officials—had listened to what workers there had to say.

In December 2015, the FBI and Wisconsin officials raided the youth correctional facility to investigate accusations that guards had beaten inmates and concealed cases of abuse and neglect. One inmate had several toes amputated after a guard slammed a metal door shut, crushing the inmate's foot. At the same time, youths at the prison—the Lincoln Hills School for Boys and the Copper Lake School for Girls—had assaulted several guards.

Working conditions at the prison had grown worse and tensions were nearing the breaking point because of severe understaffing. Its AFSCME union local had dissolved after Act 10 was passed, and many of the prison's workers quit because of stressful conditions and pay considerably lower than at many city and county jails in Wisconsin. "The prison couldn't fill their positions because of the tensions and safety issues," Spink said. "No one is taking those jobs because they [prison management] didn't listen to the people who do the jobs" to figure out what is needed to make these jobs better, safer, and more attractive to job applicants. The resulting understaffing caused those who remained to work huge overtime, making them feel exhausted, overstretched, tense, and angry.

Spink has been a state employee since 2003. A graduate of the University of Wisconsin at Whitewater, with degrees in social work and political science, he earns $44,000 a year. His wife, Hollie, who has two master's degrees, also works for the state, visiting schools across Wisconsin to evaluate the deaf and hard of hearing and to assess whether their schools comply with laws requiring that they provide these children with "appropriate" educational programs.

As a result of Act 10, Spink and his wife, like other government workers in Wisconsin, have had to contribute thousands of dollars more toward their pensions and health coverage, while their pay was frozen for six out of Walker's first seven years as governor. "Obviously, everyone has problems paying for health insurance," Spink said. "My friends in the private sector make more money, and they had bad benefits. I knew I was taking the trade-off to make less money [in the public sector] and have good benefits. Now I have the same bad benefits they do, and I make less than $22 an hour, and I have two college degrees. We have two small kids. I drive a seven-year-old car with 145,000 miles, and my wife drives a 2004 Chevy Tahoe, and that idea Walker sold that we are the haves . . ." He stopped talking, evidently to avoid spewing some four-letter words.

"We both like working with kids," Spink resumed. "We want to do community service. We made the trade-off that we might not make a lot of money, but we would retire with some dignity, and if our kids were sick, we'd be able to afford to take them to the doctor. But that all looks shaky right now."

He said things have never been as bad for his union. It's tough when "you can't just tell a worker, here is your array of features and services" from the union, such as employee assistance programs, grievance procedures, and negotiating for better benefits. "We have to explain to people that this is no longer the AAA [the American Automobile Association], where you just pay your dues and the problems are fixed automatically. Now it's all member involvement. Members have to help make things happen."

Spink is proud and defiant but doesn't hide his frustration. He and his wife consider themselves dedicated public servants, but Act 10 has not only pushed them down the economic ladder, but made them feel like scapegoats. "No one enters the social service to make a buck," Spink said. "It's because I care about what I do. And in social service, the only way to improve what you do is with the union."

Fourteen

Big Labor Gets Less Big in Politics

AFTER CELEBRATING INTO THE EARLY HOURS, the nation's top labor leaders held a triumphant news conference on November 5, 2008, and they weren't bashful about claiming much of the credit for Barack Obama's historic victory the day before. Speaking at the AFL-CIO's headquarters across Lafayette Square from the White House, John Sweeney, the labor federation's president, did some serious boasting. He said that labor's field operations had successfully reached out to 13 million union members in twenty-four states and that in just the past four days 250,000 union volunteers had made 5.5 million phone calls and visited 3.9 million union households. Sweeney also said 67 percent of union members had voted for Obama, while 30 percent backed his Republican opponent, John McCain, who often had sharp differences with unions on economic policy and other issues.

"In the defining industrial states like Ohio, Pennsylvania, Wisconsin, Michigan, and Minnesota, union voters were the firewall that stopped John McCain," Sweeney said. "In state after state, we defeated candidates with lousy voting records on worker issues and replaced them with candidates who will be champions for working families."

With regard to one constituency that tilts heavily Republican, AFL-CIO officials noted that white men overall had voted for McCain 57 percent to 41 percent, while white men who were union members favored Obama 57 percent to 40 percent. Similarly, gun owners overall backed McCain 62 percent to 37 percent, but gun owners who were union members voted for Obama 56 percent to 44 percent.

Union leaders were jubilant that day, feeling they were in the catbird seat because they believed that organized labor did more than any other outside group to help Obama win. At that news conference, labor leaders didn't hesitate to pronounce their goals—some would call them demands—for the new president and Congress. With the nation in a severe recession, union leaders called for a robust economic stimulus and job creation package. They also wanted Congress—both houses were controlled by Democrats—to enact an ambitious bill they said would enable unions to organize millions more workers and help reverse labor's decline. The bill, the Employee Free Choice Act, would allow unions to insist on a card check procedure during unionization campaigns. Card check—some labor leaders prefer to call it majority sign-up—makes it easier to unionize workers by letting unions gain recognition from an employer as soon as a majority of a workplace's employees sign pro-union cards. Under the proposed legislation, unions could choose card check instead of the traditional method in which workers vote in a secret-ballot election that takes place after the employer has typically mounted an intense antiunion pressure campaign. The bill also called for using binding arbitration to settle contract disputes whenever an employer and a newly certified union failed to agree on a contract within 120 days. One study found that 52 percent of newly unionized workplaces failed to reach a contract within one year and 37 percent didn't have a contract within two years.

Randel Johnson, the U.S. Chamber of Commerce's top official on labor policy, warned of all-out war over the legislation. "This will be Armageddon," he said. Mark McKinnon, an adviser to McCain and George W. Bush, called the bill "a political nightmare" and said businesses "are ready to riot in the street about it."

Even though unions had spent an estimated $450 million to help Obama and other Democrats during the campaign, Democratic support for labor's prized legislation was far more tepid than unions had hoped. The Employee Free Choice Act had fewer Senate co-sponsors than when it was introduced in 2007—forty versus forty-six—largely because some Democrats, pushed hard by business, got cold feet when they realized that the legislation might become a reality. In battling the bill, business groups argued, first, that secret-ballot elections were the American way and fairer than card check and, second, that mandatory arbitration would be intrusive, heavy-handed government at its worst.

(Business was hypocritical here because it often insists on arbitration in cases brought by consumers and nonunion workers.)

The lobbying was fierce. The week the legislation was introduced, 180 business executives and owners went to Capitol Hill to meet with swing senators, while 250 union officials and members met with House and Senate lawmakers. Antiunion groups ran $1 million worth of TV ads to pressure one vacillating Democrat, Senator Ben Nelson of Nebraska. By summer, unions saw they couldn't round up the sixty votes needed to overcome a filibuster. Hoping to salvage the effort, several labor leaders agreed to drop card check from the bill in exchange for a provision that would speed up union elections so companies would have less time to twist employees' arms to vote against unionizing. Some labor leaders opposed this watered-down version.

In a severe blow to America's unions and progressives and many other Americans, Senator Edward Kennedy of Massachusetts, the liberal lion who was the bill's chief sponsor, died in August 2009. With their hopes diminishing, union leaders pressed President Obama to put his all behind the bill, but that summer the White House was devoting its political juice and legislative energies to advancing the Affordable Care Act, a fight that continued into 2010. Obama asked union leaders for patience, assuring them that as soon as the health-care legislation passed—if it passed—he would push hard to enact labor's prized bill. But when Scott Brown, a Republican, won the special election to fill Kennedy's seat in early 2010, the chances of rounding up sixty votes for the Employee Free Choice Act dimmed considerably. (For many labor leaders, it stirred bitter memories of 1978, when Republicans carried out a five-week filibuster that killed Jimmy Carter's plan to help unionization efforts by increasing penalties on lawbreaking employers.)

In several other areas, Obama, despite unions' sizable role in his victory, defied organized labor's wishes. For example, he included the so-called Cadillac tax in the Affordable Care Act, which enraged many unions because it imposed a hefty tax on generous health insurance plans like those many unions had won for their members. (A 40 percent tax was to be levied when the value of policies exceeded a certain cap; for family policies, the threshold was $27,500.) Obama also angered unions by negotiating and championing the Trans-Pacific Partnership (TPP), a twelve-nation trade deal that, in labor's view, jeopardized American factory jobs and favored corporations over workers. Obama's defenders noted that most unions enthusiastically backed the Affordable Care Act overall; they also argued that the TPP was more favorable to workers than any other major trade agreement.

In retrospect, 2009 was labor's political high-water mark in recent decades, but even so unions failed to achieve their primary goal, passage of the Employee Free Choice Act.

In November 2010, the political tide went out on labor when Republicans won control of the House of Representatives, effectively killing any lingering hopes for the Employee Free Choice Act. Republicans also picked up 680 additional seats in state legislatures, the largest gains that any party had ever made in one year. That gave the GOP consolidated control of the governor's mansions and legislatures in twenty-two states.

In Wisconsin, Scott Walker, as we've seen, pushed through a law to cripple public-employee unions. In 2012, Republicans in Michigan, a cradle of labor and the UAW, enacted an anti-union-fee, "right-to-work" law that hurt union treasuries. Wisconsin lawmakers followed suit with such a law in 2015.

The GOP racked up additional gains in state legislatures in 2014 and 2016 as the Koch brothers' political network, the Club for Growth, and other conservative groups spent heavily to elect Republicans. In 2016, as soon as Republicans won the governorship in West Virginia after winning control of the legislature in 2014 for the first time since the 1930s, they enacted a right-to-work law. In Kentucky, Republicans won control of both legislative chambers in 2016 for the first time since 1920, and a right-to-work measure was the very first bill the new legislature passed.

In Iowa in 2017, soon after Republicans obtained trifecta control by winning the state senate, Governor Terry Branstad pushed through a Wisconsin-like law that gutted public-employee bargaining. "For too long," Branstad said, "union special interests have routinely won over the taxpayers." The Iowa Republican Party had made its antiunion intentions clear, its platform stating, "We call for legislation that would eliminate all public-sector unions."

In state after state, Republicans have moved to weaken unions with far more energy and discipline than Democrats have fought to strengthen them—even as Democrats gladly receive labor's money and votes and benefit from unions' phone banks and get-out-the-vote operations. The political commentator Thomas Edsall observed, "A paradox of American politics is that Republicans take organized labor more seriously than Democrats do. The right sees unions as a mainstay of the left, a crucial source of cash, campaign manpower, and votes. . . . If Republicans and conservatives place a top priority on eviscerating labor unions, what is the Democratic Party doing to protect this core constituency? Not much."

Grover Norquist has made no secret that he, to paraphrase his famous quotation about government, would love to reduce organized labor to the size where he could drag it into the bathroom and drown it in the bathtub. "Unions are the largest player in American politics, and they will be for some time," Norquist told the Conservative Political Action Conference in 2014. Giving a rough estimate of how much dues money unions collect each year, Norquist called labor "a $7 billion slush fund for the left." In fact, most union money does not go to politics. Norquist is so eager to crush unions that his antitax group created an offshoot that campaigned against the UAW's efforts to unionize Volkswagen's assembly plant in Chattanooga.

Antiunion laws have taken their toll on labor's membership and coffers; they include the right-to-work laws enacted in Indiana (2011), Michigan (2012), Wisconsin (2015), West Virginia (2016), and Kentucky (2017). Union membership in Wisconsin has plunged by a remarkable 166,000, or 43 percent, since 2009, while in Michigan it has dropped by 194,000 (to 625,000) since 2007 (the auto industry's woes helped reduce that total) and in Pennsylvania by 129,000 (to 701,000). As a result of all this, labor's vaunted political clout has inevitably—and markedly—declined. It's probably time to stop using the phrase "Big Labor."

———

Notwithstanding these downward trends, labor leaders were confident going into November 2016 that unions would put Hillary Clinton over the top. Two days before Election Day, *The Washington Post* quoted the AFL-CIO's political director, Michael Podhorzer: "Trump is making a last bet on white, non-college-educated men in Pennsylvania, Michigan and Wisconsin. That's been tried by Republican candidates before, and it hasn't worked." Podhorzer was on the money in seeing what the key states would be, but he—and organized labor—were wrong about Trump's success in winning over blue-collar whites. And Hillary Clinton was wrong, too. She was so confident about a Midwest "blue wall" assuring her victory that she didn't even campaign in Wisconsin and rarely visited Michigan.

In union households nationwide, Clinton beat Trump by eight percentage points—the smallest margin for a Democrat over a Republican since 1984. (Obama won union households by eighteen points in 2012.) Clinton's margin in union households was so modest even though the AFL-CIO had hailed her as "an unstoppable champion for working families," while it denounced Trump as "an unstable charlatan who made his fortune scamming them." In Ohio, Clinton lost to Trump in union households by nine percentage points, while Obama had won those voters by twenty-three points over Romney. Clinton won Michigan in union households by thirteen percentage points, twenty points worse than Obama had done there in 2012.

A recent academic study suggested that antiunion right-to-work laws generated the winning margin for Trump in Wisconsin and Michigan. That study found that such laws reduce the Democratic share in presidential elections by 3.5 percentage points in states with such laws. That's far more than Trump's winning margin in Michigan (0.2 percent) and Wisconsin (0.8 percent).

But labor's diminished clout wasn't the main reason Trump won over so many workers, union and nonunion. For one thing, Trump galvanized millions of blue-collar voters, many of whom live in communities that have never recovered from the tidal wave of factory closings in recent decades. Trump sensed what resonated with these voters: he promised to bring back jobs, revive manufacturing, and get tough on trade and immigration. He got applause aplenty whenever he promised to rip up NAFTA and the Trans-Pacific Partnership and to slap tariffs on imports from China and Mexico. His rhetoric was hot and visceral, and it connected. "We can't continue to allow China to rape our country—and that's what they're doing," Trump said at a rally in Indiana. Trump's tough talk went over big in midwestern communities where auto plants, metal foundries, and machine shops had closed.

But several academic studies concluded that Trump won over many white working-class males not because of their economic anxiety but because they feared a decline in social status, that they were losing their privileged positions. Diana C. Mutz, a political science and communications professor at the University of Pennsylvania and author of one of those studies, said what drove many white male voters to Trump was "not a threat to their own economic well-being; it's a threat to their group's dominance in our country over all." These white working-class men, Mutz said, felt their status was threatened by immigrants and by what they perceived as policies favoring minorities. Some Democrats asserted that these supposed fears were essentially racial resentment and even racism, that these people who were eager to keep their "privileged status" objected in particular when people of color tried to rise to their level. These studies also suggested that some white male Trump supporters felt their dominance threatened by the rise of women—a conclusion that many women saw as plain sexism, even misogyny.

Many blue-collar whites felt that their privileged status was being threatened by trade, by, for instance, the flood of Chinese goods that caused factories to close and signaled China's rise. Trump shrewdly milked these concerns. Mutz wrote in her study, "The shift toward an antitrade stance was a particularly effective strategy for capitalizing on a public experiencing status threat due to race as well as globalization." Mutz noted that voters who had shifted parties to become Trump voters between 2012 and 2016 "have done so because of increasing distance between their own views" and Hillary Clinton's "on trade, immigration, and China." "Trade opposition captures Americans' fear of takeover by more dominant economic powers," Mutz wrote.

A carefully researched new book, *Identity Crisis: The 2016 Presidential Campaign and the Battle for the Meaning of America,* found that measures of sexism and racism correlated much more closely with support for Trump than did economic dissatisfaction. The authors—John Sides, Michael Tesler, and Lynn Vavreck—found that racial attitudes "shaped the way voters understood economic outcomes." They described this as "racialized economics," "the belief that undeserving groups are getting ahead while your group is being left behind." They added that "throughout American history, the groups considered undeserving have often been racial and ethnic minorities."

The authors wrote that white voters' preference for Trump "was weakly related to their own job security, but strongly related to concerns that minorities were taking jobs away from whites." (This point echoes Arlie Russell Hochschild's findings in researching blue-collar Louisi-anans in *Strangers in Their Own Land*.) The authors also wrote that candidate Trump had demagogically asserted that "illegal immigrants are treated better in America than many of our vets" and that Clin-ton and Obama cared more about illegal immigrants than about vet-erans. Aggressively exploiting "racialized economics," Trump claimed that immigrants are "taking our jobs. They're taking our manufacturing jobs. They're taking our money. They're killing us."

In 2008, far more than in 2016, organized labor saw that racial resentment was a problem for the Democratic presidential candidate. Richard Trumka, then the AFL-CIO's secretary-treasurer and now its president, had talked with some blue-collar folks who were balking at backing Obama because he was black. Trumka addressed this force-fully in a speech to a steelworkers' convention, saying, "We can't tap dance around the fact that there are a lot of white folks" who "can't get past this idea that there's something wrong with voting for a black man." The steelworkers gave Trumka a standing ovation when he said, "There's not a single good reason for . . . any union member to vote against Barack Obama, and there's only one really bad reason to vote against Barack Obama and that's because he's not white." A video of Trumka's speech quickly went viral.

During 2016, Obama saw that Trump was scapegoating "undeserv-ing minorities," turning that into a major part of his campaign. In his farewell speech as president, Obama said, "If every economic issue is framed as a struggle between [the] hard-working white middle class and undeserving minorities, then workers of all shades will be left fight-ing for scraps while the wealthy withdraw further into their private enclaves."

———

Many working-class Americans—factory workers, construction work-ers, service-sector workers—feel that the Democratic Party has drifted away from them. Michael Korns, chairman of the Republican Party in Westmoreland County, southeast of Pittsburgh, has watched his county shift from blue to red in recent years. "Many voters feel that the Democratic Party, which they had supported for generations, has largely abandoned blue-collar workers," Korns said during the 2016 campaign. "There's also increasingly a feeling that the Republican Party has abandoned them as well, that neither party has much interest in the day-to-day economics of working people."

Trump spoke in a muscular way about blue-collar economics, about China trade, stagnant wages, factory closings—even if he failed to spell out how much he could do on any of those fronts. Clinton fell short partly because many blue-collar workers felt she wasn't their champion. Many of them thought the Democrats had become a party of the professional class, sidling up to wealthy donors at the expense of workers like themselves. Hadn't Clinton given several talks to Goldman Sachs for $225,000 each and earned $18 million making speeches? Ruy Teixeira, co-author of *The Emerging Democratic Majority,* argued that the Democrats and Clinton were foolish to pay such little heed to blue-collar voters, whether their concerns were economic anxiety or fear of losing status. In an article for the *American Prospect,* Teixeira and his co-authors had a harsh critique:

> The Democrats allowed themselves to become the party of the status quo—a status quo perceived to be elitist, exclusionary, and disconnected from the entire range of working-class concerns, but particularly from those voters in white working-class areas. Rightly or wrongly, Hillary Clinton's campaign exemplified a professional-class status quo that failed to rally enough working-class voters of color and failed to blunt the drift of white working-class voters to Republicans.

In his 2004 book, *What's the Matter with Kansas?,* Thomas Frank argued that Republicans have repeatedly outsmarted Democrats by making the political conversation focus on divisive social issues, like abortion and same-sex marriage, instead of economic issues, which usually favor Democrats. Writing a dozen years later about the 2016 campaign, Frank ruefully found that the Democrats were again falling short:

> Left parties the world over were founded to advance the fortunes of working people. But our left party in America . . . chose long ago to turn its back on these people's concerns, making itself instead into

the tribune of the enlightened professional class, a "creative class" that makes innovative things like derivative securities and smartphone apps. The working people that the party used to care about, Democrats figured, had nowhere else to go. . . . The party just didn't need to listen to them any longer.

Stanley Greenberg, a pollster who was one of Bill Clinton's key campaign strategists in 1992, wrote a searing assessment of Hillary Clinton's loss and her "working-class problem": "The Democrats don't have a 'white working-class problem.' They have a 'working-class problem,' which progressives have been reluctant to address honestly or boldly. The fact is that Democrats have lost support with *all* working-class voters across the electorate." Greenberg (resembling Mutz as well as Sides, Tesler, and Vavreck) said that many blue-collar voters felt that the Democrats too often championed trade agreements and immigrants' rights at the expense of blue-collar Americans.

As a candidate for the Democratic nomination, Bernie Sanders did far better than Clinton in rousing blue-collar voters. He did this with full-throated populist attacks—against trade agreements, Wall Street greed, income inequality, and Big Money in politics. Sanders seemed far more sincere than Trump about taking on Wall Street and fighting to raise wages. (Trump has done very little in those areas.)

If there is one lesson that Democrats should take from 2016, it's that they will have a hard time winning the presidency without making a robust appeal to blue-collar Americans of all races, whether it's a message on income inequality, trade, Wall Street's excesses, improving health coverage, or lifting workers' wages.

———

Many of the explanations for why Hillary Clinton lost have eerie echoes of Democrats falling short in decades past: the segregationist George Wallace draining votes away from the Democrat Hubert Humphrey in 1968; Richard Nixon trouncing anti–Vietnam War George McGovern in 1972; genial, upbeat Ronald Reagan defeating Jimmy Carter in 1980 and Walter Mondale in 1984. The postmortems about those Democratic losses resemble many of those in 2016, when many commentators said the Democrats were badly out of touch with blue-collar whites.

In 1969, Pete Hamill, one of the great chroniclers of working-class America, saw the rising anger of blue-collar whites. In his article "The Revolt of the White Lower Middle Class," Hamill wrote that these workers were angry at Democratic politicians for not paying enough attention to them and not doing more to improve their lives and incomes. But, Hamill observed, part of the anger was more existential: many workers were bored and frustrated with their jobs, they were getting older, they hadn't achieved as much of the American dream as they would have liked. "It is imperative for . . . politicians to begin to deal with the growing alienation and paranoia of the working-class white man," Hamill wrote. "[He] feels trapped and, even worse, in a society that purports to be democratic, ignored. . . . Any politician who leaves that white man out of the political equation, does so at very large risk."

Hamill was writing one year after George Wallace, as the candidate of the American Independent Party, received ten million votes in the 1968 presidential election. Hamill's analysis had some uncanny parallels with explanations of why many blue-collar whites backed Trump: "They want change; the America they thought was theirs has become something else in their own lifetimes, they want to go back. A lot of the people attracted to George Wallace are just people who think America has passed them by."

George Wallace promised to "stand up for the common man," sounding much like Trump, who, echoing Franklin Roosevelt, promised to fight for the "forgotten man and woman." Wallace ran for president in 1968 after Lyndon Johnson had pushed through civil rights laws that enraged many whites in the South and after LBJ had won passage of open housing laws that upset many whites in the North. In addition, Johnson's Great Society spent more federal money than ever before to help poor Americans and black communities. Egged on by Republican politicians, many whites came to resent that.

Union leaders grew alarmed that so many union members and blue-collar workers were backing Wallace, siphoning votes from labor's favorite, Hubert Humphrey, the Democratic candidate (and vice president under Johnson). John Herling, publisher of a labor newsletter, wrote of labor's frustration: "Never before has the trade union movement developed so much political muscle and organizational sophistication. Yet never before has organized labor seemed so ineffectual in combating an appeal to fear and prejudice as personified, for many, in George Wallace."

In 1972, Wallace shocked the nation by getting more than 50 percent of the vote in that year's Democratic primary in Michigan, a union stronghold, besting Humphrey and McGovern. Afterward, McGovern reflected on why Wallace had beaten him badly in Michigan, saying it was "an angry cry from the guts of ordinary Americans against a system which doesn't seem to give a damn about what is really bothering people in this country today." (Wallace's campaign was cut short when he was shot on May 15, 1972, in an assassination attempt that he survived.)

As the historian Jefferson Cowie explains in *Stayin' Alive: The 1970s and the Last Days of the Working Class,* once McGovern won the Democratic nomination in 1972, many strategists worried that he would lose blue-collar voters to Nixon just as he had lost them to Wallace. They urged McGovern to seek to put together a coalition like the one that Robert Kennedy forged in 1968, before he was assassinated: blue-collar whites along with blacks and Hispanics. Jean Westwood, chair of the Democratic National Committee, had plenty of advice for McGovern, advice that many a consultant might have given Hillary Clinton in 2016: "Make yourself the candidate of working people with particular stress on Jews and Catholics—in coalition with Blacks, Chicanos, young people, and liberal suburbanites." Westwood added that McGovern should get out in the streets and talk to "firemen, policemen, truckdrivers," visit "worker's suburbs, bowling alleys, church basements . . . amusement areas, factories," and do "talks with working wives." Another adviser urged McGovern to "ditch the movie stars, celebrities, moneyed crowds." Charles Guggenheim, a former adviser to Robert Kennedy, told McGovern, "The necessity to turn your concerns to the 'forgotten man' in America cannot be overemphasized."

The AFL-CIO remained officially neutral in the 1972 race, but it tacitly favored Nixon, even though Nixon had just a 20 percent AFL-CIO rating on the issues, while McGovern's was in the 90s. (McGovern had been a longtime friend of labor; he wrote his doctoral dissertation about the notorious Ludlow massacre of 1914, in which the Colorado National Guard and company guards attacked a strikers' tent camp, killing two dozen strikers, wives, and children.) George Meany, the AFL-CIO's president, dripped disdain toward McGovern for opposing the Vietnam War. Al Barkan, the AFL-CIO's political director, derided McGovern's supporters as "kids, kooks, Communists and other far-out 'kinky' left liberals." At the 1972 Democratic convention, Meany was shocked by the makeup of the New York delegation. "What kind of delegation is this?" Meany asked. "They've got six open fags and only three AFL-CIO people."

Running for reelection, Nixon realized that economic issues worked to the Democrats' advantage, and he worked hard to offset that advantage. "If the issues were prices and taxes, they'd vote for McGovern," Nixon told his advisers. "We've done things labor doesn't like. We've held wages down. But they'll support us for those other reasons." Nixon campaigned hard on patriotism and morality and attacked McGovern as wanting to help welfare mothers. The labor historians Melvyn Dubofsky and Joseph McCartin wrote that Nixon "merged the themes of race, crime, and welfare dependency to woo white workers." And much like many Republicans today, Nixon's vice president, Spiro Agnew, skewered Democrats as a "small and unelected elite" and "an effete core of impudent snobs who characterize themselves as intellectuals."

When Reagan ran in 1984 against Walter Mondale, a favorite of labor officials, many union leaders and Democrats were stunned when they saw so many working-class whites in Macomb County, Michigan, backing Reagan. Macomb County was prime UAW territory—a suburb of Detroit with thousands of unionized autoworkers. Like the white revolt that Hamill described fifteen years earlier, many Macomb County union members felt that politicians were neglecting them and favoring others—in this case, blacks in Detroit. Stanley Greenberg, who was teaching political science at Yale, first became well known for analyzing the "Reagan Democrats" in Macomb County:

> In the 1960s and the 1970s, the leaders who were supposed to fight for them seemed to care more about the blacks in Detroit and the protesters on campus; they seemed to care more about equal rights and abortion than about mortgage payments and crime. The resentment and disillusionment crystallized in a sense of betrayal, and the people of Macomb County rebelled. They became Reagan Democrats. . . . The Republicans had promised them a new deal and a better future, this time under the tutelage of entrepreneurs and job creators.

In essence, Greenberg is saying the Democrats made the same mistake in 2016 that they made in 1984. It's important to fight for blacks, Hispanics, the poor, and immigrants, but it's important at the same time to fight visibly for struggling blue-collar whites so that they feel that someone is paying attention, so that they don't feel forgotten or left behind, so that they feel that someone is trying to lift them, too. But even if the Democrats speak to blue-collar whites on economic issues, the question remains: Will those concerns be trumped by racial resentment?

Fred Harris, a populist Democratic senator from Oklahoma in the 1960s and 1970s, had a wise observation: the "blue-collar worker will be progressive as long as it is not progress for everyone but himself."

Part Four ◆

LABOR, TODAY AND TOMORROW

Fifteen

The Sharing—the Scraps—Economy

IT'S OFTEN CALLED THE SHARING ECONOMY, and it's often hailed as the liberating economy of tomorrow. Silicon Valley executives sound like giddy cheerleaders in championing apps like Uber, Lyft, TaskRabbit (home repairs), Instacart (grocery delivery), and Fiverr (freelance services). These boosters say these apps have ushered in a great, new era for both consumers and workers. Their message is: Bedraggled workers of the world no longer need to be chained to an office or a nine-to-five job. These apps will free workers to be their own boss and to cash in by sharing their talents (or their car) with a world full of customers via the internet. No longer need workers be wage slaves or worker drones. "Think Outside the Boss," these apps boast. You can work when you want and where you want, they say. "Why work if you can turk?" proclaims a coffee mug from Mechanical Turk, an internet marketplace where businesses offer, and workers accept, piecework jobs.

It all sounds great. But many Uber drivers and Mechanical Turk workers say that app-based work isn't all it's cracked up to be and that these gigs are often neither liberating nor lucrative. It feels less like sharing, and more like a new form of low-paid work, many gig workers say. (Gig work originally referred to jazz club musicians in the 1920s, but the term "gig economy" didn't become popular until the Great Recession as a way to describe workers juggling several part-time jobs or "gigs." Nowadays the term refers increasingly to app-based jobs.) Many gig workers complain that their pay often averages less than the minimum wage, some days as little as $3 an hour, after subtracting expenses. Many also say they need to work sixty or seventy hours a week to eke out a living. They are "less microentrepreneurs than microearners," Natasha Singer wrote in a *New York Times* profile of a gig worker. "They often work seven-day weeks, trying to assemble a living wage from a series of one-off gigs." The former labor secretary Robert B. Reich quipped that it shouldn't be called the sharing economy but instead the "share the scraps" economy.

Critics scoff at the term "sharing economy" in part because there often isn't much sharing involved. If you're driving the thirty-five miles from your San Francisco apartment to Palo Alto, it's one thing to offer a friend a ride for free—that's sharing. But it's quite another thing for an Uber or Lyft driver to charge someone $50 for that trip—that's being a taxi or livery service, even if Uber insists on calling it "ride sharing."

Many Uber drivers and other gig workers sing the praises of their platform-based work, saying it gives them flexibility and a good income. "I don't typically love driving, but the money is so good," said Brittney Barber, thirty-five, about her job driving three or four twelve-to-sixteen-hour days each week for Uber in San Francisco. (She was living 190 miles from San Francisco, and the days she drove for Uber, she slept at a friend's house there.) Many who don't earn enough on their main job turn to app-based work to make ends meet, or to make extra money to buy a car or take that longed-for vacation. A McKinsey study found that 30 percent of platform-based workers do gig work out of necessity or because their other income leaves them financially strapped. Laid off from an $80,000-a-year corporate job, Mary Acosta began driving part-time for Uber in Sarasota after sending out seventy job applications to no avail. "I'm not getting rich by any means," Acosta said, "but it's allowing me to eat, basically." One Mechanical Turk worker commented in an online forum during the Great Recession, "I have a degree in accounting and cannot find a real job, so to keep myself off of the street I work 60 hours or more a week here on mTurk just to make $150–$200. That is far below minimum wage, but it makes the difference between making my rent and living in a tent."

Tech industry executives talk up these jobs in what is variously called the digital economy, the on-demand economy, or the peer or peer-to-peer economy. Lukas Biewald, the CEO of CrowdFlower, a crowd-sourcing labor exchange like Mechanical Turk, said these apps bring "opportunities to people who never would have had them before . . . where anyone who wants to can do microtasks, no matter their gender, nationality, or socio-economic status, and can do so in a way that is entirely of their choosing and unique to them."

This dynamic, relatively new segment of the economy has gotten lots of attention from the news media, investors, and the public. There's a fierce dispute, in fact, over how many online gig jobs there are, largely because it's hard to define who is a gig or digital on-demand worker. Workers who do work through online platforms like Uber and TaskRabbit account for 0.5 percent (750,000) of the nation's workers, according to a 2016 study by two leading labor economists, Lawrence Katz and Alan Krueger, although they later pointed to a 2018 study estimating three times as many, 1.5 percent of the nation's workers, working through digital platforms.

Sara Horowitz, founder of the 300,000-member Freelancers Union, says there are millions of such workers in the United States. On the website Care.com alone, nine million people have registered to care for the elderly, babysit, or walk dogs. Some suggest that all nine million should be considered digital on-demand workers, but others say that makes no sense because those workers don't rely on platforms hour by hour like Uber drivers, "Turkers," or TaskRabbit workers.

The digital on-demand economy resembles globalization in that it has created a larger, and often a worldwide, labor pool, putting workers in the United States, Canada, Britain, Germany, and other industrial nations in competition, via the internet, with workers in India, China, and elsewhere. Like globalization, the app-based economy often pulls down wages in the industrial world, even as it creates new opportunities for workers in poorer nations. An International Labor Organization (ILO) study found that in India the median pay for Mechanical Turk workers is $1.67 an hour, putting downward pressure on what Turkers in the United States earn. Turkers in India might compete with those in the United States for such jobs as transcribing audio or identifying what is in photographs. For American Turkers, median pay is $5.63 an hour, the ILO study found, while the Pew Research Center found it's $4.99 an hour. Either number is far below the federal minimum wage of $7.25 an hour.

Uber, Lyft, Mechanical Turk, and many other app-based employers assert that their workers are independent contractors, not employees, and thus aren't covered by minimum wage and overtime laws. These companies don't feel obliged to offer these workers health coverage, paid vacations, or 401(k)s, and by treating them as independent contractors, they avoid paying Social Security, Medicare, unemployment insurance, and workers' compensation taxes. Also, if workers are considered independent contractors, they can't unionize and generally can't sue their employers for sexual harassment, racial discrimination, or overtime violations. With many Americans desperate to earn more and willing to do gigs that offer paltry pay and no benefits, "you are getting people to self-exploit in ways we have regulations in place to prevent," said Dean Baker, co-founder of the Center for Economic and Policy Research in Washington. He pointed to the myriad laws and regulations that generally assume that workers are employees covered by long-standing protections.

Many corporations turn to crowdsourcing sites because getting work done through these apps can cost less than half as much as through typical outsourcing, causing a downward pull on workers' pay, as we've seen. For example, to translate a twenty-two-minute video from English to Spanish, a professional translation firm in New York proposed charging $1,500, while on the Upwork platform, five skilled freelance translators from Argentina, Brazil, Indonesia, Mexico, and the Philippines—three of them with five-star ratings—offered to charge just $22 to $33. Biewald, CrowdFlower's CEO, has acknowledged how low wages can go, saying, "We end up paying people about $2 to $3 per hour. . . . It really depends on the level of quality that you need."

Biewald believes these platforms offer another big advantage to employers: they make "dismissing" workers less painful (hardly the case for those who are fired). "Before the Internet," Biewald said, "it would be really difficult to find someone, sit them down for ten minutes, and get them to work for you, and then fire them after those ten minutes. But with technology you can actually find them, pay them the tiny amount of money, and then get rid of them after you don't need them anymore." Biewald is part of a particular breed of Silicon Valley wizard who seems far more concerned about getting his algorithms right than about getting things right for his workers.

Beyond citing low pay and the dearth of benefits, platform workers frequently complain that they're isolated, doing work in their basement, bedroom, or car. Oftentimes, they have no communication with other workers or with their managers (which are often just apps or algorithms). These workers have an especially hard time banding together and making themselves heard by their employers, and by the world. There are some innovative efforts, however, to bring app-based workers together to exercise their collective voice and clout.

———

Rochelle LaPlante was a twenty-five-year-old social worker in Seattle helping disabled people learn to live independently when she began moonlighting on Mechanical Turk to earn extra money for Christmas presents. That was in 2007, and for ten or fifteen hours a week LaPlante did the HITs (human intelligence tasks) that she found on Mechanical Turk's website. Some HITs were simple and quick, like identifying what's in a photograph, while others took longer: transcribing audio, typing in the purchases listed on cash register receipts, watching YouTube videos to determine whether they're too vulgar or violent for children. Some HITs paid $1 or $2, but many paid just three, five, or ten cents each. At times, she could do a hundred, even two hundred an hour. "There are days the pay is amazing, and some days it's awful," said LaPlante, who has a bachelor's degree in human services from Western Washington University. Early on, she sometimes made just $5 in a day (days when there were few HITs posted and the ones posted paid very little).

LaPlante is talkative and engaging, with a quick, warm smile. She acknowledges that the work is potentially isolating, but using her MacBook together with a thirty-inch flat-panel monitor, she's often too busy rushing through HITs to worry about feeling lonely. When she signs on to Mechanical Turk, there are thousands of microtasks to choose from, with customers (known as requesters) asking workers to do anything from writing a birthday toast to responding to academic surveys to searching for people's email addresses. Helped by her knowledge of which types of HITs to do and which to avoid, LaPlante averages around $10 an hour. A Pew study found that just 8 percent of Mechanical Turk workers say they average over $8 an hour. Five hundred thousand workers have registered on the site, although an ILO study estimates that less than one-tenth of them are active.

Many Turkers complain about requesters who refuse to pay for tasks that have been completed. At times, requesters legitimately conclude that a Turker's work is deficient and they refuse to pay, but LaPlante says requesters often accept the completed tasks but deny payment, making a bogus claim that they're dissatisfied with the work. "That happens daily," LaPlante said. "There are definitely cases where it's done on purpose." Many Turkers see this as out-and-out wage theft, and some say requesters do this because they view Turkers as some nonhuman algorithm churning out work.

Many Turkers are angry that Amazon, which owns Mechanical Turk, won't intervene when requesters refuse to pay without adequate justification. Amazon seeks to dodge any responsibility by requiring Turkers to sign a "participation agreement" that says Amazon is "not involved in the transaction between Requesters and Providers" and is "not responsible for the action of any Requester or Provider." To prevent lawsuits over minimum wage violations, the participation agreement also says, "As a Provider you are performing services for a Requester in your personal capacity as an independent contractor and not as an employee of the Requester."

Recognizing that Turkers have little bargaining power, two researchers, Lilly Irani and Six Silberman, developed Turkopticon, a browser plug-in that rates requesters and gives workers a weapon against requesters who often refuse to pay Turkers. Compiling hundreds of thousands of ratings made by Turkers, Turkopticon, created in 2008, issues a red rating to requesters who repeatedly reject HITs without justification. Requesters who pay well, give clear instructions, and readily accept Turkers' work receive a green rating. Middling requesters receive yellow ratings.

"Our first goal was to give workers an ability to help each other: mutual aid," said Irani, a professor of communication at the University of California, San Diego. "But that isn't the same as voice. It doesn't mean Amazon will listen to them. But it means requesters could be pushed to listen."

Overall, Turkopticon has helped lift LaPlante's earnings. "I try to do between $12 and $15 an hour," she said. "Sometimes I far exceed that, and sometimes I'm well below." LaPlante, who moved to Los Angeles because she grew tired of the Northwest's rainy climate, now "turks" thirty hours a week, usually when her two kids, eight and six, are in school or in bed. "My husband has a job," she said. "Without that, there is no way we could live in L.A. on what I make turking."

An ILO study found that the average age of Turkers is thirty-five. Fifty-one percent work on the site ten or fewer hours a week, while 24 percent work on it twenty-one or more hours a week, according to the Pew study. Fifty-three percent say it provides a very small part of their income, while 25 percent say it provides most or all of their income. LaPlante disputes the notion that Turkers and other crowd-sourcing workers are desperate folks working out of their parents' basement. "Most Turkers are very educated, and they choose to do this," she said. "They have three children at home or are caring for a parent at home, or they have a disability, and it's hard to get out of the house. It's not just people who sit solitary in the basement. I know someone who is an attorney who does it in the evening."

Frustrated with their isolation, LaPlante and many other Turkers have done what many workers have felt a need to do—they figured out a way to communicate with each other. Turkers created online forums, like MTurk Crowd and TurkerNation, which serve as a virtual watercooler and a tool to warn against bad requesters and to share tips on how to turk more efficiently. In an innovative move for the digital world, Irani and several Stanford researchers created a virtual union hall for Turkers called Dynamo. Turkers use it to brainstorm ways to push for better pay and conditions. With more than five hundred members, Dynamo seeks to exert far more collective pressure on Amazon than the forums do. Dynamo's website proclaims, "Turkers are human beings, not algorithms." It displays a letter to Amazon's founder, Jeff Bezos, saying Turkers "deserve respect, fair treatment, and open communication."

Much like union members, Dynamo's members debate and decide on which issues to push. They have urged academic researchers to adopt ethical guidelines for when they use Turkers to complete web-based surveys or experiments. When Turkers in India were upset that Amazon paid them by check—which often took months to arrive, that is, if the checks didn't get lost in the mail—a Dynamo campaign persuaded Amazon to start paying Turkers in India through direct deposit. More recently, nearly fifty Turkers have pushed for a campaign to pressure Amazon to roll back its commissions; Amazon generally takes 20 and sometimes as much as 40 percent of what requesters pay. LaPlante is pressing for Dynamo to begin a formal campaign to create a minimum wage for academic surveys.

"I hope Dynamo continues to be a place for workers to be heard, and I hope Amazon pays attention," LaPlante said.

Inder Parmar, an Uber driver who emigrated from New Delhi to New York at age sixteen, likes neatness—he likes wearing a sports jacket and keeping his car immaculate, and seriously dislikes impolite or inebriated passengers, especially those who throw up in his backseat. Parmar was well paid and content in his years as the personal driver for a New York corporate executive, who then moved to Florida. He asked Parmar to relocate to Florida, but Parmar decided not to. "My kids were in school, and my wife had a good job in New York," he said.

Weighing what to do next, Parmar—a short, formal man with jet-black hair and Bollywood good looks, fifty-four years old, and a naturalized American—decided to drive for what was then an up-and-coming company: Uber. It was 2012, and Uber was getting off the ground in New York, having entered the city the previous year. At first, Parmar was pleased. He put in six twelve-hour days each week and often grossed $2,000 a week, sometimes $2,500, although that was before factoring in Uber's 10 percent commission and his weekly costs: gasoline ($100), tolls ($100), two car washes ($30), insurance and lease for his Toyota Camry ($400). On a good week, he could net $1,700.

Then things soured badly. Uber increased its commission to 20 percent of drivers' fares and at the same time chopped its fares as it sought to expand by undercutting the city's yellow cabs and other car services. (Uber has different rates for each city.) In July 2014, Uber cut its New York mileage rates by 28 percent and its charge per minute by 47 percent (to forty cents from seventy-five cents). These lower fares sliced into Parmar's income, although they increased the number of rides somewhat. Eighteen months later, in January 2016, Uber chopped its fares an additional 15 percent, while for many drivers Uber hiked its commission to 25 percent. As a result, Parmar said, a passenger who took a four-mile, fifteen-minute ride paid $14.80, down from $29.85 when Parmar began with Uber.

In 2015, Uber cut its fares in Atlanta, Denver, Miami, and forty-five other cities as part of its push to become the world's dominant transportation company. Since it was founded in 2009, Uber has expanded into more than 785 cities in eighty countries. It employs more than 1.1 million drivers, including over 500,000 in the United States, and Uber estimated it had an eye-popping valuation of nearly $100 billion as of April 2019. Many drivers complain that Uber has slashed fares in order to maximize market share to enable it to cash in when driverless cars arrive.

"Now, since Uber has dropped the price by 30 percent and hired so many more drivers, I'm making very little money, even though I'm still killing myself," Parmar said. "Some days after subtracting expenses, I'm making less than the minimum wage. If Uber brings in a thousand more drivers this week, they will tell everyone to welcome them, but the business is being depleted. There's one pie." Parmar complained that the pie was shared by twenty thousand drivers in 2014 and then thirty thousand in 2015, with the number of Uber, Lyft, and other app-based drivers in New York jumping to more than eighty thousand in 2018.

Parmar was especially galled by Uber's insistence that drivers' income would increase as a result of the fare cuts. After the 2016 cuts, Uber said its New York drivers were spending 39 percent less time between trips and earning more, not less, money. "I don't see how they can say drivers are making more money," Parmar said. He went to Uber's New York headquarters, in Queens, to complain about the fare cuts: "I told them, 'I'm not selling apples, I'm not selling donuts. I'm driving a car. I can do fifteen or sixteen rides a night. If the price is 30 percent less, I get paid 30 percent less.' They said the cheaper the price, the more customers you'll have. I can't drive a hundred customers a night. I'm not a machine. I cannot work eighteen hours a day." With a son in college and a daughter in graduate school, Parmar was hurting. When he grossed $2,000 a week with Uber, he netted around $1,400 a week ($72,800 per year), almost $20 an hour. But after two rounds of fare cuts, his weekly gross slipped to around $1,500 and his net to $900 ($46,800 per year). That translated to $12.50 an hour.

Parmar was earning far below the $27.70 an hour that two researchers—Alan Krueger, a Princeton economist, and Jonathan Hall, Uber's director of policy research—found to be the median gross pay (before expenses) for Uber drivers in New York in a January 2015 analysis. That comes to $58,000 a year for a forty-hour-a-week driver, far below the $90,000 a year that Uber falsely boasted that its New York drivers averaged. (Uber agreed to pay $20 million to settle a Federal Trade Commission lawsuit that accused it of misleading drivers in New York and San Francisco about pay levels.) According to Krueger and Hall's Uber-sponsored study, the median gross for Uber drivers in twenty cities was around $17.40 an hour ($16 in Chicago and just under $17 in Los Angeles). This was before Uber cut fares in forty-eight cities in early 2015. A 2016 study done by *BuzzFeed* found that Uber drivers earned just $13.17 an hour after expenses in Denver, $10.75 in Houston, and $8.77 in Detroit. And in 2018, the economist Lawrence Mishel found that Uber drivers averaged $11.77 an hour nationwide after expenses and just $10.87 after subtracting contributions for Social Security and Medicare.

Parmar insists that it's wrong for Uber to treat him as an independent contractor rather than an employee. This means Uber doesn't offer him health insurance or pay the employer's 6.2 percent share of Social Security taxes. Unlike most drivers, he is lucky that his spouse—she's a loan officer for a bank—has a job that provides family health insurance. "Uber is taking so much money from us, and they control our jobs," Parmar said. "The only independence we have is the time we work. I can start any time, and I can stop any time. Everything else is controlled by Uber." But Uber insists that most drivers prefer being independent contractors because it gives them flexibility. It says it would assign them their schedule if they were deemed employees.

Many drivers say working for Uber is fun because they meet lots of different people, but Parmar complains that many passengers act like spoiled brats. "I was tired of dealing with the way people treated me, with the dirty language," he said. "It's cheap to do UberX [the low-cost service most customers use]. Everyone is using it. They think that by paying $10 or $15 for a ride, they have a driver who is a slave to them for fifteen minutes. Young people get upset and sometimes yell at me because I get stuck in traffic. This is New York City. It's not the driver's fault. Some yell at me because I don't use Waze [a navigation app that helps drivers avoid traffic jams]. But if a police officer sees me holding my phone to use Waze, it's a $450 fine and five points on my license."

Frustrated with a string of long, low-paying weeks, Parmar decided to quit driving full-time for UberX. He switched to a friend's black-car service that pays far more and has him drive a recording company executive for thirty hours a week. He also drives for Uber's more expensive black-car service for twenty-five hours a week. (He likes that Uber's black-car customers are more polite and far less likely to be drunk.) "I had to work like a horse at UberX," Parmar says, "and I made very little money. I couldn't survive on that type of money."

———

When factory workers or office workers grow angry about stingy pay or bullying bosses, it's usually easy for them to complain to each other and discuss how to respond, whether in the office or perhaps in the employee cafeteria or a bar. For today's platform-based gig workers, though, with so many of them working from home, things are far different. Spread across the country, even the world, hunched over their computer screens, these workers rarely know each other, see each other, or talk to each other (except in various web forums). But as we saw with Rochelle LaPlante and other Mechanical Turk workers, there are some incipient efforts to band together in the gigosphere. While many obstacles exist for these workers to join together—TaskRabbit even warns its workers not to communicate with each other—their pay and working conditions are sometimes so awful that some effort to join together and speak out seems inevitable. Still, it isn't easy, because, as one professor put it, there is a pronounced power asymmetry between the platform owners, who hold all four aces, and the workers, who hold none.

Moshe Marvit, a writer who briefly toiled as a Turker, described the work in terms usually reserved for sweatshops from early last century. "Mechanical Turk may have created the most unregulated labor marketplace that has ever existed," he wrote. "Inside the machine, there is an overabundance of labor, extreme competition among workers, monotonous and repetitive work, exceedingly low pay and a great deal of scamming. In this virtual world, the disparities of power in employment relationships are magnified many times over." Janice Bellace, a Wharton Business School professor, likened it to "industrial homework," much like the garment workers of 120 years ago who sewed and stitched at home for twelve hours a day, hunched over their sewing machines inside their dark, crowded apartments.

Turkopticon was a trailblazing step to give some voice and power to platform-based workers so they could pressure requesters to improve their ways. That was followed by Dynamo, which its founders saw as a virtual union hall. "I want to help ordinary workers create a collective voice that has to be heard," said Lilly Irani, one of Dynamo's founders. Another Dynamo founder, Michael Bernstein, a Stanford University professor of computer science, added, "It's easy to come together online, act upset, and blow smoke. We wanted to take it to the next level: What does it take to come together to transform that energy into decisions and the pursuit of common goals?"

One respected advocacy group, the National Domestic Workers Alliance, which has done trailblazing work organizing nannies and housekeepers, stepped in to give a boost to Care.com's many workers—nine million have signed up for work on the site. The group got Care.com to agree to post a "Fair Care Pledge" on its website, a pledge that Care.com's eleven million customers could see and commit to. The pledge requires households to treat their workers with respect and sign a formal agreement that calls for paying at least $15 an hour and providing paid sick days, paid holidays, and paid vacation. More than 200,000 Care.com customers have signed the pledge (although it is often delicate and difficult for nannies or housekeepers, many of them immigrants with flawed English, to push their employers to comply with every part of the Fair Care Pledge).

In another innovative effort, eight German crowdsourcing companies, including Clickworker and Testbirds, adopted a code of conduct in February 2017 that pledged to treat workers with respect, pay them fairly and promptly, provide a user-friendly platform, and comply with the law. They also promised to provide a detailed description of the tasks requested and a fair estimate of how much time those tasks required. The companies said they wanted to "create a basis for a trusting and fair cooperation" between companies, clients, and crowdworkers. (Labor advocates urged the eight companies to commit to paying at least the statutory minimum wage, but the companies balked.)

Soon after, several labor unions from the United States, Germany, Sweden, Denmark, and Austria issued what they called the "Frankfurt Paper on Platform-Based Work." Going beyond the German companies' code of conduct, the unions called on crowdsourcing companies worldwide to guarantee (1) fair treatment, (2) payment of the statutory minimum wage (after subtracting expenses), (3) not to misclassify workers as independent contractors, and (4) a right to unionize and bargain collectively (even for independent contractors). In their statement, the unions invoked the ILO's founding principle, "Labor is not a commodity," adding, "We believe that information technology, shaped wisely, holds great promise for expanding access to good work."

Within the platform economy in the United States, Uber, with its more than 500,000 drivers, is by far the largest employer. As we've seen, Uber views itself simply as a technology platform (and not an employer) and its drivers as independent contractors. Because there are so many Uber drivers and because they, unlike many app-based workers, are not isolated in front of their MacBooks and PCs, it shouldn't be a surprise that the biggest explosion of organizing among on-demand workers has come from them. Unlike TaskRabbit or Mechanical Turk workers, Uber drivers often get to meet each other and complain to each other, often while waiting in airports. In numerous cities, angry drivers have joined together to picket and protest Uber's fare cuts. Union organizers took notice and viewed Uber's drivers as a field ripe for harvesting.

In New York City, organizers from four different unions—the Machinists, the International Brotherhood of Electrical Workers, the New York Taxi Workers Alliance, and the Amalgamated Transit Union—have tripped over each other trying to unionize Uber drivers. As of this writing, none of the unions has held a formal union election. In a surprising move, the International Association of Machinists and Uber announced in 2016 that they were cooperating to set up a group called the Independent Drivers Guild to represent New York's Uber drivers. The guild meets quarterly with Uber officials to discuss concerns, although their agreement bars the guild from bargaining over fares. Under the agreement, Uber is helping finance the group, a move that has caused some drivers and labor experts to call the guild a company union in cahoots with Uber, an assertion that guild officials deny.

James Conigliaro Jr., the Machinists official who founded the guild, defended his effort. "The drivers need help, and they need help now," he said. Conigliaro argued that the guild has made some important strides, like helping persuade New York's taxi commission to require Uber to put a tip option on its app.

Although they are rivals, the New York Taxi Workers Alliance and the Drivers Guild persuaded the New York City Council to enact the nation's first minimum hourly pay rate for app-based drivers as well as the first cap on the number of e-hailing vehicles in a major American city. That action, taken in August 2018, came after six New York livery drivers had committed suicide the previous year, with several complaining that the city was so saturated with Uber, Lyft, and other drivers that they were earning far too little to support their families. In December 2018, the city's Taxi and Limousine Commission set the minimum hourly pay for e-hailing drivers at $17.22 an hour, after expenses. Many Uber and Lyft drivers across the United States are hoping that their cities will copy New York and adopt a minimum hourly pay rate.

Probably the most effective effort to organize e-hailing drivers has been in Seattle, where drivers, aided by some inventive Teamster organizers, have formed the App-Based Drivers Association. One particularly unpopular move by Uber there spurred the Seattle drivers to organize; it cut fares from $2.35 a mile to $1.10. "That killed us," said Don Creery, who said his average earnings fell from around $20 an hour to $13. To offset that loss, he has been working longer days. "The flexibility they boast about evaporates as the pay goes down," Creery said. "There is not much flexibility if you have to drive ten or twelve hours a day."

Pushed by hundreds of Uber and Lyft drivers as well as the Teamsters union, the Seattle City Council unanimously approved the first law in the nation that expressly permits app-based "independent contractor" drivers to unionize. Under the measure, adopted in December 2015, Uber, Lyft, and other e-hailing companies are required to give the City of Seattle a list of their drivers, which union organizers would then have access to. Then, if a union wins the backing of a majority of a company's drivers, that company will have to bargain with the union. (Not surprisingly, Uber and Lyft drivers from many other cities have contacted Teamster organizers in Seattle to ask for guidance in enacting similar statutes.)

Lyft complained that the law "imposes" higher costs on passengers and "threatens the privacy of drivers" by letting unions obtain drivers' names and contact information. Uber sued to overturn the law, asserting that it was preempted by the National Labor Relations Act, which governs unionization efforts by private-sector workers. Uber also maintained that if independent contractor drivers joined together to push for higher fares, that would constitute price-fixing in violation of federal antitrust laws. The Teamsters and the City of Seattle argued that cities and states are free to enact laws to let independent contractors unionize (as is the case with farmworkers and government employees) because the National Labor Relations Act specifically exempts independent contractors from coverage. The Teamsters also asserted that the drivers' efforts to cooperate to raise fares wouldn't violate antitrust laws because cities can act in anti-competitive ways if state policy backs those actions. The Ninth Circuit Court of Appeals ruled that the Seattle law was not preempted by the National Labor Relations Act because the drivers are independent contractors. That court ruled, however, that because Washington's state legislature had not articulated any clear policy supporting Seattle's driver unionization law, that law doesn't appear to be protected by the so-called state action immunity defense.

This issue is likely to be litigated for years and could play a huge role in determining the extent to which online workers will be able to pressure their employers. That's precisely why the labor unions' Frankfurt paper calls for overhauling laws that prohibit independent contractors from unionizing and bargaining collectively. Under U.S. law, independent contractors are not allowed to join together to pressure and bargain with specific employers, but they are generally permitted to come together to push for legislation that helps them, by, for example, setting rates.

Creery, the Uber driver, is excited about the Seattle law and the prospect of having a union. "Without a union we can't do nothing," Creery told me. "Uber, they suck your blood like a vampire. I have faith that perhaps we can make these good jobs again."

Sixteen

The Fight for $15

THE LEADERS of the Service Employees International Union were boiling with frustration. The union's members had campaigned hard and the union had spent heavily to elect Barack Obama. And thanks to its many organizing drives, the SEIU, one of the nation's largest and most dynamic unions, had been far more successful adding members than most other unions. Yet its leaders were convinced that things were heading in the wrong direction—for workers, unions, and the nation.

It was late 2010, and the SEIU's leaders were distressed that the percentage of workers in private-sector unions was continuing to slide, to the lowest level in a century. Their huge hopes for Obama—that he would usher in far-reaching improvements for American workers and unions—had not come to pass. True, Obama had gotten the Affordable Care Act passed, reducing the number of uninsured by twenty million. But wages remained stagnant, forty-five million Americans were still in poverty, and unions were in a defensive crouch. Even though the nation wasn't close to recovering from the Great Recession, the policy conversation in Washington was focused not on creating jobs and raising wages, as SEIU officials had hoped, but on reducing the budget deficit, shrinking government, and trimming Medicare and Social Security.

Mary Kay Henry, the SEIU's president, was eager to reset the nation's conversation and trajectory in a more worker-friendly direction, an audacious goal. The SEIU, though, with nearly two million members and an annual budget of $300 million, knows how to throw its weight around.

"We were trying to figure out a way to flip the conversation," said

Scott Courtney, the SEIU's organizing director at the time. The union's big concern, he said, was that "just 7 percent of private-sector workers were in unions, and there was no way to organize workers on scale."

Labor's traditional model wasn't getting the job done, the SEIU's leaders agreed. A decade earlier, Courtney oversaw the union's operations in Ohio, West Virginia, and Kentucky, and by most measures he was quite successful there. The SEIU held unionization elections at thirty-five to forty nursing homes a year in those states, winning all but two or three of them, adding around fifteen hundred members annually. Still, a thousand nursing homes in Ohio remained nonunion.

"We're not affecting people's lives enough unionizing one business at a time," Courtney said. When the SEIU organizes those nursing homes and battles to get union contracts for each one, he explained, "You fight for nickels and dimes. Maybe you're getting a 3 percent raise every year. Three percent on ten bucks an hour is thirty cents. That's not changing anybody's life."

The SEIU had far greater ambitions; it wanted a strategy that would lift millions of workers. In 2011, the union launched a $50 million campaign, the Fight for a Fair Economy, in seventeen cities, including Cleveland, Detroit, Milwaukee, and Pittsburgh. Organizers went door to door in working-class neighborhoods to ask people about their economic problems and to urge them to get involved in efforts to fight poverty and help workers. The effort never caught fire. Indeed, it was eclipsed by the Occupy movement, which with its offbeat encampments, confrontations with the police, and inequality-is-out-of-control rhetoric, got attention aplenty for several months. The Occupy movement soon burned out, however, partly because it eschewed any formal structure. Before then, though, it injected the concepts of the 1 percent and the 99 percent into the national conversation, and it made millions of Americans realize how huge income inequality had grown.

When the Fight for a Fair Economy fell flat, the SEIU searched for another strategy, which led to Brooklyn. There, a grassroots group, New York Communities for Change, was knocking on hundreds of doors, asking low-income New Yorkers to sign a petition urging city officials to provide more affordable housing. The canvassers were surprised to discover that so many poor New Yorkers were fast-food workers, many of them overflowing with complaints about their meager wages and part-time hours. Courtney held a brainstorming session with Jon

Kest, the executive director of New York Communities for Change, and they hatched an idea: Why not begin a campaign to mobilize New York City's sixty-five thousand fast-food workers and, ultimately, the nation's nearly four million fast-food workers? That idea would turn into the biggest, most successful labor effort in decades: the Fight for $15. "We were hoping," said Henry, the SEIU's president, "to create conditions for breakthrough organizing—to spark the CIO moment of the twenty-first century to do mass-based organizing."

The SEIU and New York Communities for Change hired three dozen organizers to revisit many apartments, knock on new doors, and visit dozens of fast-food restaurants—all to urge people to join this budding movement. The movement held its first meeting in August 2012, with forty or so workers from McDonald's, Domino's, Burger King, KFC, and other chains gathering inside a teachers' union hall in downtown Brooklyn.

"When we got into that room, they were all saying the same thing," said Kendall Fells, the Fight for $15's organizing director. "Many workers were angry about their pay. You had people working ten-plus years making $7.25 an hour [the federal minimum wage], and you had workers starting out and making $7.25. Another big issue was unfair firings. One lady had been fired for eating a chicken nugget. One drank water out of a medium water cup instead of a small [one], and they fired her. I remember a guy standing up and saying, 'I make so little, and I'm struggling, and look at all the burns on my arm.' Then everybody in the room said, 'That's nothing. Look at me.' Everyone raised up their arms, showing burns. Some workers lived in homeless shelters, some were couch surfing, some slept four, five, six, seven in a one-bedroom apartment. Fast-food workers, no matter where they were in the city, no matter what brand they worked for, everybody had the same issues." The workers left that meeting fired up, with a fast-growing sense of solidarity.

At the second meeting, held one September evening, some seventy-five workers debated what their wage demands should be. "Some people at the meeting said $15, and some believed that was crazy, you would never get $15," said Alvin Major, a father of four who juggled part-time jobs at three different KFC restaurants. "Some people were even saying $20, some $25. Then people said $10, but that was too little. It came back to $15. That's enough to survive on. Fifteen is a great number."

Fells explained that the workers agreed on that number because "they thought, 'It would more than double my pay. I could figure out how to make ends meet. I think $15 may be enough to have a life and have the necessities.' It was as simple as that. It wasn't an MIT calculation." Strategists with the SEIU and New York Communities for Change also thought $15 was the right amount to ask for. They shrewdly recognized that a hugely ambitious figure like $15 would inspire—and excite— many fast-food workers.

That night, it was clear that many workers wanted a labor union. One woman who had worked at Windows on the World, the renowned restaurant atop the World Trade Center, before the September 11 terrorist attacks told the group that when workers have a union, they get a lot more and are treated better. The discussion was left vague and unresolved about how they might unionize. Would they hold individual unionization elections at hundreds of McDonald's and hope to get contracts at each one? Or might they somehow pressure McDonald's to grant union recognition in one fell swoop to workers at all of its restaurants in a certain city or state?

At a third meeting, held in October, the hundred fast-food attendees "realized that $15 and a union was a tall order," Fells said. "They realized they had to do something drastic." Many said they were willing, even eager, to go on strike. Those workers, and the Fight for $15's strategists, remembered how direct action by the Occupy movement had gotten so much attention. But the notion of fast-food workers going on strike spurred some worries. "Strikes are traditionally held at places that are already unionized, that already have a core of folks there for decades," said Jonathan Westin, then the organizing director for New York Communities for Change. "This was something completely different."

The workers agreed to strike anyway. All told, organizers had to knock on ten thousand doors to find two hundred workers who would commit to walking out. "Some folks were scared they'd be fired," Westin said. "But some weren't scared—it was kind of 'What do I have to lose? I'm already making the least money I can possibly make.'" The Fight for $15's workers and organizers decided against deploying labor's traditional weapon of an open-ended strike. They opted instead for a one-day walkout; that way they hoped to attract plenty of attention without having workers suffer the pain and privation that strikers experience during a lengthy walkout. (There was also far less risk that management would replace the strikers.)

The first strike was scheduled for November 29, 2012. As that date approached, the movement's workers and organizers had a sense of diving into the unknown. "There was a commitment to take a Hail Mary and go for fifteen and a union, to put the whole thing out there," said Héctor Figueroa, president of a large SEIU building service workers' local in New York that provided crucial early help to the Fight for $15. "Whenever you call on workers to strike, it can flop. We were worried the workers wouldn't strike. We were worried it wouldn't get much attention. We were worried the companies would respond by just cold firing everybody that participated."

The Fight for $15 went live at 6:30 a.m. at a McDonald's on Madison Avenue and Fortieth Street in Manhattan. Out front, dozens of fast-food workers from Manhattan, Brooklyn, and the Bronx gathered before sunup. They chanted, "Hey, hey, what do you say? We demand fair pay." Half a dozen TV crews were on hand. One of those chanting was Raymond Lopez, an aspiring actor who worked at that McDonald's. "In this job, having a union would really be a dream come true," said Lopez, who, earning $8.75 an hour, felt woefully underpaid. "It really is living in poverty."

Within hours, New York was abuzz about this highly unusual strike. Who ever heard of fast-food workers walking out? It was all over Twitter and Facebook. Democratic mayoral candidates tweeted out praise. *The New York Times* called it "the biggest wave of job actions in the history of America's fast-food industry."

At noon, a hundred fast-food workers protested outside a Wendy's on Thirty-fourth Street, just north of Madison Square Garden and Penn Station. Pamela Waldron, a mother of two, told reporters that she earned just $7.75 an hour after eight years at a nearby KFC. She complained that she was assigned only twenty hours of work a week, yielding income of just $8,000 a year. "I have two kids under six, and I don't earn enough to buy food for them," Waldron said. As she talked, workers chanted, "How can we survive on seven twenty-five?"

At six that evening, five hundred protesters gathered outside the lavishly lit flagship McDonald's on Forty-Second Street, just west of Times Square. Many allies joined the fast-food workers: janitors, supermarket clerks, construction workers, ministers, even some professors. The crowd shouted, "Hey, hey, ho, ho, seven-twenty-five has got to go!" All told, two hundred fast-food workers went on strike that day at twenty-seven restaurants across the city. It was a big story on the 6 p.m. and 11 p.m. local news.

"The first strike was great," said Alvin Major, the KFC worker. "A lot of people got involved." Figueroa, the SEIU leader, said, "It was like the garment workers' strikes of the early twentieth century. It really captured the imagination."

But a lot more work remained to be done.

——————

Adriana Alvarez was in a bad state. She had just given birth to her first child, she and her longtime boyfriend had broken up, and she wasn't making ends meet from her thirty-hour-a-week job at McDonald's. Her pay had been stuck at $8.50 an hour for two years. "I felt there was no purpose in life," Alvarez said. "I was at a dead-end job, and I couldn't do anything about it. You're at work, miserable, and then you go home with a miserable check."

One afternoon an organizer with the Fight for $15 visited her McDonald's, along a drab, commercial strip in Cicero, Illinois, a gritty, blue-collar town just west of Chicago. He approached her, and Alvarez, twenty-three, with long raven-black hair and penetrating dark eyes, waved him away because she was busy working the front counter. When her shift ended, he was waiting in the parking lot. He chatted up Alvarez and asked her to describe a normal workday. She launched into a monologue about understaffing and stress and getting yelled at and how at the end of many shifts she had to clock out and then spend fifteen or twenty minutes counting the cash in her register to make sure everything added up. The organizer explained that this was unlawful, off-the-clock work, and Alvarez quickly grew furious upon learning that her boss was cheating her. "The corporation was doing illegal stuff, and we treated it like normal procedure because we were told to do it," she said.

From that moment on, Alvarez plunged into the Fight for $15, soon becoming one of its leaders in the Chicago area. Within a month, fast-food workers were crowding into her basement apartment for meetings. "People would come and get everything out—about the mistreatment, about getting yelled at," she said. "Sometimes the yelling [inside the restaurants] was extremely bad; sometimes it was in front of customers."

The first time Alvarez heard of the Fight for $15 was at her mother's house. She often stopped there for food because she didn't earn enough to properly feed herself and her young son, Manny. Her mother told her, Quick, look at the TV, they're showing fast-food workers striking in New York.

"I thought it was crazy," Alvarez said. "I just kind of laughed." As for the campaign's demand for $15, her initial reaction was "We're not going to get $15. I thought it was too much. Maybe we can get ten or twelve. Honestly, I just thought it would die out," Alvarez said about the movement's prospects. "I'd just join on for a little bit, and we'll see what happens. I had no idea the movement would become so big, so important."

Alvarez, the American-born daughter of immigrants from Mexico, grew up in Cicero, a popular and good enough student. Her mother worked in a nearby chicken-processing plant, and her father was a truck driver. After high school, she attended East-West University in Chicago to study forensics, but she dropped out after a year because she couldn't afford a second year of tuition. Alvarez and her son share a bedroom in the basement apartment, which is occupied as well by another single mother with a young son because Alvarez, making $1,100 a month, on average, couldn't afford the apartment on her own.

After her first few Fight for $15 meetings, Alvarez agreed to write a petition, help circulate it for signatures, and then present it to the franchisee who owned her McDonald's and four others. "We had two years without getting a raise, and people were pretty mad," she said. "I decided, 'What do I have to lose?' We asked to be treated with respect. We asked them to follow the laws. We asked for full hours," meaning forty hours a week. Like many others, she was often scheduled for thirty hours a week; if she had worked that level of hours all year long, she would have earned around $13,000 a year. Fifty-one workers signed the petition, including twenty-nine at her McDonald's. She was furious that after they gave the franchise owner the petition, he refused to discuss it with them.

Two weeks later came a big surprise: everyone received a raise. Alvarez's pay jumped from $8.50 an hour to $9.15, and three months later came another increase, to $9.75.

As the Fight for $15 has grown, so has Alvarez's involvement. The news media often photograph or videotape the photogenic mother and son. She joined several one-day strikes, got arrested at a sit-in, and spoke out in favor of paid sick days. "Growing up, I never thought I would have to fight for something like this," Alvarez said. "I just feel it's crazy that we don't get basic things like sick days. How does a person not deserve sick days? People get sick." For one protest, the Fight for $15 flew in a fast-food worker from Denmark. "She said she makes in three days what we make in two weeks," Alvarez said. "We're doing the same kind of work. It just crushed me."

Soon after Alvarez threw herself into the Fight for $15, her McDonald's greatly cut back her hours. The Fight for $15's lawyers filed a complaint with the NLRB, and the labor board's Chicago office warned her franchise owner that it was illegal to retaliate against Alvarez for engaging in pro-worker activities. Her hours were restored.

All the clamor pressured Chicago's business-friendly mayor, Rahm Emanuel, into embracing a $13 minimum wage, in part to help him survive a reelection challenge from his left. That step pressured Alvarez's McDonald's to lift her pay toward $13, even though she works in neighboring Cicero. "The paychecks are a lot bigger now," she said. "I'm able to afford more. I can do more with Manny. I can now afford to take him to movies or the Museum of Science and Industry."

Alvarez has become one of the Fight for $15's leading spokeswomen against sexual harassment on the job; twenty-five McDonald's workers have filed complaints with the EEOC about managers demanding sex and groping their breasts and buttocks. "The public doesn't know what we go through, behind the counters, in the bathrooms, in the janitors' closets," Alvarez said. "We're sick and tired of having to deal with this."

Alvarez was flattered when Fight for $15 strategists invited her to go to Argentina to be the movement's emissary at a day of fast-food strikes there—part of an effort to make the movement global. Alvarez was a natural choice: she's bilingual, and warm and winning with people. She is also a poised (though she says nervous) speaker who thinks and speaks well on her feet. Of her visit to Buenos Aires, Alvarez said, "They were appalled when I told them that we didn't have any sick days. One worker said, 'But you're from the United States. How can that be?' I was ashamed. The fast-food workers have a union there. They get paid sick days. They get paid vacation. They get bonuses. One of the unions has a little camp where they can go on vacation. I don't know what a vacation is. People have been at my McDonald's for ten or fifteen years and never taken a vacation.

"A lot of people get scared of protesting," Alvarez added. "I'm not scared. If you have this big, old union behind you, why would you be scared? I was more scared of coming home and not being able to feed my child."

———

The two hundred workers who joined that first one-day strike in New York worried that their bosses would fire them when they returned to work the next day. At most of the restaurants, that didn't happen. Ministers and city council members accompanied many of the workers to help make sure their managers took them back. But Shalonda Montgomery, who worked at a Wendy's in downtown Brooklyn, was fired that next morning.

"I really needed this job," Montgomery said through tears. "I have a son to support."

Within two hours of the firing, organizers had summoned nearly a hundred fast-food workers and supporters to protest outside that Wendy's. The city councilman Jumaane Williams joined them and gave the manager an earful, warning of escalating protests. Montgomery's boss relented and took her back. Montgomery's experience emboldened fast-food workers far beyond New York and sent the message that workers would be taken back if they went on strike, that clergy and lawmakers had their backs.

"That was one of the most powerful moments of the first strike. It got people amped up," said Jonathan Westin of New York Communities for Change. (Westin had replaced Jon Kest as head of New York Communities of Change. Kest, who, along with Courtney, conceived the idea of a fast-food workers' movement, died of cancer six days after that first walkout.)

The November 29 strike was a shot heard round the fast-food world. Workers across the country sent messages of support, and soon the movement dispatched organizers to many cities to plan future strikes. Strategists rolled out the effort carefully, making sure it got its footing before going nationwide. Several hundred Chicago fast-food workers struck on April 24, 2013. Then came strikes in St. Louis on May 8, Detroit on May 10, Milwaukee on May 15, and Seattle on May 30. At each strike, scores of fast-food workers took to the streets, staged a loud, placard-filled protest, and generated lots of news coverage.

The campaign next flexed its muscles on July 29 by holding strikes in six cities at once. On August 29, strikes were staged in fifty cities, helping to mark the fiftieth anniversary of the famed March on Washington (held on August 28, 1963). Among those who struck was Willietta Dukes, a mother of two making $8.65 an hour after fifteen years as a fast-food worker in Durham, North Carolina. "I have seen a lot of people forming around the country, striking for better wages and to have their voices heard," Dukes said. "I think it is high time that I did something. . . . I don't want to be in poverty forever."

On December 5, 2013, the Fight for $15 held strikes in over a hundred cities. The movement was growing far beyond its founders' expectations. "The boldness and clarity of the demands really got people to rise up," said Mary Kay Henry, the SEIU's president. Scott Courtney, the SEIU's organizing director, added, "It was like the Flint strike. . . . It really inspired people elsewhere."

The Fight for $15's strategists had done some reverse engineering, taking early steps that they hoped would make the movement snowball. Largely funded by the SEIU, the movement hired a public-relations firm to set up Facebook and Twitter accounts and seed stories in the press. (As the *New York Times* labor reporter at the time, I was given the initial exclusive story about plans for that first strike in New York.) The movement underwrote several studies of the fast-food industry and laid the groundwork for wage theft lawsuits and OSHA complaints to embarrass and pressure McDonald's. After interviewing five hundred fast-food workers, the movement released a study in May 2013 saying that 84 percent of them reported being victimized by some form of wage theft. In a one-two punch, New York State's attorney general, Eric Schneiderman, announced that same day that he was launching an investigation into that very practice at fast-food restaurants.

In a study partly financed by the SEIU, researchers at the University of California, Berkeley, and the University of Illinois found that American taxpayers provided $7 billion in subsidies each year to fast-food workers, and some would say indirectly to the industry. Those subsidies took the form of Medicaid, food stamps, earned-income tax credits, and other assistance. The study noted that median fast-food pay was $8.69 an hour nationwide and that 52 percent of fast-food workers' families received some form of public assistance, compared with 25 percent of the overall workforce.

That study highlighted some misconceptions about fast-food workers. "We were battling the stereotype that fast-food workers were high school teenagers looking for pocket change, while many of them were moms and dads seeking to make ends meet," Henry said. The study found that 26 percent of fast-food workers were raising children, 68 percent were not in school, and just 18 percent were teens living with their parents.

As these studies were damaging the industry's reputation, McDonald's spectacularly shot itself in the foot, not just once, but twice. Nancy Salgado, a mother of two, earned $8.25 an hour after ten years working at a McDonald's in Chicago. When Salgado called the company's McResources help line to ask for advice on making ends meet, the help-line counselor recommended that she go to food pantries, apply for food stamps, and obtain Medicaid for her kids. In other words, McDonald's was telling her, we admit we pay you peanuts, you need to turn to the government for help. The Fight for $15's video about that help-line call went viral. The movement further embarrassed McDonald's by publicizing the obtuse advice that a McDonald's website gave workers on how to cope with their personal finances and stress. Its recommendations included "At least two vacations a year can cut heart attack risk by 50%," "Singing along to your favorite songs can lower your blood pressure," and "Breaking food into pieces often results in eating less and still feeling full." Other pointers included "Olive oil can prevent the blues" and "People who attend more church services tend to have lower blood pressure."

Its image taking a beating, the industry fought back. The National Retail Federation dismissed the Fight for $15 as "theater orchestrated by organized labor" and, absurdly, as an effort by "big labor to diminish and disparage these hard-working Americans by attacking the companies they work for." Scott DeFife, executive vice president of the National Restaurant Association, belittled the walkouts as "made-for-TV media moments" and "an effort to demonize the entire industry in order to make some organizing and political points." Heidi Barker Sa Shekhem, a McDonald's spokeswoman, scoffed at the movement, saying, "These events have not been 'strikes,' but organized rallies designed to garner media attention for which demonstrators are transported to various locations." She added, "Historically, very few McDonald's employees have participated in these organized events."

That statement enraged the Fight for $15's organizers and activists, and they hatched a plan to demonstrate otherwise. When McDonald's held its 2015 shareholders' meeting at its headquarters in a Chicago suburb, some two thousand protesters marched outside, with 101 fast-food workers sitting in and getting arrested, many of them wearing their McDonald's shirts. In ensuing months, hundreds of fast-food workers conducted sit-ins in their home cities while defiantly wearing their restaurant uniforms. (As the movement expanded from city to city, a few critics argued that it was top-down and not worker-driven enough. Those criticisms subsided as the movement registered one success after another.)

All the strikes and commotion aimed to get the national conversation to focus more on low-wage workers and to pressure McDonald's to meet with Fight for $15 leaders to discuss pay and a pathway to unionize. McDonald's rejected talks, so the movement's strategists moved to ratchet up the pressure, decisively.

- They helped arrange for a coalition of European and American unions to accuse McDonald's European operations of evading more than one billion euros in taxes by having royalty payments go through a tiny Luxembourg-based subsidiary. The European Union has launched an investigation into McDonald's tax avoidance.
- They got consumer groups in Italy to file an antitrust complaint, asserting that McDonald's had used its dominant position to vastly overcharge franchisees on rent, thereby forcing up prices to consumers. Italian antitrust authorities have launched an investigation.
- Brazil's two biggest union federations sued McDonald's largest franchisee in Latin America, accusing it of wage theft, unsanitary conditions, and not paying unemployment insurance. That mushroomed into a government investigation into unfair competition and franchise law violations, and McDonald's and its Brazilian franchisee faced potential penalties of more than $300 million.
- In the United States, McDonald's workers in nineteen cities filed complaints with OSHA, many asserting they had suffered burns on the job—

while filtering French fry grease, for instance. (McDonald's has resolved those complaints.)

- The SEIU helped persuade the NLRB's general counsel to assert that McDonald's was a joint employer with its franchisees, a move that could make it far easier to unionize McDonald's workers. (President Trump's NLRB has moved to reverse this.)

Rarely, if ever, had labor turned up the heat so much on a company outside an all-out strike. Nonetheless, McDonald's still refused to talk with the Fight for $15's leaders. In April 2015, however, the company said it would raise minimum pay at its company-owned restaurants (about 10 percent of the total) to $10 an hour by late 2016.

The "FF15" movement, growing frustrated that McDonald's wouldn't sit down and discuss wages, focused increasingly on another strategy to raise pay: pressuring government.

———

The first fight was in an unlikely place: SeaTac, a blue-collar suburb of Seattle, where Seattle's international airport is located. A coalition of unions was seeking to organize the airport's low-wage baggage handlers, airplane cleaners, and wheelchair attendants, many of them refugees from East Africa. The airlines that used the airport fought back, invoking provisions in federal law that made it especially hard to unionize airport workers.

The SeaTac organizers then embraced Plan B—a public referendum to raise the town's minimum wage to $15. As Jonathan Rosenblum recounts in his book, *Beyond $15: Immigrant Workers, Faith Activists, and the Revival of the Labor Movement,* activists first registered hundreds of working-class voters. They persuaded numerous ministers and imams to speak out for the $15 wage and mobilized many of the airport's immigrant workers to knock on doors.

In a first for the nation, in November 2013, SeaTac's voters approved a $15 minimum wage—by 77 votes out of 6,003 cast.

That victory inspired a $15 campaign in nearby Seattle. There the city's powerful labor movement pressed the Democratic mayoral candidates; the SEIU even sponsored a "low-wage workers' forum" where fast-food workers turned up the heat on the candidates to embrace a

$15 minimum. After Ed Murray, a candidate who supported $15, won the mayoral election, he indicated he might delay raising the minimum, and that caused a new surge of pressure from the left. Kshama Sawant, Seattle's first socialist city council member in a century, and the grassroots activists who backed her, threatened to sponsor a public referendum to quickly institute a $15 minimum. His hand forced, Murray appointed a labor/business advisory committee, with David Rolf, president of a large SEIU local, as its co-chair. After weeks of friction, the committee recommended a $15 minimum wage to be phased in over seven years, and the city council unanimously approved that recommendation in June 2014.

That one of the nation's major cities had adopted a $15 minimum was a tremendous victory for the Fight for $15. That triumph came just nineteen months after the first strike in New York. "Fast-food workers rightly took credit for having made plausible a minimum wage that two years ago sounded outlandish," William Finnegan wrote in *The New Yorker*.

The movement's next victory came in San Francisco, where voters overwhelmingly approved a $15 minimum in a referendum (77 percent to 23 percent). Then Rahm Emanuel jumped on the bandwagon, getting Chicago's city council to adopt a $13 minimum. In Los Angeles, the Fight for $15 mobilized union, immigrant, and African American groups to pressure Mayor Eric Garcetti and the city council to enact a $15 minimum. Garcetti at first called for a $13.25 minimum, but feeling intense heat, which included a hunger strike by fast-food workers, the council voted in May 2015 to adopt $15, and Garcetti quickly signed it into law.

The movement had so much momentum that even the pro-business New York governor, Andrew Cuomo, a centrist Democrat, championed the idea—in part to strengthen his left flank and union support in case he ran for reelection or for president. To institute a $15 minimum, Cuomo turned to the tool of setting up a "wage board," a mechanism dating from the Great Depression, when many states used such boards to set fair industry-wide pay levels. Cuomo's board held hearings across New York, and hundreds of fast-food workers testified that they couldn't survive on $8.25 an hour (then the state's minimum wage) and needed $15. Restaurant industry executives testified that $15 was absurdly high and would force them to hike menu prices and lay off workers. Cuomo sided with the workers and, in April 2016, signed a law that called for moving in steps over five years to a $15 minimum for all workers in New York City and its suburbs and moving in steps to a $12.50 minimum in the economically depressed upstate region.

With fast-food companies refusing to bargain with the Fight for $15, the wage board process became an alternative, unusually broad form of labor-versus-business bargaining. "It was like collective bargaining on steroids," Courtney said. "We were trying to bargain with society about what minimum wages and minimum living standards should be."

In what was by far the movement's biggest victory, California, the nation's most populous state, enacted a $15 minimum in April 2016 that is to be phased in through 2022. It is expected to raise pay for 5.6 million workers. Governor Jerry Brown signed it into law after being pushed by the Fight for $15, unions, and progressive groups. *The Sacramento Bee* wrote that Brown's "hand was forced" by growing concern about income inequality. Brown acknowledged that a $15 minimum could hurt business but said, "Morally and socially and politically, they [minimum wages] make every sense because it binds the community together and makes sure that parents can take care of their kids in a much more satisfactory way."

The Fight for $15 has had ripple effects in state after state. In November 2014, voters in four red states—Alaska, Arkansas, Nebraska, and South Dakota—approved minimum wage increases. In November 2016, voters in Arizona, Colorado, and Maine approved a $12 minimum, and in Washington State, $13.50. In November 2018, Missouri approved a $12 minimum, and Arkansas voters again approved a higher minimum ($11). Massachusetts enacted a $15 minimum wage law in April 2018, and New Jersey, Illinois, and Maryland followed suit in the first three months of 2019. (In those states, $15 will be reached in steps over several years.) Mary Kay Henry is understandably proud of what the Fight for $15 has accomplished. She boasts that it has directly or indirectly raised pay for twenty-two million workers across America. "The biggest lesson is that something that seems bold and audacious is completely possible and that working people are ready to stand up and fight in a way that most of us haven't seen in a generation," she said.

Fight for $15 fever even infected some well-known companies. Sheryl Sandberg, Facebook's chief operating officer, announced in 2015 that all Facebook contractors would have to pay their employees at least $15 an hour and provide fifteen paid vacation days a year. Pennsylvania's largest employer, the University of Pittsburgh Medical Center, with eighty-five thousand workers, adopted a $15 minimum wage. Pushed by their unions, Disneyland agreed to a $15 minimum for its ten thousand workers and Disney World for its thirty-eight thousand workers. Aetna embraced a $16 minimum for its employees, meaning raises for fifty-seven hundred workers. Aetna's CEO, Mark T. Bertolini, even urged the insurance company's executives to read Thomas Piketty's weighty tome on inequality *Capital in the Twenty-First Century*. In explaining why he embraced a $16 minimum, Bertolini said, "When I went out into the field to shake everybody's hands, I kept hearing the same thing: 'I can't afford the healthcare, I'm working two jobs, my family's on food stamps.'"

Target announced in September 2017 that it would raise minimum hourly pay for its 323,000 workers to $11 by late 2017 and to $15 by the end of 2020. After Congress passed more than $1 trillion in corporate tax cuts in December 2017, Wells Fargo and several other companies said they were adopting a $15 minimum in response. (The Fight for $15's leaders thought they deserved some of the credit.) Showing how far the FF15 has come, Amazon, the nation's second-largest private employer—after being criticized because thousands of its workers were on food stamps—adopted a $15 minimum wage for its 350,000 employees, which became effective in November 2018.

Notwithstanding the Fight for $15's successes, a debate had raged within the SEIU about whether the union should continue spending tens of millions of dollars to help fast-food workers who weren't SEIU members and might never be unionized. Henry convinced the union's board that an expanded campaign was needed to try to lift millions more low-wage workers, including many SEIU members. That was one reason the Fight for $15 broadened its scope to include four groups the SEIU has unionized: home-care workers, nursing-home workers, child-care workers, and adjunct professors.

This widening of the Fight for $15 has paid off. The State of Massachusetts agreed to pay thirty-five thousand SEIU home-care attendants $15 an hour, and the Los Angeles school system reached a contract with the SEIU that raised the pay of thirty-three thousand custodians, cafeteria workers, and teaching assistants to $15, from the previous $8 to $9. The SEIU's Héctor Figueroa says the Fight for $15 has helped his New

York–based local because lifting the wage floor to $15 makes it considerably easier to demand that doormen, janitors, and other workers in his union receive $20 or more an hour. The SEIU and Figueroa's local used the movement's momentum to help persuade the Port Authority of New York and New Jersey in September 2018 to establish the nation's highest targeted minimum wage—$19 an hour—for roughly forty thousand workers, including baggage handlers, cabin cleaners, and catering workers, at New York City's three major airports: JFK, LaGuardia, and Newark.

The Fight for $15's leaders often say their ambition is nothing less than to transform the service sector into the foundation for the next American middle class, just as Walter Reuther helped transform manufacturing jobs. "Factory jobs didn't start as good jobs," Courtney said. "Unionization caused them to change that. The Fight for $15 is sort of a twenty-first-century way of doing that."

———

The Fight for $15 had two original demands: a $15 minimum wage and a union. As we've seen, it has had considerable success on the first goal. The second is more complicated. McDonald's has said "there is no reason for our company . . . to meet" with the Fight for $15 or SEIU because "it does not represent any employee in a McDonald's restaurant." In fact, as of this writing, not a cent in dues money from fast-food workers has helped sustain the campaign. Indeed, the movement has deliberately shunned a traditional unionization path. Using an innovative strategy, it has sought to broaden the scope of what a union is and how worker advocacy is financed. "A lot of union organizing was niche organizing, around a small set of folks," Jonathan Westin said. "We didn't want to do that. We wanted it to be a broader-based movement around workers living in poverty."

The Fight for $15 could easily get a majority of the twenty-five-worker crews at many McDonald's to vote to unionize. But strategists fear that McDonald's and its franchisees would drag their feet for years on ever agreeing to a union contract, and that even if they did agree to a contract, they would undoubtedly reject anything close to $15, and that might seriously deflate workers' hopes. Several labor experts advised the Fight for $15 to seek to unionize all the corporate-owned McDonald's in a big city, perhaps New York or L.A., and then pressure the company until it agreed to a good contract that could become a model for hundreds of other McDonald's. "You can imagine a scenario where, if these workers succeed—just as what happened after the Flint Sit-Down Strike in 1937—it will catch the imagination of millions of people, and they'll say, 'Let's try it,'" said Ruth Milkman, a sociology professor at the City University of New York. But Fells, the Fight for $15's long-time organizing director, was thinking differently. "Our making a deal to organize a hundred restaurants, that's not going to happen," he said. "This is about lifting up tens of millions of American workers who make less than $15 an hour, who aren't making enough to live on."

The movement's hope was to create so much pressure on McDonald's that it would agree to a path to widespread unionization, perhaps giving a green light to full unionization in certain cities or states. "We were looking for a national deal with McDonald's," said the SEIU's Figueroa. "The outcome of the presidential election, the tone of Donald Trump, makes it much harder" to imagine pressuring McDonald's successfully. So the movement set out to establish a new type of labor group that is funded by workers but does not engage in collective bargaining.

In the first such example, the movement persuaded the New York City Council to enact a law in 2017 that lets fast-food workers have their employers deduct money from their paychecks and then forward that money to a workers' group. (The law applies only to fast-food restaurants.) New York's new law requires that at least five hundred fast-food workers pledge to contribute to a group before it can receive payroll deductions. The Fight for $15 has set up such a group in New York—Fast Food Justice—and it plans to help fast-food workers with immigration and housing problems, push for a higher minimum wage, and obtain transit discounts for low-wage workers. Two thousand fast-food workers have agreed to contribute $15 a month, and if Fast Food Justice achieves its goal of getting ten thousand of the city's sixty-five thousand fast-food workers to contribute, that would provide it with $1.8 million a year—enough to run an effective workers' organization. The National Restaurant Association has filed a federal lawsuit, seeking to overturn the New York law.

"This has been a lot of hard work," said Shantel Walker, an activist with Fast Food Justice whose pay working at a Papa John's in Brooklyn has jumped to $15 an hour from $7.25 since the Fight for $15 began. "I feel we've achieved a lot," she said. "People are pumped up. We want to bring change not only in the fast-food industry but in our communities. If anytime you're an everyday working person and your voice is being heard, that is a great thing."

———

Shortly before closing time one Sunday, Terrence Wise was mopping the floor at his Burger King in Kansas City, when three fast-food workers entered the store and approached him. A worker wearing a Domino's shirt asked, "Do you think you deserve better pay?"

"Yes, of course," Wise recalls telling them.

"Do you think you deserve health benefits?" the worker asked.

"Yes," Wise responded, telling them he hadn't seen a dentist in eighteen years.

"Do you think you deserve a vacation?"

"Yes," Wise said, noting he hadn't seen his mother in eight years.

That was the first time Wise heard of the Fight for $15, and within a week he was attending an FF15 meeting with a dozen other fast-food workers inside St. Mark's Lutheran Church. Little did Wise know that his joining the movement would take him to some surprising places.

Two months later, on July 29, 2013, the Fight for $15 staged its first strike in Kansas City, and Wise didn't show up for his jobs at Burger King and Pizza Hut. He instead protested alongside sixty other workers outside a McDonald's downtown. That day he worried he might get fired, yet he felt empowered, liberated even. Before the Fight for $15 came along, he said, it never crossed his mind that fast-food workers could walk out "because they don't treat us right."

Wise so impressed the other Kansas City workers with how well he spoke that they designated him their spokesman for media interviews. His early interest in the ministry had helped make him an eloquent speaker; when Wise gets going, he often speaks in the cadences of Martin Luther King Jr. Soon the Fight for $15 even had him doing interviews on national media.

He told NPR's *All Things Considered* about being homeless despite holding two jobs. "We lost our home, and we were sleeping in our minivan, me and my fiancée and my three little girls," he said. "We're in America, the richest nation on Earth, and here you have two working parents getting ready for work in the front seat of their minivan, while their three daughters are getting ready for school in the back."

On the radio show *Democracy Now!*, Wise addressed the myth that fast-food workers are overwhelmingly teenagers trying to get extra spending money. "Where I work, in both my shops, there aren't high schoolers. There are people with families," he said. "We're raising families. We're doing hard work, and we deserve to get a living wage."

Every few months, the Fight for $15 held another strike in Kansas City, with the biggest rally swelling to two thousand people—not just fast-food workers, but other low-wage workers and supporters from the faith, labor, African American, Latino, and LGBT communities. Wise and his fiancée, Myoshia, let their daughters miss school to join the protests. "It's been teaching the kids a lot," Myoshia said. "Stand up and fight—it's stuff they don't teach in school."

Kansas City's fast-food workers elected Wise to be their representative on the Fight for $15's National Organizing Committee, which holds conference calls every two weeks, connecting fast-food leaders from sixty cities. He served as emcee at a Fight for $15 convention in Chicago that brought together a thousand workers. He was even invited to speak to an NAACP convention in Las Vegas.

America's fast-food workers are disproportionately black and Hispanic, and the Fight for $15 has tied its struggle to the civil rights movement and Dr. King's struggle for economic justice. It has even joined forces with the revived Poor People's Campaign, rekindled by the Reverend William Barber. "We've seen how the civil rights movement won civil rights," Wise said. "Those things weren't given to us. People faced hoses and beatings. Some people even died. We have to bring the same pressure for today's times and make these companies listen to us. We have to do whatever it takes to win."

Wise is proud that the Fight for $15 is multiracial. "We saw how some unions would exclude women and Hispanics and blacks," he said. "We knew that wasn't the way. We knew we have to bring all workers together, whether you're black, white, Hispanic, Asian. We had to break all those barriers."

His brightest moment came when the White House organized its Summit on Worker Voice in October 2015. Not only was Wise invited to attend, but he was asked to introduce President Obama. With the president standing at his side, Wise told the White House audience that he was a second-generation fast-food worker and that "despite my working nearly two decades in this industry, I make just $8 an hour." The crowd burst into applause when his mother, JoAnn, was introduced—the Fight for $15 had brought her to the conference, the first time Wise had seen her in a decade.

"I had a chance to tell Mr. Obama how there are times I struggle and I can barely feed my three daughters," Wise said. "It hurt me to tell him that."

In Wise's view, three ingredients have been critical to the Fight for $15's success. First, it encourages workers to tell the world their own, often powerful stories. Second, fast-food workers have organized other fast-food workers. "That's the single most important thing," Wise said. "We're the ones that make these companies filthy rich, and we're the ones that are supposed to have this conversation, talking to each other, getting people involved."

The last ingredient has been the movement's extraordinary success at mobilizing workers, getting them to strike and into the streets. That has gotten the attention of McDonald's, state legislatures, and millions of Americans.

"The one thing that works is boots on the ground," Wise said. "Marching and organizing will never grow old."

Seventeen

For Farmworkers, from Worst to Best

WITH ITS SUMPTUOUS SAND BEACHES on Florida's southwest coast, Naples is a magnet for yacht owners and well-to-do retirees, boasting that it has the second-highest percentage of millionaires of any city in the nation. Drive an hour inland, past the mansions and golf courses and then the Corkscrew Swamp, and you come to Immokalee, the nation's "winter tomato capital." Immokalee (rhymes with "broccoli") is a three-stoplight town dotted with dollar stores, taco joints, dilapidated trailers, and humble homes with chickens clucking in the backyard. Its population doubles each winter as migrants from Mexico and Central America arrive, making Immokalee the heart of a Florida industry that picks 90 percent of the fresh tomatoes that Americans eat from December through May.

A dozen years ago, a typical Immokalee winter day began around 5 a.m., when nearly a thousand immigrant workers trudged to a Pantry Shelf parking lot two blocks west of Main Street. There, in the predawn gloom, crew leaders picked who would work that day and directed them onto clunky old school buses that deposited them at the fields by 6:30 or 7. The workers would often have to wait two, three, even four hours unpaid until the morning sun dried the plants and they were allowed to start picking. Only then did the crew leaders start counting their work hours; there were no time clocks. Many workers had a modest goal: to make $60 a day. They were paid forty cents for each thirty-two-pound bucket of tomatoes and had to work extremely hard picking the forty-eight hundred pounds that would yield $60 in a day. Draping bandannas over their heads and necks to protect against the sun, the pickers sprinted hour after hour to pull tomatoes off the plants, toss them into their buckets, and lug their filled buckets to a nearby flatbed truck.

Many days crew leaders cheated workers by paying them $10 or $15 less than they were due or by withholding a day's pay. When workers complained, the crew leaders sometimes beat them or fired them. The lesson: "If you didn't get paid for two or three days, you didn't bother complaining because then the crew leader wouldn't hire you again," said Lucas Benitez, an immigrant from Guerrero, Mexico, who began working in Immokalee's fields more than two decades ago, at age sixteen, and became an outspoken activist.

Even though the mercury often climbs over ninety in March and April, most tomato workers toiled without rest breaks or shade. Some fainted from the heat, thirst, the unrelenting pace, the unremitting sun, or all of the above. The only water came from local wells, frequently foul smelling and chemical tinged. (There weren't any bathrooms, so the workers relieved themselves in the fields.) Female workers had it worst of all. Crew leaders frequently groped them or demanded sex if women wanted to keep their jobs. One longtime worker told of a crew leader forcing her to the corner of the field when she was just fourteen—her screams saved her.

"It was the closest thing possible to hell on earth" was how one professor described working in Immokalee's fields.

Things had changed disconcertingly little from when Edward R. Murrow did his landmark 1960 television documentary *Harvest of Shame*, which focused on the deplorable conditions of Florida's migrant workers. "These are the forgotten people," Murrow said, "the underprotected, the undereducated, the underclothed, the underfed." Susan L. Marquis, author of a book on Florida's farmworkers, wrote, "The source and color of the workers changed over time but in many ways conditions in the fields were nearly as brutal in twentieth-century America as they had been at the time of the Civil War." There was so much forced labor in the Immokalee area that a prosecutor called it "ground zero for modern slavery." Federal prosecutors won convictions in seven cases in which crew leaders held migrants against their will. Some workers were beaten or even shot if they sought to escape. One worker said his crew chief warned newly arrived migrants, "If you want to leave, go ahead. But I'll call the bosses, and they'll feed you to the alligators."

For two years, Mariano Lucas Domingo, a Guatemalan immigrant, when not picking tomatoes, had been locked in a box truck four blocks from the parking lot where the workers gathered each morning. Cesar Navarrete, a crew leader, had offered Lucas room and board but then locked him and several others in the truck after work, charging them $20 a week "rent." The truck had no toilet or running water, so the workers urinated and defecated in a corner of the vehicle. To keep Lucas in continuous debt, Navarrete piled on charges—for meals, alcohol, even $5 for a cold shower from a garden hose. One night Lucas and two other "prisoners" punched their way through the truck's roof and escaped. Three weeks later, prosecutors indicted Navarrete and his brother, Geovanni, for forcibly keeping Lucas and a dozen other men in shacks and the truck, sometimes shackling them in chains. At the trial, Lucas testified that when he was too exhausted or ill to work, the Navarrete brothers kicked and beat him. A federal judge sentenced the brothers to twelve years in prison. In defending his client's actions, Cesar Navarrete's attorney said, "The bottom line is America wants cheap tomatoes."

———

In 1991, Greg Asbed and Laura Germino, who met as students at Brown University, moved to Immokalee to do community outreach for a legal services office that helped migrant workers. Though they had both worked in miserably poor developing nations—Asbed had worked for a community-development group in Haiti, Germino for the Peace Corps in Burkina Faso—the young married couple were shocked by what they encountered in Immokalee.

Soon after the couple's arrival, three peasant organizers from Haiti—Cristal Pierre, Jean-Claude Jean, and Mathieu Beaucicot—moved to Immokalee as refugees and began picking tomatoes. They had fled Haiti after the military overthrew its leftist president, Jean-Bertrand Aristide. Upset by the horrid working conditions in Immokalee, Asbed, Germino, and the Haitian organizers concluded that something had to be done. They teamed up with Hispanic farmworker activists, including Lucas Benitez, at a series of meetings in the nearby Our Lady of Guadalupe Roman Catholic church. In 1993, these activists founded the Coalition of Immokalee Workers (CIW), which soon rented a modest office near the parking lot where the tomato pickers gathered each morning.

This new coalition behaved differently from a traditional union. With the goal of mobilizing farmworkers, it embraced the Latin American concept of "popular education," with the slogan "Consciousness + Commitment = Change." It staged weekly skits—with the immigrants as actors—about farmwork and social justice. It sponsored Sunday morning meetings for female workers and conducted leadership training, with lessons on labor history, agribusiness, and how to speak and organize. The group preached *"Todos somos líderes"*—we are all leaders. It set up a low-power radio station to educate and entertain farmworkers. It established a program that helped uncover and investigate "modern day slavery" operations. The coalition soon became a David spoiling to take on Goliath—Florida's $650 million tomato industry.

When Pacific Tomato Growers, one of the largest producers in Florida, cut its pay rate in 1995, the pickers were primed to act. Three thousand of them went on a general strike, shutting down the fields. After five days, the strike petered out. The walkout got Pacific to rescind its wage cut, but it didn't achieve its larger goal—to get the growers to raise wages. (The rate had been stuck at forty cents a bucket since 1980.) Asbed recognized that it was hard for low-paid workers to outlast wealthy growers in such a showdown. "Poor people have a very rough time not going to work," he said. "They don't have money saved up. They don't have a safety net."

Two years later, the workers staged a second general strike. After two days, Gargiulo, then the nation's largest tomato grower, agreed to bargain with the coalition, soon agreeing to raise pay to fifty cents a bucket. The coalition hailed that victory, but the region's eight other major tomato growers refused to budge. To step up the pressure, six CIW members began a thirty-day fast just before Christmas 1997. Former president Jimmy Carter weighed in on their behalf, but the growers still refused to bargain with the coalition. The fast was not in vain, however, because Governor-elect Jeb Bush got two of Florida's largest growers to agree to raise pay by five cents a bucket.

Wages were inching upward, but working conditions remained as awful as ever. In 1999, the coalition organized a third strike, a five-day walkout that failed to get the growers to negotiate. Dozens of tomato workers then participated in a two-hundred-mile, two-week protest march from Fort Myers to the Orlando headquarters of the Florida Fruit and Vegetable Association. A pickup truck, with a ten-foot-tall replica of the Statue of Liberty standing tall in its cargo bed, led the procession. By the time the march arrived in Orlando, hundreds of demonstrators, including students from across Florida, had joined the protest, which drew substantial press coverage. Nonetheless, the growers' association still refused to negotiate, not on rest breaks, foul drinking water, or crew leaders abusing female workers. Its spokesman dismissed the march as "a transparent attempt to start a labor union." The Coalition of Immokalee Workers had run into a wall.

"The growers were so effectively insulated from pressure that they could withstand any assault that a dirt-poor community like Immokalee could muster," Asbed wrote in an essay. The growers didn't have to worry about traditional unionization because farmworkers are exempted from the National Labor Relations Act. Nor did the growers need to fear pressure from consumers because they sold to retail and restaurant chains, not to the public.

Asbed, Germino, Benitez, and the others cast about for new strategies. "You beat your head against the wall long enough, and you decide that that hurts, and you want to find another way to get around the wall," Asbed said. Just then, the industry magazine *The Packer* ran a story about Taco Bell's multiyear deal to buy tomatoes at a discounted price from a major grower, Six L's. Suddenly several lightbulbs went off. Why was the coalition focusing its pressure on the growers to raise pay when tomato-buying giants like Taco Bell were pushing down the price of tomatoes? Mightn't their protests be far more successful if they targeted image-conscious behemoths like Taco Bell instead of little-known growers? Further pushing them to target Taco Bell, one farmworker noted that its commercials, featuring a cute Chihuahua that spoke with a Mexican accent, milked Hispanic culture for Taco Bell's benefit even as its growers exploited Hispanic workers. So the coalition decided to take on giant Taco Bell, which has seven thousand restaurants worldwide.

The CIW repeatedly asked for a meeting with Taco Bell, but the company refused. The coalition escalated its pressure, announcing a national boycott against Taco Bell for its role "as a major buyer of Florida tomatoes, in perpetuating farm worker poverty." The coalition had two demands: that Taco Bell require its tomato growers to adopt a code of conduct and that it pay a penny more per pound for its Florida tomatoes, money the growers would pass on to the pickers. The demands would cost Taco Bell $100,000 a year for the ten million pounds of Florida tomatoes it purchased while substantially boosting the pickers' pay, potentially from forty cents per thirty-two-pound bucket to seventy-two cents.

The coalition mobilized and marched. (By this time, it had twenty-five hundred members and support from several foundations.) Seeking to harness consumer power to its cause, the CIW sponsored a coast-to-coast caravan that stopped in dozens of cities and college towns to urge consumers to shun Taco Bell. It adopted the slogan "Boot the Bell" to counter the chain's advertising theme, "Ring the Bell." Asbed proved a wizard at spreading the word nationwide by writing daily dispatches for the coalition's website and posting videos of its protests.

Taco Bell still refused to negotiate, insisting the dispute was between the growers and the farmworkers. "This labor dispute is four steps removed from us, and we're not going to get involved," said Jonathan Blum, a senior vice president for Yum! Brands, which owns Taco Bell, as well as KFC and Pizza Hut.

The coalition turned up the heat even more. Recognizing Taco Bell's focus on the youth market, the CIW got students at three hundred universities and fifty high schools to call for "booting the Bell," with twenty colleges closing or not letting Taco Bell open campus outlets. The coalition spawned an offshoot, the Student/Farmworker Alliance, which further spread the word. The boycott also won the backing of the National Council of Churches, the Presbyterian Church, and dozens of synagogues. Rabbi Joel Sisenwine from Wellesley, Massachusetts, visited with a delegation of rabbis and was moved by what they saw. "We Jews were slaves in Egypt," and "we find it hard to understand that there is still slavery in Florida," he said. Noelle Damico, the Presbyterian Church's boycott coordinator, told me, "We're involved in this effort because Jesus calls us to love others, not exploit people." Adding to the pressure on Taco Bell were three federal prosecutions of forced labor on Florida farms. (The CIW's work in exposing forced labor, led by Germino, had helped federal officials send a dozen crew leaders to prison and free hundreds of migrants being held against their will.) To highlight that issue, the coalition held a ten-day hunger strike outside the company's headquarters, with workers holding signs saying, "Can

Taco Bell guarantee its customers that the tomatoes in its tacos were not picked by slaves?"

Its image taking a beating, Taco Bell finally relented in 2003, two years after the boycott began, agreeing to start talks. A year passed without an agreement. The coalition grew impatient and began planning a huge protest for Yum! Brands' 2005 annual meeting in Louisville. Martin Sheen, the star of *The West Wing*, and Kerry Kennedy, a daughter of Robert F. Kennedy's, were scheduled to speak. The week before Yum! Brands' annual meeting, eighty Immokalee tomato workers boarded buses for Louisville, stopping in fifteen cities along the way to spread their message that Taco Bell perpetuated farmworker poverty.

Facing more damage to its brand and with Jimmy Carter again intervening, Taco Bell, in March 2005, reached a groundbreaking settlement with the coalition on the eve of its annual meeting, four years after the boycott began. Taco Bell agreed to pay a penny more per pound and have its tomato growers adopt a code of conduct. Jimmy Carter hailed the accord, saying, "I now call on others in the industry to follow Taco Bell's lead to help the tomato farmworkers."

The Immokalee workers next called on McDonald's to agree to the two demands that Taco Bell had accepted, as well as a third demand: that McDonald's help set up a monitoring system to ensure that tomato growers complied with the code of conduct. (At the same time, the coalition gave its effort a name: "the Campaign for Fair Food.") McDonald's rejected the CIW's demands, asserting that its own code of conduct ensured fair working conditions at its tomato farms. The coalition scoffed at McDonald's claim, maintaining that business-created codes of conduct aim mainly to burnish a brand's reputation and rarely have the rigorous monitoring needed to truly improve working conditions.

The coalition staged protests at McDonald's headquarters outside Chicago, rallied student groups and clergy, and organized the multicity "Truth Tour." It scheduled a major protest outside McDonald's shareholders' meeting, a protest to be headed by the AFL-CIO's president, John Sweeney. Also worried about its image, McDonald's agreed to the coalition's demands just before that meeting.

Even before winning that fight, the coalition had begun a campaign against Burger King, kicking it off with a protest at the company's world headquarters in Miami. The company responded with contempt, saying there was no way to assure that the extra penny a pound would ever get to the farmworkers. The company's CEO, John Chidsey, said, "It's not our job to tell the growers how much to pay their workers." Making no headway, the coalition organized an eighty-mile march from Immokalee to the Miami office of Goldman Sachs, a major private-equity investor in Burger King. During that march, tomato workers wore yellow T-shirts with a refashioned corporate logo, saying, "Exploitation King." Steven Grover, Burger King's vice president of food safety and regulatory compliance, belittled the marchers, saying, "This protest is a colossal waste of resources and time that could be focused on helping the migrant workers in Immokalee."

Three months later, a woman named Cara Schaffer contacted the Student/Farmworker Alliance, saying she was a student at Broward Community College and wanted to get involved. Schaffer was invited to join several meetings and conference calls to plan further protests. She raised suspicions, however, and CIW officials discovered in an internet search that she owned a private-security firm, Diplomatic Tactical Services. Its website said it placed "undercover operatives" and did "all types of investigative activity during strikes" and "unionization drives." When the coalition exposed Schaffer, Burger King, which had hired her to do undercover work, terminated its relationship with her.

Around the same time, someone with the screen name surfxaholic36 repeatedly attacked the coalition in comments on web stories and YouTube videos. One comment said, "The CIW is a self-serving attack organization with no real members or workers [that] creates conflict and spreads overly simplistic misinformation to unquestioning students. . . . The CIW has fooled thousands with its slick internet stories, collected millions in return and given the workers nothing." Another comment accused the coalition of "lining the leaders [sic] pockets." (The CIW didn't collect or touch the money for the penny-a-pound increment.) Journalists and the coalition uncovered that those attacks came from Burger King's Grover, who was using his middle-school daughter's screen name. Soon after Grover was outed, a badly embarrassed Burger King fired him and agreed to the coalition's demands.

Now the coalition faced an unanticipated fight from the growers' association, the Florida Tomato Exchange. The exchange's executive vice president, Reggie Brown, denounced the penny-a-pound program, saying, "It is just un-American for a third party to be involved in establishing workers' wage rates." (Don't tell that to any labor leader.) The exchange threatened a $100,000 fine to any grower that participated in the penny-a-pound program, effectively shutting it down. The penny-a-pound effort remained suspended through 2009, even as Subway and Whole Foods joined the Fair Food Program and agreed to pay a penny more per pound. The exchange dug in, even though the growers were taking a public-relations drubbing because federal prosecutors had brought new forced labor cases, including the 2008 indictment of the Navarrete brothers. When the food writer Barry Estabrook shone a harsh light on the tomato growers in a powerful article in *Gourmet,* America's "food community" also turned against the growers.

At last there was a breakthrough. Pacific Tomato Growers—one of the nation's five largest tomato producers—defied the tomato exchange's threat of a $100,000 fine and broke the more-than-decade-long logjam of growers refusing to negotiate or cooperate with the coalition. After quietly meeting for weeks with Asbed, Benitez, and other CIW representatives, Jon Esformes, an operating partner of Pacific, a fourth-generation, family-owned company, agreed in October 2010 to the coalition's new, expanded list of demands. They included the penny-a-pound increment, an elaborate monitoring system, a health and safety program, and a training program to teach workers about the code of conduct.

For Esformes, whose company employs fifteen hundred farmworkers in Florida, the agreement was an occasion to acknowledge the industry's sins. He pushed to clinch the deal right before Yom Kippur, the Jewish Day of Atonement. "It's the time of year when you're supposed to put your sins behind you," Esformes said. In announcing the settlement, he quoted the late rabbi and philosopher Abraham Joshua Heschel, saying, "Few are guilty, but all are responsible. . . . The transgressions that took place are totally unacceptable today and they were totally unacceptable yesterday."

Within days, the nation's largest tomato grower, Lipman, which used to be called Six L's, also reached an agreement with the coalition. At the time, Lipman was badly embarrassed that the Navarrete brothers had dispatched some enslaved pickers to work in its fields. Within a month, the Tomato Growers Exchange signed on, too. Finally, the CIW's vision would turn into a reality.

In a clearing just yards from Lipman's tomato fields, 150 pickers sat at plastic picnic tables listening intently, with tarps overhead to protect them from the sun. As field supervisors looked on, Gerardo Reyes, a tall, strong-voiced immigrant from Mexico, held forth in Spanish about the coalition's Fair Food Program and its code of conduct. Now rest breaks and shade tents are required, explained Reyes, who began working in Immokalee's fields in 1999 and is now on the CIW's staff. Now when the pickers reach the fields at 7 a.m., their hourly pay is to begin, he continued. Now the pickers have a right not to work when they feel unsafe, whether because of lightning, heat, or pesticides. In the past, some workers had been required to finish picking during thunderstorms.

The farmworkers listened attentively as Reyes continued. "We all have a right not to face verbal abuse," he said, explaining that supervisors are not to threaten, yell at, or swear at workers. "And this is an important right we all have—the right to be able to work without sexual harassment. We all have a right to work with dignity."

Reyes was the leadoff speaker at an hour-long training session on worker rights and safety, a key part of the groundbreaking Fair Food Program that the CIW has created with growers and with restaurant and retail chains that have signed on. Beyond banning sexual and verbal abuse, the code of conduct requires growers to comply with all laws and make accurate payments for all hours worked. The code, developed with extensive input from farmworkers, includes a complaint-resolution process and bars growers or supervisors from retaliating against workers who assert their rights. The code requires that all pickers be direct employees of growers and prohibits growers from using independent crew leaders, because crew leaders often exploited and sexually abused the pickers they hired. It also calls for ending a long-detested practice known as cupping, in which crew leaders required pickers not just to fill their buckets to the brim but to pile another ten or so tomatoes in a small mound above the rim. That meant picking an extra three pounds beyond the standard thirty-two-pound bucket, more or less giving away 10 percent of one's labor for free.

Reyes urged the workers to report violations to the program's enforcement arm, the Fair Food Standards Council, which has thirteen employees, most of them investigators. There's a twenty-four-hour hotline, which has bilingual staffers who answer calls and investigate complaints within days. The hotline's number is written on every pay stub, and callers can remain anonymous. Since the Fair Foods Standards Council was created in 2011, workers have lodged more than eighteen hundred complaints, and seventeen supervisors have been fired for sexual abuse, harassment, hitting workers, or other offenses.

The Fair Food inspectors do a far more rigorous job than similar inspectors in corporate social responsibility programs. They conduct an in-depth audit of each grower's payroll, and they interview every supervisor and at least 50 percent of each grower's workers (one strategy to ensure that workers have more of a voice). When violations are found, the council prepares a "Corrective Action Plan," and if a grower doesn't fix the problems within six months, it gets suspended from the program. Most growers are quick to correct violations, but several have been suspended. The Fair Food Program is unusually effective because its participants, including major corporations such as McDonald's and Taco Bell, have pledged to stop buying tomatoes from any grower that doesn't comply with the code. McDonald's and other companies serve, in effect, as the workers' enforcers.

Since the code went into effect, "things have changed a lot," said Angelina Velasquez, who arrived from Guatemala in 2003. She said she gets paid from the moment she gets to the field, and "they don't yell at us like they used to." Nelly Rodriguez, her co-worker, said, "It used to be commonplace for bosses to force relations with women. Now we have a right to report it, and supervisors have been fired. People used to turn a blind eye to these things. Now there are consequences." Sexual abuse and forced labor have been eliminated on Fair Food farms, the workers say.

Janice Fine, the professor who called the Immokalee of a decade ago "the closest thing possible to hell on earth," now has a very different view. "This is the best workplace-monitoring program I've seen in the U.S.," said Fine, a labor relations professor at Rutgers. "It can certainly be a model for agriculture across the U.S." Susan Marquis, dean of the Pardee RAND Graduate School, said that when she first visited Immokalee, she heard "appalling stories of abuse and modern slavery." "But now," Marquis said, "the tomato fields in Immokalee are probably the best working environment in American agriculture. They've gone from being the worst to the best." (Marquis was so moved by the coalition's accomplishments that she wrote a book about them: *I Am Not a Tractor! How Florida Farmworkers Took On the Fast Food Giants and Won.*)

The CIW scored a huge victory in 2014 when Walmart, the world's largest retailer, well known for being vehemently antiunion, joined the Fair Food Program on its own accord. Not long before, some Arizona tomato growers that Walmart relied on had their tomatoes rot in the fields because they couldn't attract enough pickers due to their dismal wages and working conditions. Walmart turned to the CIW's Fair Food Program because it was looking for both a dependable supply of tomatoes and ethically sourced produce. Walmart then helped to extend the program to tomato fields far from Immokalee: in Georgia, South Carolina, Virginia, Maryland, and New Jersey—an enormous boost to the program. In fact, Walmart has spread the program to some bell pepper growers (and Whole Foods to strawberry growers). Thus far fourteen companies have joined the Fair Food Program, including the giants Chipotle and Trader Joe's. Wendy's has steadfastly resisted pressure to join, and CIW launched a nationwide boycott against it in 2016.

A vital part of the Fair Food Program is its "sheriff," Laura Safer Espinoza. After retiring from her job as a New York State Supreme Court judge, she had moved to Fort Myers, thirty-five miles northwest of Immokalee, and volunteered to do some work for the CIW. When the Fair Food Standards Council was established to police the fields, Safer was an obvious choice to head it. As the council's executive director, Judge Laura, as she is called, oversees investigations and enforcement. She fires wayward supervisors, writes "Corrective Action Plans" for growers that violate the code of conduct, and decides when errant growers should be suspended and when readmitted.

"Standards are really nice, but if there aren't meaningful consequences that stand behind them, you have nothing," she said. "I wouldn't want to be part of something with standards that are merely aspirational. There are very few times in a person's life that you can be part of something that is making systemic and real change for so many people who have been disenfranchised and marginalized for so long. Whatever little piece I can play, I consider it an honor." Safer often tells of a farmworker who used to complain about having to wake her kids at 4 a.m. and drop them off with a neighbor an hour later, when she had to head to the parking lot. But nowadays that worker can wake her children hours later, have breakfast with them, and walk them to school before leaving for the fields.

Greg Asbed is understandably proud that thanks to the Fair Food Program, 35,000 farmworkers have had their wages and working conditions significantly improved. The MacArthur Foundation, duly impressed, awarded him a "genius" grant in 2017 for his "exceptionally creative" efforts in advancing worker rights. In explaining the coalition's strategy, Asbed said the group "can't be a labor union" that bargains with growers because neither federal law, nor Florida law provides farmworkers with any protections if they seek to unionize. Thus, Asbed said, the coalition instead became "a standards-setting organization." Through its quarter century of protests, it has persuaded companies and growers to embrace those standards along with an elaborate system of enforcement. Asbed has given the coalition's model a name: "worker-driven social responsibility." He contrasts it with corporate-driven social responsibility programs, like Western companies' hugely flawed "social responsibility" programs in Bangladesh that repeatedly "inspected" apparel factories but didn't prevent the Tazreen fire, which killed 112 workers in 2012, or the Rana Plaza building collapse, which killed 1,130 workers in 2013.

"The Fair Food Program has created a model of protection of human rights in a corporate supply chain that has never existed before," Asbed said. In his view, four essential tools are needed for a social responsibility program to truly help workers: (1) worker-to-worker education to train people on their rights; (2) a twenty-four-hour complaint hotline; (3) rigorous and thorough investigations and audits; and (4) enforcement that has market consequences. Asbed said corporations' much-ballyhooed social responsibility programs often fail because many of them do quick, superficial inspections that don't have tough market consequences when violations are found. "Enforcement needs teeth to work," he said.

CIW created its elaborate program to lift workers with virtually no government involvement. It has all been done within the private sector. Asbed sees some parallels with food safety and *E. coli* outbreaks. "The food buyers said to the growers, If you don't meet these food safety standards, we won't buy from you," he said. "We condition purchases on compliance with a human-rights set of standards." He's proud that Fair Food Program tomatoes now carry a green "Fair Food" label saying, "Consumer Powered, Worker Certified." The program, he said, has been a model in harnessing consumer power so that the "voice of the marginalized" worker "is raised in chorus with the powerful voice of consumers."

Beau McHan, a top manager in Pacific Tomato's Immokalee operations, has unhappy memories of the coalition's first general strike in 1995, triggered by Pacific's decision to cut wages. "They said we're this evil corporation," McHan recalled. But now he, Pacific Tomato, and the coalition are working hand in hand to improve conditions. His company has invested $50,000 in a new drinking water system and $5,000 a year for shade tents. "We found that we had a lot more similarities than differences," McHan said. "We also believe in human rights."

"We are tomato farmers," he added. "We're trying to make a profit. Yet everyone wants to know that they're changing the world for the better."

Eighteen

How Los Angeles Became Pro-Labor

EACH SUMMER AS A CHILD, Maria Elena Durazo crisscrossed California's Central Valley with her parents, helping them pick grapes, strawberries, and peaches. The seventh of eleven children, Durazo remembers times, long past midnight, when the police rousted her sleeping family from riverbanks and ravines for trespassing. Despite their hard work, her parents, immigrants from Mexico, often couldn't afford housing. When Durazo was five, her infant brother died after her parents were unable to afford a doctor for him. A priest took up a collection for the burial.

It was only thanks to financial aid that Durazo was able to attend St. Mary's College, a school outside San Francisco, where she became an activist in the Chicano movement. After graduation, she took a job with the International Ladies' Garment Workers' Union as an organizer in L.A.'s garment district. She juggled that job with going to the Peoples College of Law, and after law school Durazo, who says fighting for workers is in her blood, became an organizer for the hotel workers' union in Los Angeles.

She soon grew disgusted with that union local's white male leadership. Even though two-thirds of the local's members were Latino, its president, Scotty Allan, refused to hold membership meetings in Spanish, have a translator at meetings, or print union materials in Spanish. Durazo grew angrier still that Allan was going easy on management, with wages and benefits for L.A.'s hotel workers slipping well below those in other major cities. Fed up, she led an insurgent slate that challenged Allan. Fearing that Durazo would win, Allan accused her slate of stuffing ballot boxes, prompting the parent union to put the L.A. local into trusteeship. It sent in a troubleshooter, Miguel Contreras, to fix the mess.

At first, Durazo, idealistic firebrand, viewed Contreras, canny pragmatist, as an adversary, a water carrier for the old guard. But Contreras convinced her that he, too, was all about improving the lives of low-wage workers. He, too, was the child of farmworkers. As a teenager, Contreras had worked for Cesar Chavez, promoting the United Farm Workers' grape boycott; one summer he was arrested eighteen times for violating an injunction against picketing. Within a year, Durazo and Contreras were married.

In 1989, with the trusteeship ending, Durazo was overwhelmingly elected president of the local, UNITE HERE Local 11. She injected it with her fierce energy and drive. To pressure recalcitrant hotels, she at times orchestrated elaborate efforts to block traffic, such as having Local 11 members place a dozen beds in the middle of a major L.A. boulevard and having several housekeepers make the beds right then and there.

Durazo was pushing to revive her local at a time when L.A.'s unions were weak, not least because the city's business community had long made L.A. one of the most antiunion cities outside the South. Moreover, when Durazo took her local's helm, L.A.'s economy was going through a turbulent time. It had boomed with aircraft and other defense plants during World War II, but in the 1980s and into the 1990s middle-class manufacturing jobs were disappearing from the area, while low-wage service-sector jobs were exploding, with immigrants from Mexico and Central America filling positions as dishwashers, janitors, home-care aides, and hotel housekeepers. In Los Angeles, there was increasingly a two-tier, high-low economy, with the middle hollowing out.

In April 1992, a jury acquitted four L.A. police officers on charges of using excessive force in the beating of Rodney King, an African American man arrested after a high-speed chase. To many Angelenos, that verdict was an affront to justice. A bystander had made a widely televised video showing the police repeatedly kicking and pummeling King as he lay on the ground. King suffered skull fractures, broken bones, and permanent brain damage.

Three hours after the not-guilty verdict was announced, rioting erupted in South L.A., one of the city's poorest areas, with people setting fires and looting grocery stores, electronics shops, and liquor stores. During five days of rioting, 63 people were killed, 2,383 injured, and 12,000 arrested, with an estimated $1 billion in property damage. L.A. residents were stunned by the rampage, and city leaders reluctantly acknowledged that the underlying cause wasn't just fury with the verdict but also poverty and inequality.

City leaders were at a loss for how to respond. A secretive white business elite, the Committee of Twenty-Five, had long run the city, but it had largely broken down, partly because many L.A.-based corporations had merged and moved their headquarters elsewhere. The leaders who remained named Peter Ueberroth, the organizer of the 1984 Summer Olympics in L.A., to oversee efforts to rebuild. Business and government pledged $4 billion to the plan, but they ultimately came up with only $800 million. The effort fizzled.

Meanwhile, Durazo and Contreras were cooking up their own, very different plan to rebuild L.A. and battle its poverty and inequality. They decided to create a scrappy new worker advocacy group that would be equal parts policy incubator, liaison with community groups, and mobilizer of the public. "We needed a new entity to look at things differently," Durazo said. "We needed to find a way to come up with policies that the government would institute." The new group, she explained, was to form alliances with other organizations to leverage labor's limited power.

Durazo turned to an activist friend to head the group. Madeline Janis had been executive director of the Central American Refugee Center, which helped resettle refugees from El Salvador and Guatemala. Like Durazo, Janis was a fighter, having protested apartheid and U.S. interference in Central America while a student at Amherst College. For Durazo, Contreras, and Janis, the objective was to create an organization that would promote policies and build politics to lift L.A.'s low-wage workers.

"Miguel and Maria Elena had this vision—let's build a coalition of progressive forces that can change the city's direction," said Peter Dreier, a professor of urban policy at Occidental College. "They had a broader vision than most other groups."

They named their new group the Tourism Industry Development Council, and at first it focused on helping hotel workers, although Janis—forever bubbling with ideas—soon expanded its scope. She ultimately renamed the group the Los Angeles Alliance for a New Economy (LAANE), indicating the group's ambitious goals. It was founded at an opportune time for anyone who wanted to expand labor's reach. With the once-mighty Committee of Twenty-Five fading, there was an opening for a new progressive group to influence policy, and LAANE was brilliant at seizing that opening.

In its twenty-five-year history, LAANE has spearheaded numerous efforts that have helped, all told, more than 120,000 workers. Among its achievements, it won enactment of one of the nation's first and most far-reaching living-wage laws and orchestrated passage of an innovative $15.37 minimum wage for the city's hotel workers. It got L.A.'s transit authority to hire more African Americans on once-segregated construction projects and got real estate developers to agree to pay a living wage to the workers in their buildings as well as hire workers from poor neighborhoods and pledge not to oppose unionization. LAANE formed a pioneering labor-environmentalist coalition that has cut truck pollution by 90 percent at the ports of Long Beach and Los Angeles. In an innovative effort to bolster manufacturing, its offshoot, Jobs to Move America, persuaded L.A.'s transit agency (as well as Chicago's and Boston's) to use their purchasing power to get Japanese and Chinese companies to build rail and bus factories in the United States, creating more than twenty-five hundred new manufacturing jobs.

Not bad for a group that was founded with $60,000 and Janis as its sole employee. (It now has thirty employees and a budget of $4 million, much of it coming from foundations.) "It was the best $60,000 our union ever spent," said Kurt Petersen, a current co-president of Local 11. Harold Meyerson, a longtime writer on labor, has called LAANE "the nation's most innovative and effective force for raising the incomes of low-wage private-sector workers."

———

During LAANE's first two years, Janis focused on exposing poverty among L.A.'s nonunion hotel workers. Then, in 1995, a crisis erupted that pushed the group to center stage. Richard Riordan, the Republican mayor, called for L.A.'s airport commission to award new franchises for the restaurants and shops at LAX. As a result, the new franchise owners laid off three hundred workers and hired lower-wage, nonunion replacements.

Many Angelenos were outraged. Janis and Durazo considered fighting just for reinstatement of the workers, but they realized that if they succeeded, it would in ways be a hollow victory because the workers would have considerably worse wages and benefits than before. Janis had an epiphany: "The crisis at the airport lit up a lightbulb on how can we use government as a way to help lift up workers. Instead of dealing with policies just to win the jobs back, we used it [the airport crisis] to fight for a better set of policies to set a new standard for cities."

Durazo, who chaired LAANE's board, has a husky voice, raucous laugh, and charge-ahead style. She is a born organizer who relishes a good fight. Janis is more cerebral, hugely inventive in formulating policy solutions for ten-sided problems. She also doesn't shrink from battle, although all the brickbats and vilification from business and the right sometimes get her down. The duo teamed up with Jackie Goldberg, a labor-friendly city council member, to pursue a two-step strategy. First, they pushed for a worker retention bill to prevent future layoffs when the city awarded new franchises. Second, they pushed for a living-wage bill, even though Mayor Riordan strongly opposed such a law, and most council members were hardly fans of labor. "A lot of people told me I was crazy to push these proposals," Janis said.

Durazo, Contreras, and Janis realized that they had to transform L.A.'s politics if they were to get a living wage enacted, and they embraced three strategies to that end. Their first strategy was to forge a broad, living-wage coalition, and they built a coalition that L.A. had never seen before: unions; community groups; immigrant groups; African American, Asian, and Latino groups; and of course clergy. Religious leaders formed a new group, Clergy and Laity United for Economic Justice, and their joining the fight made many council members start taking the living-wage cause seriously. One of the group's leaders was the Reverend James Lawson, who had played a key role in the Memphis sanitation strike three decades earlier. "The 'living wage' in Los Angeles and around the country would clearly be something that [Martin Luther] King would support," Lawson told the *Los Angeles Times*. "The living wage . . . reflects the best tradition of religious activism."

The second strategy was, in Janis's words, "taking the city to city hall." After graduating from UCLA Law School, Janis had worked as a real estate lawyer and had repeatedly seen developers and business lobbyists huddle with council members the day before an important vote, often to discuss donations and deals. Janis set out to have people power trump lobbyists' power. LAANE directed a stream of clergy, community leaders, and rank-and-file workers to meet with council members. Restaurant workers and janitors from LAX argued for a living wage by telling council members how they could barely make ends meet. "We took thousands of people to city hall," Janis said. "We had festivals. We took people from old-age homes. We took schoolkids. We took many workers."

This coalition also took its campaign to all fifteen city council districts. Recognizing that it needed ten votes to override Riordan's anticipated veto, LAANE focused on winning over council members from conservative parts of the San Fernando Valley. "Clergy from every denomination began faxing in their support to their council members every day," Durazo said. "People expected that from Watts, but not from the [San Fernando] Valley."

Contreras oversaw a brilliant third strategy. He undertook a mobilization that convincingly transformed the city and county of Los Angeles from red to blue in politics, while helping flip the state assembly from Republican to Democratic. In 1994, Contreras left the hotel workers' union to become political director of the Los Angeles County Federation of Labor, and two years later he became overall head of that 800,000-member federation. Knowing that two million Hispanic immigrants had moved to L.A., Contreras transformed the labor federation from a lethargic group dominated by well-paid white construction workers into a labor-Latino powerhouse that battled for low-wage workers. Contreras was tired of seeing labor serve as an ATM for politicians, giving money and getting little back. He wanted to turn unions into a potent, on-the-ground political force that elected politicians who delivered for workers.

It was an era when California's immigrants were ripe to be mobilized. They were furious that the Republican governor, Pete Wilson, had championed Proposition 187, the successful 1994 ballot initiative that barred undocumented immigrants from receiving government aid and services, including public education, food stamps, and nonemergency medical aid. Under Contreras, L.A.'s labor federation mobilized tens of thousands of immigrant workers—huge numbers registered to vote, and many who couldn't register became politically active. "He saw that in a city of immigrants you don't have to vote to get involved in politics," Professor Dreier said. "You can make phone calls and knock on doors."

With Contreras at the helm, L.A.'s unions became a major force in city council races. The labor federation sought to oust some longtime Democrats who were wishy-washy on union issues and replace them with candidates Contreras described as "warriors for labor." The best known was Hilda Solis, who ousted Congressman Marty Martínez, a nine-term pro-NAFTA centrist Democrat. (Solis later became President Obama's first secretary of labor.)

One organizing victory in particular showed labor's growing clout—and Contreras's touch. In 1999, the SEIU unionized seventy-four thousand Los Angeles home-care workers in one fell swoop; Contreras had made that possible by persuading L.A. County's commissioners to declare the county the employer of the seventy-four thousand aides. That was the nation's single biggest unionization victory since Ford Motor Company's workers unionized in 1941.

Thanks to all this mobilizing and politicking, the city council enacted the worker retention law over Riordan's veto. The bigger showdown was supposed to be over the living-wage bill, but LAANE did such an impressive job lining up support that the bill passed 12–0, showing how Janis, Durazo, Contreras, and their allies had hugely transformed the council. (Three council members who opposed the bill abstained, rather than vote no and thereby anger the muscular, new labor-Latino coalition.) The new law covered around five thousand workers—parking-lot attendants, library janitors, airport newsstand workers—less than 1 percent of L.A.'s workforce, but for LAANE it was a vital first step. Janis explained, "That's how you create change, not thinking that you're going to have to change the wages of a million people at once, but that you can have incremental goals . . . that build on each other." (Contreras died of a heart attack in 2005, and Durazo was elected head of the Los Angeles Federation of Labor the following year.)

L.A.'s living-wage law was the nation's third and broadest, going beyond the first two enacted in Baltimore and New York. Unlike theirs, it applied not just to companies that received city contracts but also to those getting city subsidies and leases. Moreover, the L.A. law called for both a living wage and health coverage. Janis traveled across the United States to push the idea of a living wage, and ultimately dozens of cities enacted such a law. She also brainstormed other ways to lift L.A.'s low-wage workers, and soon she and Goldberg settled on a new strategy.

In 1998, a prominent developer proposed a huge project in Goldberg's district (Hollywood). It was to include upscale retail shops, a high-end hotel, and the giant theater where the Oscar ceremonies are held each year. Janis and Goldberg realized that this project could become a vehicle for a new policy that would ensure that the community and workers benefited, and not just the developer. They called their idea a "community benefits agreement" (CBA). They warned the developer that unless it signed such an agreement, they could easily block the project because they had two powerful levers. First, under city council tradition, members could essentially veto projects proposed for their districts (the project was in Goldberg's district). Second, because Hollywood was a run-down area at the time, the project qualified for tax abatements—$90 million worth. Goldberg and Janis warned that they could rally the council to block those abatements. "I was determined that if we were going to put money into [this project], the employees would be treated well," Goldberg said. "We wanted development, [but] we basically decided that all boats should rise." She had warned the developer, TrizecHahn, "You don't want to open your project with picket lines."

TrizecHahn signed the nation's first community benefits agreement. It promised that the new upscale hotel would retain workers from the previous hotel on the site and promised that the hotel's workers would receive the same pay and benefits as L.A.'s unionized hotel workers. The company also agreed that the living-wage law would cover the janitors, security guards, and parking attendants it hired for the project's mall and parking garage. It also promised to recognize a union at the Oscar awards theater (now called the Dolby Theatre). When choosing retail tenants, TrizecHahn would favor those that paid a living wage and provided health insurance. It also promised to hire many people from the area—68 percent of the hotel's employees would come from neighboring zip codes. Harold Meyerson wrote that the agreement meant "working-class Hollywood would have a direct share in Hollywood's revival."

A new pro-worker tool, the community benefits agreement, was born. The idea has spread to more than twenty other cities and helped tens of thousands of workers. LAANE has used it in dozens of projects, including the huge L.A. Live development around the Staples Center, home of the Los Angeles Lakers. On that project, which included stores, condominiums, and office buildings, the developer agreed that the luxury hotels that came to the site—ultimately a Ritz-Carlton and JW Marriott—wouldn't oppose unionization. The developer also agreed that half the hotel workers would be from the neighborhood, that African Americans would have some front-of-the-house hotel jobs, and that one-fifth of the new housing units would be for low-income residents.

"Community benefits agreements are all driven by the vision that the economy needs to serve the people who are in it," Janis said. "People have a limited idea of what community benefits agreements can do. We can make a community benefits agreement whatever we want it to be. . . . It's the right of people to contract." Roxana Tynan, who worked as Goldberg's economic development deputy, pointed to another benefit of these agreements: "A CBA creates not just a measurable victory, but a certain accountability, a way that promises have to be lived up to—on wages, number of jobs, number of affordable housing units."

Ultimately, LAANE concluded that instead of battling for agreements on project after project, it would be smarter to get the City of Los Angeles to adopt a policy that universalized the CBA's basic ingredients, including living-wage and local hiring provisions, in every major L.A. project that sought zoning changes or subsidies. The city and its development agency adopted that policy in several steps between 2002 and 2008.

Many developers dislike community benefits agreements, saying they obstruct free enterprise and blackmail entrepreneurs. To that, Janis responded, "We were pursuing a very capitalistic notion. Public money is an investment on behalf of the community and taxpayers. We're saying that the developers who receive the benefit of public investment should give a return on that investment to the community."

———

After this string of victories, LAANE held a retreat to brainstorm additional ways to lift L.A.'s workers. It decided to focus on six industries—hotels, construction, recycling, waste hauling, retail, and port trucking—and that led to numerous hard-fought campaigns over the next decade.

In early 2014, in ways leapfrogging the Fight for $15, LAANE and its allies proposed a $15.37 minimum wage for L.A.'s hotel workers, nearly double the city's then-minimum wage of $8 ($15.37 was then the "living wage" for L.A.'s airport workers). In waging the fight, LAANE provided a textbook model of how to win despite fierce industry opposition. The effort focused on hotel workers because so many of them lived in poverty and because the hotel workers' union was one of LAANE's main backers. "Our goal is to shrink the number of low-wage workers in Los Angeles," Durazo said. "This campaign comes from the need to do something forceful about income inequality."

The business community immediately sought to kill the effort. Bob Amano, executive director of the Hotel Association of Los Angeles, denounced the proposal as "a drastic pay increase," saying that "when the city is desperately seeking more hotel rooms," this "is definitely not the way to go." Carol Schatz, chief executive of the Central City Association, a business group, said enacting a $15.37 wage would be "highly irresponsible" and "the economic impacts could be huge."

Having faced such opposition before, LAANE proceeded to do what it does so well—mount a full-court press to persuade the city council. To kick off the campaign, called Raise L.A., LAANE held a news conference in city hall in January 2014 at which three council members joined officials from dozens of allied groups, including the American Civil Liberties Union, the Natural Resources Defense Council, and the Jewish Labor Committee.

From February on, a stream of clergy members—often joined by hotel workers—met with council members. "We try to map who is the rabbi, who is the priest, who are their friends in the district. Are there people they went to high school with?" said Roxana Tynan, the former Jackie Goldberg aide who, in 2012, succeeded Janis as LAANE's executive director. (Term limits forced Goldberg to leave the city council in 2001, and at that point LAANE hired Tynan as its community benefits coordinator.) LAANE asked clergy to meet repeatedly with wavering council members, like Mitch O'Farrell, who represented Hollywood, Goldberg's former district. Rick Hoyt, a Unitarian minister, went to see O'Farrell, telling him, "The argument that hotel owners can only make a profit by abusing their workers is a nonstarter. They're in the wrong business if their plan requires that hotel workers not be able to support themselves and their families."

Hotel owners commissioned a study that said the $15.37 wage would cause the loss of fourteen hundred jobs. LAANE responded with its own report, calling that estimate hugely inflated and outlining the benefits of a $15.37 wage. LAANE also created an online, interactive map that detailed the number of hotel workers who lived in each council district and estimated how a $15.37 wage would benefit each district. That map showed, for instance, that 675 hotel workers lived in O'Farrell's district and that a $15.37 wage would lift their overall pay by $3.4 million a year and increase consumer spending in his district by $1.9 million.

When several corporate groups attacked the proposal, LAANE took pains to show that the idea had significant business backing, too. Raise L.A. supporters knocked on the doors of thousands of small businesses, and ultimately 750 of those business owners signed a petition backing the $15.37 wage, with hundreds placing "Raise L.A." stickers in their windows. To demonstrate there was strong grassroots support, LAANE's organizers got seventeen neighborhood councils, representing 750,000 L.A. residents, to endorse the recommended wage.

LAANE made deft use of social media, steering message after message to the Facebook and Twitter accounts of wavering members like O'Farrell. For months, Raise L.A. activists went to nearly every community event and farmers' market in O'Farrell's district, getting ten thousand of his constituents to sign a petition. Most Sunday mornings, Julia Gould, then a senior at Occidental College, set up a table at the Hollywood Farmers Market, where she asked shoppers to sign a petition backing the $15.37 wage. She also urged shoppers to write on a whiteboard their reasons for supporting the higher wage. One shopper wrote, "To live a healthy life, you need a living wage." A community organizer working with Gould photographed these shoppers and their hand-scrawled messages and then posted those photos on Facebook and Twitter and directed them to O'Farrell's social media accounts. "We were trying to show him that his constituents cared about this," Gould said.

On the afternoon of the vote, hundreds of hotel workers packed the city council's ornate chambers. In tense remarks minutes before the vote, O'Farrell acknowledged his ambivalence. He pointed to the study forecasting a loss of jobs, but he nonetheless announced he would vote for the $15.37 wage. "At the end of the day, between the intellect and the heart, the heart wins out," O'Farrell said. Evidently, hearing from myriad constituents, including many hotel workers, helped make sure his heart won out.

The council approved the bill, 12–3, and the crowd erupted with cheers. "I'm overjoyed," said Magdali Martinez, a hotel room attendant and mother of three who was making $11.42 an hour at the time. "This is really going to help my family. We don't have enough money coming in. We often have to choose between falling behind on our gas bill or our phone bill." Martinez, whose husband works at an auto body shop, said that thanks to the $15.37 law, her pay has jumped to $18 an hour (longtime room attendants like her had their pay bumped well above $15.37). As a result, she can now work just one job, instead of two, and the couple can now afford to send their son to dental school in their native Guatemala.

Mayor Garcetti promptly signed the $15.37 wage into law. "LAANE," he said, "has helped bring a sense of urgency for social justice in a town where people are falling behind."

His wife, Amy Wakeland, has served as head of LAANE's advisory board and called LAANE "perhaps the most important organization working on economic justice issues in the city." Garcetti had originally backed a $13.25 minimum wage for Los Angeles, but the council's overwhelming support for the $15.37 hotel wage went far to persuade him to sign a $15 citywide minimum into law eight months later, thereby fulfilling one of LAANE's ambitious goals.

———

LAANE often gets attacked from the right. Riordan, the former mayor, called it "a shill for labor unions," while Carol Schatz of the Central City Association said, "LAANE purports to combat poverty and promote new jobs, but it only supports union jobs." LAANE's leaders say these critics miss the mark. "The vast majority of the workers who have benefited from our policies are not members of a union and probably never will be," says Roxana Tynan, LAANE's executive director. In fact, LAANE has evolved greatly since its founding. It now sees itself not simply as a labor union adjunct but as a community group and an environmental group. It has broadened its scope because it recognizes that to improve people's lives, it is necessary not just to help workers on workplace matters but to help assure them affordable housing, clean air and water, and much more. With union power in decline, LAANE has concluded that the most effective way to lift workers, and their communities, is to work closely with other groups, including community and environmental groups.

Of all the local worker advocacy groups in the nation, LAANE has been the most effective in allying itself with green groups to help both workers and the environment. For example, in 2005, sixteen thousand trucks rumbled each day into the neighboring Ports of Los Angeles and Long Beach—together the nation's largest seaport—often waiting hours to pick up goods, spewing diesel particulates and befouling neighboring communities. Angry residents and environmentalists demanded that the ports require a new generation of cleaner trucks that would cut pollution by 90 percent. All these new trucks would cost nearly $2 billion, and it was unclear who would pay for them.

LAANE joined with environmental groups to analyze the situation. Most port truck drivers couldn't afford the more than $100,000 to buy new-generation trucks. Eighty-eight percent of the drivers were independent contractors, and although they grossed $75,000 a year on average, they netted just $29,000 after factoring in fuel, insurance, and other costs. Their pay averaged just $12 an hour.

LAANE, with strong support from L.A.'s then mayor, Antonio Villaraigosa, teamed up with environmental groups to develop an ingenious clean air plan that the two ports adopted in 2008. The ports required that within five years only new-generation trucks could be used. The ports levied a supplemental $35 fee per shipping container and then used the money from that levy to provide loans and subsidies to help companies and drivers buy new trucks. In addition, the Port of Los Angeles required trucking companies to treat their drivers as employees, not independent contractors. This meant that the trucking companies would have to pay for overtime and cover many of the truckers' costs, including fuel and insurance. It also enabled the truckers to unionize.

By 2013, truck pollution at the ports had dropped by 90 percent. But a federal appeals court ruled that the Port of Los Angeles couldn't require trucking companies to treat their drivers as employees. That was a huge blow to many drivers who once again found themselves as low-paid independent contractors. As employees, many were earning enough to pay down the debt on their new trucks, but as contractors many were soon in default. Fortunately, LAANE and several lawyers got California's labor commissioner, Julie Su, to rule that trucking companies had been illegally misclassifying more than fifteen hundred drivers as independent contractors. Those rulings increased those drivers' pay and bargaining power (although the labor commissioner's ruling didn't cover all trucking companies and drivers).

As innovative as this port trucking effort was, LAANE's campaign to improve L.A.'s waste-hauling industry was arguably more imaginative. In 2011, city officials were alarmed that the main garbage landfill in L.A. would soon reach capacity. They were also upset that the private-sector waste haulers that served businesses and multifamily buildings, picking up 77 percent of the city's trash, recycled merely one-fifth of what they collected. Many Angelenos complained that trucks from seven or eight different waste-hauling companies would rumble down their streets each day, clogging roads, belching pollution, and endangering pedestrians. At the time, the city's 125 trash haulers won contracts by submitting the lowest bid (and often paying dismal wages).

"Our commercial waste industry was the Wild West—there were no recycling standards, no job standards," said Greg Good, who was LAANE's point man on fixing the waste-hauling chaos. "The system incentivized a race to the bottom."

After nearly two years of studying the industry, LAANE and its environmental allies put forward a far-reaching plan to bring order to the chaos. Their plan called for dividing L.A. into eleven zones, with an exclusive waste-hauling franchise awarded for each zone through competitive bidding. To win a ten-year franchise, companies would have to pledge to use clean trucks, recycle a high percentage of trash, pay a living wage, assure safe working conditions, and promise not to oppose unionization. The plan was called Don't Waste L.A.

Before going public with the plan, LAANE published a twenty-six-page research report that examined the waste industry's problems. "You can't come into city hall with a half-baked idea and hope to succeed," Good said. For months, he and Adrian Martinez, a lawyer with the Natural Resources Defense Council, attended meetings in dozens of California communities to learn how their trash collection systems worked. "If you want to get something done, LAANE is the go-to group," Martinez said. "They're successful because they find areas where environmental and community groups can really align with them on environmental matters and on unjust practices that harm workers." (LAANE has had great success with the staffing strategy it uses for each of its campaigns, including its waste industry campaign. It creates a four-person team: a director, a researcher, a communications person, and an organizer who rallies community support and forges alliances with other groups.)

Among the workers who supported the waste initiative was Margarita Castro, a recycling worker who spent her days picking plastics and paper off a conveyor belt that carried trash past her. "We work in the sun and in the rain—there's no shade," Castro said. "You're standing with no protection at all. No rain boots. A lot of accidents can happen." A truck once drove over a pipe that went flying and smashed into her right heel. A co-worker slipped and broke a tailbone, another nearly lost a finger, another stepped on a nail. The workers, Castro complained, were given flimsy gloves and ineffective paper masks to cover their mouths. She praised the franchise system, saying it would force recycling companies to mend their ways: "They'll have to work differently, with more protections."

Gary Toebben, president of the Los Angeles Area Chamber of Commerce, lambasted the plan as a plot to "use city rules and regulations to unionize the industry." He warned that the plan would push dozens of smaller haulers out of business and significantly raise prices for trash collection. The plan's goals, he said, could have been achieved by setting minimum requirements for waste-hauling companies—and without a franchise plan. Good disagreed. He said the franchise system was the best way to ensure a stable industry with clean trucks, solid wages, and safe workplaces.

In 2014, the Los Angeles City Council, after being pressured by a LAANE-led coalition of thirty groups, approved the eleven-zone waste plan, which has been renamed RecycLA. It has increased recycling, improved pay and safety, and reduced pollution and the number of trucks. As the system got off the ground, customers complained that the waste-hauling companies were charging unexpected fees and skipping many pickups, but month by month it was working more smoothly.

Waste experts in many cities view L.A.'s new system as a model.

"LAANE's an inspiration for us," said Matt Ryan, executive director of the Alliance for a Greater New York, a labor-environmental group. "They're proof that you can change an economy, lift workers, and improve the environment at the local level."

———

Much like Madeline Janis, her savvy predecessor, Roxana Tynan knows how to strategize, mobilize, build alliances, push boundaries, write smart, well-researched reports, and speak movingly and convincingly, whether at a city council hearing, a rally of port truck drivers, or a $5,000-a-table fund-raiser that includes Hollywood stars. She has been on a crusade to spread LAANE's model and successes to other cities. She's hoping that LAANE-like groups will spring up elsewhere and build alliances—and power—to lift workers, communities, and the environment. LAANE helped to create the Partnership for Working Families, a group with affiliates in Boston, Chicago, Hartford, Minneapolis, Phoenix, and a dozen other cities. Those groups are seeking to copy many of LAANE's successes.

"Given the dysfunction of the federal government, our sense is that in a country as huge and complex as ours, cities should serve as the laboratories for change," Tynan said. "We're trying to be a laboratory for experimentation about what makes the economy work for more people." To Tynan, the power that comes from forging labor-community-environmental alliances will help roll back the political gains that antiunion, antiprogressive forces have made in state after state. She says worker advocates need to build out from the cities, where they have built power, and then seek to win control of state governments. "Part of our mission is to make links between labor, community groups, environmental groups, and affordable housing advocates because that's the only way we can win stuff," Tynan said. "On our own, none of us is strong enough to win improvements for workers or the community at large."

Tynan became a union activist in college, at Yale, inspired by UNITE HERE's efforts to help the school's food-service and administrative workers. Raised in London and Los Angeles, she said her parents were "Champagne Socialists." Her British father was a drama critic for *The New Yorker* magazine and co-author of the bawdy Broadway musical *Oh! Calcutta!* After college, Tynan worked as an organizer for the Culinary Union in Las Vegas in its unusually successful effort that has unionized nearly every hotel on the Strip.

Her message for worker advocates and their progressive allies is that one can only build power from the bottom. "Our real message is that power gets built in place and gets built through long-standing coalitions and through leadership development," she said. "And it gets built through the day-to-day work of organizing folks through permanent institutions. There is no shortcut to that. Fancy-ass ideas like universal basic income are meaningless if there is no power to win anything."

Tynan has little patience for critics who dismiss LAANE as a bunch of out-of-control leftists seeking to tear down capitalism. "We have business support," she said. "Developers work with us. Not only do we not have horns, but we have a fundamentally pro-growth agenda. We just want to ensure that all boats are rising." At LAANE's annual fund-raiser, prominent developers buy tables for $10,000. Its 2015 fund-raiser—some call it "labor's prom"—was held at the Beverly Hills Hilton and honored *Modern Family*, with its stars Ed O'Neill and Sofía Vergara in attendance. "The beauty of LAANE—even though they tap into Hollywood—is that at the end of the day they're standing up for workers," said Kurt Petersen, Local 11's co-president.

"When all is said and done," says Tynan, "we have a pretty conservative vision that people should earn enough money so they can take care of themselves and their families, live somewhere decent, and send their kids to schools that they like. This whole idea that raising wages is a left idea is nutty. You can't make an economy work if people don't have money to spend."

Nineteen

Best Foot Forward

KAISER PERMANENTE IS GIGANTIC—it has 12 million health plan members and 210,000 employees, including 57,000 nurses. It also has 39 hospitals and 680 other medical facilities spread over eight states and the District of Columbia. It is a giant in labor relations, too, often hailed as having the nation's best labor-management partnership, quite an accomplishment in a nation where labor-management relations are often uninspired or rancorous. At Kaiser, doctors, supervisors, nurses, lab assistants, and kitchen workers, among others, pull together to improve patient service and increase efficiency, morale, and employee safety. Kaiser and its thirty-plus union locals, representing 123,000 workers at Kaiser, have formed the nation's largest, longest-lasting labor-management partnership.

Examining one small corner of this partnership can reveal a lot.

Each morning, Candy Maldonado, a pharmacy technician at the Kaiser Permanente Medical Center in San Jose, had a mess to clean up—she had to track down ten or so diabetes outpatients who had missed their telephone appointments with Kaiser pharmacists the day before. Those appointments are vital because the pharmacists use them to check on those patients' blood sugar levels and, if need be, adjust their insulin intake and diet. Maldonado's pharmaceutical department serves thousands of outpatients, and its three Spanish-speaking pharmacists devote one day a week each to telephone appointments with Latino diabetes patients—in theory, twenty-five appointments of twenty minutes each. But 40 percent of those patients weren't answering the phone for their appointments. As a result, a sizable chunk of each pharmacist's day was wasted, many diabetes patients were not receiving the monitoring and advice they needed, and techs like Maldonado had to spend hours chasing down patients to reschedule. Within Maldonado's department, there was much concern about the "FTKA" metric—failure to keep appointments. It was a glaring sign of inefficiency at a company that puts a big focus on metrics and efficiency.

Maldonado was in a position to address this problem. She is "union co-lead" of her department's unit-based team, and she joined with the team's "management co-lead," Griffin Marie Edwards, a supervisor, to strategize on how to deal with these FTKAs. Kaiser Permanente has over thirty-five hundred such unit-based teams (known at UBTs) at its hospitals and medical offices. Teams can include everyone from doctors to lab assistants who join together to tackle problems, improve service, and save money (which, employees know, can translate into bonuses or larger raises). Kaiser says that in 2016 alone, forty-eight hundred separate UBT projects achieved cost savings of over $48 million. Kaiser instructs its UBTs to follow the company's "value compass," which places patients in the middle and stresses four goals: best service, best quality, most affordable, and best place to work.

At one of its monthly meetings, Maldonado's UBT—the department's seventy-one employees select seven co-workers to lead the UBT—decided that reducing the number of missed telephone appointments would be its official project. The team tasked Maldonado with surveying the diabetes patients to ask why they often missed their appointments. Because she is bilingual and talkative, puts people at ease, and is a good listener, she was perfect for the job. After speaking with more than a hundred patients, Maldonado reported back about their responses: " 'I don't have a lunchtime or break.' 'I work a lot of overtime.' 'It's mandatory overtime.' 'I can't pick up the phone at work.' 'I left my phone somewhere.' 'I forgot about my appointment.' 'Something happened in my family.' They were ill. Sometimes out of the country. They didn't hear the phone." Maldonado added that many patients feared unpleasantness. They told her, " 'The doctor is going to yell at me.' 'I'm going to be in trouble.' 'My blood sugar is bad.' 'My mother died of diabetes. I know I'm going to die of diabetes, too.' "

With this information, the UBT's members brainstormed and then decided that Maldonado should phone reluctant patients and make clear that the pharmacists wouldn't yell at them and that they shouldn't be embarrassed if their blood sugar is high. Previously, patients received automatic telephone reminders several days before their appointment, but those reminders were usually in English. Under the revised approach, Maldonado would call many patients the morning of their appointments, and if they didn't pick up, she would leave a voice mail in Spanish. In the past, Maldonado made her calls from a blocked number that prevented patients who missed her call from phoning back. The team recommended unblocking her number so patients who missed her "reminder" could call back. With many patients missing their appointments because they were at work, the pharmacists expanded their schedules; they now often do telephone appointments until 7 p.m. and on weekends.

As a result, in just three months, the rate of missed appointments dropped to 18 percent from 40 percent. This means that pharmacists are now using their time more efficiently and that diabetes patients are having better health results and fewer hospitalizations (saving Kaiser Permanente money). Another benefit: Maldonado doesn't have to spend nearly as many hours chasing after those who missed appointments. Kaiser's employees realize that increased efficiency saves money and can help them; for instance, when Kaiser does worse financially, that can endanger their pensions.

Maldonado and Edwards boasted of numerous other smart ideas their UBT came up with. When a pharmacist or pharmacy technician missed a few days of work, outpatients' messages often weren't picked up or responded to for several days—a big snag in serving people. So the UBT created a buddy system to ensure that whenever someone misses a day of work, her "buddy" checks her emails and phone messages to assure prompt responses to patients.

Each day, the pharmacy techs have to send faxes filled with instructions to twelve dialysis centers. The techs complained about having to spend hours and hours feeding the fax machines, maintaining them, waiting for confirmations, and phoning the dialysis centers to make sure they saw the faxes. The UBT came up with a time- and money-saving solution: send the faxes by computer, which ensures automatic "fax received" responses by computer. This move has saved untold hours.

At the very first meeting of Maldonado's UBT, its leaders decided to ask the department's employees to vote on what issue they most wanted addressed. The answer was, do more for staff recognition. "That was a big deal," Maldonado said. The team created an accolades box. "If you catch someone doing an awesome job or they do something that really helps you, to acknowledge them, you write that down and put it in the box," she said. "At our [the department's] monthly meeting, we read them aloud so everyone could get little accolades. We saw that morale went up." Those who receive accolades earn coupons they can use to get umbrellas, baseball caps, and other items for free in the medical center's store (Kaiser Permanente covers the cost of the coupons).

Maldonado, a member of the Service Employees International Union, says morale and working conditions are much better at Kaiser than at the nonunion hospital where she once worked. "Here I'm automatically guaranteed a raise," she said. "I don't have to jump through hoops to get one. You used to have to say, 'Pretty please.'" As part of their three-year contract that expired in September 2018, Kaiser's workers in California received annual raises of 3 percent, 3 percent, and 4 percent—considerably better than most workers nationwide.

"The labor-management partnership is awesome," Maldonado said. "You can bring any idea to your manager, and our manager is willing to work with you and your union if there is a problem. It's not management versus employee or labor."

————

It was not always thus. Denise Duncan has troubling memories of what Kaiser Permanente was like in the 1990s, when she was a nurse at a Kaiser hospital in suburban Los Angeles. The company was downsizing hospital units, laying off workers, and demanding draconian pay cuts. "They drove right through our contract and tried to cut everything—everything from wages and benefits to reducing our sick time," Duncan said. "Anything that had a dollar sign attached to it they tried to cut."

Duncan's union—its unwieldy name is the United Nurses Associations of California/Union of Health Care Professionals—voted to strike. At the time, Duncan was furious that Kaiser had veered away from its labor-friendly history. Kaiser Permanente grew out of a health-care program created in the 1930s and 1940s for construction, shipyard, and steel mill workers at unionized companies run by Henry J. Kaiser, one of that era's foremost industrialists. The company also had roots in a twelve-bed hospital that Dr. Sidney Garfield set up in the Mojave Desert for hundreds of workers on the New Deal's Colorado River Aqueduct project. To keep that hospital afloat, the workers' insurance companies agreed, in an innovation for the time, to set up a prepaid insurance plan that cost five cents per worker per day. That enabled Garfield's hospital to survive and focus on preventive care and not just emergencies.

That system worked so well that in 1938 Henry Kaiser called on Garfield to set up a similar, though much larger, health-care program for 6,500 workers and their families at what was, to that time, the largest construction project in American history—the Grand Coulee Dam, on the Columbia River in Washington State. When the dam was nearly completed and soon after the United States had entered World War II, Kaiser asked Garfield to oversee health care for the 200,000 workers at his fast-expanding shipyards—in Richmond, California, Portland, Oregon, and Vancouver, Washington—and at his steel mill in Fontana, California. (Kaiser's shipyards, far ahead of their time, had child-care centers for their many "Rosie the Riveters.")

When the war ended, the shipyards' workforce dropped from ninety thousand to thirteen thousand, and Garfield's medical group dwindled, too. He wanted to continue his prepaid practice, but his path forward and financing were unclear. The International Longshore and Warehouse Union came to the rescue, telling Garfield that if his practice would continue taking care of the union's members, the union would steer all of its members to him, and encourage other unions to do likewise. (While the East Coast longshoremen's union was known for its Mafia ties, the West Coast longshoremen's union was known for its leftist politics and rank-and-file militancy.)

Joined at the hip with labor, Kaiser grew from 154,000 health plan members in 1950 to more than 6 million in 1990. While Kaiser Permanente, a nonprofit, didn't invent prepaid medical plans, it was one of the first to build a large-scale, prepaid integrated model. It was also one of the nation's first HMOs. In the late 1980s and the 1990s, however, competition from several aggressive new HMOs badly squeezed Kaiser by pushing down prices and wooing away customers. To deal with this squeeze—Kaiser's losses totaled $900 million from 1995 to 1997—Kaiser's management consultants recommended layoffs, cutting wages, closing medical units, and perhaps shutting or selling its hospitals in Southern California.

That's when Kaiser Permanente's traditionally good labor relations soured. The company strong-armed its weakest unions into accepting concessions and then demanded that all of its union locals swallow the same medicine. In the early 1990s, Kaiser's biggest union, the SEIU, and many of its nurses' unions had held repeated protests and strikes. In 1995, the situation once again reached the boiling point. That year Denise Duncan's union, outraged by Kaiser's demand for a 12 percent wage cut, voted to go on strike unless Kaiser dropped its demands for concessions. "People who had been with Kaiser for twenty years were angry," Duncan said. "They felt that the family had broken up."

Duncan was an unlikely union activist, having grown up in an antiunion family in Oklahoma. After nursing school, she worked at a nonunion hospital but later jumped at the opportunity to take a higher-paying job at a new Kaiser hospital in the Woodland Hills section of Los Angeles. She left her Huntington Beach home at 5 a.m. to arrive on time for her 7 a.m. to 3 p.m. shift, but several times each week the badly understaffed hospital ordered her to work an additional shift, until 11 p.m.

For months, Duncan complained to management about being forced to work grueling double shifts. They ignored her pleas. Finally, she told her union's president of her problem, one that many other nurses had. The union president confronted the hospital's managers; they hired more nurses and addressed other issues, and the problem was fixed. "They cleaned it up, and that made me a believer in the power of unions," Duncan said. She proceeded to become a shop steward, a union vice president, and eventually union president.

In 1996, furious at Kaiser's tough line, Duncan's union and Kaiser's other unions formed a bargaining coalition and asked the national AFL-CIO to mount a pressure campaign against Kaiser. To turn up the heat, the AFL-CIO urged the local governments of Oakland and several other cities to take over Kaiser's hospitals. It also publicized a government report that gave bad grades to Kaiser's facilities in North Carolina.

Some union officials voiced fears that this campaign could destroy the institution that, despite its demands for concessions, was still providing solid wages and benefits. "We might do permanent damage to them [Kaiser Permanente] and to our 55,000 union members," acknowledged Peter diCicco, an AFL-CIO strategist who became the first head of Kaiser's union coalition. In addition, all the turmoil and cutbacks had some Kaiser officials, doctors, and workers worried that Kaiser was violating its commitment to guarantee quality care. As one worker put it, "This is not the Kaiser we came to work for."

The AFL-CIO's president, John Sweeney, told Kaiser's CEO, David Lawrence, that Kaiser had two choices: war or partnership. The federal government's top mediator arranged a face-to-face meeting between the two men. "We were like dogs sniffing each other," Lawrence said about his meeting with Sweeney. "Our hackles were up."

Lawrence agreed to hear an AFL-CIO presentation about the benefits of labor-management partnerships. He was far more moved by it than he had expected. "I honestly had to fight to keep from crying," he said. "It was like, holy crap, this really is exciting to listen to. This is exactly what we had to do. I responded by saying health care involves teams. You can't do it without teams. If we're fighting with each other, we can't take care of patients."

Lawrence and Sweeney embraced peace over war, and after nearly a year of negotiations the two sides established an unusually broad partnership. Kaiser's unions gained consensus decision making at many levels and an agreement promising "maximum possible employment and income security." That developed into one of the nation's best employment security programs. If a worker's job is eliminated, the worker gets up to a year of regular pay while receiving free training for a new position. Ninety-five percent of the time those workers are placed in other jobs at Kaiser, as happened with more than one hundred records clerks whose positions were eliminated when Kaiser converted to electronic medical records.

As part of the partnership, Kaiser pledged not to fight unionization efforts at its nonunion facilities and to allow the use of card check. In exchange, Kaiser's unions pledged to help persuade other unions and the public to sign up with Kaiser. Together, management and labor vowed to improve the quality of Kaiser's health care and make it a better place to work. "Sometimes out of crisis and determined effort comes a willingness to try a better alternative," Sweeney said.

One major union, the California Nurses Association, with twelve thousand members at Kaiser at the time, opposed the partnership, saying it would force unions to surrender their weapons in exchange for an ineffective partnership. "Our job," the union said, "is to fight corporate power, not partner with it." Early on, Denise Duncan also opposed the partnership: "I said hell no. We had such contentious bargaining that we felt people we had worked with had sold us down the river. I didn't think there'd be a chance of a partnership. I didn't think we could sit across the table and collaborate on anything." But now, two decades later, she says, "I was wrong. I learned a powerful lesson. You frequently have more in common [with management] than not. Frequently you want the same thing, you just may differ on how to get there."

Kaiser Permanente's popularity and reputation for quality have increased greatly since the partnership began in 1997. Kaiser has swelled from 8.7 million health plan members to 12 million, and its unionized workforce has jumped from 55,000 two decades ago to 123,000. "At a time when union membership has been declining in America, Kaiser's partnership and union coalition have helped unions grow tremendously," said Hal Ruddick, the executive director of the Coalition of Kaiser Permanente Unions from 2013 to 2018. That coalition broke into two in 2018 because most of Kaiser's union locals grew angry at the head of Kaiser's largest local, SEIU United Healthcare Workers West, asserting that he wanted to dominate and reduce the power of other unions in the coalition.

Health-care workers in California line up for jobs at Kaiser because it is known for having the best wages and benefits. Indeed, many California hospitals complain that they train nurses fresh out of nursing school for several years, only to have the nurses desert them for better-paying Kaiser hospitals. Tom Schneider, a labor relations consultant to many health-care companies, said, "Kaiser is the benchmark in every negotiation. Unions always hold Kaiser out. They say, 'Well, they have this at Kaiser.' They [management] respond, 'We can't match Kaiser,' and there's all this hair pulling over it."

"Kaiser," Duncan said, "has gone in twenty years from being in a very scary place, at the brink of closing its doors, to being one of the most respected health-care providers in the country."

When Dennis Dabney, a Kaiser executive, goes to human resources conventions, other corporate officials view him suspiciously. Some see Kaiser's cooperation with its unions as a fool's errand; some view it as apostasy.

"They say I'm crazy, that you're out of your mind," said Dabney, who is Kaiser's senior vice president in charge of labor relations and its labor-management partnership. "You get a lot of pushback. It's so foreign to them. Many take it personally. It's an insult to them." Dabney believes the partnership has, in ways large and small, improved service, cut costs, and lifted morale. "It's not a human resources program. It's a business strategy," he said. "That's what makes it different. At Kaiser, labor has been there from the beginning."

One of the partnership's biggest early successes came after a consultant recommended that Kaiser close its optical laboratory in Berkeley, California, saying that this would save $800,000 a year. Livid about that recommendation, the lab's 210 unionized workers insisted on some collaborative brainstorming. They came up with 250 ideas to improve operations, ideas that helped persuade Kaiser to keep the lab open. One idea was to adopt a new, broader utility worker classification, a major, cost-saving departure from the previous narrow job classifications that undermined efficiency. The lab also embraced a "gainsharing" recommendation in which workers would earn more if revenue, quality, and customer satisfaction improved.

After a year, the lab's annual income rose 19 percent, while productivity increased 8 percent per worker. Turnaround time on the lab's 350,000 eyeglass orders fell from 2.7 days to 1.3 days. All this helped save the lab over $800,000 a year, including $250,000 saved by reducing breakage and reworking. Thanks to all these improvements, the workers received a 2.7 percent pay bonus that year. Tony Gately, Kaiser's regional medical group director at the time and a longtime skeptic of unions, said, "I was impressed by how much labor knew about the business. They had ideas, but before, they never surfaced or if they did, they never went anywhere."

Nowadays, one of the partnership's biggest challenges is negotiating a new company-wide contract every three or four years for 123,000 workers in more than thirty union locals affiliated with twelve different national unions. The negotiations involve a cast of hundreds. Two months before the contract deadline, 150 union representatives and management officials, plus two dozen mediators/facilitators, begin meeting on weekends. They break into smaller committees to focus on specific issues, like training, reducing absenteeism, and safeguarding pensions. Then all 150 come back together to recommend an agreement for endorsement by union delegates. This agreement goes to local union members for ratification before becoming a national contract.

Bargaining with so many people can be daunting, Dabney acknowledged. "I realized you've got to get 120,000 people to ratify an agreement," he said. "Everyone in that room was a mini-ambassador. They will all go back to talk about how they were involved in the bargaining."

At times, the two sides surprise themselves with the progress they make. Many managers complained about absenteeism, that employees were using all of their allotted sick days, that too many workers saw their sick days as an "entitlement" and not an "insurance policy." Some Kaiser executives insisted on reducing the number of sick days that employees could take, but union negotiators warned that such a move would shatter morale. Instead of an angry deadlock, the partnership's negotiating committee reached a creative solution that pleased both sides—a sick leave bank for long-term illnesses and an annual cash-out for unused sick leave, a move that discouraged the casual or improper use of sick days.

When Dabney tells executives at other companies about such successes, they're dubious. "They say, Labor gets in your way and labor is not trying to help you," Dabney said, adding, "Labor doesn't get in our way. They help us. How many companies do you know that have unions working on promoting their growth?" (Kaiser's unions send representatives to health fairs to talk up Kaiser.)

Denise Duncan and other coalition union leaders sometimes go to conventions with Dabney to sing the praises of Kaiser's labor-management partnership. "Between negotiating cycles, we spend the rest of our time working to make Kaiser Permanente the best place to receive health care," she told a convention in Chicago. "Frontline workers have saved millions of dollars, decreased waste, and saved jobs. It's extraordinary what frontline staff can do."

A few examples:

• At one Kaiser medical center, a disconcertingly high percentage of patients who showed up for their scheduled colonoscopies hadn't done the proper dietary prep work. As a result, many weren't able to have their colonoscopies that day, throwing off the schedules of doctors and nurses and causing underutilization of the facility. The UBT, after studying the problem, assigned nurse practitioners to walk those patients ever so patiently through the dietary instructions to make sure they prepped correctly. As a result, the percentage of patients who didn't do the proper dietary prep plunged.

- In one maternity ward, nurses who spent much of their days feeding babies began suffering back and shoulder problems. The UBT recommended buying ergonomically suitable chairs, and most of the aches and pains went away.
- At a Kaiser medical center in Portland, Oregon, all the patients had to check in at the front desk on the first floor. Many mornings a thirty-minute line formed, and the medical units upstairs had to wait for patients to arrive, wasting doctors' and nurses' time. The UBT delved down and discovered the root of the problem: the first-floor printers were far too slow churning out all the needed paperwork. The medical center bought some high-speed printers, and, presto, the long lines disappeared.
- Kaiser Permanente spends millions of dollars each year to purchase blood for transfusions its patients need. One UBT organized a company-wide blood drive, seeking donations from Kaiser employees. They responded generously, saving Kaiser over $1 million a year.
- At one medical center, nurses who were preparing medications were often distracted and made mistakes because co-workers, doctors, patients, and phone calls interrupted their work, causing them to lose track or forget something. The UBT's solution: whenever nurses are preparing medications, they're to stand on a blue mat, designated a "quiet zone." The mat signifies that others are prohibited from talking to those nurses until they've finished preparing medications. The error rate plummeted.

In the sickle-cell department at Kaiser's medical offices in Inglewood, just outside Los Angeles, almost 20 percent of patients were not going to their scheduled appointments. Many were poor and hurting, many had problems arranging transportation, many didn't want to see a doctor soon after being released from the hospital. Many who missed appointments ended up having to be readmitted to a hospital within weeks of being discharged from one. Dismayed by the high rate of missed appointments, Pippa Stewart, who runs Inglewood's highly respected sickle-cell program, said, "At the end of the day, it meant we weren't taking care of our members."

The center's UBT created what Kaiser calls a "smart goal": it set an objective of cutting the rate of missed appointments by a third. Stewart's team invited in dozens of sickle-cell patients to discuss why so many had missed appointments. "We had a come-to-Jesus moment," Stewart said. "I asked, 'Are my nurses treating you well? Are my physicians treating you well? Is the building clean?'" Some patients responded with suggestions on how to handle parking and phone calls better.

Stewart and the UBT's other leaders decided on several steps. They would make reminder calls to patients the day before their appointments and stress the importance of not missing appointments. They set up more telephone appointments for those who had a hard time getting to the medical center or didn't want to go to a center a few weeks after being discharged from the hospital. They teamed with social workers to help arrange transportation for sickle-cell patients who needed rides to their appointments. Within six months, the rate of missed appointments fell significantly—from 20 percent to 14 percent.

Jacqueline Wadsworth, one of the leaders of Inglewood's UBT and a nurse for forty-seven years, sings the praises of unit-based teams. "It's taking ownership," she said. "When people take ownership, they're more productive. We do the work. We're on the front lines. It's good for us to have a voice in the process."

Dabney is proud of smart, well-run unit-based teams like the one in Inglewood. "I've been doing traditional labor relations for thirty years," he said. (He used to work for an auto-parts company in Michigan.) "This [partnership] is better. The solutions work better. The company works better." Sometimes Dabney wonders, "If it's so positive and works so well, why aren't more people doing this? People say, why take a risk? The in-thing now is to be antiunion. If you say something positive about a union, a lot of people will boo you out of a room. We're trying to open people's minds about partnerships."

Duncan also says the partnership is great, but she adds, "It's like your marriage. You have to keep working on it."

———

It was 7:50 in the morning, and the electronic sign outside Johnson Senior High in St. Paul, Minnesota, read "18 degrees." More than two hundred people huddled out front, chanting, "One, two, three, four. Students are what we're fighting for." Most of the demonstrators— whites, blacks, Native Americans, and Hmong—were wearing red ski caps, red having become the #RedforEd symbol of teacher militancy nationwide. The demonstrators—not just teachers, but also many parents and students—carried picket signs that read, "We Demand the Schools *All* Our Children Deserve," "St. Paul Students Can't Wait for Pre-K and School Nurses," and "St. Paul Students Can't Wait for Smaller Classes." Dressed in a bright red down jacket, a teachers' union leader bellowed into a bullhorn, calling for high-quality pre-K and ending racial inequities in St. Paul's schools.

The crowd soon filed past the three-foot-high snowbanks and into Johnson High's warmth for a communal breakfast of coffee and donuts. This wasn't a walkout, union officials said. It was a walk-in. This wasn't a protest, they insisted, but a celebration of what the community wanted. All this was a sharp contrast to what happens in those communities where parents and taxpayers view teachers' unions as a greedy, malevolent force. In St. Paul, that story has been turned on its head. That early morning "celebration" showed an extraordinary union-community partnership that was built over a decade. That partnership grew out of the vision of a middle school English teacher named Mary Cathryn Ricker.

Working with many devoted colleagues, Ricker forged a teacher-parent coalition that has turned the St. Paul Federation of Teachers (SPFT) into a model of what a farsighted teachers' union can demand and win: not just higher pay, but smaller class sizes, pre-K for all four-year-olds, and more music teachers, librarians, social workers, and nurses. In other unusual moves, the SPFT has won contract language for teacher visits to students' homes to improve parent-teacher relations and for forming school-based teams that seek to reduce the disproportionate number of suspensions of students of color. With achievements like these, the St. Paul Federation of Teachers—an affiliate of both the National Education Association and the American Federation of Teachers—has been hailed as a leading example of an innovative labor strategy called "bargaining for the common good."

Ricker grew up in the Minnesota Iron Range town of Hibbing (Bob Dylan's hometown), where her father was a math teacher and president of the local teachers' union. Strong-voiced and self-assured, she followed in her father's footsteps, and a dozen years into teaching in St. Paul, she was getting fed up with the abuse being heaped on teachers and public schools. One day she grew especially enraged when she heard a Republican state senator say on TV, "We all know Minneapolis and St. Paul schools suck."

"I was appalled," Ricker said. "I didn't even know you could say 'suck' on television." Conservatives, as they often do, were beating up on teachers' unions, castigating them for inflating salaries, pushing up taxes, and protecting bad teachers. Ricker realized that for conservatives who detest unions, taxes, and "big government," it's convenient (and smart politics) to blame teachers' unions for public schools' woes, rather than blame systemic, expensive-to-fix problems like poverty and racial inequities.

"I could have closed my classroom door and turned out all the noise," Ricker said of the teacher bashing and union bashing. "Or knowing enough about myself, I could challenge myself to do something about it."

With union militancy in her blood, Ricker of course chose the latter course. She's a solid, unpretentious midwesterner with a straightforward style, shoulder-length chestnut hair, and conservative, schoolteacherish glasses. Back then (2005), Ricker informed the SPFT's president that she planned to run for the local's top post. Already on the union's executive board, she thought the local's leader was far too passive about responding to the attacks against teachers and public schools. The incumbent decided not to run, and Ricker easily won the presidency. The SPFT represents thirty-six hundred teachers and other school employees in a city of 300,000, where over two-thirds of the thirty-nine thousand public school students qualify for free or reduced-price lunch and three-quarters are children of color. (Around one-fourth are of Hmong descent.)

Ricker's first goal was to counter the anti-teacher, antiunion narrative. Teachers' unions, she realized, were good at saying what they were against—school vouchers, for instance—but not good at saying what they were for. As a result, many Americans viewed them as establishment groups intent on preserving education's much-derided status quo. So Ricker pulled together a group of union leaders and teachers to write a mission statement that would be a sharp departure. Called "A New Narrative for Teachers, Educators, and Public Education," the statement hardly touched on pay and pensions. Instead, it was all about student success, social justice, and partnering with the community. Its tenets included: "We are committed to building a just and equitable society. . . . We believe in honoring the value of and cultivating each student. . . . We believe educating students is a craft that requires talented and committed professionals. . . . We believe working with community is essential to student success."

Nick Faber, an elementary school science teacher who helped write the narrative, said, "It moved us away from just being reactive. It told the story we wanted to tell about public education and who we are. It was clear that if the public believed that teachers are in their jobs to have June, July, and August off and that the role of unions is to just protect bad teachers, then we'd never get anywhere on our goal of creating the schools that St. Paul students deserve—unless we changed the narrative."

From day one, Ricker and her team sought to transform and rev up the local, which had been a traditional-style union run by a handful of officers, with scant rank-and-file participation. "We were dusty," Ricker said. "We had to dust ourselves off." The local was hugely proud that in 1946 it held what many historians say was the first organized strike by an American teachers' union. That strike demanded increased school spending to buy textbooks, renovate dilapidated schools, and reduce class sizes (some had fifty students).

Ricker hired two tough, smart organizers from the Service Employees International Union, and they, along with the SPFT's officers pushed to involve lots more rank-and-file teachers. Each of St. Paul's sixty schools had a shop steward, but now the union set up a contract action team in each school to create more teacher—and student and parent—pressure to advance the union's contract goals. That created a new set of activists and new opportunities to get involved.

With two young children, Ricker soon realized the demands on her were impossible. She was tasked to write reports single-handedly, draft contract language, help with professional development, and meet with shop stewards, principals, school board members, and state lawmakers. "The first big learning experience for me," Ricker said, "was realizing that not only should I not be doing this alone, but we would be better if we did this with as many members as possible."

Plenty of St. Paul teachers were ready to join with Ricker to rev up the union, and soon a nucleus of dedicated, whip-smart teacher activists formed around her. "One of the strengths of SPFT is that it's solution-driven," said Sarah Johnson, a third-grade teacher who helps run the union's professional development program. "The SPFT isn't a place where you just come and complain and whine. You tap into members and the community and you discuss: How are we going to work together to figure this out?"

Ricker talks of two models of labor unions: the soda machine model and the gym member model. The soda machine—Ricker calls it a pop machine—is there, you walk by it every day, hardly ever using it. "But the day you need that pop, you want it immediately," Ricker said. And then you walk away. As for the other model, "We know that a lot more real progress gets made when a lot of us go [to the gym], and we get stronger and healthier. We know we make progress when we work side by side."

The union's new narrative was noble, but it was just words. Ricker and her team knew they had to turn their narrative and vision into action, to show that the union wasn't just about helping teachers but was also about helping students and the community. To that end, the SPFT seized on a provision of Minnesota law that many labor leaders abhorred, requiring that all government-union bargaining sessions be open to the public. Many union officials feared that parents might shriek at such open sessions when they heard a union's opening demand for, say, a 6 percent raise. But the SPFT decided it would turn the bargaining sessions into a public-relations tool and public spectacle, where parents and students could see the union battling for them on many issues.

For the 2009 contract talks, the union urged special education teachers to attend and to invite members of the families they served. At one session, the union had its bargaining team sit with the audience and the special ed teachers move to the negotiating table to advocate for themselves. The special ed teachers and families felt newly involved, empowered, and valued as a result.

The SPFT took things to the next level in 2011, encouraging anyone involved in the education of St. Paul's children to attend that year's bargaining sessions. The union and school district agreed to schedule negotiations the same time each week, Thursdays from 5 p.m. to 7 p.m., making it easier for teachers and the public to attend. Aside from the negotiators, only eight people went to the first session; after several months, nearly a hundred teachers and parents attended each session.

In those negotiations, the union was pushing, among other things, for smaller class size and strengthening "peer review," a much-praised practice that helps assess and improve teachers, especially struggling ones (and helps ease out—some would say weed out—poorly performing teachers). "The people who came and watched us negotiate ended up gaining trust in us," Ricker said.

For the 2013 negotiations, the union decided to take an unusual leap. While the SPFT boasted of its union-community partnership, it was always the union, not the community, that formulated contract demands. But this time would be different. The union set up two monthly study groups composed of teachers, parents, and community members. One group read *The Schools Our Children Deserve* by Alfie Kohn; the other read Barnett Berry's *Teaching 2030: What We Must Do for Our Students and Our Public Schools—Now and in the Future*. The study groups were tasked with answering three questions: What are the schools St. Paul students deserve? Who are the teachers St. Paul students deserve? What kind of profession do those teachers deserve?

In addressing those questions, the study groups made numerous recommendations for what the union should seek in its next contract: smaller classes, less standardized testing, increased access to preschool, more school nurses, librarians, and social workers, and more help for teachers' aides to become teachers (a move that would help diversify St. Paul's largely white teaching force). The SPFT's executive board voted to incorporate the study groups' twenty-nine recommendations in its contract proposals.

"There's the adage 'Two heads are better than one,'" Ricker said. "That's exponentially true when you bring more people into developing the best contract language to meet the needs of students."

One day, Ricker had an epiphany—there's no limit, except your imagination, on what can be put into a contract to improve the schools. To that, she added a corollary: "There is nothing our contract negotiations can't try when it comes to the common good." The union presented the twenty-nine proposals at the first bargaining session in May 2013, but the district's negotiators said they would bargain on only seven of them. The district insisted that the twenty-two other proposals—including the ones on class size, librarians, and social workers—were matters of "management prerogative" and not "mandatory" subjects the district had to negotiate.

The audience was appalled that the district wouldn't discuss these matters. When word spread, the SPFT suddenly had more community support. (Some schools in poorer neighborhoods didn't—and still don't—have librarians or full-time nurses or social workers.) Paul Rohlfing, one of the organizers Ricker hired, said that inviting the public into the negotiating sessions had turned out far better than expected. "We saw it as a feature and not a bug, an opportunity to create leverage," he said. "It became an incredibly powerful way to put gas in the tank. Parents would come in skeptical, saying, 'I don't understand why I'm at this bargaining session. What does it mean for my child?' But they came away radicalized, ready to go to the barricades for things like smaller classes. This approach was a big risk, and it's paid off massively."

Four months after bargaining began, the school district demanded mediation—a move that would close the sessions to the public. Ricker's response: "We knew we had the upper hand if we could rally the community." And rally they did. Teachers knocked on doors and collected sixty-five hundred signatures supporting their demands. That fall hundreds of families put out yard signs—some called them "snowbank signs"—with slogans like "St. Paul Kids Deserve Librarians" and "St. Paul Kids Deserve Pre-K." Most schools held early-morning walk-ins, like the one outside Johnson Senior High. Some days twenty-five hundred students, parents, and teachers participated.

On the eve of a planned strike vote, the two sides hunkered down in a twenty-three-hour bargaining session that led to a settlement. Ricker and her negotiating team came away exhausted but gratified; the talks had made progress in every area in which the study groups had made recommendations, winning more librarians, nurses, social workers, and pre-K slots, among other goals.

For the SPFT, those negotiations were a tremendous success. Randi Weingarten, the president of the American Federation of Teachers, was so impressed with Ricker's vision and achievements that she asked Ricker to run on her slate, and Ricker was elected the AFT's executive vice president in July 2014. (She left that post to become Minnesota's commissioner of education in January 2019.) Ricker's successor at the SPFT was Denise Rodriguez, a longtime Spanish teacher, who was succeeded in turn by Nick Faber, the elementary school science teacher who helped write the union's break-the-mold narrative.

Under Ricker's successors, the union has forged ahead with its community-minded approach. The SPFT called on the school district, albeit unsuccessfully, to require all of its vendors and contractors to pay their workers at least $15 an hour. It urged the district to refuse to do banking with any institution that evicted students' families during the school year. After a police officer killed Philando Castile, an African American cafeteria aide beloved by many St. Paul students, the SPFT joined numerous Black Lives Matter protests.

Kirinda Anderson, the mother of an eleven-year-old, applauds the union's unorthodox approach. "You don't just fight for the teachers," she said. "You fight for the fact that children deserve to have a nurse. You fight for the fact that children have a right to recess. You fight for janitors who have kids in the St. Paul schools to earn a living wage. You fight so parents with kids in school aren't foreclosed on during the school year. It's like a beaded chain. We're all connected together."

To Faber, the SPFT's current president, the union has a vital role in identifying and championing issues that improve education, often ones that the school district hasn't focused on. For example, having heard of Sacramento's program of teachers visiting students' homes, Faber pushed St. Paul to adopt the idea. Such a practice helps get parents more involved in their children's education and enables teachers to develop strong relationships with parents so that the first time a teacher communicates with parents isn't a tension-filled moment about bad grades or detention.

Faber, trim, intense, and, like Ricker, a gifted public speaker, said he presented that idea to the district three times, asserting, "This is really powerful for our unions, our parents, our children. But they said no." At that point, Faber told the district, "Let's take it to the bargaining table and you have to listen." The union got the home visit program into its contract. The contract, in Faber's view, is a great tool for turning good ideas into concrete, enforceable reality.

Dan McGrath, the longtime executive director of TakeAction Minnesota, a coalition of thirty progressive groups, said the SPFT is unusual because both Ricker and Faber had community organizing experience; they know how to work with and mobilize the community. McGrath said the union's work-with-the-community approach was not only smart but necessary. "SPFT has figured out they cannot just bargain on their own behalf and expect to get ahead," he said. "That's not a winning recipe for teachers and not a winning recipe for schools." In other words, in solidarity with the community, there is increased strength.

———

For the 2018 negotiations, the SPFT adopted a hugely ambitious goal: fixing the school district's chronic underfunding problem. In search of more money, the union's researchers concluded that three of the biggest corporations in St. Paul—U.S. Bank, Wells Fargo, and Ecolab, a $14 billion company that provides services to assure clean water, food, and energy—were not paying an equitable share of taxes.

"We have to talk about getting the corporate elite in this country to pay their fair share toward education funding," Faber said, "or else it will continually be a political football that when we get a Democrat in control, we suddenly have a little more money, but not enough, and when we get a Republican in, we have even less."

As a central demand, the union wanted the school district to join it in seeking to pressure U.S. Bank, Wells Fargo, and Ecolab to "voluntarily" contribute more money toward St. Paul's schools or to urge state lawmakers to increase taxes to assure more school funding. The SPFT teamed up with other progressive groups, including TakeAction Minnesota, the SEIU, MN350 (an environmental group), and CTUL (a Twin Cities workers center) to picket those corporations. To apply more pressure, the SPFT formed so-called Tiger teams (Tiger is an acronym for "Teaching and Inquiring about Greed, Equity, and Racism"). To create these teams of activists, the union gives teachers, students, parents, and other community members a crash course in populist economics, teaching them about income inequality, CEO salaries, how Minnesota has cut corporate taxes, and how school funding has suffered.

School district officials resisted the SPFT's call to pressure those three corporations—a move that surprised the union because it had helped elect four of the school board's seven members. Now a union that prided itself on fighting for the community found itself dividing the community. Ian Keith, a former SPFT president, wrote an op-ed criticizing the union for choosing "a premature path of confrontation, finger-pointing, fearmongering, and power politics." Steven Marchese, the school board's vice-chair and director of the Minnesota Bar Association's pro bono program, usually applauds the SPFT's focus on community and students, but in this case, Marchese said, "the union took a very adversarial approach." To his mind, the union was using the same hardball playbook as in previous negotiations, even though it had helped elect a friendlier board. "It was a strange way to try to build toward something better," Marchese said. "Their tactics were not very helpful and almost drove the district over the cliff."

The teachers voted to authorize a strike when the board continued to reject the union's call to join in confronting U.S. Bank, Wells Fargo, and Ecolab. (The union was also demanding more support staff for special ed students and more teachers for students who were learning English.) Board members said Ecolab was already a generous donor to several schools, and they feared that the union's approach would blow up current relationships. The board members also complained that the SPFT acted as if it knew what was better for the community than the elected school board did. At the last minute, the school district avoided a strike by agreeing to some of the union's demands, among them, to hire thirty additional English as a second language teachers.

To some St. Paul residents, the union's confrontational approach didn't seem like bargaining for the common good. Faber disagreed, saying, "Bargaining for the common good doesn't mean the absence of conflict. It means pushing ideas that benefit the community." McGrath of TakeAction Minnesota defended the union's strategy. The school board is the key decision maker on how much school funding is available, he said, and the union was seeking new ways to get additional money to make the board's life easier and the schools better. "The union was trying to pull the levers to create forward motion for the good of teachers and the good of the community," McGrath said.

The SPFT, which has the highest teacher salaries in Minnesota, has become such a model that the National Education Association, the nation's largest labor union, has created the St. Paul Institute, where SPFT officials teach educators from across the nation about strategies on how to bargain for the common good.

"I don't think there's anything the St. Paul Federation does that can't be done in other school districts," said Rohlfing, who teaches at the institute. "People tell me, 'But that won't work here.' The fundamental fluid dynamics of organizing campaigns remain the same wherever you are—rural, suburban, or urban, conservative or liberal. It would be great for students and schools if we could see this happen in more places."

Twenty

Teachers Catch #RedforEd Fever

IN 2015, Jay O'Neal left his teaching position in a suburb of Pittsburgh to take a job as an eighth-grade English teacher in Charleston, West Virginia. "I was shocked at how low the salaries were," said O'Neal, who moved because the University of Charleston had hired his wife. In his second year there, O'Neal received a modest "step" raise, but "when I opened my pay stub in the fall to see how much I was making, I thought there was some mistake," he said. "It was $30 less a month than the first year." O'Neal soon learned that the state's health insurance agency for public employees was taking substantially bigger premiums from his paycheck because that small raise had bumped him into a higher "premium" bracket.

Emily Comer also began teaching in Charleston in 2015, as a high school Spanish teacher, right after she obtained a master's degree in education. She had $70,000 in student debt, and her salary was $38,000. "I don't have any kids, but I wonder, could I afford to have children on a teacher's salary?" Comer said. "Could I afford the day care?" She soon discovered that other teachers were far more exercised about the annual increases in health-care premiums than about the low salaries. "People kept saying our health care is getting worse and worse. When is it going to stop?"

O'Neal and Comer first met in the summer of 2017 as activists fighting to save the Affordable Care Act from the Republicans' repeal efforts. O'Neal, thirty-seven at the time, belonged to the National Education Association, while Comer, twenty-seven, belonged to the other big teachers' union, the American Federation of Teachers. They were both unhappy that the two unions often fought each other in vying to recruit teachers, and they were also dismayed that their unions had failed to achieve more for teachers. West Virginia doesn't allow teachers' unions to bargain collectively, and as a result those unions' leaders devoted much of their energy to lobbying state lawmakers to increase teacher pay and get the state health insurance agency—the West Virginia Public Employees Insurance Agency, known as PEIA—to stop raising premiums so steeply year after year.

"It felt like all our union leadership had been doing was lobbying, and we knew that wasn't enough," Comer said. "'Will you pretty please improve our health plan' is not a particularly good way to get something."

Comer and O'Neal began strategizing about what to do. Having just finished Jane McAlevey's book *No Shortcuts: Organizing for Power in the New Gilded Age,* Comer got several other teachers to read it and discuss it. They took several lessons from it, among them that advocacy is rarely enough for workers to make significant gains; mobilizing and organizing are needed, too.

"Another thing we took from the book is the sense that *you* are the union, that members of the union are the union," Comer said. "We talked to people who were really upset about PEIA. They'd say, 'What are the unions doing? The unions have never done anything for us.' We told them, 'You pay dues. You are the union.' We used that message to get people to step up."

In October 2017, O'Neal set up a Facebook group, West Virginia Teachers United, explaining that he "created it to work across different unions to try to make some changes and fix things." For the first month or so, the Facebook group had only about a hundred members, but then PEIA announced a new policy that would significantly raise many teachers' premiums by basing them not just on a teacher's salary but also on his or her spouse's income. That further irked teachers, and by January 1 the Facebook group had grown to a thousand members. (O'Neal and Comer, who joined him in managing the Facebook page, changed its name to WV Public Employees United.) Comer simultaneously helped organize efforts on the ground—getting dozens of teachers to attend education forums, legislators' town halls, and PEIA meetings to call for raising pay and fixing health coverage. "We bird-dogged candidates," Comer said. "We confronted legislators. We were getting that on camera and posting video. We were really turning up the heat." They urged teachers to email lawmakers about pay and PEIA, and when several lawmakers sent back dismissive responses, ruling out the idea of a halfway decent raise, teachers posted screen shots of the email exchanges on the Facebook page.

"They were insensitive to us," Comer said. "They showed the legislature didn't care about us." She complained that the legislature, heeding the wishes of campaign donors, had sliced the corporate tax rate as well as taxes on fracking in enacting $425 million in tax cuts over the previous decade. That in turn squeezed school budgets and depressed teacher salaries. In West Virginia, the state legislature, not the individual school district, plays the dominant role in determining and financing raises. West Virginia's teachers hadn't received an across-the-board raise in four years.

On January 6, one teacher wrote on the Facebook page, "Just curious if there are any talks of striking." Some teachers applauded the idea, but many said it was too early, that far more mobilizing and organizing were needed. The mood changed drastically four days later, however, when Governor Jim Justice, a billionaire coal-mining heir and the state's richest man, gave his State of the State address and called for raises of 1 percent a year for the next five years for teachers and other public employees.

"My feeling was, 'Are you kidding me?'" O'Neal said. "The changes from PEIA would eat all that up." Many teachers realized that if inflation averaged 2 percent a year and raises were 1 percent, that would effectively erode their paychecks by 5 percent over five years. "That really escalated things," Comer said. "As soon as lunch started the next day, all that teachers wanted to talk about was the governor's speech." His proposal called for an annual raise of just $404 for teachers. With its teacher pay averaging $45,622 in 2016, West Virginia ranked forty-eighth among the states in educators' salaries. There were 725 unfilled spots for teachers across the state, partly because teachers could easily take, and commute to, jobs in neighboring Virginia and Maryland that paid $12,000 or $15,000 more.

A few days after the governor's speech, PEIA launched a new "wellness app," Go365, that PEIA all but demanded teachers use. Teachers who met the fitness goals of walking a certain number of steps each day would receive gift cards, while those who fell short would see their premiums jump by $25 a month. Teachers who refused to use Go365—many viewed it as invasive and insulting—would have their annual deductibles increase by $500. "People were already furious, and that just added fuel to the fire," Comer said. "People were saying, 'When are we going on strike?'" By the end of January, O'Neal and Comer's Facebook group had exploded to twenty thousand members.

Republicans control West Virginia's state legislature, and pushed by conservative groups like the Koch brothers–funded Americans for Prosperity, lawmakers enacted one corporate tax cut after another. The teachers were seething: the cuts were starving the schools and sabotaging education. Even though government employee unions were weak in the state, the teachers adopted a militant stance: we're fed up and we're not going to take it anymore. Teachers usually view themselves as professionals, but many felt like a beaten-down proletariat with bachelor degrees, often needing to work a second or even third job to get by.

Teachers in three southern counties with a history of miner militancy took the lead. On February 2, roughly a thousand teachers from Mingo, Wyoming, and Logan Counties flocked to the state capital for a one-day strike. They called it #FedUpFriday. "We come from these mountains," said Katie Endicott, a high school English teacher in Gilbert, fifteen miles south of where the famous Battle of Blair Mountain took place. "We come from an area that is known for [people] standing up for what they believe in. We believe we're following in their footsteps."

In the Battle of Blair Mountain, ten thousand coal miners battled three thousand lawmen and strikebreakers in 1921 in what was the largest uprising since the Civil War. Estimates of the dead range from twenty to a hundred.

At Jay O'Neal's middle school, people were live streaming the February 2 protests on their mobile phones. "We were all watching it during lunch," O'Neal said. "It was like the genie got out of the bottle. Everyone said, 'My gosh, we want to be part of this.'"

At a town hall meeting on February 6, Governor Justice sought to show the teachers he got their message. "I am absolutely all in on education. All in," he said. "I've said judge me by my deeds." But Justice clumsily suggested that the angry teachers were "dumb bunnies," a remark that further enraged the teachers.

That week, the heads of West Virginia's two teachers' unions, seeing the anger coursing through the rank and file, asked teachers in the state's fifty-five counties to vote on whether to back a "work action." The West Virginia School Service Personnel Association, representing custodians, cafeteria workers, and bus drivers, joined in that move. On February 11, union leaders counted the ballots, with a large majority endorsing a job action. At that point, teachers and other school employees in more than a dozen counties started doing "walk-in" protests just before school started. On February 17, the three unions announced there would be a statewide educators' strike beginning Thursday, February 22. Their demands: an immediate 5 percent raise and fixing PEIA's finances so premiums weren't always soaring.

On February 21, seeking to avert a strike, Governor Justice signed legislation that would give teachers and school service personnel a 2 percent raise in July 2019, and 1 percent more in 2020 and 2021. He had earlier gotten PEIA to jettison the Go365 penalties and promise not to raise premiums through mid-2019. But it was too little too late. The teachers were already mobilized, organized—and furious. On February 22, more than ten thousand teachers flooded into Charleston and protested inside and outside the State Capitol, chanting, "Enough is enough" and "Fired up and fed up." One teacher's protest sign read, "55 Strong Can't Be Wrong," while many teachers wore bunny ears or bunny outfits.

"It was the most incredible, beautiful thing I experienced in my entire life," Comer told me. "It was transformational. It was a giant celebration. It was so removed from the everyday routine where you pass each other in the hallways. All of a sudden, you're all picketing and chanting together."

West Virginia's attorney general warned that the strike was illegal and that the teachers would be punished. But school superintendents in all fifty-five counties announced that schools were closed, throwing their weight behind the teachers and undermining the attorney general's threat to fine them for missing work. The teachers had worked hard to win the support of parents, and during the strike teachers in many districts made sure that food got to the tens of thousands students who relied on school lunches.

The strikers wore bright red, for they were part of what became known as the #RedforEd movement. As for the derivation of #RedforEd, many teachers point to a Facebook group created in Florida in 2011 called

"Wear Red for Public Ed." The choice of color, it is said, was inspired by the color of little red schoolhouses and the apples given to teachers, and even teachers' red pencils. Red was the color worn by Chicago's striking teachers in 2012, but some of the teachers' detractors asserted that red was obviously inspired by Communism.

The West Virginia strike was a shot heard round the teaching world. Caitlin Emma, an education writer, observed, "Teachers, many of them women, are redefining attitudes about organized labor, replacing negative stereotypes of overpaid and underperforming blue-collar workers with a more sympathetic face: overworked and underappreciated nurturers who say they're fighting for their students as much as they're fighting for themselves."

About three-fourths of the teachers in West Virginia and nationwide are women, and many striking teachers say they were inspired in part by the women's marches after Donald Trump won election. "There are a bunch of men sitting in an office right now telling us that we don't deserve anything better," said Amanda Howard Garvin, an elementary school art teacher in Morgantown, West Virginia. She said that women were standing up to say, "No. We're equal here"—and we deserve better pay.

"People like to dismiss West Virginia as Trumpland," O'Neal said. "But that's a simplification. A lot of people here didn't vote for Trump. And you also have a lot of people who voted for him, but who are involved in the strike. Everyone is now saying, I know when I'm being screwed over. Enough is enough. Folks are waking up."

On Wednesday, February 28, Governor Justice and union leaders announced a deal: a 5 percent raise and the creation of a task force to fix PEIA. But hundreds of teachers standing outside the capitol derided the settlement, fearing that the legislature would not enact the promised raise and viewing the task force as an excuse for inaction. The teachers shouted, "We're not going back in for that" and "We got sold out." They also yelled to the union leaders, "We are the union bosses!" They were mindful that the senate president Mitch Carmichael had said the day before, "It would be completely frivolous and ridiculous to embrace this [5 percent] proposal." He suggested that any available money be used to shore up PEIA's finances.

Hearing the rank and file loud and clear, Dale Lee, president of the West Virginia Education Association, had a message for lawmakers:

"Until this bill passes at 5 percent, we will be out indefinitely." On March 5, the state senate passed a 5 percent raise, which the state house had already approved. The teachers rejoiced and ended their nine-day strike.

"It looked like we weren't going to win. But we fought our asses off," Comer said. "Is 5 percent enough? Absolutely not. Was PEIA fixed? Absolutely not. But it's incredible that we won even a 5 percent raise. That's a huge win. But this isn't over by any means. We have to keep organizing."

In retrospect, O'Neal wishes the teachers had demanded a larger raise, tied to a rollback of the tax cuts for fracking. But he rejoiced. "We started a national strike wave," he said. "Unions can't use the same old formula of just trying to lobby for legislation and just ask for a meager raise. They're going to have to be more aggressive because we've been getting blown away by the Koch brothers."

———

Alberto Morejon, a twenty-five-year-old history teacher at Stillwater Junior High School in Oklahoma, was watching a television report about the West Virginia teachers' strike when he realized that he, too, could start a Facebook group. He began it on March 1 and named it "Oklahoma Teacher Walkout—The Time Is Now!" By the next morning, it had twenty-four thousand members. Oklahoma teachers poured into the Facebook group because they, too, were fed up. "People are ready to have their voices heard," Morejon said at the time. "If we want to keep good teachers, we need to pay them."

Oklahoma's forty-two thousand public school teachers hadn't received an across-the-board raise in a decade. Their average salary was $45,276, less than West Virginia's and every other state except Mississippi's. With pay so low, Oklahoma couldn't attract enough certified teachers, forcing its schools to fill two thousand spots with emergency-certified staff who didn't have teaching degrees. "You can go anywhere else and make $15,000 more as a first-year teacher," said Brenda Frieling, an elementary school teacher in Norman. Shawn Sheehan, Oklahoma's 2016 Teacher of the Year, and his wife took teaching jobs in Texas, where, together, they will earn $40,000 more than in Oklahoma.

Todd Henshaw, a teacher and baseball coach at Liberty High School in Mounds, complained that his base salary was just $38,000, even though he had been teaching for twenty-two years. "We have two teachers leaving, going to Texas," he said. "Signed contracts for sixty thousand dollars. I just have to say, I think the legislators are out of touch." Oklahoma's lawmakers, like West Virginia's, were preoccupied with cutting taxes, especially for the wealthy and the oil and gas industry. A capital-gains tax cut gave two-thirds of the benefits to the state's eight hundred richest families, while in 2015 the legislature chopped Oklahoma's production tax on oil and gas drilling from 7 percent to 2 percent, making it the lowest such rate in the nation. That reduced the state's revenues by more than $300 million a year.

Many teachers and parents felt that the legislature was starving the schools. Since 2008, state funding per pupil had plunged by 28 percent, adjusted for inflation. Teachers talked of ramshackle desks and tattered, outdated textbooks held together by duct tape, with one first grader discovering she had the same textbook that the country singer Blake Shelton used in 1982. Oklahoma's State Science and Engineering Fair was canceled in 2017, but a retired teacher rescued it by donating $50,000 from his savings.

With West Virginia's educators erupting, Oklahoma's teachers made clear to lawmakers that they had better boost teacher pay and school funding or Oklahoma would be the next red state to face a strike. "Oklahoma teachers have felt hopeless and powerless for years," said Mickey Miller, a high school economics teacher with a master's degree who holds three jobs, including one loading and unloading luggage at the airport. Oklahoma's teachers, he said, "began saying, 'Wait a second, they did it there [West Virginia], they were able to get all counties to go out. Why can't we do that here?'"

On March 6, the Oklahoma Education Association called for a statewide strike beginning April 23, believing the state's #RedforEd movement needed several weeks to deepen its roots and broaden its reach. Two days later, after Morejon and many other teachers had criticized the union as being sluggish and out of sync with rank-and-file anger, the union embraced Morejon's call for a strike on April 2. Alicia Priest, the union's president, announced the demands: raises of $10,000 for teachers and $5,000 for support staff, and an $800 million tax increase for school funding, state employee raises, and improved health care.

Governor Mary Fallin, a Republican with a record of slashing taxes, moved quickly to try to ward off a strike. Working with the legislature, Fallin signed a bill that increased teacher salaries by $6,100 on average and those of support staff by $1,250, paid for by the state's first tax increase since 1992. She pushed through legislation to raise $400 million by legalizing sports betting and instituting new or higher taxes on oil and gas production, motor fuels, tobacco, and hotel rooms.

But the teachers wanted more. "We have come too far to accept this offer that does nothing but put a band aid on a severe wound," Morejon said. Teachers "will have no choice but to close down the districts." With the legislature giving them raises averaging 14 percent, the teachers adroitly pivoted, focusing on calls for increased school spending.

On April 2, the State Capitol was a sea of red, with more than fifty thousand protesters—teachers, students, and parents—rallying inside and outside the legislative halls. Teachers circled the building, waving signs that ridiculed Fallin. Some teachers set up tents, while a high school band played Twisted Sister's "We're Not Gonna Take It." Dozens of school superintendents had closed the schools in their districts in support.

Fallin wasn't cowed. As with Governor Justice's "dumb bunnies" comment, she belittled the strikers. "Teachers want more," she told CBS News. "But it's kind of like having a teenage kid that wants a better car." Serving her last year as governor, Fallin pushed back against the strike by saying she had just signed a 20 percent increase in school funding, adding, "We must be responsible not to neglect other areas of need in the state such as corrections and health and human services."

The two sides were at an impasse. Thousands of teachers were demanding more, but the legislature's Republican majority, having just voted large raises for teachers, was in no mood to enact another tax increase to reward them further. In a video that went viral, Kevin McDugle, a Republican state representative, said, "I'm not voting for another stinking measure [for the teachers] when they're acting the way they're acting." Some Republicans seemed to go out of their way to undercut the teachers, with the legislature voting to repeal a $5-a-night hotel tax that was meant to raise $45 million a year for education funding.

After nine days on strike, many teachers wanted to continue the walkout into a third week to keep up the pressure, but the Oklahoma Education Association's leaders, backed by many school superintendents and teachers, called for ending the walkout, worried that it had reached the point of diminishing returns. On April 12, Priest, the union's president, announced an end to the strike. "There comes a time, when if what you're doing is not getting the results you seek, there is wisdom in shifting focus," Priest said. For Priest, the next focus was evident. "We got here by electing the wrong people to office," she said. "We have the opportunity to make our voices heard at the ballot box."

Tensions were boiling over when the strike ended. Many teachers felt the union wasn't tough enough; they were frustrated they had won little beyond what the legislature had approved before the strike. At the same time, many GOP lawmakers were fuming, convinced that the striking teachers were petulant and ungrateful, having walked out even though the legislature had passed a sizable tax increase to finance education.

The teachers thought their movement was an irresistible force, but the Republican legislature, after having voted the raises and increased funding, proved to be far more unmovable than the teachers had anticipated. So the teachers sought to move the legislature in Priest's way: by changing its composition. Dozens of Oklahoma teachers announced they were running for the state legislature in 2018. In what the *Tulsa World* said was "perhaps the most extraordinary primary season in state history," a dozen Republican legislators lost their primaries. All twelve had earned the teachers' wrath during the strike.

Craig Hoxie, a high school physics teacher in Tulsa who was making less than $50,000 a year after nineteen years of teaching, set out to unseat the house majority whip, Terry O'Donnell. Hoxie said he decided to run while he was participating in the teachers' 110-mile march from Tulsa to Oklahoma City during the strike. "We need to rebuild an education system that's been destroyed," he said. "The legislature has been gutting our funding, and we have to stop it from constantly degrading our schools."

———

"When West Virginia happened, people thought, 'Hey, we could do that,'" said Joe Thomas, the president of the Arizona Education Association. But Thomas, an astute strategist, knew that his union, the state's main teachers' union, shouldn't take the lead. He was confident others would step up.

Days after West Virginia erupted, Rebecca Garelli, a sixth-grade science teacher in Phoenix, contacted Jay O'Neal for advice, and she, too, started a Facebook group, calling it Arizona Educators Get Organized. About fifteen hundred people joined the first day. "People started calling for a strike right away," Garelli said. "I freaked out." Feeling overwhelmed, she shut down the Facebook group two days after starting it.

Noah Karvelis, a twenty-three-year-old elementary school music teacher in Tolleson, a Phoenix suburb, took the baton from Garelli and started a new Facebook group that same day, March 4. He called it Arizona Educators United (AEU), and by the next morning it had fifteen thousand members. "Little did I know what I was getting into," said Karvelis, who was earning just $34,000 as a second-year teacher. With Garelli and half a dozen others helping him administer the Facebook group, it soon swelled to fifty-two thousand members. Teachers posted tales of overcrowded classrooms and photos of their paychecks—to show how puny they were. Some paychecks came to less than $1,000 every two weeks.

Thomas, whose union had twenty thousand members out of the state's fifty-five thousand public school teachers, posted a question to the Facebook group, "Have you seen what's happening in West Virginia? What's the atmosphere at your school?" Karvelis responded that the teachers at his school seemed ready to strike, but Thomas cautioned that before taking such bold action, it was vital to know whether large numbers were truly ready to act. If a strike were called and teachers walked out at only two or three dozen schools, that wouldn't be nearly enough to move Arizona's conservative governor and legislature to increase teacher pay and school funding. To build solidarity and gauge support for a walkout, Karvelis asked teachers to wear red shirts to school. "I created a Facebook event with the info and the call for action for March 7," Karvelis said.

That Wednesday, just three days after he had created the Arizona Educators United group, thousands of teachers wore red to class. That's because many were seeing red. The state's funding for schools, adjusted for inflation, had plunged 36.6 percent since 2008, the largest drop of any state. That left Arizona forty-ninth in spending per student. Arizona had the highest average class size after Nevada, and its average teacher salary was $47,403, placing it forty-third. Arizona's school counselors had an average caseload of over 920 students, the highest in the nation. Pay was so inadequate that two thousand teaching positions were unfilled. One teacher in Yuma quit and took a teaching post in California, commuting an hour each way and doubling his pay. Heightening teachers' dismay, Arizona's Republican governor, Douglas Ducey, was offering them just a 1 percent raise for 2018.

Week by week, the #RedforEd Wednesdays snowballed. Karvelis, Garelli, Thomas, and several others formed an informal steering committee, and they decided it was time to escalate. They called for a protest at the State Capitol on March 28. That day two thousand teachers rallied outside the statehouse, many wearing stickers saying, "I don't want to strike, but I will." One teacher carried a sign saying, "Don't Make Me Go All West Virginia on You." At that protest, Arizona Educators United announced its demands for an immediate 20 percent pay increase, restoring $1 billion in school funding cuts, and no more tax cuts until Arizona's per-pupil spending caught up to the national average (the legislature had cut taxes nearly every year for three decades).

"Things were exploding at the seams," said Karvelis, who was an unlikely leader—he had been a senior at the University of Illinois just two years earlier. "People organized independent marches in their town. People were passing out #RedforEd signs to local businesses. They were lining overpasses with red. It was incredible." Thomas, the longtime union leader, felt suddenly rejuvenated, after his union had repeatedly failed to get the legislature to boost education funding. "West Virginia made us believe in ourselves again," he said. "We [the union] were very good at talking with the legislature and at community town halls and letter-writing campaigns. We had done everything you're supposed to do, but we were ignored."

Garelli, who had been a teacher in Chicago before moving to Arizona for the warmer weather, noticed that it was far harder to get teachers to protest in Arizona than in Chicago. (She had been involved in the Chicago Teachers Union's successful 2012 strike.) "Compared to Illinois, there's definitely a different mind-set, showing people how to use their voice for the first time," Garelli said. "Chicago is a fighting city—people are protesting all the time. They're not scared to speak up. Here, there was some real fear to overcome. Here people ask, 'Am I going to get in trouble if I wear a red shirt to school? Will I get in trouble if I paint #RedforEd on my car windows?' The Facebook page was important to put up photos and show people you're not alone. That was the key to overcoming the fear factor."

In West Virginia, O'Neal and Comer had operated independently of the two big teachers' unions, while in Oklahoma, Morejon was often at loggerheads with union leaders. But in Arizona, Arizona Educators United and the union worked closely together, even though many teachers objected to the union's role. "Some people said, 'The union has been too slow. The union has gotten us into this mess. They're just about electing Democrats,'" Karvelis said. "They were skeptical about the union's role in Oklahoma. They said if we bring in the union, we'll lose the grassroots thing." Some conservative teachers didn't like or trust unions, and some feared that the union's involvement would make the Republican legislature less receptive to the teachers' message.

Notwithstanding these worries, the partnership between the AEU and the union worked out very well for both groups. "We were the engine that drove the bus," Garelli said. "We had the people. They had the resources. They had communications resources, an email system, political know-how." Karvelis added, "We didn't have funding. We didn't have staff. We didn't have insurance. We didn't have anything. There wouldn't have been water or Porta Potties at the rallies without the union."

For his part, Thomas hailed AEU and its wizardry in using Facebook. "Social media was everything," Thomas said, recognizing that it's far faster and more efficient to get a message to fifty thousand teachers via Facebook than through five hundred separate shop steward meetings with teachers. The union was happy to let Arizona Educators United carry the ball, while it played a secondary role. "I just want to fix the schools," Thomas said. "This is not about an Arizona Education Association win. I don't care who scores the touchdown. I just want to win."

#RedforEd's leaders called for walk-ins across the state, beginning April 11. That day, teachers, students, parents, and school support staff gathered outside school entrances before the opening bell and then walked inside arm in arm. Every school had a captain, and those captains counted a total of 110,000 participants in the walk-ins on April 11. That week, the captains asked all school employees to vote on whether they supported a strike, and on April 19 #RedforEd announced that 78 percent of the state's teachers and support staff backed a walkout if their demands were not met.

With the movement getting huge media coverage, Governor Ducey, who was running for reelection, announced that the state would give teachers raises totaling 20 percent—10 percent in 2019 and 5 percent in 2020 and 2021. The teachers were pleased but dubious because it wasn't clear whether Ducey's plan provided funding for even the first 10 percent raise. Nor did Ducey offer raises to school librarians, school counselors, cafeteria workers, and custodians. Convinced that Ducey wasn't furnishing nearly enough money to pay for the raises, Thomas said, "He might have just as well promised everyone a unicorn or a pony."

Many teachers disliked Ducey ever since he led the opposition to a 2012 referendum that sought to raise the state sales tax as a means to increase school funding. Ducey, a former CEO of Cold Stone Creamery, and many GOP legislators distrusted #RedforEd because Thomas had endorsed Ducey's Democratic opponent, while Karvelis was campaign manager for a Democratic candidate for state superintendent of public instruction.

Heightening the tensions, some conservative critics of the teachers attacked Karvelis after they learned that he had been a campaign volunteer for Bernie Sanders while in college. Maria Syms, a GOP state representative, savaged Karvelis in an op-ed, writing that he and several "comrades" had moved to Arizona "to use teachers and our children to carry out their socialist movement." Accusing Karvelis of "channeling Leninism," she attacked him for being a fan of Howard Zinn and Noam Chomsky, well-known left-wing writers. Soon many Republicans were engaged in McCarthyist red-baiting of #RedforEd.

Many Republican teachers had joined the movement—among them Laura Fox, a music teacher in Gilbert, a Phoenix suburb, who was angry that salaries in her school district hadn't risen in a decade. Divorced, she worked evenings at McDonald's to support herself and her seventeen-year-old daughter. Fox, who remains a fan of Barry Goldwater's, said, "I'm a Republican, but because I'm a teacher there are people in this state who are so brainwashed that they call me a socialist. They say I'm a Communist. It's crazy." Despite her conservative politics, she enthusiastically joined the #RedforEd movement, calling it "amazing."

After Ducey promised the raises totaling 20 percent, he and the legislature did little to meet the teachers' demands or to reassure them that there would be adequate funding for the raises. At an impasse, AEU called for a statewide strike on April 26, with a march on the capitol. #RedforEd leaders expected ten thousand, maybe fifteen thousand protesters; Arizona is a deep red state with weak unions and without a history of protest. Organizers and rank-and-file teachers alike were astounded when tens of thousands of red-shirted protesters—teachers, students, parents—filled block after block in downtown Phoenix. Estimates of the crowd ranged from fifty thousand to seventy-five thousand, with aerial photos showing a spectacular bright red ribbon extending through downtown. Teachers carried signs, saying, "I am standing up for your child," and bands, as in Oklahoma City, played Twisted Sister's "We're Not Gonna Take It," along with "The Star-Spangled Banner."

"We were shocked, amazed. We never imagined that we'd have nearly that many people," said Karvelis. Suddenly a twenty-three-year-old who spent his days speaking to thirty third graders was speaking before a crowd of over fifty thousand. Thomas said, "It was the most incredible, beautiful display of public support for education I've ever seen."

Even though schools were shut statewide, the legislators, as in Oklahoma, were in no mood to bow to the teachers' demands, especially because the governor had made what they considered an extremely generous offer. As the strike continued, with many parents strongly backing it, the governor and the legislature budged and agreed to extend raises to all school staff. The legislature also voted a $400 million increase in school funding, a down payment to finance the initial 10 percent raise.

That fell far short of the $1 billion increase in funding that #RedforEd had demanded, but convinced that the legislature wouldn't do anything further, the strike's leaders, after informally canvassing teachers at the capitol, decided to end the walkout after six days. Many teachers complained that the decision hadn't been put to a formal vote, but #RedforEd leaders feared that a formal vote would take two or three days, prolonging the strike and trying the public's patience.

"We knew the right move was to go back," Garelli said. "We knew we had squeezed every dollar we could in this legislative session." While #RedforEd had laid down its strike weapon, it was planning a new battle that it was confident it would win: a ballot initiative for November 2018. The teachers collected 270,000 signatures for an "Invest in Ed" initiative that would raise $690 million a year to increase school funding. It would nearly double state income tax rates for the richest Arizonans, to 8 percent for individuals earning more than $250,000 a year and for households over $500,000, and to 9 percent for individuals earning more than $500,000 and for households over $1 million. These were among the five highest state tax rates in the nation. "We've learned that these legislators will only do so much," Karvelis said, "and that then you have to take the power into your own hands. That's what this initiative does."

Republicans and business leaders denounced the initiative, saying it would undermine the tax base by discouraging businesses from investing in Arizona and rich retirees from moving to the state. In a stinging setback for teachers, the Arizona Supreme Court threw the initiative off the ballot in August 2018, saying its language was unclear. The union called the ruling a Ducey-orchestrated "low blow" that cheated voters out of the opportunity to increase school funding. Not surprisingly, the union was intent on pushing a new "Invest in Ed" initiative.

After the #RedforEd strikes, some teachers hailed Facebook as a magical tool for organizing, but Karvelis says it's not enough. "Facebook pages are great for mobilizing people, but they're not great for long-term organizing," he said. For that, "unions are vital," Karvelis added. "We need to make the union what it can be. . . . We need to grow it, and make sure it reflects what the people want."

Garelli views Arizona's #RedforEd movement as a definite success, saying the fact that "this movement" got "a right-wing government to make concessions is a big deal." She said something that could apply equally to all six states that had major teacher walkouts in 2018—West Virginia, Oklahoma, Arizona, Kentucky, Colorado, and North Carolina (the latter three had less sweeping strikes). "Fifty percent of the win here has been that we now have a strong, organized mass movement," Garelli said. "And we're not going away. People now have the courage to fight."

———

In January 2019, thirty-two thousand Los Angeles teachers went on strike at an especially inauspicious time—there was drenching rain day after day. As they picketed outside their schools, many teachers donned red ponchos; some even laminated their picket signs and song sheets. They chanted "Teachers want what students need" and "Hey hey! Ho ho! We're fighting to keep class size low!" Many teachers complained of having thirty-eight, forty, forty-two students in a class and of schools that had no librarian or had a nurse only one day a week. Thousands of parents joined the picket lines, many drivers honked in support, and taco trucks showed up to feed the striking teachers. Steve Lopez, a columnist for the *Los Angeles Times,* wrote, "The best thing about the strike, hands down, was the way it galvanized a usually disengaged public."

These teachers in the nation's second-largest school district were clearly inspired by the landmark Chicago teachers' strike of 2012, by the walkouts in West Virginia, Oklahoma, and Arizona, and by the notion of bargaining for the common good. Their union, United Teachers Los Angeles, had an unusually ambitious list of demands aimed at improving education, including far more nurses, librarians, and school counselors, less standardized testing, more green space on school campuses, and fewer "random" searches that made students feel like criminals. The teachers also demanded a moratorium on charter schools in L.A., asserting that charters were hurting the majority of schoolchildren (overwhelmingly minority, overwhelmingly low-income) by taking away precious space and money from traditional schools. The union was standing up to a charter-friendly school board that was elected thanks to $9.7 million in campaign funding by billionaires such as Eli Broad and the Walton family, the heirs of Walmart's founder. The union argued that it was absurd that L.A.'s schools were so underfunded when the school district had a $2 billion rainy day fund and the state a $21 billion surplus.

Alex Caputo-Pearl, the union's president, said the teachers were focused on the "broader common good, and not so much about a narrow . . . contract." The school board had offered a 6 percent raise over two years before the strike, and the teachers settled for 6 percent. That showed this strike was really about issues far beyond teacher pay. With California's governor and L.A.'s mayor working vigorously to settle the dispute, the school district got the teachers to end their six-day strike by promising to hire three hundred more nurses and eighty-two more librarians. This assured a full-time nurse in every school and a librarian in every middle and high school. The teachers also won commitments to reduce class size in grades four through twelve by four students per class over three years. The union won promises to reduce random searches in twenty-eight schools and create thirty "community schools" that will have wraparound services, including after-school programs, health care, and adult education. The union even got the school board to commit to urging state officials to order a moratorium on new charter schools in L.A. until a study was completed on those schools' effects on the district.

As soon as the settlement was announced, the teachers at one school broke into a dance line to the song "Celebrate" by Kool and the Gang. Caputo-Pearl said, "We won because you—at nine hundred schools across the entire city, with parents, with students, with community organizations—you walked the line." He hailed the settlement as "a very broad compact around things that get at social justice, educational justice, and racial justice." Arlene Inouye, an English-as-a-second-language teacher who became the union's chief negotiator, added, "I think every" teacher "feels that, 'I won this, we won this all together. We do have collective power. We can't do it individually, but we can do it together.'"

Twenty-One

How Workers Can Regain Their Power

LABOR LEADERS OFTEN SUGGEST that there are easy, straightforward ways to reverse the decline in worker power and labor unions. Enact a card check law, they say—that would make it far easier to unionize workers. Move from company-by-company bargaining to the industry-wide bargaining that exists in many European countries—that would create higher standards for millions of workers in different industries.

To be sure, if those ideas were adopted, it would be a boon for workers and unions alike. But today's political realities make it extremely hard to get Congress to enact union-friendly or worker-friendly measures. Despite overwhelming public support for such worker-friendly ideas as increasing the minimum wage and enacting a paid sick days' law, many in Congress seem allergic to both ideas. Ever since the National Labor Relations Act was enacted in 1935, Congress has rejected every push to make it easier for unions to grow, including efforts by Presidents Johnson, Carter, Clinton, and Obama. Time and again, Republicans have used the filibuster to defeat these efforts—most frustratingly in 1978, when a five-week filibuster torpedoed legislation that would have helped unionization campaigns by imposing tougher penalties on law-breaking companies.

Nowadays, the political landscape in Washington and many states is in many ways more hostile toward labor than at any time in decades. That landscape will have to change hugely if Washington is to enact any legislation that gives workers more power or helps unions. If we hope to create a more favorable environment for workers, we as a nation will first need to overhaul our campaign finance system. That system is dominated by ultra-wealthy, conservative (and vehemently antiunion) donors like the Koch brothers and Sheldon Adelson as well as powerful corporations and dark money groups.

In the 2016 election cycle, the Koch brothers' network alone spent around $750 million—two to three times as much as all of organized labor. There was also heavy spending by conservative groups like the Club for Growth and the U.S. Chamber of Commerce. As we saw, corporations and business executives contributed $3.4 billion in the 2016 election cycle, sixteen times as much as labor. That of course makes lawmakers far more attentive to businesses' concerns than to workers' concerns.

Unfortunately, thanks to the Supreme Court's rulings in *Citizens United* and other cases, the hallowed ideal of one person, one vote has given way to a lopsided situation where billionaires like the Koch brothers, Adelson, and Tom Steyer have thousands of times the political voice and power of a schoolteacher, store clerk, or steelworker. (Adelson and his wife donated more than $110 million to help Republicans in the 2018 campaign and more than $20 million to help Trump in 2016.) Everyone who believes in one person, one vote, and every workers' advocate, should support a constitutional amendment to curb Big Money's outsize influence in our elections.

Eighty-four percent of Americans agree that corporations and wealthy individuals have too much sway in our elections, with more than 84 percent of Democrats and 72 percent of Republicans backing restrictions on campaign spending. Nonetheless, amending the Constitution to limit Big Money's influence will be a daunting challenge because billionaire donors will spend heavily to defeat such an effort and preserve their immense power.

Even without a constitutional amendment, we can and should expand public financing in political campaigns as widely as we can. This would reduce the domination of the wealthy and amplify the voice of average Americans. Under a measure that New York City voters approved in 2018, residents have their campaign donations matched eight to one in mayoral and city council races, while thirteen states give publicly financed grants to gubernatorial candidates once they achieve a threshold of support through small contributions. Seattle has a particularly innovative program, called Democracy Vouchers, that enables even low-wage workers to donate to campaigns. Voters are given four vouchers of $25 each that they can contribute to city council and mayoral candidates. Good ideas like these should be extended to presidential, Senate, and House campaigns.

John Sarbanes, a congressman from Maryland, has made a smart proposal to limit rich donors' inordinate influence in House campaigns. Under his plan, if candidates agree not to accept donations of more than $1,000, every donation they receive of $150 or less from residents of their state would be matched six to one by public funds. This proposal, Sarbanes said, "addresses the need to build a movement to take government back from big money." (The Democratic-controlled House passed a bill in March 2019 that includes a Seattle-like voucher experiment and Sarbanes's six-to-one match for House and presidential campaigns.)

Much of Bernie Sanders's 2016 campaign was a crusade against Big Money and its distorting influence on government. "The need for real campaign finance reform is not a progressive issue. It is not a conservative issue. It is an American issue," Sanders said. "Our vision for American democracy should be a nation in which all people, regardless of their income, can participate in the political process, can run for office without begging for contributions from the wealthy and the powerful."

When the National Labor Relations Act was enacted in 1935, its chief sponsor, Senator Robert F. Wagner, a Democrat from New York, saw it as a vehicle to give millions of workers more bargaining power vis-à-vis their employers. That act gave workers a federally guaranteed right to unionize; if a majority of employees at a workplace voted to unionize, the employer was required to recognize the union and bargain for a contract. That landmark law had another lasting result: giving workers far more power in politics. It enabled millions of Americans to pool their voices and dues money to help elect worker-friendly candidates and win laws like the minimum wage, Medicare, and the Occupational Safety and Health Act.

With union power in decline, American workers badly need new strategies to amplify their voices. Beyond the many worker centers that have sprouted up, one important way would be to create a major new national workers' group—let's call it the American Association of Working People (AAWP). When I first heard Janice Bellace, a professor of business ethics at the Wharton School, propose this idea in 2017, she said American workers could use a group like AARP to help speak for them and represent their interests (supplementing what unions are doing). This new association could fight for workers on myriad issues: raising the minimum wage, pushing for paid parental leave and sick days, and enacting stronger protections against sexual harassment. It could issue reports and hold conferences on the dangers in particular industries, like construction and mining, or on how non-compete clauses and industry oligopolies limit opportunities and pay increases for workers. It could add a powerful voice that helps counter business lobbies like the U.S. Chamber of Commerce and the National Restaurant Association. Basic membership in this organization should be affordable, perhaps $50 or $75 a year, with sustaining memberships of $200. If a million Americans join, it could become a potent new pro-worker voice.

To bring more attention to workers' concerns, some of the nation's leading advocacy groups should create departments that focus on worker issues (or expand such departments if they already exist). Here I'm thinking of groups like the National Organization for Women, the NAACP, Planned Parenthood, AARP, the American Civil Liberties Union, and UnidosUS (formerly the National Council of La Raza). Environmental groups like the Sierra Club and the Environmental Defense Fund could establish departments that focus on environmental health and safety for workers. It would be wonderful if the National Rifle Association focused on worker issues, too.

The nation's news media should devote more resources to reporting on worker matters. Few news organizations still have full-time workplace reporters. *The New York Times, The Washington Post,* ProPublica, *Bloomberg, BuzzFeed,* and *The Huffington Post* still do, but not *The Wall Street Journal,* the *Los Angeles Times,* the *Chicago Tribune,* or the Associated Press or most daily newspapers—all when there are hundreds of business reporters and nearly constant reports on every blip in the stock market. If workers face major problems and no one reports on them, that will often mean workers' interests are ignored.

A few advocacy groups have developed inventive ways to use the internet to fight for workers. OUR Walmart, an association of over ten thousand Walmart workers, has developed a mobile phone app, WorkIt, that uses IBM's Watson artificial intelligence bot to answer workers' questions on issues like Walmart's parental leave or sick days policies. OUR Walmart's leaders say WorkIt helps them identify what's bothering Walmart workers and can be used to mobilize workers to push Walmart to improve policies.

Coworker.org has been by far the most successful group in harnessing new technologies to help workers. Coworker.org has used online petitions to get well-known companies to change unpopular policies—for instance, it got Netflix to improve its parental leave policy. After Starbucks barred employees from having visible tattoos, Kristie Williams, a barista, started a petition urging the company to drop that policy. Helped by Coworker.org, Williams got twenty-five thousand baristas worldwide to sign on, and Starbucks soon reversed itself. After that victory, the network of Starbucks baristas won improvements on scheduling and paid parental leave and persuaded Starbucks to stop prohibiting employees from having unusual hair colors like blue and purple. One Coworker.org petition helped persuade Uber to adjust its app to make tipping available to all U.S. drivers, while another called on Comcast to crack down on sexual harassment at its call centers. Coworker.org is strategizing to figure out how to use the internet to rally and lift workers in bigger and more important ways, perhaps to unionize. It played a big, behind-the-scenes role in organizing the November 2018 protest by twenty thousand Google workers against sexual harassment. Coworker.org may have only a fraction of the power that Walter Reuther's UAW once had, but every innovative idea helps.

———

Even as unions have grown weaker, their public approval ratings have climbed in recent years, with 62 percent of Americans voicing approval of unions, the highest level since 2003. The surge has probably come because many Americans felt powerless and victimized during the Great Recession and during the painfully slow economic recovery that followed. Many no doubt felt angry that their wages, adjusted for inflation, remained dismayingly flat for many years even as corporate profits and stock prices were soaring to new records.

In other promising news for unions, their highest approval ratings are coming from young workers, those eighteen to thirty-four—perhaps because those millennials are eager for some tool to help them economically after they faced such an unfriendly entry-level job market during and after the Great Recession. Moreover, many millennials have seen how much the union-backed Fight for $15 has done to lift wages and inspire young workers. In addition, many millennials are unhappy with capitalism's inequities; a 2018 Gallup poll found that 51 percent of that group have a positive view of socialism, higher than the 45 percent with a positive view of capitalism.

Another hopeful note for labor is that a 2017 poll found that 46 percent of nonunion workers say they would vote to join a union if they could, up from 32 percent in 1995. That means 55 million nonunion workers want to unionize. Add that to the 14.8 million workers already in unions, and that means if workers were given the union representation they desired, America's overall unionization rate would be 44 percent.

Instead, just 6.4 percent of private-sector workers are union members, and just 10.5 percent of the workforce overall. By far the biggest obstacle to unions' growth is fierce employer opposition, which is encouraged by the extraordinarily weak penalties that companies face when they break the law battling unions. As we have seen, the main penalty that employers often face for such lawbreaking is having to post a notice on the bulletin board admitting they broke the law and promising not to do it again. Researchers have found that nearly 20 percent of rank-and-file union activists are fired during organizing drives, a percentage that is so high because the punishment is so puny. It's almost foolhardy for antiunion companies not to fire the two or three workers heading an organizing drive. Such firings often cripple the campaign, while the NLRB might order the lawbreaking company to pay $5,000 or $10,000 in back wages two or three years later, long after the union drive has fizzled. For a major company, that's not even a slap on the wrist.

To deter frequent lawbreaking by employers, the National Labor Relations Act should be strengthened so it has real teeth. To prevent unlawful firings for union activity, the NLRA should have fines that bite—$100,000 for a first firing, $200,000 for a second one, and increasing from there. There should also be sizable financial penalties when employers demote workers or cut their hours for backing a union or when employers illegally spy on workers or threaten to close a plant if it unionizes. If companies egregiously violate labor laws by firing the workers spearheading a unionization drive, then corporate executives should also face penalties with real bite, such as large personal fines. It shouldn't be just the pro-union workers whose lives are turned upside down. There also needs to be swifter and surer means to reinstate union supporters who are improperly fired during organizing drives.

Some labor experts say new laws are needed to embolden workers to speak up more. One audacious proposal is to replace America's at-will employment system (in which most workers can be fired for any cause, or no cause) with a rule that says workers can only be fired for "just cause." Representative John Lewis has introduced legislation to make workers' rights like civil rights—if workers are fired for backing a union, they could file civil rights lawsuits just like workers who are fired because of their race or religion. As a result, companies would face punitive and compensatory damages—far greater penalties than the NLRA's toothless ones. If the original National Labor Relations Act included muscular penalties, instead of feeble ones, America's labor unions would probably have organized many millions more workers than they have.

———

Few Americans realize how tilted the playing field is when unions seek to organize a workplace. Managers have access to workers 24/7 and often show antiunion videos in lunchrooms and break rooms. Companies often require employees to attend meetings where high-priced consultants tell them that unions are corrupt and dishonest and only want their dues money, and that workplaces like theirs have closed down after unionizing. While employers flood the zone with antiunion propaganda, companies—thanks to the Supreme Court's *Lechmere* ruling—have the right to prohibit union organizers from setting foot on company property. In that 1992 case, the employer barred organizers from putting flyers on workers' windshields in the employee parking lot.

Before requesting a union election, organizers often get two-thirds of employees to sign cards saying they support a union. But once the NLRB schedules an election and management mounts an all-out antiunion drive, unions often lose the vote. Unions deserve a fairer shot. If an employer requires workers to attend hour-long meetings to hear antiunion speeches, union organizers should be given equal access, either to speak at such a meeting or to have equal time with employees. (Many labor leaders have called for banning such "captive audience meetings," arguing that they give employers a big advantage and unfairly compel workers to hear antiunion propaganda.) Union organizers should also be allowed to distribute flyers and talk to workers in parking lots and lunchrooms. The Supreme Court has ruled that employers' property rights trump workers' rights, but with things so skewed against unions, Congress and the courts should adjust that balance.

Labor leaders have long called for a law that would let unions, when organizing workers, opt for card check. They see card check as a faster, fairer way to unionize, especially because election campaigns are often tilted lopsidedly in favor of employers. As discussed earlier, with card check, unions seek recognition as soon as a majority of employees at a workplace sign cards saying they favor a union. Many companies denounce card check, asserting, with scant evidence, that "union thugs" bully workers into signing pro-union cards. Corporate lobbyists argue that card check that is based on a simple majority of 50 percent plus one of workers should not be allowed because, they say, some of the signatures are undoubtedly coerced. To overcome these assertions of coercion, no matter how unsubstantiated, Congress should consider a law saying that when unions obtain 60 percent of employee signatures on cards, employers shall be required to grant union recognition and bargain.

If unions are voted in, many companies follow a let's-sabotage-the-union playbook. They drag out contract negotiations for months, trying to convince workers that unions are weak and worthless. After many months without a contract (during which there are no raises), management often works with antiunion employees who collect signatures to hold a decertification vote to oust the union, feeding on workers' impatience and frustration. (Such votes can't be held within a year of the union first being certified. Under federal law, it's illegal for companies to help gather signatures for decertification votes.) To stop such undermining of unions, the NLRA should be amended so that if an employer and a new union don't agree on a contract within four months, a federal arbitrator will issue a binding recommendation on what a fair contract should be (based on the two sides' last, best, and final offers).

Even without new laws, government can take some important steps to increase workers' voice and power.

Here's a simple one: Health and safety is a concern in every workplace, whether it has to do with hazardous machinery, high stress levels, or aches from standing all day or slumping over one's keyboard. Because safety is so important, California, Michigan, and the twenty other states that have their own state OSHA programs should require every workplace with fifty or more workers to have a health and safety committee that meets monthly, with workers choosing the employee representatives on these committees.

States can give unions a boost by embracing a system, popular in Scandinavia, in which unions administer unemployment benefits. Such a system—known as the Ghent system, after the Belgian city where it was first developed—helps keep unions visible and strong and helps them attract members. Under this system, unions could also match workers with jobs or run skills-training programs. Remembering how Frances Perkins gave states considerable leeway in shaping their unemployment insurance systems, some labor-friendly governors should experiment with such a system.

State and city labor commissioners are often overburdened and short staffed as they investigate minimum wage, overtime, and off-the-clock violations. Using a strategy known as co-enforcement, San Francisco's Office of Labor Standards Enforcement has turned to several worker groups to help it investigate violations and interview workers. San Francisco's labor office gives out $700,000 a year in grants to worker groups, including the Chinese Progressive Association and Young Workers United. This money helps these groups hire investigators who not only probe for violations but also train and encourage workers to speak up.

While unions would love to have the system of industry-wide or sectoral bargaining common in Europe, Congress is unlikely to approve such a policy, and American unions are generally not strong enough to pressure companies into industry-wide agreements. But a type of industry-wide bargaining can be required at the state level. As we saw earlier, when Governor Andrew Cuomo of New York set up a wage board to determine what a "living wage" should be for fast-food workers, that turned into a type of industry-wide bargaining, albeit in a nonunion industry. Cuomo held a series of hearings across New York State, where unions and the restaurant industry butted heads over what a living wage should be for fast-food workers. Cuomo then served in effect as arbitrator and determined that there should be a $15 minimum wage in New York City and its suburbs and $12.50 upstate. In theory, this industry-wide type of bargaining could also be done for hotels, nursing homes, nail salons, and other fields. California, Massachusetts, New Jersey, and several other states also have "wage board" laws, and they could be used for more such industry-wide bargaining.

In 2018, Seattle's City Council enacted a law that takes the wage board concept to a new level that may well be copied by other cities. Pushed by the National Domestic Workers Alliance and other groups, the City Council created a "standards board" to improve pay and conditions for Seattle's thirty thousand domestic workers. The thirteen-member board will make recommendations on minimum pay, overtime, paid time off, and health benefits for nannies and housekeepers, with the expectation that the council will enact those proposals into law. Some Uber and Lyft drivers hope to get Seattle's City Council to create a similar board to set minimum pay levels for app-based drivers. (In ways, New York City's Taxi and Limousine Commission served as such a board when it set $17.22 an hour as the minimum for the city's app-based drivers.)

Volkswagen has established a fascinating model of worker representation at its assembly plant in Chattanooga. Employee groups that have the support of more than 15 percent of the workforce qualify to meet monthly with VW's human resources officials. Groups with more than 45 percent support, somewhat like works councils in Germany (discussed below), get to meet every two weeks with the plant's executive committee. VW has adopted this system not for collective bargaining but to assure worker input. VW recognizes the value of meeting with employee representatives to address sources of friction and improve morale, efficiency, and working conditions.

As fewer workplaces are unionized in the United States, we as a nation should look increasingly to the VW model or, more broadly, to minority unions as a voice for workers, to ensure that workers have input and their views are not forgotten. These models could also serve as stepping-stones toward traditional unionization. American law is binary on this—employers are free to totally ignore worker groups that have not demonstrated majority support, but once a union wins an election showing majority backing, then the employer has to recognize and bargain with it.

Germany's system of worker voice and representation is often viewed as the best in the world. Under German law, all corporations with more than two thousand employees are required to give worker representatives just under half the seats on their supervisory boards. These boards set a broad agenda to help guide a company's board of directors, which must include one worker (and which functions like a U.S. corporate board). Supervisory boards don't make operational decisions, although they often foster a mind-set that promotes worker interests—for instance, to invest heavily in worker training or to discourage outsourcing overseas.

In Germany, union contracts are usually industry-wide, meaning there will be one contract covering all of the country's steelmakers or supermarkets. To help adapt these contracts to local conditions and give workers more of a voice, nearly every workplace has a works council—a consultative committee, made up half of management and half of worker-chosen representatives (white-collar and blue-collar). These councils develop policies on work hours, safety, training, vacation schedules, and pay incentives to boost production and quality. These councils also reduce tensions and prevent strikes by addressing sore points or explaining to workers why certain problems can't be resolved.

As hostile as many American business executives are to the idea of workers' speaking up, forward-thinking companies should borrow some of Germany's ideas. Germany certainly has some of the world's most successful and respected companies—BMW, Daimler, Siemens—with German workers known for their know-how, dedication, and excellence in manufacturing. One poll found that 53 percent of Americans support letting workers at large companies elect representatives to their corporation's board of directors, while just 22 percent opposed the idea. Upset that corporate America's focus on maximizing profits has shortchanged workers, Senator Elizabeth Warren of Massachusetts has introduced the Accountable Capitalism Act, which would require corporations with more than $1 billion in annual revenues to have their employees elect at least 40 percent of the board members. Warren's bill would also require those corporations to obtain a federal charter that would obligate their directors to consider the interests of all corporate stakeholders, including employees, and not just the interests of shareholders.

Barring a radical change in American politics, Congress is unlikely to enact Warren's bill or any other legislation that requires companies to adopt even a smidgen of Germany's worker-inclusive capitalism. In his book *Only One Thing Can Save Us: Why America Needs a New Kind of Labor Movement,* Thomas Geoghegan, a Chicago labor lawyer, has proposed several smart steps to nudge corporate America in the German direction. Because nonprofit hospitals need charters from their states, Geoghegan suggests that states require those hospitals, as a condition of getting their charters renewed, to let nurses, kitchen workers, and other employees elect half of their board members. With regard to for-profit corporations, Geoghegan recommends that states exempt companies from the state income tax if they let employees elect one-third of their board members. Geoghegan would also have the White House issue an executive order that gives preference in awarding federal contracts to corporations that let workers elect several members to their board of directors.

Many of today's nonunion worker groups have the existential worry that they'll wither and die if foundations ever stop funding them. Pushed by the Fight for $15, New York City enacted a first-in-the-nation law that aims to solve that problem. That law, as we discussed, enables fast-food workers to make voluntary contributions from their paychecks to worker groups to help assure those groups a steady source of funding. The law requires restaurants to deduct those contributions and forward the money to a worker group, but only if the group first gets five hundred workers to pledge to make contributions.

In New York, as discussed previously, a group called Fast Food Justice hopes to get ten thousand fast-food workers to contribute and in that way obtain $1.8 million a year in funding to fight for workers. If this technique succeeds in providing adequate financing, expect worker groups in many other cities to push for similar laws.

Sympathetic billionaires who want to lift struggling workers and their families should consider giving a few hundred thousand dollars to up-and-coming worker groups. As we saw with the Coalition of Immokalee Workers or with a group like the hugely successful Workers Defense Project in Austin, Texas, donating to worker groups might be a more effective way to lift thousands of low-income or moderate-income families than, say, donating to a charter school.

In the 1960s, John Kenneth Galbraith and other commentators wrote that two slow-moving, heavily bureaucratic behemoths dominated the American economy—big business and big labor. They warned that these cumbersome institutions might have a hard time adapting to economic change. In subsequent decades, business has adjusted, becoming far more agile in order to stay competitive—adopting new technologies, closing underutilized factories, firing underperforming CEOs, moving production to lower-cost countries. While some of these strategies are unpopular, there's no denying that corporate America is dynamic and thriving—anything but slow moving.

In contrast, many labor unions remain sluggish and bureaucratic. Too many have changed little since the 1960s. Many are top-heavy and, as before, devote much of their resources to handling grievances—an important activity, but one that doesn't help unions grow. Today, as before, many unions spend little money or energy on organizing, and many union presidents remain at their organization's helm for fifteen or twenty years, even as their unions decline.

If labor is ever going to reverse its slide, unions need to become more agile and innovative and put more emphasis on growth. Every union, both national and local, should be required to spend at least 30 percent of its budget on organizing, that is, expansion. For organized labor, it's now or never, grow or grow irrelevant.

Many union officials have little incentive to organize (and we shouldn't forget that incentives play a major role in how people act). For labor leaders, organizing is stressful and risky. Union presidents can look bad if their union spends six months and $500,000 on an organizing drive and it ends up failing (often because the company mounted an effective beat-back-the-union crusade). For many union officials, it's easier not to bother with stress-inducing organizing drives.

Unions should have long ago adopted incentives to encourage their leaders to do more organizing, perhaps by barring them from getting raises unless they expand their unions through organizing (and not through mergers). Or perhaps union officials should be given a bonus every time their union adds a thousand members. Or perhaps their pay should be cut in proportion to any decline in membership; a 5 percent drop in membership would mean a 5 percent pay cut. That might persuade union leaders to take organizing and growth more seriously.

Too many labor leaders remain in office for a decade or two, even when their unions are shrinking. Far too many unions have a democracy deficit; it's easy for union leaders to remain in power because they control their union's newspaper, emails, website, and bureaucracy. Moreover, challengers usually have scant chance of winning because they are often little known and poorly funded. Unions should consider adopting conditional term limits; for instance, the top officials of national and local unions could be limited to eight years of service if their union membership has declined since they took office. (Admittedly, this might be too harsh if a union is in a shrinking industry or if a major plant closed.) Or perhaps this variation: If a union leader has been elected to two four-year terms and wants a third term, then he or she must win two-thirds support in a referendum. If the leader meets that threshold, then he or she can run for reelection. For a fourth term, a leader must survive a 75 percent referendum. (Employers must be strictly prohibited from interfering in any way in such votes.)

Unions also need to do a better job communicating. Many unions are headed by shrewd tacticians who do a fine job wrestling with management at the bargaining table but do far less well conveying labor's message on television or to the public, or even to workers in their industry. To get labor's message across—and, importantly, to attract and inspire young workers (and to obtain TV and radio bookings)—every national union should appoint a smart, appealing young spokesperson or policy director. If union presidents fear that this person will eclipse them in the public eye, that's a risk that must be taken to do what's best for the nation's workers.

———

If a workers' movement is ever to rebound and flourish in the United States, it will need to excite millions of Americans. It will need ideas that will lift workers and their children, ideas that increase opportunity, upward mobility, and economic security. A workers' movement has to lead the fight for higher wages and against increased income inequality.

Some unions—not enough of them—stand for a vision of social and economic justice. A workers' movement will have to do the same. It needs to stand for something more than whether workers get a 1.8 percent or a 2.1 percent raise. It will need a message that inspires, the way that the Fight for $15's audacious demands inspired millions of workers.

A workers' movement needs to fight for more security and stability in the lives of workers—a stronger safety net for all workers (including portable benefits for gig economy workers) and greater protections when workers lose their jobs, and not just a solid unemployment insurance program, but improved and expanded training and retraining.

A workers' movement needs to be a powerful, unrelenting voice against unjust treatment, whether wage theft, sexual harassment, dangerous conditions, or bullying bosses. It needs to be a loud and fierce opponent of discrimination, whether by race, gender, religion, or age.

A workers' movement should seek to ensure that every worker has a voice and feels empowered to speak up and speak out, to be valued, rather than dismissed and drowned out.

A workers' movement should be an outspoken leader in fighting for a true democracy in which voting rights are not trampled upon and corporations and the rich do not dominate elections and policy making.

A workers' movement needs to ensure that workers are well trained and productive not just to help workers increase their income but also to keep employers competitive and profitable so that employers can share their prosperity with their workers. ("I even believe in helping an employer function more productively," Sidney Hillman, the president of the clothing workers' union, once said. "For then, we will have a claim to higher wages, shorter hours, and greater participation in the benefits of running a smooth industrial machine.")

A workers' movement needs to serve as a countervailing force to corporate power, whether in fighting wage freezes, health-care cuts, or corporate mergers that restrict competition and hurt consumers and workers alike. A workers' movement should also stand up to corporations and oligopolies that gouge workers and their families, whether it's banks, drug companies, airlines, cable companies, or internet providers.

It's hard to say what form (or forms) a future workers' movement should or will take. It could be in a newfangled form, perhaps like some of the innovative groups we have discussed, or it could be in the form of traditional unions, notwithstanding the sizable obstacles that workers face in unionizing. The important thing is that there be movement, energy, vision, and moral courage. To succeed, as we've seen, often takes two seemingly contradictory things: individual agency and group solidarity. It will take individual workers' agency to speak out. That, of course, must be met with solidarity from other workers. If progress, if greater justice is to be achieved, people need to speak up, stand up, and join together.

If a workers' movement is to grow and have a future, it of course needs to attract the young. Some efforts, like the Fight for $15 and the Freelancers Union, have done this. But too many unions remain uninspired and uninspiring. Fortunately, a few recent union drives have excited young workers, among them the successes in unionizing digital media workers, adjunct professors, and grad student workers. Some of the contracts won by these workers have achieved truly impressive gains: huge raises, an end to particularly objectionable practices, and a path from insecure gig jobs to steady employment. These are the types of gains that many workers long for.

Labor should go back to first principles and, as always, fight for fairness, for a more balanced economy with less poverty, more opportunity, more economic security, and more work-life balance. To this end, labor could champion universal health coverage, free community college, free public universities, more and better apprenticeships, paid parental leave, a paid vacation law, more generous Social Security benefits, a fairer tax system, and vastly expanded infrastructure and green jobs programs that create hundreds of thousands of good jobs. (Alexandria Ocasio-Cortez and others have called this last idea a "Green New Deal.) A workers' movement should also fight for affordable housing, first-class public schools, excellent public transportation, and clean air and water. (And it goes without saying that labor should try to do these things without causing budget deficits to explode.)

It's still the same old story. Today's workers want what Rose Schneiderman, the great labor activist and speaker, called for a century ago: "The worker must have bread, but she must have roses, too"—to have "the sun and music and art."

For all his imperfections, the goals that Samuel Gompers laid out for labor still ring true: "What does labor want? . . . We want more schoolhouses and less jails; more books and less arsenals; more learning and less vice; more constant work and less crime, more leisure and less greed; more justice and less revenge; in fact, more of the opportunities to cultivate our better natures."

Acknowledgments

In writing this book, I very much felt that I was standing on the shoulders of labor historians and writers who came before me. I learned so much from their fine work. I owe a huge debt to Irving Bernstein, Jefferson Cowie, Kirstin Downey, Philip Dray, Melvyn Dubofsky, Sidney Fine, Michael Honey, Nelson Lichtenstein, Joseph McCartin, Annelise Orleck, Leon Stein, David Von Drehle, and many others. I am also hugely grateful to many experts on industrial and labor relations—there are far too many to name here—whose research, work, and wisdom I have turned to and relied on over the years.

I owe tremendous gratitude to my wife, Miriam, for helping and encouraging me in ways large and small throughout this project. I am greatly thankful to my editor at Knopf, Jonathan Segal, who suggested that I write a history of American labor and who is such a wizard at editing and shaping a book. I also thank my agent, Vicky Bijur, who has been an unwavering source of support and has invariably provided good advice.

The Russell Sage Foundation generously supported my research, and I especially thank Sheldon Danziger and Claire Gabriel there. I also thank the Ford Foundation, and Laine Romero-Alston in particular, for its travel grant to help me research this book. I also want to thank the Institute of Politics at the University of Chicago, especially David Axelrod and Alicia Sams, for its support.

I feel huge gratitude to many people at *The New York Times* who variously served as colleagues, mentors, and teachers. I appreciate that the *Times* gave me the freedom to roam the country for nearly two decades to write about the important issues facing American workers. I thank Jill Abramson, Fred Andrews, Dean Baquet, Susan Chira, Max Frankel, Soma Golden Behr, Dave Jones, Bill Keller, John M. Lee, Joe Lelyveld, Dean Murphy, Mike Oreskes, Joyce Purnick, Howell Raines, Jim Roberts, and many others.

I feel deep gratitude to the journalists who continue to shine a needed light on what's happening to America's workers, among them Lydia DePillis, Josh

Eidelson, Alexia Fernández Campbell, Steve Franklin, Michael Grabell, Sarah Jaffe, Dave Jamieson, Dave Moberg, Hamilton Nolan, Danielle Paquette, Margot Roosevelt, Noam Scheiber, Alana Semuels, and Ken Ward Jr. I am also indebted to an earlier generation of labor journalists, including Nancy Cleeland, Peter Kilborn, Ken Noble, Bill Serrin, Frank Swoboda, and the incomparable A. H. Raskin. (And there are many economics reporters to whom I am indebted as well.)

Over the past four years, I discussed and debated many issues in this book with Kirk Adams, Rosemary Batt, Craig Becker, Kim Bobo, Peter Dreier, Cynthia Estlund, Janice Fine, Steve Franklin, Charlotte Garden, Tom Geoghegan, Kent Hirozawa, Robert Kuttner, Mark Levinson, Wilma Liebman, Ray Markey, Harold Meyerson, and Cristina Tzintzún. I appreciate their insights and wisdom.

I also owe thanks to the Economic Policy Institute for, month after month, providing extremely helpful statistics and reports on trends involving the nation's 150 million workers.

I also thank the friends who put me up (and put up with me) as I was traveling to research this book: Aixa Gannon, Larry Gordon, Harold and Nancy Krent, Jonathan Siegel, and Leda Siskind. I thank Rabbi David Schuck for ever so patiently and wisely instructing me about Judaism's teachings on ethics and labor.

Lastly, I shall forever be thankful to my late parents, Mortimer and Cyril Greenhouse, who repeatedly taught me, as Dr. King taught, that all labor that helps humanity has dignity and that every worker, no matter how low paid or humble, deserves respect.

Notes

Introduction

xii income inequality has grown worse: "Crisis Squeezes Income and Puts Pressure on Inequality and Poverty," Organization for Economic Co-operation and Development, May 2013, 4.

xiv That effort showed how unionization: Steven Greenhouse, "Union Claims Texas Victory with Janitors," *New York Times,* Nov. 28, 2005, A1.

xiv He said unions need to help: Michael Sean Winters, "Labor Unions Are Prophetic, Innovative, Pope Says," *National Catholic Reporter,* July 6, 2017.

xv One in five adults: "Report on the Economic Well-Being of U.S. Households in 2017," Federal Reserve Board, May 2018, 2.

ONE Losing Our Voice

3 Many of the laid-off workers: Julia Preston, "In Turnabout, Disney Cancels Tech Worker Layoffs," *New York Times,* June 17, 2015, A18. When word leaked to the news media about these layoffs, it became a front-page story, and Disney grew so embarrassed that it rescinded many of the layoffs—but not Keith Barrett's.

3 At one point, her shift supervisor: Maura Dolan, "California's Top Court Tells Employers to Give Workers a Chair," *Los Angeles Times,* April 5, 2016, A1. Jamie Workman left on maternity leave far earlier than she had planned because of the requirement that she stand for eight hours.

4 Too sick to work the next day: "Sick and Fired: Why We Need Earned Sick Days to Fix the Economy," Family Values at Work.

6 Indeed, labor's share of national income: OECD Employment Outlook 2018, 566.

6 four in ten American adults: "Report on the Economic Well-Being of U.S. Households in 2017," Federal Reserve System, May 2018, 21.

6 Forty million Americans: Alisha Coleman-Jensen et al., "Household Food Security in the United States in 2016," U.S. Department of Agriculture, Report No. 237, Sept. 2017.

7 Not only have his appointees: Steven Greenhouse, "How Trump Betrays 'Forgotten' Americans," *New York Times,* Sept. 3, 2018.

8 "Voice means discussing with an employer": Richard B. Freeman and James L. Medoff, *What Do Unions Do?* (New York: Basic Books, 1984), 7.

8 In recent years, far more companies: Conor Dougherty, "Losing the Right to a New Job," *New York Times,* May 14, 2017, BU1; Steven Greenhouse, "Noncompete

Clauses Increasingly Pop Up in Array of Jobs," *New York Times,* June 9, 2014, B1; Paul Wyche, "Noncompete Decrees: Jimmy John's Makes Hourly Workers Sign and Gets a Lawsuit," *Fort Wayne Journal Gazette,* Oct. 26, 2014, 1H.

8   For instance, if one or two hospital chains: Neil Irwin, "Tying Behemoths to Stagnant Pay and Low Growth," *New York Times,* Aug. 26, 2018, A1.

8   Similarly, the United States is the only: Jody Heymann et al., "Contagion Nation: A Comparison of Paid Sick Day Policies in 22 Countries," Center for Economic and Policy Research, May 2009.

8   In France, by contrast: Rebecca Ray, Milla Sanes, and John Schmitt, "No-Vacation Nation Revisited," Center for Economic Policy Research, May 2013.

9   The only other countries: Jessica Deahl, "Countries Around the World Beat the U.S. on Paid Parental Leave," NPR, Oct. 6, 2016.

9   "While there are many 'progressive' groups": Jacob S. Hacker and Paul Pierson, *Winner-Take-All Politics: How Washington Made the Rich Richer—and Turned Its Back on the Middle Class* (New York: Simon & Schuster, 2011), 56–57.

9   Union members earn 13.6 percent: "The Benefits of Collective Bargaining: An Antidote to Wage Decline and Inequality," Economic Policy Institute, April 14, 2015.

9   Seventy-five percent of unionized workers: "Employee Benefits in the United States—March 2018," Bureau of Labor Statistics, July 20, 2018.

9   Eighty-three percent of union members: Employment Benefits Survey, Retirement Benefits, March 2017, Bureau of Labor Statistics.

9   Unions also help reduce the gender pay gap: Elise Gould and Celine McNicholas, "Unions Help Narrow the Wage Gap," Economic Policy Institute, April 3, 2017.

10 African American union members: Cherrie Bucknor, "Black Workers, Union, and Inequality," Center for Economic and Policy Research, Aug. 2016.

10 One study found that the decline: Steven Greenhouse, "Labor's Decline and Wage Inequality," *New York Times Blogs* (*Economix*) Aug. 4, 2011. A study by Richard Freeman of Harvard and other economists found that a 10 percent increase in the percentage of unionized workers in a community is associated with a 3 to 4.5 percent increase in the income of all the area's children—partly because unions push for better schools and a higher minimum wage. Noam Scheiber, "A Link Between Unions and Children's Prospects," *New York Times,* Sept. 10, 2015, A20; Richard Freeman et al., "Bargaining for the American Dream: What Unions Do for Mobility," Center for American Progress, Sept. 9, 2015.

10 Two economists at the International Monetary: Florence Jaumotte and Carolina Osorio Buitron, "Power from the People," *Finance & Development,* 52, 1 (March 2015), 39.

10 Labor unions have done more: Jake Rosenfeld, *What Unions No Longer Do* (Cambridge, Mass.: Harvard University Press, 2014), 158–71.

10 "schools for democracy": Robert D. Putnam, "Democracy," in *The Democracy Sourcebook,* ed. Robert Dahl, Ian Shapiro, and José Antonio Cheibub (Cambridge, Mass.: MIT Press, 2003), 158.

10 "The labor movement was the principal force": Martin Luther King Jr., *All Labor Has Dignity* (Boston: Beacon Press, 2011).

11 From 2010 to 2017, there were fewer: "Work Stoppages Involving 1,000 or More Workers, 1947–2017," Bureau of Labor Statistics.

11 Partly because of imports and outsourcing: Jon Greenberg, "MSNBC's Ed Schultz: Trade Deals Closed 50,000 Factories," *PunditFact,* April 23, 2015.

11 Corporations have increasingly used temps: David Weil, *The Fissured Workplace: Why Work Became So Bad for So Many and What We Can Do to Improve It* (Cambridge, Mass.: Harvard University Press, 2014), 5–14.

11 (Indeed, a new term has been coined): See Guy Standing, *The Precariat: The New Dangerous Class* (London: Bloomsbury, 2011).

12 experts like the McKinsey Global Institute: James Manyika et al., "Jobs Lost, Jobs Gained: Workforce Transitions in a Time of Automation," McKinsey Global Institute, Dec. 2017, 11, 14.

12 while two Oxford professors predict: Carl Benedikt Frey and Michael A. Osborne, "The Future of Employment: How Susceptible Are Jobs to Computerisation?," Oxford Martin Programme on Technology and Employment, Sept. 17, 2013, 1.

12 from 1973 to 2016, a period of waning: "The Productivity-Pay Gap," Economic Policy Institute, Aug. 2018. This study found that employee productivity rose 77 percent from 1973 to 2016, while compensation rose 12.4 percent.

12 Hard though it may be: Drew DeSilver, "For Most U.S. Workers, Real Wages Have Barely Budged in Decades," Pew Research Center, Aug. 7, 2018.

12 CEOs at the largest 350 corporations: Dominic Rushe, "US Bosses Now Earn 312 Times the Average Worker's Wage, Figures Show," *Guardian,* Aug. 16, 2018.

12 Nearly fifty million American workers: Irene Tung, Yannet Lathrop, and Paul Sonn, "The Growing Movement for $15," National Employment Law Project, Nov. 2015, 5.

12 The top 1 percent of households: Chad Stone et al., "A Guide to Statistics on Historical Trends in Income Inequality," Center for Budget Policies and Priorities, Aug. 29, 2018.

12 Americans average 1,780 hours: "Hours Worked," OECD Data, data.oecd.org/emp /hours-worked.htm.

13 For college graduates who entered: Elise Gould, Zane Mokhiber, and Julia Wolfe, "Class of 2018: College Edition," Economic Policy Institute, May 10, 2018; Elise Gould, Zane Mokhiber, and Julia Wolfe, "Class of 2018: High School Edition," Economic Policy Institute, June 14, 2018.

13 The federal minimum wage of $7.25: Today's minimum wage is also 30 percent below its 1976 level, when Gerald Ford, a Republican, was president.

13 Indeed, the ratio of America's federal minimum wage: Christopher Ingraham, "The U.S. Has One of the Stingiest Minimum Wage Policies of Any Wealthy Nation," *Washington Post,* Dec. 29, 2017.

The reference is to the thirty-six industrial nations in the Organisation for Economic Co-operation and Development.

13 Although the percentage of workers: Leo Troy, "Trade Union Membership, 1897– 1962," National Bureau of Economic Research, 1965.

13 (although they forget that unionization): James T. Bennett and Bruce E. Kaufman, *What Do Unions Do? A Twenty-Year Perspective* (New Brunswick, N.J.: Transaction Publishers, 2007), 62.

14 When journalists at *Gothamist:* Andy Newman and John Leland, "DNAinfo and Gothamist Are Shut Down After Vote to Unionize," *New York Times,* Nov. 3, 2017, A21.

14 Only after a local newspaper: Spencer Soper, "Inside Amazon's Warehouse," *Allentown (Pa.) Morning Call,* Sept. 18, 2011, A1.

14 According to a *New York Times:* Jodi Kantor and David Streitfeld, "Inside Amazon: Wrestling Big Ideas in a Bruising Workplace," *New York Times,* Aug. 15, 2015, A1.

14 A biography of Tesla's co-founder: Matt McFarland, "The 22 Most Memorable Quotes from the New Elon Musk Book, Ranked," *Washington Post,* May 11, 2015; Michael Schaub, "Elon Musk: I Never Told a Male Underling to Miss His Child's Birth," *Los Angeles Times,* May 13, 2015, 1.

15 (Unions have sometimes been far too slow): For a powerful story about how a major corporation and a labor union were delinquent in addressing serious sexual harassment problems, see Susan Chira and Catrin Einhorn, "After #MeToo, 'What About Us?,'" *New York Times,* Dec. 20, 2017, A1.

15 Fowler wrote a blog post: Susan Fowler, "Reflecting on One Very, Very Strange Year at Uber," Feb. 19, 2017.

15 "No one felt they could go": Chris Togneri, "Massey Miners Pour Out Anger to House Committee," *Pittsburgh Tribune Review,* May 25, 2010. Workers generally feel more emboldened to speak up at unionized employers—and far more protected when they do.

16 It was unclear where: Carolyn Thompson, "Buffalo Crash Opened Window into Pilots' Life," Associated Press, June 7, 2009.

16 He had driven eight hundred miles: Joan Lowy, "Driver Fatigue Cited as Cause of Crash That Injured Comedian," Associated Press, Aug. 11, 2015.

16 A survey done by the National Restaurant Association: Lisa Graves and Zaid Jilani, "The Restaurant Industry Ran a Private Poll on the Minimum Wage. It Did Not Go Well for Them," *Intercept,* April 17, 2018.

16 poll found that Americans: Noam Scheiber and Dalia Sussman, "Inequality Troubles Americans Across Party Lines, a Poll Finds," *New York Times,* June 4, 2015, A1; "Americans' Views on Income Inequality and Workers' Rights," *New York Times,* June 3, 2015; Elise Gould and Jessica Schieder, "Work Sick or Lose Pay? The High Cost of Being Sick When You Don't Get Paid Sick Days," Economic Policy Institute, June 28, 2017.

16 In the 2015–16 election cycle: "Business-Labor-Ideology Split in PAC & Individual Donations to Candidates, Parties, Super PACs, and Outside Spending Groups," Center for Responsive Politics, www.opensecrets.org.

Even if one adds an estimated $100 million, even $200 million, for labor's other campaign efforts, like phone banking and door knocking to get out the vote, which are not considered direct political contributions, labor is still hugely outspent.

The Center for Responsive Politics notes, "An important caveat must be added to these figures: 'business' contributions from individuals are based on the donor's occupation/employer. Since nearly everyone works for someone, and since union affiliation is not listed on FEC reports, totals for business are somewhat overstated, while labor is understated. Still, the base of large individual donors is predominantly made up of business executives and professionals. Contributions under $200 are not included in these numbers, as they are not itemized."

17 "Today, we celebrate those who have taken": Paul Krugman, "Disdain for Workers," *New York Times,* Sept. 21, 2012, A29.

TWO A Worker's Struggle Never Ends

27 Those strikers were enraged: See Stephen Franklin, *Three Strikes: Labor's Heartland Losses and What They Mean for Working Americans* (New York: Guilford, 2001).

28 "Paying wages well above market levels": Steven Greenhouse, "At Caterpillar, Pressing Labor for Concessions," *New York Times,* July 23, 2012, A1.

28 "Frankly, if we're not competitive": Mina Kimes, "Caterpillar's Doug Oberhelman: Manufacturing's Mouthpiece," *Bloomberg BusinessWeek,* May 16, 2013.

28 "I always try to communicate": Ibid.

28 "It is class warfare": Mary Mitchell, "It's Corporate Greed, Plain and Simple," *Chicago Sun-Times,* July 29, 2012, 15.

28 In 2015, three years after this strike: Lauren Leone-Cross, "Caterpillar Announces Production Line Moves from Joliet to Mexico," *Joliet (Ill.) Herald-News,* March 21, 2015.

THREE Helping Workers Hit the Jackpot

35 Housekeeping jobs are arduous: Steven Greenhouse, "Hotel Rooms Get Plusher, Adding to Maids' Injuries," *New York Times,* April 21, 2006, A20.

35 And then there's the strain: For an excellent piece about a housekeeper's life, see Dan Barry, "A Force of Labor and of Politics in Las Vegas Hotels," *New York Times,* Nov. 6, 2016, A18.

38 "I didn't want him to become president": Sergio Bustos and Nicholas Riccardi, "Divided America: Will Trump Energize the Latino Vote?," Associated Press, Aug. 7, 2016.

38 "The Culinary is the most potent": Jack Healy, "Trump Hotel Workers Campaign for a Union, over the Boss's Objections," *New York Times,* July 30, 2016, A11.

38 "It was really like an army": Scott Sonner, "Labor, Latinos Helped Nevada Buck Red Tide," Associated Press, Nov. 10, 2016.

38 "the dominant political force in the state": Matt Viser, "GOP Tests Left's Energy with Nev. Ground Game," *Washington Post,* Oct. 23, 2018, A1.

39 After a state senator from Las Vegas: Michael Scott Davidson, "Yvanna Cancela Wants to Fight for Working Families as Member of Nevada Senate," *Las Vegas Review-Journal,* Feb. 4, 2017.

40 In 2016, the Culinary helped the Democrats: Brendan Morrow, "2016 Nevada Early Voting Final Results," Heavy.com, Nov. 6, 2016.

40 As a result, more than 95 percent: Workers can choose to be members of their union and pay full union dues or can opt out of being union members and pay so-called agency fees, which is the amount of union dues, minus the amount the union spends on politics and lobbying.

41 At six hotels, the workers: Dorothee Benz, "Labor's Ace in the Hole," *New Political Science* 26, no. 4 (Dec. 2004): 531.

42 Headquarters dispatched some crack organizers: Harold Meyerson, "Las Vegas as a Workers' Paradise," *American Prospect,* Jan. 2004, 38.

42 "The union was run": Quoted in Benz, "Labor's Ace in the Hole," 532.

42 The union persuaded Wynn: Meyerson, "Las Vegas as a Workers' Paradise."

43 But UNITE HERE and its labor allies: Benz, "Labor's Ace in the Hole," 535.

44 "The last thing you want": Steven Greenhouse, "Local 226, 'the Culinary,' Makes Las Vegas the Land of the Living Wage," *New York Times,* June 3, 2004, A22.

44 "You are not going to stop technology": Eduardo Porter, "Hotel Workers Fear the Robot at the Front Desk," *New York Times,* Sept. 25, 2018, A1.

44 "The Culinary was among the pioneers": Benz, "Labor's Ace in the Hole," 549.

FOUR The Uprising of the Twenty Thousand

49 Some apparel factories even charged: Leon Stein, ed., *Out of the Sweatshop: The Struggle for Industrial Democracy* (New York: Quadrangle/New York Times Book Company, 1977), 51.

49 "The shop we worked in": Clara Lemlich Shavelson, "Remembering the Waistmakers General Strike, 1909," *Jewish Currents*, Nov. 1982, 301.

49 To the foreman, Lemlich added: Stein, *Out of the Sweatshop*, 66, quoting Lemlich in *New York Evening Journal*, Nov. 28, 1909.

50 At another, the boss required: Ibid., 50, 79.

50 At many factories, the women: Annelise Orleck, *Common Sense and a Little Fire: Women and Working-Class Politics in the United States, 1900–1965* (Chapel Hill: University of North Carolina Press, 1995), 72–73.

50 "an organizer and an agitator": Ibid., 4.

51 "She was a model of a new sort": David Von Drehle, *Triangle: The Fire That Changed America* (New York: Atlantic Monthly Press, 2003), 7.

51 On some blocks, people lived: Philip Dray, *There Is Power in a Union: The Epic Story of Labor in America* (New York: Anchor Books, 2010), 257.

51 "the lowest-paid, most degrading": Ray Stannard Baker, "Plight of the Tailors," *McClure's Magazine*, Dec. 1904, quoted in Stein, *Out of the Sweatshop*, 22.

51 But with her expertise: Von Drehle, *Triangle*, 7.

51 In July 1909, two hundred garment workers: Ibid., 8, 16.

52 On the evening of Friday, September 10: Ibid., 6, 11.

52 "Like rain the blows fell": Orleck, *Common Sense and a Little Fire*, 49.

52 "one of America's first": Von Drehle, *Triangle*, 44.

52 "kicking, punching, and tearing of hair": Ibid., 50.

53 "I will split your head open": Dray, *There Is Power in a Union*, 259.

53 Police headquarters and city hall: Alice Henry, *The Trade Union Woman* (New York: D. Appleton, 1915), 91.

53 The Women's Trade Union League: Dray, *There Is Power in a Union*, 259–60.

53 "Most male labor leaders": Orleck, *Common Sense and a Little Fire*, 45.

53 "willing hands lifted the frail little girl": Stein, *Out of the Sweatshop*, 70, quoting *New York Call*, Nov. 23, 1909.

54 More than two thousand workers: Irving Howe, *World of Our Fathers* (New York: Harcourt Brace Jovanovich, 1976), 298–99.

54 "If we stick together": Orleck, *Common Sense and a Little Fire*, 61.

54 "the Lexington and Bunker Hill": Von Drehle, *Triangle*, 65.

54 "such as has never been known": Sarah Comstock, "The Uprising of the Girls," *Collier's*, Dec. 25, 1909, 20.

54 "farbrente meydlekh": Howe, *World of Our Fathers*, 300.

55 "was up at six for the picket line": Paula Scheier, "Clara Lemlich Shavelson: 50 Years in Labor's Front Line," *Jewish Life*, Nov. 1954, 7.

55 The Women's Trade Union League collected: Carol Hymowitz and Michaele Weissman, *A History of Women in America* (New York: Bantam Books, 2011), 251.

55 "It was too late": Scheier, "Clara Lemlich Shavelson," 9–10.

55 "We ain't here to protect": Stein, *Out of the Sweatshop*, 76, quoting *New York Tribune*, Dec. 11, 1909.

55 "The girls, headed by teen-age Clara": Howe, *World of Our Fathers*, 299–300.

56 "The brutality of the police": Reminiscences of Frances Perkins (1951–1955), pt. 1, 50, Columbia University Oral History Research Office Collection.

56 One of the most famous strikers: Von Drehle, *Triangle*, 63–66.

56 Hearing of this, George Bernard Shaw: Stein, *Out of the Sweatshop*, 83, quoting from F. E. Sheldon, *A Souvenir History of the Strike of the Ladies Waist Makers' Union* (New York: International Ladies' Garment Workers' Union, 1910).

57 "We can't live our lives": "Miss Morgan Aids Girl Waist Strikers," *New York Times*, Dec. 14, 1909, 1.

57 "welfare of 40,000 striking girls": Von Drehle, *Triangle*, 69.

58 When a magistrate ordered four: Ibid., 69–76.

58 "bejeweled, befurred, belaced, begowned audience": Stein, *Out of the Sweatshop*, 78, quoting *New York Call*, Dec. 16, 1909.

58 "The only chance for fair treatment": Tarbell quoted in Ibid., 86.

59 "These young, inexperienced girls": Miriam Finn Scott, "What the Women Strikers Won," *Outlook Magazine*, July 2, 1910, 480.

59 "They used to say that you": Scheier, "Clara Lemlich Shavelson," 8.

59 (The Uprising inspired the Cloakmakers): Melvyn Dubofsky and Joseph A. McCartin, *Labor in America: A History*, 9th ed. (Malden, Mass.: Wiley Blackwell, 2017), 174–75.

59 "Ah—then I had fire in my mouth!": Scheier, "Clara Lemlich Shavelson," 9.

59 "I am still at it": Jim Dwyer, "One Woman Who Changed the Rules," *New York Times*, March 23, 2011, A21.

FIVE Out of These Ashes

60 More than a ton of such scraps: Leon Stein, *The Triangle Fire* (New York: Lippincott, 1962; repr., Ithaca, N.Y.: ILR Press, 2001), 33.

61 Seeing that a fire: David Von Drehle, *Triangle: The Fire That Changed America* (New York: Atlantic Monthly Press, 2003), 118–19.

61 "They were packed by the door": Stein, *Triangle Fire*, 38–39.

61 "The bins under the remaining": Von Drehle, *Triangle*, 122.

62 "The only way for you to get out": Ibid., 131.

62 "She was young and very pretty": Stein, *Triangle Fire*, 47. Her name was sometimes given as Clotilde and her last name as Terranova and Gerranova. Von Drehle, *Triangle*, 282.

62 On the ninth floor, Anna Gullo: Anna Gullo, interview with Leon Stein, Sept. 10, 1957, Cornell University Kheel Center Archives, trianglefire.ilr.cornell.edu; Stein, *Triangle Fire*, 55; Von Drehle, *Triangle*, 156.

63 "I pulled my scarf tighter": Rose Glantz Hauser, interview with Leon Stein, Sept. 4, 1958, Cornell University Kheel Center Archives; Stein, *Triangle Fire*, 55.

63 "Girls were lying on the floor": Stein, *Triangle Fire*, 60–61.

63 "All the way down": Ibid., 61–64.

64 "I heard a loud noise": Abe Gordon, interview with Leon Stein, June 19, 1958, Cornell University Kheel Center Archives; Stein, *Triangle Fire*, 57–58.

64 Managers had often kept that door: Stein, *Triangle Fire*, 26–27.

64 "Call the firemen!": Von Drehle, *Triangle*, 154.

64 "The crowd yelled 'Don't jump!'": "141 Men and Girls Die in Waist Factory Fire;

Trapped High Up in Washington Place Building," *New York Times,* March 26, 1911, 1.

64 "The firemen raised": William G. Shepherd, *Milwaukee Journal,* March 27, 1911, quoted in Leon Stein, *Out of the Sweatshop: The Struggle for Industrial Democracy* (New York: Quadrangle/New York Times Book Company, 1977), 188–93.

65 Wolf Muslin Undergarment Company: Peter Applebome, "In Newark, Wresting a Fatal Factory Fire from Oblivion," *New York Times,* Feb. 23, 2011, A22; Mary Alden Hopkins, "The Newark Factory Fire," *McClure's Magazine* 36 (1910–11): 663.

65 "The neglect of factory owners": Stein, *Triangle Fire,* 28.

66 "I would be a traitor": *Survey,* April 8, 1911, quoted in ibid., 196–97.

67 "It was the most horrible sight": Reminiscences of Frances Perkins (1951–1955), pt. 1, 126, Columbia University Oral History Research Office Collection.

67 "seared on my mind": Peter Dreier, *The 100 Greatest Americans of the 20th Century: A Social Justice Hall of Fame* (New York: Nation Books, 2012), 113.

67 "the day the New Deal was born": "Her Life: The Woman Behind the New Deal," Frances Perkins Center, francesperkinscenter.org.

68 One of her most memorable moments: Kirstin Downey, *The Woman Behind the New Deal* (New York: Anchor Books, 2010), 11–13.

68 As a Hull House volunteer: Ibid., 20.

68 As part of her Hull House work: Von Drehle, *Triangle,* 197; Downey, *Woman Behind the New Deal,* 21.

69 (The league—and its calls): Philip Dray, *There Is Power in a Union: The Epic Story of Labor in America* (New York: Anchor Books, 2010), 278–79.

69 In her new job, Perkins: Downey, *Woman Behind the New Deal,* 29.

69 Through persistent lobbying: Ibid., 43. Because of industry pressure, cannery workers were excluded from that law, but the following year it was amended to include those workers.

69 "there were hundreds of other factories": Reminiscences of Frances Perkins, pt. 1, 132.

69 At the urging of Addams: Downey, *Woman Behind the New Deal,* 46–49.

69 Soon Al Smith, a state assemblyman: Lecture by Frances Perkins, Sept. 30, 1964, Kheel Center for Labor-Management Documentation and Archives, Ithaca, N.Y.

70 They named Perkins the commission's chief: Downey, *Woman Behind the New Deal,* 52.

70 "plain-spoken, plainly dressed": David M. Kennedy, *Freedom from Fear: The American People in Depression and War, 1929–1945* (New York: Oxford University Press, 1999), 259.

70 "We used to make it our business": Frances Perkins, *The Roosevelt I Knew* (New York: Viking Press, 1946; New York: Penguin Books, 2011), 22.

71 The legislature also required: Downey, *Woman Behind the New Deal,* 51.

71 "In New York I could see": Adam Cohen, *Nothing to Fear: FDR's Inner Circle and the Hundred Days That Created Modern America* (New York: Penguin, 2009), 310.

71 Theirs was a strained marriage: Downey, *Woman Behind the New Deal,* 62–74.

71 "As a rule," Smith said: Perkins, *Roosevelt I Knew,* 55.

71 "Unemployment is just as much": Ibid., 99.

72 "If it could be done there": Ibid., 23.

72 "'Why don't I get a job'": Ibid., 92.

73 "It was time to consider": Ibid., 144.

73 "Ever mindful of the Triangle fire": Downey, *Woman Behind the New Deal,* 122.

73 "he wanted his conscience kept": Ibid., 123–24.

73 "Labor can never become reconciled": Cohen, *Nothing to Fear*, 193.

74 "They didn't care about": Reminiscences of Frances Perkins, pt. 1, 59.

74 "One could not escape": Perkins, *Roosevelt I Knew*, 205.

74 "I'd much rather get a law": Reminiscences of Frances Perkins, pt. 1, 58; Cohen, *Nothing to Fear*, 168.

74 "Only in climbing trees": Downey, *Woman Behind the New Deal*, 117.

75 Green recommended that every industry: Cohen, *Nothing to Fear*, 232, 240.

75 "Democracy in industry means fair participation": Quoted in Clyde W. Summers, "Industrial Democracy: America's Unfulfilled Promise," *Cleveland State Law Review* 28 (1979): 29, 34.

76 In her short, heartfelt remarks: Perkins, *Roosevelt I Knew*, 207–11.

76 "I have come to the conclusion": Downey, *Woman Behind the New Deal*, 203–4.

77 "I see no reason why": Perkins, *Roosevelt I Knew*, 270.

77 "socialized medicine": Downey, *Woman Behind the New Deal*, 243.

77 "You care about this thing": Perkins, *Roosevelt I Knew*, 269.

77 "the very thought of 'retirement'": Kennedy, *Freedom from Fear*, 261.

78 his move ultimately excluded 9.4 million: Ibid., 268–69; Downey, *Woman Behind the New Deal*, 241. The financing through worker contributions was more regressive than Perkins would have liked.

78 A *Washington Post* article: Franklin Waltman, "Roosevelt Signs Security Bill to Benefit 30 Million Citizens," *Washington Post*, Aug. 15, 1935, 1.

78 That landmark law created the first: Downey, *Woman Behind the New Deal*, 266–68. Perkins originally opposed a flat, nationwide minimum wage, saying it lacked adequate flexibility. She instead wanted to set minimum wages by industry, with adjustments by region, sensitive to the cost of living. The business community opposed any minimum wage, while many northern members of Congress worried that any law that established lower minimums for the South would encourage industry to flee from the North to the South. The AFL president, Green, backed a flat, nationwide minimum with a forty-hour week, but some other labor leaders fought a national minimum, fearing that it would ultimately undercut efforts to unionize workers. Some northern lawmakers complained that the twenty-five-cent and forty-cent minimum were mere subsistence pay, but many southern lawmakers opposed anything higher.

79 "If I were a Jew": Ibid., 274–75.

79 "The Roosevelt pattern of government": Jerry Kluttz and Herbert Asbury, "The Woman Nobody Knows," *Collier's*, Aug. 5, 1944, 21, 30.

SIX Standing Up by Sitting Down

80 "not big, but colossal": Irving Bernstein, *The Turbulent Years: A History of the American Worker, 1933–1940* (Boston: Houghton Mifflin, 1969; Chicago: Haymarket Books, 2010), 510.

80 "I know everything": Sidney Fine, *Sit-Down: The General Motors Strike of 1936–1937* (Ann Arbor: University of Michigan Press, 1969), 41.

81 "a shabby shrine": Bernstein, *Turbulent Years*, 519.

81 According to a Senate committee report: Fine, *Sit-Down*, 38–41. The La Follette Commission report estimated that UAW membership had dropped from 26,000 to 120, but Fine said it "never remotely approached that level in 1934 because it

would have represented such a huge percentage of GM workers in Flint at that time."

81 "Where you used to be a man": Ibid., 59.

81 "thousands of men": Russell B. Porter, "The Assembly Lines Hum: The Song of the Speed-Up," *New York Times Magazine*, Feb. 28, 1937, 10.

81 "Speed, speed, speed": "Speed, Speed, and Still More Speed! That Is Flint," *New York Times Magazine*, Jan. 31, 1937, 9.

81 "We didn't even have time": Fine, *Sit-Down*, 56–57.

82 "We was only beggars": Ibid., 52.

82 In a 1936 speech in Detroit: Franklin D. Roosevelt, "Address in Detroit," Oct. 15, 1936, American Presidency Project.

83 "A moderately conservative bookmaker": Bernstein, *Turbulent Years*, 509.

83 "We may take it as probable": Bruce Kaufman, "The Future of U.S. Private Sector Unionism: Did George Barnett Get It Right After All?," *Journal of Labor Research* 22, no. 3 (Summer 2001): 433.

83 "We knew that if we could": Oral History of Wyndham Mortimer, interview by Jack W. Sheels, June 20, 1960, 27, Walter Reuther Library, Wayne State University.

83 Workers at the Goodyear tire plant: Walter Galenson, *The CIO Challenge to the AFL: A History of the American Labor Movement, 1935–1941* (Cambridge, Mass.: Harvard University Press, 1960), 134.

84 "That could not happen": Fine, *Sit-Down*, 128.

84 Undermining that schedule: Ibid., 144–46. The Cleveland sit-down followed UAW walkouts at far less strategic GM plants in Atlanta and Kansas City. In *Sit-Down*, Fine explains that the fear that GM would transfer the dies is the "usual account" for what triggered the strike. But Fine notes that Bud Simon, the chairman of the shop committee in Flint No. 1, gave another reason—that the plant would soon face a temporary shutdown because it was running out of glass, the result of a strike at Libbey-Owens-Ford. Simon said the workers, eager to ratchet up the pressure on GM, wanted the plant to be shut down due to their own strike and not because GM was ordering a temporary closing due to a shortage of glass. By that alternative account, the story of the dies was fabricated.

85 This aroused suspicions: Ibid., 144–45. GM said that this story was untrue, maintaining that it had shipped only part of one die to Pontiac because of a machinery failure there.

85 Soon a shout came: Bernstein, *Turbulent Years*, 522–26; Fine, *Sit-Down*, 144–45.

85 "the great General Motors automotive system": Bernstein, *Turbulent Years*, 525.

85 "the most critical labor conflict": Galenson, *CIO Challenge to the AFL*, 134.

85 "When the speed-up comes": Bernstein, *Turbulent Years*, 501. Maurice Sugar, the UAW's general counsel, wrote the song.

86 Lewis, the CIO's president: Fine, *Sit-Down*, 157–58, 170.

86 "We will form a line": Ibid., 201.

86 "can seize premises illegally": Ibid., 332–33.

87 "We wanted peace!": A. H. Raskin, "From Sit-Downs to 'Solidarity,'" *Across the Board*, Dec. 1981, 14.

87 Several policemen opened fire: Fine, *Sit-Down*, 1–13; Bernstein, *Turbulent Years*, 529–30.

87 "everything be done by the troops": Bernstein, *Turbulent Years*, 534.

87 Many GM supporters found Murphy's behavior: Fine, *Sit-Down*, 240.

88 Complicating Murphy's role: Bernstein, *Turbulent Years*, 532–33.

88 "Collective bargaining cannot be justified": "Reply of W. S. Knudsen, General Motors Executive, to Auto Union Head on Strike," *New York Times*, Jan. 1, 1937, 10.

88 The alliance's leaders asserted: Fine, *Sit-Down*, 188–89.

88 When UAW leaders learned of Knudsen's meeting: Ibid., 252–54.

89 "And what do you do when a man": Philip Dray, *There Is Power in a Union: The Epic Story of Labor in America* (New York: Anchor Books, 2010), 463.

89 Sloan was appalled: Reminiscences of Frances Perkins (1955, 1957, 1960, 1961), pt. 6, 204–5, Columbia University Oral History Research Office Collection.

90 "We have decided to stay": Fine, *Sit-Down*, 278.

90 "I shall then walk up": Raskin, "From Sit-Downs to 'Solidarity,'" 16.

90 "a Yellow-Bellied Cur Dog": Fine, *Sit-Down*, 308.

91 "We are going to go down there": Ibid., 278–81.

91 "You can't put those men": Ibid., 293–94.

91 On the other hand, GM feared: Galenson, *CIO Challenge to the AFL*, 136.

91 For years, GM had vigorously: The AFL backed General Motors on this issue, undercutting—and infuriating—the UAW and Lewis by opposing exclusive representation.

92 Outside the plant hung: Russell B. Porter, "Strikers at Plant March as Victors," *New York Times*, Feb. 12, 1937, 1.

92 "I never saw a night like that": Victor Reuther, *The Brothers Reuther* (Boston: Houghton Mifflin, 1976), 170–71.

92 Its membership nationwide soared: Fine, *Sit-Down*, 329.

92 It inspired a tidal wave: Nelson Lichtenstein, *State of the Union: A Century of American Labor* (Princeton, N.J.: Princeton University Press, 2002), 48, 51.

92 "Sitting down has replaced": Fine, *Sit-Down*, 331.

93 "that the decision-making power": Ibid., 338.

93 "The inhuman high speed": Ibid., 328.

SEVEN Walter Reuther, Builder of the Middle Class

94 Union membership rose 63 percent: Gerald Mayer, "Union Membership Trends in the United States," Congressional Research Service, Aug. 31, 2004, 23.

95 FDR's military planners even borrowed: Walter Reuther radio speech, "More Airplanes for Defense," Dec. 28, 1940, available at Wayne State University Library, reuther100.wayne.edu.

95 GM and its workers: Nelson Lichtenstein, *The Most Dangerous Man in Detroit* (New York: Basic Books, 1995), 221; Greg Wallace (general manager of the GM Heritage Center), telephone interview with author, April 30, 2007.

95 "rejected the cash-register approach": Damon Stetson, "Walter Reuther: Union Pioneer with Broad Influence Far Beyond the Field of Labor," *New York Times*, May 11, 1970, 38.

96 "The smart, dancing-eyed Reuther": Philip Dray, *There Is Power in a Union: The Epic Story of Labor in America* (New York: Anchor Books, 2010), 509.

96 "We are not going to operate": John Barnard, *American Vanguard: The United Auto Workers During the Reuther Years, 1935–1970* (Detroit: Wayne State University Press, 2005), 213.

96 He proposed that war factories: Victor Reuther, *The Brothers Reuther* (Boston: Houghton Mifflin, 1976), 247.

96 "there can be no permanent prosperity": Kevin Boyle, *The UAW and the Heyday of American Liberalism, 1945–1968* (Ithaca, N.Y.: Cornell University Press, 1995), 24.

96 "Walter Reuther is the most dangerous man": Lichtenstein, *Most Dangerous Man in Detroit*, 230.

96 "more dangerous menace than the Sputnik": Adam Clymer, "Barry Goldwater, Conservative and Individualist, Dies at 89," *New York Times*, May 29, 1998.

97 "At my father's knee": Thomas Featherstone, "No Greater Calling: The Life of Walter P. Reuther," Walter Reuther Library, Wayne State University, reuther100.wayne.edu.

97 "nameless, faceless clock numbers": Ibid.

97 "They picked my feet up": Lichtenstein, *Most Dangerous Man in Detroit*, 84.

98 Moreover, Reuther argued that GM: Ibid., 278–79.

98 "I am greatly exercised": Ibid., 230.

99 "We shall resist the monopolistic power": Reuther, *Brothers Reuther*, 250.

99 "Mass purchasing power is our new frontier": Lichtenstein, *Most Dangerous Man in Detroit*, 231, 235.

99 "If fighting for a more equal": Ibid., 231.

100 Luce put Reuther on the cover: Ibid., 237.

100 There were 4,985 strikes: "Analysis of Work Stoppages 1956," Bureau of Labor Statistics, Bulletin No. 1218, June 1957, 12.

101 After the UAW's picket lines: Reuther stubbornly maintained that the settlement was worth more than eighteen and a half cents because GM's local factory managers could sprinkle some modest raises on top of that.

102 He also recognized that Reuther: Lichtenstein, *Most Dangerous Man in Detroit*, 277–79.

102 Thirteen months later, his brother: Ibid., 271–72.

102 Wilson's innovative contract proposal: Ibid., 278–79. Reuther had one nagging fear about a cost-of-living adjustment: that a decline in prices could at times result in a decrease in wages, something that would no doubt upset the rank and file.

103 The new Republican Congress moved: Ibid., 261.

104 "If you make $258 an hour": Ibid., 283.

104 The deal was so widely celebrated: Walter W. Ruch, "Reuther's Stock Goes Up; What's Next? Detroit Asks," *New York Times*, May 28, 1950, E7.

104 "industrial statesmanship of a very high order": Lichtenstein: *Most Dangerous Man in Detroit*, 280.

104 By the early 1960s, over half: Lizabeth Cohen, *A Consumers' Republic: The Politics of Mass Consumption in Postwar America* (New York: Vintage, 2003), 154; Lichtenstein, *Most Dangerous Man in Detroit*, 287.

105 "The activities of many unions": Fred K. Foulkes, *Personnel Policies in Large Nonunion Companies* (Englewood Cliffs, N.J.: Prentice-Hall, 1980), 153, quoted in Jake Rosenfeld, *What Unions No Longer Do* (Cambridge, Mass.: Harvard University Press, 2014), 74.

105 (Worker productivity overall increased): "The Productivity-Pay Gap," Economic Policy Institute, Aug. 2018.

105 "Other peoples find it hard to believe": Dwight D. Eisenhower, "Address in Detroit at the National Automobile Show Industry Dinner," Oct. 17, 1960, American Presidency Project.

105 "The United States comes closest": Cohen, *Consumers' Republic*, 126.

106 Nonetheless, thanks to unions lifting: Harold Meyerson, "The Forty-Year Slump," *American Prospect,* Nov. 12, 2013.

106 "This rally is not the end": Michael Kazin, "The White Man Whose 'March on Washington' Speech You Should Remember Too," *New Republic,* Aug. 20, 2013.

106 His frequent adversary, Henry Ford II: "Nation's Leaders Mourn a Giant of Labor," *Detroit Free Press,* May 11, 1970, 8.

106 "made the worker to an amazing degree": Cohen, *Consumers' Republic,* 155.

EIGHT I *Am* a Man

107 One morning a foreman: Zack McMillin, "Paving the Way; Sanitation Strike Veteran Remembers Past, Cherishes Progress," *Memphis Commercial Appeal,* Feb. 17, 2008, V1.

108 "You could tell a worker": Michael K. Honey, *Going Down Jericho Road* (New York: Norton, 2007), 50.

109 "You work two weeks": Ibid., 58.

109 But the department's white sewer: Ibid., 100–101.

109 "Anything that you did that the supervisor": Ibid., 62.

109 On February 1, 1968, with the rain: Ibid., 1–2.

110 Jones rejected the city's offer: Ibid., 68–69.

111 The next morning, 1,144: Taylor Branch, *At Canaan's Edge: America in the King Years, 1965–68* (New York: Simon & Schuster, 2006), 693.

111 "You keep your back bent over": Honey: *Going Down Jericho Road,* 104.

111 "My God, what in the hell": Ibid., 108.

111 "His daddy would turn over": Ibid., 111.

111 "City employees can't strike": Ibid., 117–19.

112 "When a public official orders": *At the River I Stand,* directed by David Appleby, Allison Graham, and Steven John Ross, California Newsreel.

112 "What crime have they committed": Honey, *Going Down Jericho Road,* 113.

112 That newspaper maintained that outsiders: Ibid., 131.

113 "This was done to me": Ibid., 197–208.

113 The placards read, "I *Am* A Man": Ibid., 212.

114 "If you can't get a decent salary": Ibid., 282–83; *At the River I Stand,* directed by Appleby, Graham, and Ross.

114 "If America doesn't use its vast resources": Branch, *At Canaan's Edge,* 695.

115 "Memphis is the Washington campaign": Honey, *Going Down Jericho Road,* 380.

115 "You can't win without us": Ibid., 242.

115 "I've never seen a community": David J. Garrow, *Bearing the Cross: Martin Luther King Jr. and the Southern Christian Leadership Conference* (New York: William Morrow, 1986), 606.

115 "You are demanding that this city": Branch, *At Canaan's Edge,* 719.

115 "What does it profit a man": Michael K. Honey, *To the Promised Land: Martin Luther King and the Fight for Economic Justice* (New York: Norton, 2018), 153–54.

116 "We can all get more together": Martin Luther King Jr., *The Radical King* (Boston: Beacon Press, 2016), 250–51.

117 Hundreds of demonstrators sought refuge: Honey, *Going Down Jericho Road,* 353–54.

117 One student leader said: Ibid., 350.

117   As part of its long campaign: Branch, *At Canaan's Edge*, 735.

117   "Either the movement lives or dies": Honey, *Going Down Jericho Road*, 381.

117   King had expansive ambitions: The second march was originally scheduled for April 5, but the date was moved back because of a court injunction and because the later date would make it easier for national labor groups to participate.

118   "[E]ither we go up together": Martin Luther King Jr., "I've Been to the Mountaintop," *King Institute Encyclopedia*, Stanford University, April 3, 1968, kingencyclopedia .stanford.edu.

118   "Like anybody, I would like": Ibid.

119   "Nonviolence was murdered in Memphis": Honey, *Going Down Jericho Road*, 445.

119   "He believed, especially, that he was sent": Ibid., 482.

119   "We are not going to recognize": Ibid., 468.

120   "I say to Mayor Loeb": *At the River I Stand*, directed by Appleby, Graham, and Ross.

120   Unlike Loeb, the council agreed: Loeb petulantly maintained that the settlement wasn't a union victory because the union was not technically made exclusive bargaining agent and because a federal credit union, rather than the city, would handle the dues checkoff.

120   "White supremacy thus fell": Honey, *Going Down Jericho Road*, 491.

120   "our Flint sit-downs": Jefferson Cowie, *Stayin' Alive: The 1970s and the Last Days of the Working Class* (New York: New Press, 2010), 61.

120   "We have been aggrieved many times": Honey, *Going Down Jericho Road*, 493.

NINE   Mighty Labor Strikes Out

126   "You should be treated like a pilot": Joseph A. McCartin, *Collision Course: Ronald Reagan, the Air Traffic Controllers, and the Strike That Changed America* (New York: Oxford University Press, 2011), 64–69.

126   But that action brought the FAA: Ibid., 80–87.

126   But the FAA fired eighty controllers: Ibid., 10–24.

126   In 1972, a commission the FAA: Philip Dray, *There Is Power in a Union: The Epic Story of Labor in America* (New York: Anchor Books, 2010), 622.

127   federal employees' pay slipped 3.1 percent: McCartin, *Collision Course*, 199.

127   The FAA further irked: Ibid., 218. In what many controllers viewed as another insult to their professionalism, the FAA sent out a memo ordering them to "discharge their private financial obligations" in a way that didn't create "an unfavorable image to the Federal Government." In short, the agency told them that if they didn't pay their debts, they would be fired.

128   Many controllers grew angrier: Dray, *There Is Power in a Union*, 623.

128   "Our studies show that the only": McCartin, *Collision Course*, 221, 225.

129   "You can rest assured": Dray, *There Is Power in a Union*, 625; Warren Brown, "Poli Concedes He Misjudged Reagan Stand," *Washington Post*, Aug. 9, 1981, A1; William Yardley, "Robert E. Poli, Leader of Pivotal Strike by Air Traffic Controllers, Is Dead at 78," *New York Times*, Sept. 22, 2014, A23.

129   With a large militant faction: McCartin, *Collision Course*, 236–40.

129   "Our greed should not exceed": Ibid., 240.

129   "Some had said that our demands": Ibid., 227.

129   Reagan's aides estimated: Ibid., 257.

130   Lewis rejected PATCO's demand: Richard Witkin, "Air Control Strike Canceled as

Union and U.S. Reach Pact," *New York Times,* June 23, 1981, A1; McCartin, *Collision Course,* 261.

130 "crossed into uncharted territory": McCartin, *Collision Course,* 262.

130 "I vow to you": Ibid., 260.

130 To Poli's shock, only 75 percent: Richard Witkin, "Air Control Union Breaks Off Talks as a Strike Looms," *New York Times,* Aug. 3, 1981, A1.

130 They rallied the controllers: Dray, *There Is Power in a Union,* 627.

131 "perhaps the most overpaid": McCartin, *Collision Course,* 257. Complicating matters, a Democratic congressman had badly embarrassed Reagan by disclosing that Reagan's campaign staff, when angling for PATCO's endorsement, had agreed to have the FAA administrator fired. Many viewed that promise as an illegal campaign quid pro quo. This discomforting disclosure pushed the administration to dig in to demonstrate that it was not doing special favors for PATCO. Richard Witkin, "Air Control Union Eases Strike Threat," *New York Times,* June 20, 1981, sec. 1, 1.

131 "call Reagan's resolve into question": McCartin, *Collision Course,* 278.

132 "You're making a mistake": Ibid., 287, 289.

132 "This is twice what other government employees": Ronald Reagan, Remarks and a Question-and-Answer Session with Reporters on the Air Traffic Controllers Strike, Aug. 3, 1981, Reagan Library Archives, www.reaganlibrary.archives.gov.

133 "Take This Job and Shove It": McCartin, *Collision Course,* 294.

133 Poli denounced Reagan's remarks: Richard Witkin, "U.S. Begins Sending Dismissals to Controllers and Jails Five," *New York Times,* Aug. 6, 1981, A1.

133 "It's all over now": McCartin, *Collision Course,* 294, 299.

133 "believes this is desertion": Howell Raines, "Tower Power: Controllers Discover the Ceiling After Reagan Hits It," *New York Times,* Aug. 9, 1981, sec. 4, 1.

133 Indeed, Nixon's labor secretary: A. H. Raskin, "The Air Strike Is Ominous for Labor," *New York Times,* Aug. 16, 1981, sec. 3, 1.

133 Reagan had reminded his cabinet: McCartin, *Collision Course,* 243–45.

133 Those labor leaders thought: Ibid., 284, 291.

133 "You can't win this strike": Ibid., 284, 291.

133 "massive damage to the labor movement": William Serrin, "A Crucial Time," *New York Times,* Aug. 6, 1981, D21.

134 sent out 11,345 dismissal notices: McCartin, *Collision Course,* 297–300, 305.

134 After three days, the FAA: Richard Witkin, "U.S. Begins Sending Dismissals to Controllers and Jails Five; Up 'Slightly' in 3d Day," *New York Times,* Aug. 6, 1981, A1. The FAA's director, J. Lynn Helms, said that was up from 64 percent on the first day (higher than the number Drew Lewis gave). But FAA officials said they handled just 50 percent of flights at the major airports the first day.

134 In a crushing blow: Dray, *There Is Power in a Union,* 632–33; McCartin, *Collision Course,* 307–8.

135 "We cannot, as citizens, pick and choose": Howell Raines, "Reagan Addresses Union Convention," *New York Times,* Sept. 4, 1981, A11.

136 *The Washington Post* noted: Dan Balz and Lee Lescaze, "President Facing New Problems in Efforts to Restrain Spending; Reagan Returns," *Washington Post,* Sept. 4, 1981, A1; McCartin, *Collision Course,* 306.

136 The courts ordered PATCO: McCartin, *Collision Course,* 319.

136 "The administration," Nordlund wrote: Willis J. Nordlund, *Silent Skies: The Air Traffic Controllers' Strike* (Westport, Conn.: Praeger, 1998), 14.

136 "Reagan's breaking of the PATCO strike": McCartin, *Collision Course,* 330, 341–42.

TEN Labor's Slide Picks Up Speed

137 "Suddenly people realized, hell": Jonathan D. Rosenblum, *Copper Crucible: How the Arizona Miners' Strike of 1983 Recast Labor-Management Relations in America* (Ithaca, N.Y.: ILR Press, 1998), 48.

137 "Managers are discovering that strikes": Herbert E. Meyer, "The Decline," *Fortune,* Nov. 2, 1981, 66.

138 "Ronald Reagan recast the crimes": Martin Jay Levitt, *Confessions of a Union Buster* (New York: Crown, 1993), 217.

138 "If the President of the United States": William Serrin, "Industries, in Shift, Aren't Letting Strikes Stop Them," *New York Times,* Sept. 30, 1986, A18.

138 "maintain an image as corporate": James J. Brudney, "To Strike or Not to Strike," review of *The Betrayal of Local 14: Paperworkers, Politics, and Permanent Replacements,* by Julius Getman, *Wisconsin Law Review* (1999): 65, 70.

138 Elmer Chatak, an AFL-CIO official: Serrin, "Industries, in Shift."

138 "not in tune with economic realities": William Serrin, "Fury Etches Strikers' Life in Crumbling Fight at Arizona Mines," *New York Times,* July 30, 1984, A8.

139 "I had decided to break": Rosenblum, *Copper Crucible,* 91.

139 Fifteen months after the walkout began: Paul Davenport, "Copper Workers Vote to Oust Unions; Sides Debate Whether Strike Over," Associated Press, Jan. 25, 1985. Lopez said, "There is nothing to keep the company from doing anything it wants. The scabs will realize that soon."

139 Louisiana-Pacific instead insisted: Louisiana-Pacific's proposal called for raising wages to $8.50 in the second year. David Staats, "Bitter Strike Could Weaken Timber Unions," Associated Press, July 14, 1984.

139 Within six months, one-third: Again, those voting were the replacement workers and the strikers who had crossed the picket line.

140 Just two weeks earlier: Kathy Sawyer, "Greyhound Agreement Announced; Union Employees Still Must Ratify Bus-Line Accord," *Washington Post,* Dec. 4, 1983, A1.

140 "The ultimate weapon of the union": Leslie Wayne, "Steering Greyhound Through the Strike," *New York Times,* Dec. 18, 1983, sec. 3, 6.

140 "there was always a sense": Peter Kilborn, "Replacement Workers: Management's Big Gun," *New York Times,* March 13, 1990, A24.

140 "Union members and leaders": Bill Keller, "Unionists See Labor Day '84 as a Time to Weigh Setbacks," *New York Times,* Sept. 3, 1984, sec. 1, 1.

140 The decline in strikes was good: Arne L. Kalleberg, Michael Wallace, and Lawrence E. Raffalovich, "Accounting for Labor's Share: Class and Income Distribution in the Printing Industry," *Industrial and Labor Relations Review* 37 (April 1984): 386–402.

140 Jake Rosenfeld, a labor relations expert: Jake Rosenfeld, *What Unions No Longer Do* (Cambridge, Mass.: Harvard University Press, 2014), 94.

142 rate of profit was falling, too: Lane Windham, *Knocking on Labor's Door: Union Organizing in the 1970s and the Roots of a New Economic Divide* (Chapel Hill: University of North Carolina Press, 2017), 3–4, 65–67.

142 "the standard of living of the average American": Steve Rattner, "Volker Asserts U.S. Must Trim Living Standard," *New York Times,* Oct. 18, 1979, 1.

142 In late 1979 and early 1980: Ruth Milkman, *Farewell to the Factory: Auto Workers in the Late Twentieth Century* (Berkeley: University of California Press, 1997), 80.

143 "unions are good for industrial society": Nelson Lichtenstein, *State of the Union:*

A Century of American Labor (Princeton, N.J.: Princeton University Press, 2002), 220.

143   In the two decades after 1973: Ibid., 213.

144   In the airline industry: David A. NewMyer et al., "Airline Unions Since Deregulation: The Views of Selected Airline Unions," *Journal of Aviation/Aerospace Education and Research* 2, no. 2 (Winter 1992): 34.

144   A decade later, after deregulation: "Labor's Challenge," *Journal of Commerce,* Sept. 3, 1991, 4A.

144   In 1979, before deregulation: Brian S. Moskal, "How the Teamsters Lost Their Grip," *Industry Week,* Nov. 26, 1984, 68; Thomas L. Friedman, "The Rocky Road for Truckers," *New York Times,* Jan. 24, 1982, sec. 3, 1.

144   "The only way we can increase": Martha M. Hamilton, "Railroads Are Rolling Toward Some Basic Changes; Individual Talks May Replace Industry-Wide Labor Bargaining," *Washington Post,* June 7, 1987, H1.

144   "The Gompers gospel of 'more'": A. H. Raskin, "Frustrated and Wary, Labor Marks Its Day," *New York Times,* Sept. 5, 1982, sec. 3, 1.

145   There is a famous anecdote: "Walter Reuther Quote Collection," United Auto Workers, April 20, 2016, uaw.org. (There are varying accounts about the exact words exchanged between Reuther and the Ford executive.)

145   IBP usually built its slaughterhouses: Christopher Drew, "A Chain of Setbacks for Meat Workers," *Chicago Tribune,* Oct. 25, 1988, 1.

145   Similarly, the number of West Coast: Richard A. Greenwald, "Working the Docks: Labor, Management, and the New Waterfront," *Review of Business* 25, no. 3 (Fall 2004): 16.

146   "It used to be that companies": William Glaberson, "An Uneasy Alliance in Smokestack U.S.A.," *New York Times,* March 13, 1988, sec. 3, 1.

146   A study by three Harvard economists: Aaron Bernstein, "Shaking Up Trade Theory," *Business Week,* Dec. 6, 2004, 116.

146   "Now capital has wings": William Greider, *One World, Ready or Not: The Manic Logic of Global Capitalism* (New York: Simon & Schuster, 1997), 24.

147   By 2010, institutional investors owned: Michael Useem, *Investor Capitalism: How Money Managers Are Changing the Face of Corporate America* (New York: Basic Books, 1996), 25; "Growth in Institutional Investing: A Role in Market Liquidity?", Knowledge @ Wharton, Nov. 5, 2012.

147   "far and away the most influential manager": Geoffrey Colvin, "The Ultimate Manager," *Fortune,* Nov. 22, 1989, 185.

147   From 2006 to 2014, the five hundred: Harold Meyerson, "How to End the Stock Buyback Deluge," *Washington Post,* Dec. 31, 2015, A17.

148   Taken together, CEOs' desire: Thomas Heath, "Whose Cash Is It, Anyway? Get in line. Shareholders, Workers, Politicians, Executives and Raiders Eye Trillions in Corporate Piggy Banks," *Washington Post,* April 15, 2018, G05.

148   In the intervening years, many CEOs: Rick Wartzman, "It's Time for Top CEOs to Realign Their Interests—Beyond Those of Elevating Shareholders Above All," *Fast Company,* June 28, 2018.

148   These activists drew fuel: Milton Friedman, "A Friedman Doctrine—the Social Responsibility of Business Is to Increase Its Profits," *New York Times Magazine,* Sept. 13, 1970, 32; Michael C. Jensen and William H. Meckling, "Theory of the Firm: Managerial Behavior, Agency Costs, and Ownership Structure," *Journal of Financial Economics* 3, no. 4 (Oct. 1976): 305–60.

148 "The paramount duty of management": Thomas A. Kochan, *Shaping the Future of Work: What Future Worker, Business, Government, and Education Leaders Need to Do for All to Prosper* (New York: Business Expert Press, 2015), 56–57.

149 "After God had finished the rattlesnake": Jack London, "Definition of a Strike-breaker," quoted in *National Letter Carriers v. Austin,* 418 U.S. 264 (1974), 268.

150 "This is a sign of increased": Steven Greenhouse, "More Lockouts as Companies Battle Unions," *New York Times,* Jan. 23, 2011, A1.

150 "unconditional surrender of the union": Jim Spencer, "Employers Get Control by Turning to Lockouts," *Minneapolis Star Tribune,* Oct. 29, 2012, 1A.

150 "just another way of trying to break": Greenhouse, "More Lockouts as Companies Battle Unions."

150 After twenty arduous months: Rose French and Mike Hughlett, "Sugar Workers Approve Contract," *Minneapolis Star Tribune,* April 14, 2013, 1B.

151 "They're using the excuse": Steven Greenhouse, "Locked Out, and Worked Up," *New York Times,* Dec. 4, 2015, B1.

151 The agreement called for: The union agreed that future hires would not have retiree health coverage—probably some thirty or thirty-five years in the future. But the union set up a worker-financed fund to pay for such coverage.

152 "a tremendous victory for a very brave": Dan Majors, "Steelworkers, Allegheny Technologies Agree on Tentative Deal," *Pittsburgh Post-Gazette,* Feb. 23, 2016, Business sec., A1.

ELEVEN Corporations Turn Up the Heat

153 Uber vigorously denied: Steven Greenhouse, "Uber on the Road to Nowhere," *American Prospect,* Dec. 7, 2015; Danny Westneat, "Uber's Ride Gets a Bit Bumpier," *Seattle Times,* Sept. 2, 2015, A1.

154 Months later, the company: Steven Greenhouse, "As T-Mobile Rises, Questions Emerge over Treatment of Workers, Consumers," *Inside Sources,* Feb. 23, 2016.

154 "We like driving the car": Jake Rosenfeld, *What Unions No Longer Do* (Cambridge, Mass.: Harvard University Press, 2014), 7.

154 As soon as that contract provision: Bill Lueders, "Managers at Menards Stand to Lose Big Money If Unions Form," *Progressive,* Dec. 8, 2015.

155 As Dave Jamieson wrote: Dave Jamieson, "This Is What It's Like to Sit Through an Anti-union Meeting at Work," *Huffington Post,* Sept. 3, 2014.

155 "Flashing a photograph of himself": Nick Wingfield, "Amazon Warehouses Prove Infertile Soil for Unions, So Far," *New York Times,* May 17, 2016, B1.

156 "Union busting is a field": Martin Jay Levitt, *Confessions of a Union Buster* (New York: Crown, 1993), 1.

156 Union busting has become: John Logan, "The Fine Art of Union-Busting," *New Labor Forum* 13 (Summer 2004): 2, 78.

156 They range from shady outfits: Kris Maher, "Unions' New Foe: Consultants," *Wall Street Journal,* Aug. 15, 2005, B1.

156 That study also found: Kate Bronfenbrenner, "No Holds Barred: The Intensification of Employer Opposition to Bargaining," Economic Policy Institute, May 20, 2009. This study is based on a survey of 1,004 unionization elections. Some critics have questioned Bronfenbrenner's findings because she relies on surveys that union organizers completed about what antiunion tactics they witnessed during union-

ization drives. Bronfenbrenner says the information from union organizers was often corroborated by the NLRB and by journalistic accounts and that her findings have been largely consistent over four such studies she conducted over eighteen years.

157 When a Fruit of the Loom factory: Kate Bronfenbrenner, "We'll Close! Plant Closings, Plant-Closing Threats, Union Organizing, and NAFTA," *Multinational Monitor*, March 1997, 8–14.

157 "We are not competitive": Kate Bronfenbrenner, "Raw Power, Plant-Closing Threats, and the Threat to Union Organizing," *Multinational Monitor*, Dec. 2000, 26.

157 "The Union *never* got a contract": Ibid., 27.

157 "I always thought that unions": Steven Greenhouse, "How Walmart Persuades Its Workers Not to Unionize," *Atlantic*, June 8, 2015.

158 "Our decision to expand": David Koenig, "Wal-Mart Will End Meat Cutting at 180 Stores; Denies Link to Union Vote," Associated Press, March 3, 2000.

158 Walmart closed that store: Charmaine Noronha, "Canada High Court Rules for Wal-Mart in Union Case," Associated Press, Nov. 27, 2009. In 2009, Canada's Supreme Court ruled 6–3 that Walmart had the right to shut down the Jonquière store, saying that labor law doesn't oblige an employer to stay in business. The majority said Walmart's move did not hinder the employees from exercising their rights under the national labor code. But in 2014, the Canadian Supreme Court ruled, 5–2, that the closing was illegal under Quebec law because it modified working conditions for the employees without a valid reason when it shut the store down. Quebec laws say conditions may not be altered during a unionization process.

158 "Walmart has sent a clear": Statement from Stuart Appelbaum, PR Newswire US, Feb. 11, 2005.

159 "It was pretty critical": Jim Defede, "NLRB Sides with Workers Fired by Hospital," *Miami Herald*, May 4, 2004, 1B.

159 In a further slap: Forrest Norman, "Blunt Trauma," *Miami New Times*, Jan. 20, 2005.

160 "Many years have passed": Defede, "NLRB Sides with Workers Fired by Hospital."

160 One study found that one in three: Bronfenbrenner, "No Holds Barred."

160 A 2007 study concluded: John Schmitt and Ben Zipperer, "Dropping the Ax: Illegal Firings in Union Election Campaigns," Center for Economic and Policy Research, Jan. 2007, 3, 17.

161 The award was so small: "Unfair Advantage: Workers' Freedom of Association in the United States Under International Human Rights Standards," Human Rights Watch, 2000, 10.

161 "defying the law was far cheaper": Jacob Hacker and Paul Pierson, *Winner Take-All Politics* (New York: Simon & Schuster, 2011), 129. Illegally firing the one or two rank-and-file leaders of a union drive might cost $5,000, $10,000, perhaps $20,000, in back pay if and when the NLRB orders them reinstated a few years after being fired. But the fruits of such a move—keeping out a union—might save a nursing home or retailer at least $100,000 annually because it might not have to pay the higher wages and benefits that a union contract would bring.

161 A Human Rights Watch report: "Unfair Advantage," 18.

161 "Firing is the single most potent": Steven Greenhouse, "Report Faults Laws for Slowing Growth of Unions," *New York Times*, Oct. 24, 2000, A20.

161 a fascinating study of all the unionization drives: John-Paul Ferguson, "The Eyes of the Needles: A Sequential Model of Union Organizing Drives, 1999–2004," *Industrial and Labor Relations Review* 62, no. 1 (Oct. 2008): 6; John-Paul Ferguson

and Thomas A. Kochan, "Sequential Failures in Workers' Right to Organize," MIT Sloan School of Management, March 2008.

162 When the UAW sought to unionize: Steven Greenhouse, "Automaker Gives Its Blessings, and G.O.P. Its Warnings," *New York Times,* Feb. 12, 2014, B3.

162 Tennessee's governor, Bill Haslam: Karl Henkel, "Records: Tenn. Gov Tried to Sway VW Vote," *Detroit News,* April 2, 2014, D3.

162 "When we recruit other companies": Joey Garrison, "Haslam Tries to Keep UAW out of State," *Tennessean,* Feb. 6, 2014, D1. Senator Corker, a former mayor of Chattanooga, also warned that a UAW victory would damage efforts to attract business and would "drive up costs" and "make the facility less competitive." Steven Greenhouse, "Outsiders, Not Auto Plant, Battle U.A.W. in Tennessee," *New York Times,* Jan. 29, 2014, B1.

162 "We're concerned about the impact": Greenhouse, "Automaker Gives Its Blessings."

163 "Unions are a big driver": Greenhouse, "Outsiders, Not Auto Plant, Battle U.A.W. in Tennessee."

163 When the UAW sought: Jeff Amy, "Nissan Workers in Mississippi Vote on Whether to Unionize," Associated Press, Aug. 2, 2017.

163 "Detroit is the perfect example": Jeff Amy, "Rally Opens Union Push at Nissan Motor Plant in Mississippi," Associated Press, July 11, 2017.

163 They started bonfires: Philip Dray, *There Is Power in a Union: The Epic Story of Labor in America* (New York: Anchor Books, 2010), 504–7.

163 "legacy of slavery, sharecropping": Ibid., 502.

164 "We'll make the unions understand": Seanna Adcox and Jim Davenport, "State of State: Haley Urges Tax Cuts, Tort Reform," Associated Press, Jan. 19, 2012.

164 "You've heard me say many times": Rudolph Bell, "South Carolina: Union Jobs Aren't Welcome Here," *USA Today,* Feb. 20, 2014.

164 The political arm of a leading: Josh Eidelson, "Boeing Workers' Vote Wednesday Could Be an 'Earthquake in the South,'" *Bloomberg,* Feb. 14, 2017.

164 "Organized labor has no place": Bell, "South Carolina: Union Jobs Aren't Welcome Here."

164 Politicians are free to fight: Steven Greenhouse, "In Bid for Revote, Union Claims Tennessee Officials Frightened Workers," *New York Times,* April 5, 2014, B3. Samuel Estreicher, an NYU labor law professor, said the NLRB has ordered new unionization votes to be held "when laboratory conditions have been undermined—and it doesn't necessarily have to be through actions of the employer." But Julius G. Getman, a labor law professor at the University of Texas, warned that telling governors how far they can go could be problematic. "When you start telling politicians what they can or cannot say, it becomes a firestorm," he said.

164 "The local students are violently opposed": Noam Scheiber, "U.A.W. Accuses Nissan of 'Scare Tactics' as Workers Reject Union Bid," *New York Times,* Aug. 6, 2017, A19.

TWELVE Labor's Self-Inflicted Wounds

166 The economist John Kenneth Galbraith: John Kenneth Galbraith, *American Capitalism: The Concept of Countervailing Power* (Boston: Houghton Mifflin, 1952).

167 In 1960, the sociologist Daniel Bell: Nelson Lichtenstein, *State of the Union: A Century of American Labor* (Princeton, N.J.: Princeton University Press, 2002), 167.

167 Moreover, the automatic dues: Alice Lynd and Staughton Lynd, eds., *Rank and File: Personal Histories by Working-Class Organizers* (Boston: Beacon, 1973), 3–4.

168 "Why should we worry about": Charles Craver, *Can Unions Survive?* (New York: New York University Press, 1993), 3.

168 "In appearance, he is a cross": Timothy J. Minchin, *Labor Under Fire: A History of the AFL-CIO Since 1979* (Chapel Hill: University of North Carolina Press, 2017), 19.

168 within four years Meany had slashed: Ibid., 23.

168 "tended to enter a state of atrophy": Rick Fantasia and Kim Voss, *Hard Work: Remaking the American Labor Movement* (Berkeley: University of California Press, 2004), 84.

169 "lacks the social vision": Melvyn Dubofsky and Warren Van Tine, *Labor Leaders in America* (Urbana: University of Illinois Press, 1987), 298.

169 "disarmed on the shop floor": Minchin, *Labor Under Fire,* 128–29.

169 "as little more than a self-aggrandizing": Lichtenstein, *State of the Union,* 141–42.

169 "the American labor movement is sleepwalking": Quoted in ibid., 167.

170 Three Genovese crime family members: Ira Henry Freeman, "3 Convicted of Plot in Riesel Blinding," *New York Times,* Dec. 7, 1956, 1; Lawrence Van Gelder, "Victor Riesel, 81, Columnist Blinded by Acid Attack, Dies," *New York Times,* Jan. 5, 1995, B11.

171 "had a devastating impact": Lichtenstein, *State of the Union,* 162.

171 The indictments said the money: Melissa Burden and Robert Snell, "Ex–Fiat Chrysler Exec Indicted for UAW Payoffs," *Detroit News,* July 27, 2017, A1. In January 2018, the Fiat Chrysler executive pleaded guilty to making illegal payoffs. In July 2019, Holiefield's widow was sentenced to eighteen months in prison after pleading guilty. By April 2019, two high-level UAW officials had also pleaded guilty.

172 The barons of labor turned: Homer Bigart, "War Foes Here Attacked by Construction Workers," *New York Times,* May 9, 1970, 1.

172 "dirty-necked and dirty-mouthed group": Dubofsky and Van Tine, *Labor Leaders in America,* 344.

172 "people named Jack who look like Jill": Rick Perlstein, *Nixonland: The Rise of a President and the Fracturing of America* (New York: Simon & Schuster, 2010), 695.

172 Indeed, he voiced regret: Greg Mantsios, *A New Labor Movement for the New Century* (New York: Monthly Review Press, 1998), 59.

172 "It's been very inspiring": Steven Greenhouse, "Labor and Academia in a Campus Meeting," *New York Times,* Oct. 6, 1996, sec. 1, 39.

173 "For a lot of students": Steven Greenhouse, "Lessons in Labor: A Course for Summer; Students Plunge into Union Activities," *New York Times,* Aug. 9, 1996, B1.

173 "the removal of all girl employees": Nelson Lichtenstein, *The Most Dangerous Man in Detroit* (New York: Basic Books, 1995), 200.

173 Indeed, worried that this influx: Lichtenstein, *State of the Union,* 92.

173 That was one reason more than three thousand: Eileen Shanahan, "3,000 Delegates at Chicago Meeting Organize a National Coalition of Labor Union Women," *New York Times,* March 25, 1974, 27.

174 At the time, there were just: Minchin, *Labor Under Fire,* 178–79.

174 "'You can't organize women'": Ibid., 103.

174 In 1902, W. E. B. Du Bois: Carolyn Shenaz Hossein, *The Black Social Economy in the Americas: Exploring Diverse Community-Based Markets* (New York: Springer, 2017), 25.

174 "the practice of labor unions": Manning Marable and Leith Mullings, *Let Nobody*

Turn Us Around: Voices of Resistance, Reform, and Renewal (Lanham, Md.: Rowman and Littlefield, 2009), 211.

175 "Caucasians are not going to let": Robert H. Zieger, *For Jobs and Freedom: Race and Labor in America Since 1865* (Lexington: University Press of Kentucky, 2014), 62.

175 The journalist Ida B. Wells: Herbert Hill, "Labor Unions and the Negro: The Record of Discrimination," *Commentary,* Dec. 1, 1959, 479.

175 "If employers can keep": A. Philip Randolph, "Our Reason for Being," *Messenger,* Aug. 1919, 11–12.

176 "White and black workers": Quoted in Jervis Anderson, *A. Philip Randolph: A Biographical Portrait* (Berkeley: University of California Press, 1986), 289.

176 "The fact that the American": Gunnar Myrdal, *An American Dilemma: The Negro Problem and Modern Democracy* (New York: Routledge, 2017), 1:402.

176 "Who the hell appointed you": Paul Delaney, "A. Philip Randolph Is Dead, Pioneer in Rights and Labor," *New York Times,* May 17, 1979, A1.

177 "Discrimination does exist in the labor movement": Martin Luther King Jr., "If the Negro Wins, Labor Wins" (address to AFL-CIO Convention, Dec. 11, 1961), in Jonathan Birnbaum and Clarence Taylor, *Civil Rights Since 1787: A Reader on the Black Struggle* (New York: New York University Press, 2000), 424–25.

178 "practice either total exclusion": Hill, "Labor Unions and the Negro."

178 "Our needs are identical": King, "If the Negro Wins, Labor Wins," 423.

178 "we had to meet the threats": From Samuel Gompers, *Seventy Years of Life in Labor,* quoted in Stanford M. Lyman, "The 'Chinese Question' and American Labor Historians," *New Politics* 7, no. 4 (Winter 2000).

179 "perhaps the most important": Ibid.

179 "as a race were cruel": Hill, "Labor Unions and the Negro."

179 "this Asiatic contamination": Lyman, " 'Chinese Question' and American Labor Historians."

179 "Surely, America's workmen have enough": Report of Proceedings of the Twenty-Fifth Annual Convention of the American Federation of Labor, 1905, quoted in ibid.

179 Unhappy about that exemption: Robert Lazo, "Latinos and the AFL-CIO: The California Immigrant Workers Association as an Important New Development," *Berkeley La Raza Law Journal* 4, article 2 (1991): 27–28.

179 It was only after Communist organizers: Ibid., 30.

179 By 1942, the CIO had: Ibid.

180 "You're going to win": Miriam Pawel, *The Crusades of Cesar Chavez* (New York: Bloomsbury, 2014), 115. Pawel's book is an excellent, comprehensive biography of Chavez.

180 Stung by the boycott, twenty-six: Steven Roberts, "26 Grape Growers Sign Union Accord; Boycott Nears End," *New York Times,* July 30, 1970, 1.

180 "I couldn't tolerate seeing kids": Mindi McNeil, "Women's History Month Celebrates: Dolores Huerta," KUVO, March 24, 2018.

180 "blend[ed] the nonviolent resistance": Robert Lindsey, "Cesar Chavez, 66, Organizer of Union for Migrants, Dies," *New York Times,* April 24, 1993, sec. 1, 1.

181 "The union's survival, its very existence": Pawel, *Crusades of Cesar Chavez,* 2.

181 "With this resolution, the AFL-CIO": Alice Ann Love, "Labor Leaders Call for Loosening Immigration Restriction," Associated Press, Feb. 16, 2000.

THIRTEEN The Assault on Public-Sector Unions

183 "We can no longer live": Lee Berquist and Jason Stein, "Walker Looks at Show-down with State Employee Unions," *Milwaukee Journal Sentinel,* Dec. 8, 2010, A1.

186 Walker then boasted that his bold: Jason Stein and Patrick Marley, *More Than They Bargained For: Scott Walker, Unions, and the Fight for Wisconsin* (Madison: University of Wisconsin Press, 2013), 56–57.

186 "This may sound melodramatic": Jason Stein and Patrick Marley, "Selling Act 10," *Isthmus,* March 7, 2013, 9. Walker's words were recorded by a blogger who had tricked him into thinking he was talking with the conservative billionaire David Koch. There is a debate among historians over whether Reagan's hard-line stance toward PATCO and his victory in that showdown made much of an impression on the Soviet Union or contributed in any way toward the fall of Communism.

186 He called it a "budget-repair bill": "Governor Walker Introduces Budget Repair," Targeted News Service, Feb. 11, 2011.

186 Republicans hated those unions': Stein and Marley, *More Than They Bargained For,* 68.

186 Because Republicans had large majorities: Ibid., 69.

187 "My God, this is going to cause": Ibid., 50, 57, 63.

188 "This is a King moment": John Nichols, *Uprising* (New York: Nation Books, 2012), 21.

188 "We know what this is about": Stein and Marley, *More Than They Bargained For,* 75.

188 "If they succeed in Wisconsin": Michael Cooper and Kathryn Seelye, "Wisconsin Leads Way as Workers Fight State Cuts," *New York Times,* Feb. 19, 2011, A1.

188 "The process of collective bargaining": Franklin D. Roosevelt, Letter on the Resolution of Federation of Federal Employees Against Strikes in Federal Service, Aug. 16, 1937. Roosevelt wrote this in a letter to Luther C. Steward, president of the National Federation of Federal Employees. www.presidency.ucsb.edu/.

188 Although those measures would save: Scott Bauer, "Wis. Governor Wants to Cut Union Rights in Budget," Associated Press, Feb. 11, 2011.

189 "If we win this battle": Jason Stein, Patrick Marley, and Lee Berquist, "Walker Wins; Battle Shifts," *Milwaukee Journal Sentinel,* March 11, 2011, A1.

189 For example, the state's main teachers' union: Molly Beck, "Unions Lose 38% of Members Since Act 10," *Wisconsin State Journal,* Jan. 27, 2017, A1; Dave Umhoefer, "For Unions in Wisconsin, a Fast and Hard Fall Since Act 10," *Milwaukee Journal Sentinel,* Nov. 27, 2016, 1.

189 If he had, labor unions: Stein and Marley, *More Than They Bargained For,* 23.

189 "It appears Walker's motive": "Another Black Mark for Wisconsin," *Sheboygan Press,* March 11, 2011, A5.

189 "I'm just trying to balance": Monica Davey and Steven Greenhouse, "Wisconsin May Take an Ax to State Workers' Benefits and Their Unions," *New York Times,* Feb. 12, 2011, A11.

189 Democratic lawmakers, labor leaders: James B. Nelson, "Wisconsin Gov. Scott Walker Says Wisconsin Is Broke," *PolitiFact Wisconsin,* March 3, 2011.

189 "Wisconsin can balance its budget": Nichols, *Uprising,* 48–49.

190 Walker said that he: Scott Walker, *Unintimidated: A Governor's Strategy and a Nation's Challenge* (New York: Sentinel, 2013), 61.

190 "to help bring our state's budget": Jason Stein, Patrick Marley, and Steve Schultze,

"Mad City Showdown: Budget Battle," *Milwaukee Journal Sentinel,* Feb. 19, 2011, A1.

190 "The reforms have done exceptionally well": Steven Greenhouse, "The Wisconsin Legacy," *New York Times,* Feb. 23, 2014, BU1.

191 "We couldn't negotiate or maneuver": Ibid. Here's another example of how curbing collective bargaining helped school districts' finances: Instead of raising teachers' pay, the Mequon-Thiensville School District, near Milwaukee, froze teacher salaries for two years, saving $560,000. It saved an additional $400,000 a year by increasing employee contributions for health care.

191 "As a result of Act 10": Ibid.

191 "I don't see how unions": Steven Greenhouse, "Countering the Siege," *New York Times,* April 13, 2011, B1. Professor Jones has since moved to the University of Minnesota.

191 the Lynde and Harry Bradley Foundation: Jane Mayer, *Dark Money: The Hidden History of the Billionaires Behind the Rise of the Radical Right* (New York: Doubleday, 2016), 307.

192 The political action committee at Koch: Brad Knickerbocker, "Why Did Wisconsin Gov. Scott Take a Call from 'David Koch'?" *Christian Science Monitor,* Feb. 24, 2011.

192 That PAC also gave $1 million: Judith Davidoff, "Scott Walker Hopes to Deliver on a Longstanding GOP Priority—the Weakening of Public Sector Unions," *The Capital Times,* Feb. 23, 2011, p.1.

192 John Menard Jr., Wisconsin's richest man: Mary Spicuzza and Jason Stein, "Menard Gave to Walker Group; Report Says State Billionaire Contributed $1.5 Million to Wisconsin Club for Growth," *Milwaukee Journal Sentinel,* March 25, 2015, A3. Menard's contribution created a huge controversy because in 2013 and 2014 the Wisconsin Economic Development Corporation, which was chaired by Walker, awarded $1.8 million in tax credits to Menard's chain of home-improvement stores.

192 (For many years, Menard's chain): Mayer, *Dark Money,* 309.

192 "on a wave of dark money": Ibid., 307–8.

192 "public employee unions skew": Brian Fraley, "The Time Is Now to Reform Labor Laws Which Threaten Our State's Future," MacIver Institute, Nov. 24, 2010.

192 "Some people in the Walker campaign": Patrick Healey and Monica Davey, "Conservatives and Their Cash Lined Up Early Behind Walker," *New York Times,* June 8, 2015, A1.

192 "Any chance we'll ever get": Jason Stein and Patrick Marley, "In Film, Walker Cites 'Divide and Conquer' Plan," *Milwaukee Journal Sentinel,* May 11, 2012, A1.

193 In all, Walker raised over $30 million: Dana Bash and Stacey Samuel, "Dollars Roll in from Far Beyond Wisconsin for Recall," *CNN Wire,* June 5, 2012.

193 "I hope I'm [an] inspiration": Cooper and Seelye, "Wisconsin Leads Way."

193 Conservative think tanks, GOP politicians: See, for instance, Steven Brill, "The Rubber Room," *New Yorker,* Aug. 31, 2009, 30.

194 "The gravy train was running": Umhoefer, "For Unions in Wisconsin, a Fast and Hard Fall Since Act 10."

194 (A 2012 study by three business school professors): David Lewin, Jeffrey H. Keefe, and Thomas A. Kochan, "The New Great Debate About Unionism and Collective Bargaining in U.S. State and Local Governments," *Industrial and Labor Relations Review* 65, no. 4 (Fall 2012): 747, 756–57. Lewin, Keefe, and Kochan found that the pay gap was smaller for local government employees (4.1 percent) than

for state employees (8.3 percent). The authors found that this doesn't mean that unions fail to increase the pay of public-sector workers; they do, but far less than many of labor's critics suggest. The authors found that public-employee unions win their members 3.7 percent higher pay on average than nonunion public-sector workers—far less than the 14.1 percent wage increases that they said private-sector unions win for their members, compared with nonunion workers.

194 "If Act 10 is enacted": Grover Norquist, "Why Republicans (and Trump) May Still Win Big in 2020—Despite 'Everything,'" Ozy.com, May 28, 2017.

195 "Government unions have pushed": Mark Janus, "Why I Don't Want to Pay Union Dues," *Chicago Tribune,* Jan. 6, 2016, 19.

195 "I'm not anti-union": Andrew Hanna and Caitlin Emma, "Supreme Court Could Cripple Public Unions in Run-Up to 2018 Midterms," *Politico,* Feb. 25, 2018.

195 "a landmark victory for rights": David G. Savage, "High Court Strikes a Blow Against Unions," *Los Angeles Times,* June 28, 2018, A1.

195 "is not a free rider on a bus": Rick Pearson, "State Worker Behind Landmark Union Lawsuit Leaving Post; Mark Janus to Join Conservative Think Tank, Tour Country," *Chicago Tribune,* July 23, 2018, C6.

195 (The Court overturned its unanimous): In *Abood,* the Supreme Court sought to balance the union's interest in obtaining fees from everyone it represented with workers' First Amendment interests. In seeking to strike that balance, the *Abood* ruling held that government employees did not have to pay that part of union dues, roughly 20 percent, that goes for campaigning, lobbying, and other political activities.

196 She slammed the majority: Dylan Matthews, "6 Excerpts That Explain the Supreme Court's Big Anti-union Ruling," *Vox,* June 27, 2018.

196 "a case brought by individuals": Ed Pilkington, "Exclusive: How Rightwing Groups Wield Secret 'Toolkit' to Plot Against US Unions," *Guardian,* May 15, 2018.

196 "keeping the labor movement afloat": Bill Scher, "Unions Can't Save Us Now," *Politico,* June 27, 2018.

196 Nonetheless, the National Education Association: Madeline Will, "Union Membership Is at a High for the American Federation of Teachers. Will It Last?," *Education Week,* July 1, 2018, 1.

196 The group, funded by a billionaire-backed: Josh Eidelson, "Koch Brothers–Linked Group Declares New War on Unions," *Bloomberg News,* June 27, 2018.

196 "proven plan for bankrupting": Steven Greenhouse, "The Door-to-Door Union Killers: Right-Wing Foundation Takes Labor Fight to the Streets," *Guardian,* March 10, 2016.

197 "They're really not advocating": Eidelson, "Koch Brothers–Linked Group Declares New War on Unions."

FOURTEEN Big Labor Gets Less Big in Politics

201 After celebrating into the early hours: "AFL-CIO President John Sweeney and AFSCME President Gerald McEntee Hold a News Conference on the Election Results," Political Transcript Wire, Nov. 5, 2008.

202 One study found that 52 percent: Kate Bronfenbrenner, "No Holds Barred: The Intensification of Employer Opposition to Organizing," Economic Policy Institute, May 2009. (Based on a survey of NLRB elections from 1999 to 2003.)

202 "This will be Armageddon": Steven Greenhouse, "After Push for Obama, Unions Seek New Rules," *New York Times,* Nov. 9, 2008, A33.

202 "a political nightmare": Steven Greenhouse, "Bill Easing Unionizing Is Under Heavy Attack," *New York Times,* Jan. 9, 2009, A12.

203 Antiunion groups ran $1 million: The House, which normally would have taken up the bill first, decided against voting on it until the Senate acted. House leaders wanted to protect some centrist, business-friendly Democrats from having to stick their necks out in case the Senate didn't pass the bill.

204 In retrospect, 2009 was labor's: Some labor leaders complained that Obama didn't fight hard enough for the Employee Free Choice Act, while others acknowledged that the sixty votes were never going to be there when business opposition was so fierce.

204 "For too long," Branstad said: Dave Dreeszen, "Unions Outraged as GOP Fast-Tracks 'Tweaks' to Iowa Labor Law," *Sioux City Journal,* Feb. 7, 2017.

204 "We call for legislation": Ed Tibbetts, "Iowa Collective Bargaining Battle Is Joined," *Quad-City Times,* Feb. 8, 2017, A1.

205 "A paradox of American politics": Thomas B. Edsall, "Republicans Sure Love to Hate Unions," *New York Times,* Nov. 18, 2014.

205 "a $7 billion slush fund": Ibid.

205 Antiunion laws have taken: The Missouri legislature enacted a right-to-work law in 2017, but Missouri voters overwhelmingly voted to repeal it in a referendum in August 2018. To further drain union treasuries, Republicans in Wisconsin, Michigan, and Iowa also enacted legislation prohibiting any state or local government agency from collecting government workers' dues and forwarding that money to unions in a practice known as a dues checkoff.

205 "Trump is making a last bet": Karen Tumulty and Dan Balz, "Battleground Fight Intensifies," *Washington Post,* Nov. 5, 2016, A1.

206 "an unstoppable champion for working families": John Harris, "AFL-CIO Announces Support for Clinton, Slams Trump as an 'Unstable Charlatan,'" *Washington Post,* June 16, 2016.

206 In Ohio, Clinton lost to Trump: Ted Hesson and Marianne Levine, "Unions Investigate Their Poor Showing for Clinton," *Politico,* Nov. 11, 2016.

206 A recent academic study suggested: James Feigenbaum, Alexander Hertel-Fernandez, and Vanessa Williamson, "From the Bargaining Table to the Ballot Box: Political Effects of Right to Work Laws," National Bureau of Economic Research, Jan. 20, 2018.

206 "We can't continue to allow": Nick Gass, "Trump: 'We Can't Continue to Allow China to Rape Our Country,'" *Politico,* May 2, 2016.

207 "not a threat to their own": Niraj Chokshi, "Trump Voters Driven by Fear of Losing Status, Not Economic Anxiety, Study Finds," *New York Times,* April 24, 2018.

207 "The shift toward an antitrade stance": Ibid.

207 "Trade opposition captures Americans' fear": Tom Jacobs, "Research Finds That Racism, Sexism, and Status Fears Drove Trump Voters," *Pacific Standard,* April 24, 2018.

207 "racialized economics": John Sides, Michael Tesler, and Lynn Vavreck, *Identity Crisis: The 2016 Presidential Campaign and the Battle for the Meaning of America* (Princeton, N.J.: Princeton University Press, 2018), 175.

208 Arlie Russell Hochschild's findings: Arlie Russell Hochschild, *Strangers in Their Own Land: Anger and Mourning on the American Right* (New York: New Press, 2016).

208 "taking our jobs": Sides, Tesler, and Vavreck, *Identity Crisis,* 176.

208 "We can't tap dance around the fact": Don Gonyea, "Union Leader Confronts Race Issue in Campaign," NPR, Oct. 10, 2008.

208 "Many voters feel that the Democratic Party": Steven Greenhouse, "Trump's Rust Belt Allure," *New York Times,* July 3, 2016, SR6.

209 Many of them thought the Democrats: Joan C. Williams, "What So Many People Don't Get About the U.S. Working Class," *Harvard Business Review,* Nov. 20, 2016.

209 "The Democrats allowed themselves": Robert Griffin, John Halpin, and Ruy Teixeira, "Democrats Need to Be the Party of and for Working People—of All Races," *American Prospect,* June 1, 2017.

209 "Left parties the world over": Thomas Frank, "Millions of Ordinary Americans Support Donald Trump. Here's Why," *Guardian,* March 7, 2016.

210 "The Democrats don't have": Stanley Greenberg, "The Democrats' 'Working-Class Problem,'" *American Prospect,* June 1, 2017.

211 "It is imperative for": Pete Hamill, "The Revolt of the White Lower Middle Class," *New York,* April 14, 1969.

211 "Never before has the trade union movement": Quoted in Jefferson Cowie, *Stayin' Alive: The 1970s and the Last Days of the Working Class* (New York: New Press, 2010), 83.

212 "an angry cry from the guts": Ibid., 100.

212 "Make yourself the candidate": Ibid., 116.

212 "The necessity to turn": Ibid., 90.

213 "What kind of delegation is this?": Ibid., 105. Another labor leader complained, "There is too much hair and not enough cigars at this convention."

213 "If the issues were prices": Ibid., 124.

213 "merged the themes of race": Melvyn Dubofsky and Joseph A. McCartin, *Labor in America: A History,* 9th ed. (Malden, Mass.: Wiley Blackwell, 2017), 350.

213 "an effete core of impudent snobs": "President 'Proud' to Have Agnew in Administration," *New York Times,* Oct. 31, 1969, 1.

213 "In the 1960s and the 1970s": Stanley B. Greenberg, *Middle Class Dreams: The Politics and Power of the New American Majority* (New Haven, Conn.: Yale University Press 1996), 26.

214 "blue-collar worker will be progressive": Quoted in Cowie, *Stayin' Alive,* 80.

FIFTEEN The Sharing—the Scraps—Economy

217 "Why work if you can turk?": Trebor Scholz, *Uberworked and Underpaid: How Workers Are Disrupting the Digital Economy* (Malden, Mass.: Polity Press, 2017), 13, 57.

218 "less microentrepreneurs than microearners": Natasha Singer, "Check App. Accept Job. Repeat," *New York Times,* Aug. 17, 2014, BU1.

218 "share the scraps" economy: Robert Reich, "In New Economy, Workers Get Stuck with the Scraps," *San Francisco Chronicle,* Feb. 28, 2015, C8.

218 (She was living 190 miles): Carolyn Said, "Driving Long Distances Just to Drive Some More: Long-Distance Uber, Lyft Drivers' Crazy Commute, Marathon Days, Big Paychecks," *San Francisco Chronicle,* Feb. 19, 2017, A1.

218 A McKinsey study found: James Manyika et al., "Independent Work: Choice, Necessity, and the Gig Economy," McKinsey Global Institute, Oct. 2016.

218 "I'm not getting rich": Emily Le Coz, "Uber Says Proposal a Killer. If Rules Pass as Written, Ride-Sharing Service Will Leave Sarasota," *Sarasota Herald Tribune,* Sept. 6, 2015, B1.

218 "I have a degree in accounting": Posting of Maynard420, Reply to $3 for 30 Minute Transcription Job, to Turker Nation, quoted in Alek Felstiner, "Working the Crowd: Employment and Labor Law in the Crowdsourcing Industry," *Berkeley Journal of Employment and Labor Law* 32, no. 1 (2011): 166.

218 "opportunities to people who never": Moshe Z. Marvit, "How Crowdworkers Became the Ghosts in the Digital Machine," *Nation,* Feb. 5, 2014.

219 Workers who do work through: Lawrence F. Katz and Alan B. Krueger, "The Rise and Nature of Alternative Work Arrangements in the United States, 1995–2015" (NBER working paper No. 22667, Sept. 2016); Diana Farrell, Fiona Greig, and Amaar Hamoudi, "The Online Platform Economy in 2018: Drivers, Workers, Sellers and Lessors," JPMorgan Chase Institute, Sept. 2018.

219 the ILO study found: Janine Berg, Marianne Furrer, Ellie Harmon, Uma Rani, M Six Silberman, "Digital Labour Platforms and the Future of Work" (Geneva: International Labor Organization, 2016), 50. The study found that the average (mean) pay for Turkers in the United States was $6.54 per hour, and in India, $2.53.

219 while the Pew Research Center: Paul Hitlin, "Research in the Crowdsourcing Age, a Case Study," Pew Research Center, July 11, 2016.

220 With many Americans desperate: Singer, "Check App. Accept Job. Repeat."

220 Many corporations turn to crowdsourcing: Rachel Emma Silverman, "Big Firms Try Crowdsourcing," *Wall Street Journal,* Jan. 17, 2012.

220 For example, to translate a twenty-two-minute: "Online Labour Exchanges: The Workforce in the Cloud," *Economist,* June 1, 2013. The World Bank estimates that such online freelancing—indeed, the online outsourcing industry worldwide—will generate more than $15 billion a year in revenues by 2020. Siou Chew Kuek et al., "The Global Opportunity in Online Outsourcing," World Bank, June 2015, 3.

220 "We end up paying people": Steven Hill, *Raw Deal: How the "Uber Economy" and Runaway Capitalism Are Screwing American Workers* (New York: St. Martin's Press, 2015), 11–12.

220 "Before the Internet," Biewald said: Marvit, "How Crowdworkers Became the Ghosts in the Digital Machine."

221 A Pew study found: Hitlin, "Research in the Crowdsourcing Age." The ILO study found that 10 percent of Turkers average $10 or more an hour. Janice Berg, "Income Security in the On-Demand Economy: Findings and Policy Lessons from a Survey of Crowdworkers" (Geneva: International Labor Organization, 2018), 11.

221 Five hundred thousand workers: Berg, "Income Security," 3; "Online Crowdsourcing for Psychology Ain't Without Pitfalls," *Mashable,* March 17, 2017.

222 "not involved in the transaction": Steven Greenhouse, "On Demand and Demanding Their Rights," *American Prospect* (Summer 2016): 41.

222 "Our first goal was to give": Ibid.

222 An ILO study found: Berg, "Income Security," 5.

223 Fifty-three percent say: Hitlin, "Research in the Crowdsourcing Age." Thirty-two percent of U.S. Turkers have a bachelor's degree, while 49 percent have some college, with a substantial portion of them pursuing a bachelor's degree.

224 Then things soured badly: Danielle Furfaro, "Uber Slashes Prices 15%; Taxi War Fare as Uber Drops Prices," *New York Post,* Jan. 29, 2016, 1. Fares dropped to $1.75 per mile from $2.15 and the minimum fare to $7 from $8.

224 it had an eye-popping valuation: Michael J. de la Merced and Kate Conger, "Uber IPO Seen Hitting $100 Billion," *New York Times,* April 12, 2019, B1.

225 After the 2016 cuts: Ivan Pereira, "Wallets on Empty: Uber Drivers Rally Against Recent Fare Reductions," *Newsday,* Feb. 2, 2016, 26.

225 Parmar was earning far below: Jonathan V. Hall and Alan Krueger, "An Analysis of the Labor Market for Uber's Driver-Partners" (NBER working paper No. 22843, Jan. 22, 2015), 18.

225 (Uber agreed to pay $20 million): Sara Ashley O'Brien, "Uber to Pay $20 Million for Misleading Drivers," *CNN Wire,* Jan. 19, 2017.

225 According to Krueger and Hall's: Hall and Krueger, "Analysis of the Labor Market for Uber's Driver-Partners," 18.

226 This was before Uber cut: Mike Isaac, "Uber Cuts Fares in 48 Cities, Raising Some Concern Among Drivers," *Bits* (blog), *New York Times,* Jan. 9, 2015.

226 A 2016 study done by *BuzzFeed*: Caroline O'Donovan and Jeremy Singer-Vine, "How Much Uber Drivers Actually Make per Hour," *BuzzFeed News,* June 22, 2016.

226 And in 2018, the economist Lawrence Mishel: Alison Griswold, "Uber Drivers Make About as Much Money as Minimum Wage Workers," *Quartz,* May 16, 2018.

226 But Uber insists that most drivers: Carlos Oliva, an Uber driver in Los Angeles, said, "Even if Uber wanted to make me an employee, I wouldn't want to be one. I would quit before I would accept an offer to be an Uber employee. I value my freedom as an independent contractor too much, and I don't want Uber to tell me when or where I have to drive." Steven Greenhouse, "The Uber Challenge," *American Prospect* (Winter 2016): 30.

227 there is a pronounced power asymmetry: Scholz, *Uberworked and Underpaid,* 15, paraphrasing David Graeber, anthropology professor at the London School of Economics.

227 "Mechanical Turk may have created": Marvit, "How Crowdworkers Became the Ghosts in the Digital Machine."

227 Janice Bellace, a Wharton Business School: Greenhouse, "On Demand and Demanding Their Rights," quoting Bellace, director of the Huntsman Program in International Studies and Business at Wharton.

228 "It's easy to come together": Tom Abate, "Stanford Engineers Collaborate on Research to Help Online Groups Organize Themselves," *Stanford Report,* March 23, 2015.

228 More than 200,000 Care.com: Palak Shah, the National Domestic Workers Alliance official in charge of promoting the Fair Care Pledge, told me, "I was worried that there were a lot of people out there in the gig economy speaking for workers who were not from worker organizations." Her group, she explained, "wanted to offer a road map" to people who were eager to attract a steady, quality workforce—which, no secret here, often means paying and treating your workers well."

228 "create a basis for a trusting": "Eight German Labor Platforms Sign 'Crowdsourcing Code of Conduct 2.0,'" *Fair Crowd Work,* March 17, 2017, faircrowd.work.

228 Soon after, several labor unions: "Frankfurt Paper on Platform-Based Work," Dec. 6, 2016.

229 "Labor is not a commodity": The coalition called for revamping "laws that prohibit platform-based workers classified as independent contractors from organizing and negotiating collective agreements with platform operators." The coalition included the Service Employees International Union, a large Teamsters local in Seattle, and Germany's largest union, IG Metall.

229 "The drivers need help": Noam Scheiber, "Uber Has a Union of Sorts, but Faces Doubt on Its Autonomy," *New York Times,* May 12, 2017, BU1. David Plouffe, Uber's strategic adviser, said that the guild—in ways an experiment—could help Uber communicate better with drivers. "Communication is important," Plouffe said. Jing Cao and Eric Newcomer, "Uber and Union Agree to Form Drivers Guild in New York City," *Bloomberg Technology,* May 10, 2016.

230 Lyft complained that the law: Phuong Le, "Seattle's Uber Unionization Measure a New Economy Test Case," Associated Press, Dec. 15, 2015.

231 That court ruled, however: Gene Johnson, "Appeals Court Reinstates Challenge to Seattle Rideshare Law," Associated Press, May 11, 2018.

SIXTEEN The Fight for $15

232 "We were trying to figure out": Courtney resigned from his position as executive vice president and organizing director of the SEIU in October 2017 amid an investigation into "sexual misconduct." SEIU officials said Courtney had, in violation of union rules, failed to report to his superiors that he had been dating subordinates. Josh Eidelson, "Labor Leaders Confront Harassment in Ranks," *Boston Globe,* Nov. 8, 2017, B12.

233 There, a grassroots group: New York Communities for Change is a successor group to Acorn, doing community organizing that focuses on the poor and low-wage workers.

234 "When we got into that room": Fells resigned from his position as the Fight for $15 organizing director in November 2017, after SEIU officials said Fells had failed to report Fight for $15 employees' abusive behavior "toward staff, predominantly female staff." Fells declined to comment. Eidelson, "Labor Leaders Confront Harassment in Ranks."

236 "In this job, having a union": Steven Greenhouse, "With Day of Protests, Fast-Food Workers Seek More Pay," *New York Times,* Nov. 30, 2012, A29.

236 "the biggest wave of job actions": Ibid.

236 "I have two kids under six": Ibid.

239 "The public doesn't know": Kari Lydersen, "'I'm Not on the Menu': McDonald's Workers Strike over 'Rampant' Sexual Harassment," *Guardian,* Sept. 18, 2018.

240 Montgomery's boss relented: Lore Croghan, "Workers Flip Out: Wendy's Employees Rally to Save Fired Colleague," *New York Daily News,* Dec. 4, 2012, 47.

241 "I have seen a lot of people": Michael A. Fletcher, "Low-Wage Workers Plan Walkout," *Washington Post,* Aug. 20, 2013, 10.

241 In a one-two punch: Emily Jane Fox, "NY Attorney General Investigating Fast Food Wage Theft," *CNN Money,* May 16, 2013.

241 In a study partly financed: Susan Berfield, "Fast-Food Wages Come with a $7 Billion Side of Public Assistance," *Bloomberg Businessweek,* Oct. 16, 2013; Sylvia A. Allegretto et al., "Fast Food, Poverty Wages: The Public Cost of Low-Wage Jobs in the Fast-Food Industry," University of California, Berkeley Labor Center, Oct. 15, 2013.

242 When Salgado called the company's: Alexander Abad-Santos, "Instead of Raises, McDonald's Tells Workers to Sign Up for Food Stamps," *Atlantic,* Oct. 24, 2013.

242 Its recommendations included: Josh Eidelson, "McDonald's Tells Workers to 'Sing Away Stress,' 'Chew Away Cares,' and Go to Church," *Salon,* Nov. 19, 2013.

242 The National Retail Federation dismissed: Karen McVeigh, "US Fast-Food Workers Stage Nationwide Strike in Protest at Low Wages," *Guardian,* Aug. 29, 2013.

242 "made-for-TV media moments": Steven Greenhouse, "A Day's Strike Seeks to Raise Fast-Food Pay," *New York Times,* Aug. 1, 2013, A1.

243 "events have not been 'strikes'": Steven Greenhouse, "A Broader Strategy on Wages," *New York Times,* March 31, 2015, B1.

243 When McDonald's held its 2015: Alejandra Cancino and Jessica Wohl, "Protesters Swarm McD's; Crowd Asks for Increase in Wages at Chain's HQ," *Chicago Tribune,* May 21, 2015, C1.

243 Those criticisms subsided: One critic noted that the movement's main PR firm had prepared a "Strike in a Box" document to help organizers arrange strikes in various cities. The document told organizers to pick a restaurant to focus on and said, "Is it an iconic brand? Does the brand help tell a story, locally and/or nationally? Do we have spokespeople? Trained? Reliable? Experienced? Do we have stories? Compelling worker stories, Horror stories about site practices (wage theft, sexual harassment, etc.)." Arun Gupta, "Beyond the Fight for 15: The Worker-Led Fast Food Union Campaign Building Power on the Shop Floor," *In These Times,* Oct. 25, 2016.

244 In April 2015, however: The Fight for $15 claimed credit for that raise, but McDonald's said it was merely responding to a tighter labor market.

244 As Jonathan Rosenblum recounts: Jonathan Rosenblum, *Beyond $15: Immigrant Workers, Faith Activists, and the Revival of the Labor Movement* (Boston: Beacon Press, 2017).

245 "Fast-food workers rightly took": William Finnegan, "Dignity: Fast-Food Workers and a New Form of Labor Activism," *New Yorker,* Sept. 15, 2014.

246 "Morally and socially and politically": David Siders, "Jerry Brown Signs $15 Minimum Wage in California," *Sacramento Bee,* April 4, 2016.

246 Sheryl Sandberg, Facebook's chief: Sam Thielman, "Facebook to Raise Minimum Wage to $15 an Hour for Contractors and Vendors," *Guardian,* May 13, 2015.

247 "When I went out into the field": David Crow, "Mark Bertolini, Aetna CEO: Mindful of Mortality," *Financial Times,* March 13, 2016.

248 "there is no reason for our company": Steven Greenhouse, "How to Get Low-Wage Workers into the Middle Class," *Atlantic,* Aug. 19, 2015.

248 But strategists fear that McDonald's: Fight for $15 strategists feared that even if the movement unionized and won a great contract from a dozen or a few dozen restaurants, the parent company might seek to take away those franchisees' contracts or help a new, nonunion franchise operator set up shop across the street to hurt the unionized restaurants.

249 "You can imagine a scenario": Greenhouse, "How to Get Low-Wage Workers into the Middle Class."

249 "We were looking for a national deal": The Fight for $15 was hoping to have the NLRB rule that McDonald's is a joint employer with its franchisees. That would have made it far easier to unionize many McDonald's at once. The Obama NLRB's general counsel backed that position, but the business-friendly Trump NLRB is seeking to make it harder for McDonald's and other companies to be declared joint employers.

249 In the first such example: Such funding is a rare bird. It would in effect be a non-union dues checkoff.

249 The National Restaurant Association: The Restaurant Law Center—the legal arm of the National Restaurant Association—has sued in federal court, seeking to block the law. The center asserts that requiring restaurants to forward money to worker groups is unconstitutional forced speech under the First Amendment. Steven Greenhouse, "Fast-Food Workers Claim a Labor Victory in New York," *New York Times,* Jan. 10, 2018, B2.

250 "We lost our home": Allison Aubrey, "Activists Gather to Push for $15 Federal Minimum Wage," *All Things Considered,* Aug. 13, 2016. Some conservative critics attacked Terrence Wise because a public-relations agency helped arrange his broadcast interviews. The Fight for $15's public-relations agency, BerlinRosen—just like public-relations agencies for myriad other causes—helped arrange for Wise's appearance on various broadcast outlets.

251 "Where I work, in both my shops": " 'We Are Slowly Dying': Fast-Food Workers Launch Strike for Living Wage and Right to Unionize," *Democracy Now!,* Aug. 2, 2013.

252 "I had a chance to tell Mr. Obama": Robert Townsend, "KC Man 'Ecstatic' After Meeting President Obama at 'Worker Voice' Summit," fox4kc.com, Oct. 8, 2015.

SEVENTEEN For Farmworkers, from Worst to Best

254 "If you didn't get paid": Philippe Diederich, "Fairness in the Fields," *Sarasota Magazine,* Sept. 1, 2014.

254 "It was the closest thing possible": Tracie McMillan, "Labor Gains: Tracing the History of the Fair-Food Movement," *Modern Farmer,* Jan. 4, 2016, quoting Janice Fine, professor of labor studies and employment relations at Rutgers.

254 "The source and color of the workers": Susan L. Marquis, *I Am Not a Tractor! How Florida Farmworkers Took on the Fast Food Giants and Won* (Ithaca, N.Y.: ILR Press, 2017), 3.

254 "ground zero for modern slavery": Barry Estabrook, "Politics of the Plate: The Price of Tomatoes," *Gourmet,* March 2009.

254 "If you want to leave": John Bowe, "Nobodies," *New Yorker,* April 21, 2003.

255 Lucas testified that when: Estabrook, "Politics of the Plate."

255 "The bottom line is America wants": Steve Beardsley, "Brothers Receive 12-Year Prison Terms," *Naples Daily News,* Dec. 20, 2008, B2.

257 "a transparent attempt to start": Susan Jacobson, "Tomato Pickers March to Orlando for 'Living Wage,'" *Orlando Sentinel,* March 3, 2000, Osceola sec., 1.

257 "The growers were so effectively insulated": Greg Asbed, "Coalition of Immokalee Workers: '¡Golpear a Uno es Golpear a Todos!' To Beat One of Us Is to Beat Us All!," in *Bringing Human Rights Home,* ed. Cynthia Soohoo, Catherine Albisa, and Martha F. Davis, vol. 3, *Portraits of the Movement* (Westport, Conn.: Praeger, 2007), 18.

257 "You beat your head against": Charles Osgood and Mark Stressman, "At What Cost Do We Americans Enjoy Our Fruits and Vegetables?," CBS News Sunday Morning, Aug. 9, 2015.

257 The coalition escalated: Paul King, "Students: No Quiero Taco Bell on UCLA Campus," *Nation's Restaurant News,* Dec. 1, 2003, 6.

258 "This labor dispute is four steps": Bruce Schreiner, "Florida Farmworkers Take Grievances to Fast-Food Giant," Associated Press, May 17, 2002.

258 "We Jews were slaves in Egypt": "Rabbis Travel to Frontlines of a Battle for Labor Rights," *Jewish Advocate*, Dec. 9, 2011, 6.

259 "I now call on others": "USA: Taco Bell Does Deal to Boost Farmworkers' Pay," *Just-Food Global News*, March 9, 2005, www.just-food.com/.

260 "It's not our job to tell": Elaine Walker, "Group Wants Burger King to Pay More for Tomatoes," *Miami Herald*, Sept. 1, 2007, C1.

260 "This protest is a colossal waste": Adrian Sainz, "Tomato Pickers Protest at Burger King HQ over Low Wages," Associated Press, Nov. 30, 2007.

260 Its website said it placed: Tiffany Ten Eyck, "Tomato Pickers Say Burger King Spies on Allies, Pretends to Be Students," *Labor Notes*, May 2008, 5.

260 When the coalition exposed: Elaine Walker, "Burger King's Virtual Missteps 'a Cautionary Tale,'" *Miami Herald*, May 18, 2008, E1.

260 "The CIW is a self-serving attack organization": Amy Bennett Williams, "Tomato Pickers Feeling Spied On," *Fort Myers News-Press*, April 13, 2008, 1A.

260 Another comment accused: Amy Bennett Williams, "Burger King VP Puts Self on Grill," *Fort Myers News-Press*, April 28, 2008, 1A.

261 "It is just un-American": Walker, "Group Wants Burger King to Pay More for Tomatoes."

261 When the food writer Barry Estabrook: Estabrook, "Politics of the Plate."

261 They included the penny-a-pound increment: Laura Wides-Munoz, "Fla. Tomato Pickers Announce New Deal with Growers," Associated Press, Oct. 13, 2010.

261 "Few are guilty, but all": Amy Bennett Williams, "Tomato Grower, Harvesters Strike Historic Accord," *Fort Myers News-Press*, Oct. 14, 2010, A1.

262 a long-detested practice known as cupping: Workers say that disputes over cupping sometimes became violent as crew leaders insisted on having many tomatoes added above the rim, and the pickers refused, saying that was improper and unfair.

263 "This is the best workplace-monitoring program": Steven Greenhouse, "In Florida Tomato Fields, a Penny Buys Progress," *New York Times*, April 25, 2014. A1.

263 "appalling stories of abuse": Ibid.

264 Walmart turned to the CIW's: Ibid. Jack L. Sinclair, then executive vice president of Walmart's grocery division, praised the CIW, saying, "These guys have a pretty good set of standards in place that we think will allow our growers to get a consistent level of labor."

264 Safer often tells of a farmworker: Diederich, "Fairness in the Fields."

266 "voice of the marginalized": Greg Asbed and Steve Hitov, "Preventing Forced Labor in Corporate Supply Chains: The Fair Food Program and Worker-Driven Social Responsibility," *Wake Forest Law Review* 52 (July 2017): 526.

EIGHTEEN How Los Angeles Became Pro-Labor

267 Durazo grew angrier still: Hillel Aron, "The Wage Warrior," *Los Angeles Magazine*, Dec. 1, 2013, 126; Marita Hernandez, "Organizer Wins Post of President; Latina Leads Takeover of Union from Anglo Males," *Los Angeles Times*, May 6, 1989, pt. I, 1.

268 King suffered skull fractures: Anjuli Sastry, "When LA Erupted in Anger: A Look Back at the Rodney King Riots," NPR, April 26, 2017.

270 Jobs to Move America: Steven Greenhouse, "Connecting Public Transit to Great Manufacturing Jobs," *American Prospect,* April 9, 2018.

270 "the nation's most innovative": Harold Meyerson, "L.A. Story," *American Prospect,* July–Aug. 2013, 28.

271 "The 'living wage' in Los Angeles": "Los Angeles Times Interview: 'James Lawson; Standing Up for Rev. King's Beliefs,'" *Los Angeles Times,* Jan. 19, 1997, M3.

272 "Clergy from every denomination": Meyerson, "L.A. Story."

273 "He saw that in a city": Steven Greenhouse, "The Fight for $15.37 an Hour," *New York Times,* Nov. 23, 2014, BU1.

273 "That's how you create change": Jose Cardenas, "She's Working Overtime for L.A.'s Living Wage Battle," *Los Angeles Times,* Aug. 21, 2000, E1.

273 Moreover, the L.A. law called for: If a company covered by the law didn't provide health coverage, it had to pay $1.25 more per hour.

274 "I was determined that": Harold Meyerson, "No Justice, No Growth: How Los Angeles Is Making Big-Time Developers Create Decent Jobs," *American Prospect,* Nov. 2006, 39.

274 "working-class Hollywood would have": Ibid.

275 "Community benefits agreements": In 2005, Janis co-wrote a book about these agreements. Julian Gross, Greg Leroy, and Madeline Janis, *Community Benefits Agreements: Making Development Projects Accountable* (Washington, D.C.: Good Jobs First, 2005).

275 Many developers dislike community benefits: But some developers have come to like these agreements, saying it's easier to deal with a community coalition that puts forward one unified set of demands, instead of having to fight individually with a dozen or two not-in-my-backyard groups.

275 It decided to focus on six industries: LAANE has close ties to UNITE HERE and the Teamsters, but because UNITE HERE and the Service Employees International Union have been fighting for years, LAANE has largely steered clear of working in industries that the SEIU focuses on, like health care and building services. See David Agnew, "Breaking the Bank: Unions Fight a Civil War over Amalgamated Bank," States News Service, June 17, 2013.

276 Carol Schatz, chief executive: Howard Fine, "Hotels Seek Say on Worker Pay: Minimum-Wage Increase Seemed Like Done Deal," *Los Angeles Business Journal,* Feb. 3, 2014, 1.

278 The council approved the bill: Under the law, the $15.37 wage applies only to hotels with more than 125 rooms.

278 "perhaps the most important organization": Emily Alpert Reyes, "Economic Justice Group, Which Has Succeeded in Bringing Divergent Interests Together, Has Become a Political Powerhouse," *Los Angeles Times,* Jan. 3, 2015, AA1.

278 "a shill for labor unions": Greenhouse, "Fight for $15.37 an Hour."

279 It has broadened its scope: This parallels Jane McAlevey's teachings that unions should take a "whole worker" approach to organizing and not just serve the worker in the workplace. Jane McAlevey, *Raising Expectations (and Raising Hell): My Decade Fighting for the Labor Movement,* with Bob Ostertag (New York: Verso, 2014), 14–16, 27–59.

279 Their pay averaged just $12: Bill Mongelluzzo, "Crossroads for Drayage; Clean-Air Proposals, TWIC Produce Uncertainty for Port Trucking Industry," *Journal of Commerce,* Jan. 7, 2008, 23.

283 Tynan has little patience for critics: In 2016, the City of Los Angeles fined LAANE

$30,000 for violating L.A. ethics rules on lobbying. From 2011 to 2014, LAANE had failed to report on disclosure forms any payments to its registered in-house lobbyists and failed to list any people they had lobbied or subjects they had lobbied on. LAANE said that it was an innocent oversight and that it had misunderstood the city's rules on reporting lobbying expenses. It revised its filings to indicate that it had spent over $175,000 lobbying between 2011 and 2014. Emily Alpert Reyes, "Ethics Panel Fines Two Groups $47,000," *Los Angeles Times,* Feb. 17, 2016, B1.

NINETEEN Best Foot Forward

285 Kaiser instructs its UBTs: Peter M. Lazes, Maria Figueroa, and Liana Katz, "How Labor-Management Partnerships Improve Patient Care, Cost Control, and Labor Relations," Cornell ILR School, Feb. 1, 2012, 8.

290 "This is not the Kaiser": Thomas A. Kochan et al., *Healing Together: The Labor-Management Partnership at Kaiser Permanente* (Ithaca, N.Y.: Cornell University Press, 2009), 35.

290 "We were like dogs sniffing": Kellie Applen, "How Our Partnership Came to Be" (video sponsored by Kaiser Permanente), Oct. 1, 2017, www.lmpartnership.org.

290 "I honestly had to fight": Ibid.

290 "Sometimes out of crisis": Kochan et al., *Healing Together,* 39.

290 "Our job," the union said: Ibid., 43–44. The California Nurses Association also voiced fears that the unions in the partnership would be required to promote Kaiser "regardless of the facts" and "the decreasing quality of care at Kaiser."

292 "I was impressed by how much": Ibid., 61.

293 Instead of an angry deadlock: Ibid., 105–6.

296 With achievements like these: Marilyn Sneiderman and Secky Fascione, "Going on Offense During Challenging Times," *New Labor Forum,* Jan. 2018; Joseph A. McCartin, "Bargaining for the Common Good," *Dissent* (Spring 2016).

298 That strike demanded increased: Curt Brown, "1946 St. Paul Teachers' Strike Got Everyone's Attention," *Minneapolis Star Tribune,* Feb. 3, 2018.

300 The union set up two monthly study groups: Alfie Kohn, *The Schools Our Children Deserve: Moving Beyond Traditional Classrooms and "Tougher Standards"* (Boston: Houghton Mifflin, 1999); Barnett Berry, *Teaching 2030: What We Must Do for Our Students and Our Public Schools—Now and in the Future* (New York: Teachers College Press, 2010).

301 "We knew we had the upper hand": Mary Cathryn Ricker, "Teacher-Community Unionism: A Lesson from St. Paul," *Dissent* (Summer 2015).

303 "a premature path of confrontation": Ian Keith, "This St. Paul Teacher Opposes Authorizing a Strike," *Minneapolis Star Tribune,* Feb. 2, 2018.

TWENTY Teachers Catch #RedforEd Fever

306 Having just finished Jane McAlevey's: Jane F. McAlevey, *No Shortcuts: Organizing for Power in the New Gilded Age* (New York: Oxford University Press, 2016).

307 With its teacher pay averaging: Christine Hauser, "Thousands of West Virginia Teachers Strike for a Second Day," *New York Times,* Feb. 28, 2018, A11.

307 There were 725 unfilled spots: "Teachers to Continue Walkout over Pay, PEIA Benefits," *Huntington (W.Va.) Herald-Dispatch,* Feb. 25, 2018.

308 "We come from these mountains": Jess Bidgood, "'I Live Paycheck to Paycheck': West Virginia Teacher Talks About Walking Out," *New York Times,* March 2, 2018, A10.

308 "I am absolutely all in": Brad McElhinny, "'Dumb Bunnies' in WV Teacher Crowds Protest Comment by Governor Justice," *WV Metro News,* Feb. 25, 2018.

310 "Teachers, many of them women": Caitlin Emma, "Teachers Are Going on Strike in Trump's America," *Politico,* April 12, 2018.

310 "No. We're equal here": Michelle Goldberg, "The Teachers Revolt in West Virginia," *New York Times,* March 6, 2018, A26.

310 "People like to dismiss West Virginia": "The Strike Is On: An Interview with Jay O'Neal," *Jacobin,* March 2018.

310 "We're not going back in": Ibid.

310 "It would be completely frivolous": Ryan Quinn, "Schools to Remain Closed in All 55 Counties of W.Va. Today," *Charleston Gazette-Mail,* March 1, 2018, 1A.

311 "Until this bill passes at 5 percent": Jake Zuckerman, "Legislature Divided over Pay Raise Bill," *Charleston Gazette-Mail,* March 4, 2018, 1A.

311 "People are ready to have their voices": David Bitton, "Teacher Walkout Looming as Educators Seek Pay Raise," *Stillwater (Okla.) News Press,* March 7, 2018.

311 "You can go anywhere else": Emma, "Teachers Are Going on Strike in Trump's America."

311 Shawn Sheehan, Oklahoma's 2016: Caleb Slinkard, "Sheehans' Departure Highlights Depth of State's Education Funding Woes," *Norman (Okla.) Transcript,* Oct. 17, 2017.

312 "We have two teachers leaving": Rivka Galchen, "The Teaching Moment," *New Yorker,* June 4–11, 2018, 38.

312 same textbook that the country singer: Andrea Diaz, "This Okla. Student Is Excited She's Reading a Textbook Used by Blake Shelton. Her Mother Is Not," CNN.com, April 5, 2018.

312 Oklahoma's State Science and Engineering Fair: Galchen, "Teaching Moment."

312 "Oklahoma teachers have felt hopeless": Eric Blanc, "It's Oklahoma's Turn to Strike," *Jacobin,* March 2018.

313 "Teachers want more": Moriah Balingit, "Okla. Governor's Slam Vexes Teachers," *Washington Post,* April 5, 2018, A4.

313 "We must be responsible not to neglect": Randy Krehbiel, "Tempers Stay Cool at Capitol as Thousands of Teachers Descend on Lawmakers," *Tulsa World,* April 2, 2018.

313 "I'm not voting for another": Ben Felder, "Observations from Day 2 of the Teacher Walkout," *Daily Oklahoman,* April 3, 2018.

314 "There comes a time": Emily Sullivan, "Union Leader Calls for an End to Oklahoma Teachers' 9-Day Strike," NPR, April 14, 2018.

314 "We got here by electing": Dana Goldstein and Elizabeth Dias, "Protest in Oklahoma Ends, but Without Adding to Modest Gains in Funding," *New York Times,* April 13, 2018, A13.

314 "perhaps the most extraordinary primary": Randy Krehbiel, "Six More House Incumbents Ousted in GOP Runoff Elections," *Tulsa World,* Aug. 29, 2018.

315 The state's funding for schools: Michael Leachman, Kathleen Masterson, and Eric Figueroa, "A Punishing Decade for School Funding," Center for Budget and Policy Priorities, Nov. 29, 2017.

316 One teacher in Yuma: Dale Russakoff, "The Teachers Movement," *New York Times*, Sept. 9, 2018, MM54.

318 Accusing Karvelis of "channeling Leninism": Maria Syms, "#RedforEd Movement Deserves Some Better Advocates," *Arizona Republic*, April 26, 2018, A12.

320 "learned that these legislators will only do so": "The Outcome in Arizona," *Jacobin*, May 2018.

320 The union called the ruling a Ducey-orchestrated: Steven Greenhouse, "Billionaires v Teachers: The Koch Brothers' Plan to Starve Public Education," *Guardian*, Sept. 7, 2018.

320 "Facebook pages are great for mobilizing": Mary Ellen Flannery and Amanda Litvinov, "Why We Are Red for Ed," *NEA Today*, Oct. 12, 2018.

320 "this movement" got "a right-wing government": "Outcome in Arizona."

321 Steve Lopez, a columnist: Steve Lopez, "The Public Had Teachers' Backs; Amid a Failure of Leadership, the People of L.A. Sided with Educators," *Los Angeles Times*, Jan. 23, 2019, A1.

321 Alex Caputo-Pearl, the union's: Dakota Smith, "A New Movement in L.A.?; Striking Teachers Highlighted City's Education Inequality and Drew Supporters to the Streets, but Lasting Effects Are Unclear," *Los Angeles Times*, Jan. 24, 2019, A1.

322 Caputo-Pearl said: "We won": Barbara Madeloni, "L.A. Teachers Win Big and Beat Back Privatizers," *Labor Notes*, Feb. 1, 2019, 1.

322 He hailed the settlement: Madeline Will, "The New Flavor of Teacher Strike: More Than Just Pay Raises," *Education Week*, Jan. 25, 2019.

322 Arlene Inouye, an English-as-a-second: Eric Blanc, "After LA's Strike, 'Nothing Will Be the Same,'" *Jacobin*, Jan. 1, 2019.

TWENTY-ONE How Workers Can Regain Their Power

323 Congress has rejected every push: Under President Johnson, Republicans blocked a push to repeal Section 14(b) of the Taft-Hartley Act, which enabled states to adopt right-to-work laws. Facing a filibuster, President Clinton failed to muster the sixty votes needed to ban the use of permanent replacement workers during strikes. Under President Obama, even with the Democrats holding sixty Senate seats, labor couldn't win passage of a bill that would have made card check the law of the land.

324 There was also heavy spending: Lisa Mascaro, "Koch's Quiet Sway in White House; Bannon's Ouster Could Boost Billionaire's Network to Shape Conservative Policies," *Los Angeles Times*, Aug. 21, 2017, A1.

324 As we saw, corporations and business: "Business-Labor-Ideology Split in PAC & Individual Donations to Candidates, Parties, Super PACs, and Outside Spending Groups," Center for Responsive Politics, www.openscrets.org.

324 (Adelson and his wife donated): Peter Stone, "Mega-donor Adelson with Access and Influence, Scores Two Pro-Israel Victories," McClatchy, May 14, 2018; Mark Landler, "Defiantly Fulfilling a 2016 Vow," *New York Times*, Dec. 7, 2017, A1.

324 Eighty-four percent of Americans: Nicholas Confessore and Megan Thee-Brenan, "Poll Shows Americans Favor an Overhaul of Campaign Financing," *New York Times*, June 2, 2015; Pew Research Center, "Beyond Distrust: How Americans View Their Government," Nov. 23, 2015.

324 Voters are given four vouchers: Gene Johnson, "Judge Upholds Seattle's Novel

Campaign-Finance Vouchers," *Seattle Times,* Nov. 4, 2017, B2. Seattle has allocated $3 million in public money for these vouchers.

325 "addresses the need to build": To encourage donations by those of modest means, Sarbanes's proposal calls for contributors to get a 50 percent tax refund for their first $50 in donations to any candidate. To qualify for matching funds, candidates would have to reject contributions from any PAC that receives contributions of $150 or more. Harold Meyerson, "A Campaign Finance Idea Whose Time Has Come," *Washington Post,* March 26, 2015.

325 "The need for real campaign finance reform": Bernie Sanders, "Getting Big Money out of Politics and Restoring Democracy," berniesanders.com. To help limit the influence of dark money, whether from corporations or ultrarich donors, Senator Tom Udall of New Mexico has made proposals that would require quick disclosure. Any time candidates receive a contribution of over $1,000, they would be required to report that within forty-eight hours, and whenever an outside group spends $10,000 or more on a campaign-related expenditure, that, too, would have to be disclosed within forty-eight hours.

To discourage members of Congress from tilting unduly toward business and shortchanging the interests of workers, lawmakers should be barred from becoming lobbyists for five years after leaving office. That would go a long way toward ensuring that lawmakers serve the public interest instead of corporate interests.

326 Basic membership in this organization: Such an organization might need some foundation support to get off the ground. If this new "AAWP" gains critical mass, it might, for instance, offer lower-cost, consumer-friendly insurance or credit cards to its members or perhaps even travel discounts. That might help attract members (and strengthen the group's treasury). But first and foremost, such a group's focus should be not on marketing but on fighting for American workers.

327 One Coworker.org petition helped: Coworker.org invites workers to launch petition campaigns on workplace issues, and then Coworker helps them, using Facebook, Twitter, Instagram, and other networks, to attract co-workers to sign. In other petition drives, workers at Publix supermarkets won the right to wear beards, while Chipotle and Starbucks workers have urged their companies to end what they say is systematic understaffing.

327 Even as unions have grown weaker: Lydia Saad, "Labor Union Approval Steady at 15-Year High," Gallup, Aug. 30, 2018.

327 In other promising news: The public's view of unions fell sharply in 2008–9, when GM and Chrysler were sinking into bankruptcy and many states' and cities' budget deficits were rising because of the recession.

328 Moreover, many millennials have seen: Shiva Maniam, "Most Americans See Labor Unions, Corporations Favorably," Pew Research Center, Jan. 30, 2017.

328 In addition, many millennials are unhappy: Frank Newport, "Democrats More Positive About Socialism Than Capitalism," Gallup, Aug. 13, 2018.

328 Add that to the 14.8 million: Thomas Kochan et al., "Worker Voice in America: A Current Assessment and Exploration of Options" (working draft, Massachusetts Institute of Technology, Institute for Work and Employment Research, Jan. 17, 2018). In that poll, the National Opinion Research Corporation surveyed 3,915 workers. Its finding that 46 percent of American workers wanted to join unions was an increase from 32 percent in 1995 (and 30 percent in 1970).

328 Researchers have found that nearly: John Schmitt and Ben Zipperer, "Dropping

the Ax: Illegal Firings During Union Election Campaigns," Center for Economic and Policy Research, Jan. 2007, 17, cepr.net.

329 One audacious proposal: Moshe Z. Marvit and Shaun Richman, "A Better Way to Protect Workers," *New York Times,* Dec. 29, 2017, A23.

329 As a result, companies would: Richard D. Kahlenberg and Moshe Z. Marvit, "A Civil Right to Unionize," *New York Times,* March 1, 2012, A31; Richard D. Kahlenberg and Moshe Z. Marvit, *Why Labor Organizing Should Be a Civil Right* (New York: Century Foundation, 2012).

329 In that 1992 case: *Lechmere Inc. v. NLRB,* 502 U.S. 527 (1992).

330 Union organizers should also: A big problem is that managers often hold one-on-one meetings with employees where they subtly or none too subtly intimidate workers into opposing the union. Managers often do two illegal things: asking workers how they feel about the union and urging them to promise to vote against the union. The first thing is considered unlawful spying and intimidation, and the second is often considered illegal intimidation. Once workers tell their boss that they'll vote against the union, they're often reluctant to break that "promise." There is no easy solution to this frequent intimidation. Workers usually don't know it's illegal, and if they complain about these one-on-one meetings, they could face retaliation.

331 Under this system, unions: Matthew Dimick, "The Ghent System and Progressive Federalism," *OnLabor,* Feb. 3, 2017, onlabor.org.

331 This money helps these groups: In Seattle, the city has distributed $1 million to ten groups, including the pioneering Fair Work Center, which educates workers and has developed an app to report violations. Janice Fine, a labor relations professor at Rutgers, has proposed that industries with bad compliance records be required to contribute to an enforcement fund that would help worker centers hire investigators and trainers. The worker centers, Fine says, should then encourage employees to elect representatives to oversee efforts to uncover violations at their workplaces and report them. Janice Fine, "'Alt Labor' from the Margins to the Center, the Policy Turn and Using Enforcement to Build Structure: A Presentation to the Shanker Institute," Rutgers University School of Management and Labor Relations, Dec. 2016, www.shankerinstitute.org.

332 In theory, this industry-wide type: David Madland, "Wage Boards for American Workers," Center for American Progress, April 9, 2018; Dylan Matthews, "The Emerging Plan to Save the American Labor Movement," *Vox,* April 9, 2018.

333 These councils also reduce: The worker representatives are often union members or union officials.

333 One poll found that 53 percent: Dylan Matthews, "Workers Don't Have Much Say in Corporations. Why Not Give Them Seats on the Board?," *Vox,* April 6, 2018.

334 In his book *Only One:* Thomas Geoghegan, *Only One Thing Can Save Us: Why America Needs a New Kind of Labor Movement* (New York: New Press, 2014), 208–11.

334 In New York, as discussed previously: Steven Greenhouse, "Fast-Food Workers Claim a Labor Victory in New York," *New York Times,* Jan. 10, 2018, B2; Max Zahn, "The Future of the Low-Wage Worker Movement May Depend on a Little-Known New York Law," *In These Times,* Aug. 15, 2017. To avoid falling under federal regulations that apply to labor unions—such as rigorous financial reporting requirements—Fast Food Justice says it won't engage in union-like bargaining or

handle workers' grievances, for instance, for a terminated employee. Fast Food Justice is also seeking to avoid being considered a union because it fears having the New York City law overturned on the basis that it is preempted by the federal law covering unions, that is, the National Labor Relations Act.

In suing to have the New York law overturned, the National Restaurant Association asserts that requiring restaurants to merely administer the forwarding of workers' contributions violates the restaurants' First Amendment rights.

334 the hugely successful Workers Defense Project: Steven Greenhouse, "A Union in Spirit," *New York Times,* Aug. 11, 2013, BU1.

334 In the 1960s, John Kenneth Galbraith: John Kenneth Galbraith, *The New Industrial State* (Princeton, N.J.: Princeton University Press, 2007). 322–24, 338–40.

335 For organized labor, it's now: This might mean devoting less money and staff to current members' grievances and getting more member-volunteers to handle grievances.

337 (portable benefits for gig economy workers): Nick Hanauer and David Rolf, "Shared Security, Shared Growth," *Democracy: A Journal of Ideas* (Summer 2015).

337 ("I even believe in helping"): Ruth L. Horowitz, *Political Ideologies of Organized Labor: The New Deal Era* (New Brunswick, N.J.: Transaction, 1978), 215.

338 A workers' movement should also fight: Some of these programs would cost tens of billions of dollars, but many of them could be funded by clawing back some of the more than $1.5 trillion in the 2017 tax cuts that go to corporations (when corporate America was already enjoying record profits) and to the 1 percent (when the 1 percent already had its highest share of income since the 1920s). To be clear, I support tax cuts to help middle-income, moderate-income, and low-income workers, and a higher earned-income tax credit for lower-paid workers. But I'm for responsible tax cuts—not tax cuts that cause the federal debt to soar, forcing our children and their children to pay for them.

338 "What does labor want?": Melvyn Dubofsky and Joseph A. McCartin (eds.), *American Labor: A Documentary History* (New York: Springer, 2016) 123–26. Also, "What Does Labor Want?," The Samuel Gompers Papers, Volume 11, 1893 (Chicago), 32, 34n; 1897. gompers.umd.edu/ind11a-l.htm.

Index